NINETEEN THIRTY-ONE
Political Crisis

NINETEEN THIRTY-ONE

Political Crisis

BY

R. BASSETT

READER IN POLITICAL SCIENCE,
UNIVERSITY OF LONDON

LONDON
MACMILLAN & CO LTD
NEW YORK · ST MARTIN'S PRESS
1958

MACMILLAN AND COMPANY LIMITED
London Bombay Calcutta Madras Melbourne

THE MACMILLAN COMPANY OF CANADA LIMITED
Toronto

ST MARTIN'S PRESS INC
New York

PRINTED IN GREAT BRITAIN

TO THE MEMORY OF

J. THOMAS BAXTER

CONTENTS

vii

INTRODUCTION

On Monday, August 24, 1931, H.M. King George V accepted the resignation of the Labour Ministry which had been in office since June of 1929. The outgoing Prime Minister (J. Ramsay MacDonald) then accepted the King's commission to form a National Government on a comprehensive basis for the purpose of dealing with the existing financial emergency. By the evening of Tuesday, August 25, the new Cabinet had been formed. It included the Leader of the Conservative Party (Stanley Baldwin) and the acting Leader of the Liberal Party (Sir Herbert — now Viscount — Samuel). By then the three directing executives of the Labour Movement had announced their decision to enter into vigorous opposition, a decision endorsed by the Parliamentary Labour Party on August 28. The Conservative and Liberal Parties on the same day agreed to support the new Government. On October 7 — much had happened in the interim — Parliament was dissolved. At the ensuing General Election on October 27, the National Government secured an overwhelming majority in the House of Commons. MacDonald then reconstructed his Ministry. His second National Government terminated in June of 1935.

The political crisis of 1931, which resulted in the formation of the National Government and its subsequent electoral triumph, has probably had an influence upon the course of British politics greater even than that of 1846, with which it has sometimes been compared. In the outcome, undesigned and unexpected, it brought to an end a period of political uncertainty and governmental instability which had characterized the previous decade. It led to a clarification of the political situation by promoting an alignment into two main parties. The disintegration and decline of the Liberal Party was accelerated; the Conservative Party was enabled to broaden its basis and transform its policy; while, for the Labour Party, the crisis marked the end of one vitally important stage on the path to power, and provided the opportunity for a fresh advance. Labour's longer-run prospects, it is true, were over-shadowed at the time, and for another decade, by the shock of the crisis itself, by the crushing electoral defeat which followed, and by the slowness of the subsequent recovery. What happened, or rather what is supposed to have happened, in 1931, made a deep and still potent impression in Labour Party circles. It aroused embittered and still continuing controversy. MacDonald's conduct, in particular, has been subjected to savage criticism. 'The denunciations heaped upon MacDonald's head by many who had previously idolized him were', wrote the late Viscount Simon, 'the most violent I have ever known in British politics.'[1]

Any change of Government is a major political event. The resignation of the second minority Labour Government would in itself have been unusually exciting because of its occasion, its causes, and its unavoidable consequences. The formation, in time of peace, of any kind of Coalition or 'National' Government, though often suggested during the previous months, would in any event have produced a radical transformation in the political situation and considerable controversy. But it was MacDonald's retention of the Premiership which provided the great surprise and sensation. Labour's first Prime Minister became the head of a Ministry which included the Leaders of the Conservative and Liberal parties; and sensation was added to sensation when his action was quickly repudiated by the Labour Party organization. The course of events, moreover, led unexpectedly to a General Election in which the former Labour Premier, with his Conservative, Liberal and Labour allies, fighting against the bitter opposition of the Labour Party and its Liberal associates, gained the greatest electoral victory, both personal and political, so far recorded in British experience.

Our political history provides no near parallel to the events of 1931. It is not surprising that they have figured prominently in commentaries upon our political system. The crisis raised interesting and important constitutional issues, and on that plane as well as on those of party politics and personalities there has been much controversy.

A re-examination of the crisis itself, and of the various controversies arising therefrom, is desirable on several grounds. In the first place, accounts emanating from Labour sources (as most

[1] *Retrospect*, p. 168.

accounts have done) have usually been much distorted by partisan and personal bias. The Labour Party's sensational defeat in the election of October 1931 aroused its enduring resentment and has coloured for it the whole story of the formation of the National Government. Disapproval and dislike of that Government's formation, and still more of the subsequent Election, have also warped in some degree the versions presented by influential Conservative commentators. Secondly, references to the crisis made in the course of academic writing (the two groups overlap) have often been both inadequate and inaccurate. Thirdly, new and authoritative information has been made available in recent years, notably in Sir Harold Nicolson's *King George the Fifth*. Finally, the appointment of Mr Harold Macmillan as Prime Minister after Sir Anthony Eden's resignation in January 1957, has revived interest in the constitutional aspects of the 1931 crisis.

The fact that there are still some gaps in our knowledge provides no sufficient justification for refraining from dealing with what is known, and with the partial, partisan or careless versions of the crisis which have been widely popularized. Such versions have had and continue to exercise much influence. The need for the kind of examination attempted in the following pages has been strengthened by the publication in recent years of two books of considerable importance. In Mr R. T. McKenzie's *British Political Parties* (1954), there are numerous allusions to the 1931 crisis, and although the author makes no attempt to present an account of what happened, he unquestioningly accepts the most melodramatic of the interpretations of MacDonald's actions given us by Labour critics. Mr C. L. Mowat's *Britain between the Wars, 1918–1940* (1955) is in a different category. It is the first full-length history of the period which has appeared, and for that reason, and because of his relatively detached and scholarly approach, his treatment of the 1931 crisis is of much interest and importance. It is none the less open to a considerable number of objections.

During the crisis weeks, and for some time afterwards, much relevant information was lacking. That, however, did not prevent assertions being made for which there was little or no supporting evidence: indeed, it provided scope for such assertions. The information supplied in more recent years by Sir Harold Nicolson and others has filled many gaps in our previous knowledge which others had tried to fill from their imaginations. It must be emphasized, none the less, that a great deal written about the crisis, both at the time and subsequently, was inconsistent with the facts currently available to the student of affairs.

Any account of the 1931 crisis must rest, first of all, upon the official and other statements made at the time, including the explanations then given by the political leaders to party meetings; and secondly upon the revelations of Cabinet discussions made in the course of the Parliamentary debates in September 1931 and later during the General Election campaign. The information available to the general public from these sources has since been supplemented either by political leaders themselves or by their authorized biographers.

The key personalities in the formation of the National Government on August 24, 1931, were, of course, King George V, the Prime Minister (MacDonald), the Conservative leader (Baldwin), and the acting Liberal leader (Samuel). Of these four men, Lord Samuel is to-day the only survivor. His *Memoirs*, published in 1945, are important, but not always accurate in detail. Mr G. M. Young produced in 1952 what purported to be the official biography of Baldwin: he had but scanty material at his disposal, and made disappointing use of it. His book adds little or nothing to our knowledge of the 1931 crisis; and the same thing is true, unfortunately, of Mr A. W. Baldwin's admirable biography, *My Father* (1955). An official biography of MacDonald remains to be written. That is the major difficulty. MacDonald's own case has not yet been fully presented (a fact to which no allusion is made even by Mowat), nor, so far as one can judge, is it likely to be available in the near future. Yet MacDonald, of course, was the central figure. On the other hand, the Royal Archives relative to King George V have now been examined, more particularly by Sir Harold Nicolson, whose book (published in 1952) gave us for the first time a detailed and authoritative account of the part played by the King.

For many years, the only detailed account of the crisis written by a leading participant was Snowden's *An Autobiography*, which appeared in 1934. As Chancellor of the Exchequer, Philip Snowden (afterwards Viscount Snowden) was one of the two chief representatives of the Labour Cabinet (the other, of course, was MacDonald) in the complex negotiations which preceded its break-up; and his book is of major importance, although not always reliable when dealing with matters outside his own direct experience, and one which has to be read in the light of his well-known personal antipathy to MacDonald.

Of the other members of the Labour Cabinet (the full Cabinet list is given in Appendix VI), Sidney Webb (Lord Passfield) wrote a brief account of the crisis, *What Happened in 1931: A Record*, published at the very beginning of 1932 in *The Political Quarterly* for January–March 1932, and subsequently reprinted as a Fabian tract (No. 237). Through the kindness of the Passfield Trustees, the present writer has had the opportunity of consulting Webb's papers on the crisis. The Trustees have also generously given him permission to quote extensively from Webb's own documents and from Beatrice Webb's diaries for this period. The latter have been edited and published by Mrs Margaret Cole (*Beatrice Webb's Diaries, 1924–1932*), and in all but a few instances the references given below are to this edition. Webb's 'record' of 1932 added little to our knowledge; but its 'avowedly hypothetical' parts have been eagerly and widely used by subsequent commentators. Nothing of importance was revealed in J. H. Thomas's *My Story*. The same is true of Lord Parmoor's *A Retrospect*, which, in its comments on the constitutional aspects of the crisis, is much confused. The account given by J. R. Clynes in his *Memoirs, 1924–1937*, is deplorable and useless. In her *Life of Arthur Henderson* (1938), Mrs Mary Agnes Hamilton appears to have relied mainly upon the account in Snowden's autobiography. Certain other biographies, such as R. W. Postgate's *George Lansbury* and T. N. Graham's *Willie Graham*, are of relatively little value.

Of the junior Ministers in the Labour Government, Mr Emanuel Shinwell's *Conflict without Malice* has given us an important letter of MacDonald's; Dr Hugh Dalton has published his *Memoirs* (1953), which throw some indirect light on the subject; while Lord Attlee's autobiography *As It Happened* (1954) adds nothing.

Shortly after the formation of the National Government and before the reassembly of Parliament on September 8, 1931, two documents were prepared for the use of the Labour ex-Ministers. The first of these was a Memorandum on the proceedings of the Labour Cabinet's Economy Committee; the second a Memorandum on the subsequent discussions in Cabinet. Although not detailed stage-by-stage records, they provide much confirmatory evidence, and references to them are made in the following pages.

In the negotiations preceding the resignation of the Labour

Cabinet, the leading parts on the Conservative side were played by Neville Chamberlain and Sir Samuel Hoare (now Viscount Templewood). Mr Keith Feiling's *Life of Neville Chamberlain* (1946) provides some important evidence, and Lord Templewood's *Nine Troubled Years* (1954) valuable confirmation.

On the basis of all the material now available, it is possible to clear up nearly all the disputed points. At the same time it must be stressed that examination of MacDonald's papers is likely to throw much fresh light on the subject. In this connection, I am grateful to Mr Malcolm MacDonald for the permission he has kindly given me to quote from his important letter of January 6, 1932, to Lord Passfield.

In the preparation of this book, the author has deliberately refrained from personal discussions with persons who played a part in the crisis. Experience suggests that memories are usually unreliable after such an interval of time. There is a danger, too, that undue weight may be given to the recollections of those who may be willing to indulge in them. It is hoped that this book will provoke any who have further information to make it available to the public.

Objections may be raised in some quarters to the attention given to the mistakes and shortcomings of other commentators. The author, however, has no apology to make for criticisms which he believes to be both justified and necessary. Distaste for controversy in these matters is often expressed nowadays; but much harm has been done by allowing errors and distortions to circulate unrefuted. The pose of contemptuous silence so frequently adopted is neither convincing nor effective. For his part, the author will welcome corrections and criticism.

CHAPTER I

THE BACKGROUND (1)

THE THREE-PARTY SYSTEM

W hat happened in 1931 can be properly understood only in the light of the extremely confused political situation which then existed. To-day (1957) the domestic political scene is dominated by two great parties, the Conservative and Labour Parties. That has been so, and to a steadily increasing degree, throughout the years following the Second World War and the abrupt ending of the war-time Coalition in the early summer of 1945; although the process was well under way before the War came. During this period, both major parties have held office with substantial majorities in the House of Commons; the Labour Party, for the first time in its history, from 1945 to 1950; the Conservative Party, for the first time since 1929, from 1955 to date. It is true that in 1950–51 the Labour Government had an extremely slender majority in the House of Commons, and that in the three-and-a-half years immediately following the Conservative Government's majority, though larger, was still unusually small. It is also true that neither party has yet succeeded in obtaining a majority of the votes cast at a General Election, although both have come very near doing so. For the Liberal Party still survives, despite crippling electoral discouragement, and is much stronger in the country than its tiny representation at Westminster might suggest. Minor parties also exist; and certainly the influence of the Communist Party is not to be measured by the fact that it has no avowed representative in the House of Commons. None the less it is both usual and legitimate to speak of a Two-Party alignment or 'system' in present circumstances. But no such system functioned in the period between the Wars, nor had functioned, even leaving the Irish Nationalists out of account, for at least a decade before. In the 'twenties and early 'thirties, indeed, it was customary to speak of 'the Three-Party system', and that phrase over-simplified the position, since the Liberal Party seldom operated as a unity, and then only in a formal sense.

This state of affairs may be attributed simply to the emergence of the Labour Party, founded as the Labour Representation Committee in 1900, and constituted a Party after the General Election of 1906. But, although it may now seem that the new Party had plainly come to stay, that was not so clear then or for some time to come.

In the years immediately preceding 1914, the advance of the Labour Party appeared to have been checked. The party was confronted by the difficulties against which any third party has to contend under our electoral system. Much Labour and even Socialist opinion was consequently expressed through the Liberal Party. Labour's parliamentary representation was for the most part dependent upon Liberal support or acquiescence. In the House of Commons from January 1910 onwards, the Labour Party constituted little more than a Left Wing of the Liberal Party; its ability to act as an independent political force being severely restricted by the desirability of maintaining the Liberal Government in office. In these years, it did not appear at all likely that the Labour Party would ever become a successful competitor for office with the Liberals and Conservatives. Its future as an independent Party was itself uncertain. A merger with the Liberals was a possibility. When James Ramsay MacDonald (Secretary of the Labour Party from its inception and, from 1911, Chairman and Leader) wrote his important but strangely neglected work, *Socialism and Government*, in 1909, his view of the evolution of the Labour Party embraced two alternatives. One was, of course, its gradual rise to the position of one of two great parties; but there was another, the adoption of its principles and objects by one of the two great parties. During the years 1910–14 the second seemed more likely to happen than the first. In this period, too, Labour's parliamentary leaders had to contend against a wave of disillusionment and anti-parliamentarianism in the Labour movement. It was a phase of militant industrial action and development in Trade Union organization, influenced by and promoting Syndicalism, then the popular revolutionary doctrine of the Left.

LABOUR AND THE FIRST WAR

The development of British political parties was profoundly

affected, indeed distorted, by the events of the first week of December 1916. The deposition of Asquith from the Premiership and his replacement by Lloyd George led to a split which proved fatal to the Liberal Party. The methods by which the change was accomplished provoked personal and group enmities which in turn intensified and prolonged the breach. Had it not been for this embittered and enduring cleavage in the Liberal ranks, it is more than doubtful if the Labour Party would have become one of the two main parties in the State. Certainly the process would have been much slower than it actually proved to be. Nor would it have been anything like so rapid, if indeed it had occurred at all, but for the impact of the First War itself, despite the fact that that War gave rise to serious internal dissensions in Labour's ranks.

Down to the last moment British participation in the War was opposed by the great majority of Labourites and Liberals (including the majority of the Liberal Cabinet). On August 3, 1914, after Sir Edward Grey's famous speech, MacDonald, speaking as Leader of the Labour Party and with its full authority, criticized Grey's policy and declared for neutrality, in concise and forthright terms. Two days later, after the declaration of war, the National Executive of the Labour Party passed a compromise resolution which, while not refusing co-operation in the war effort, condemned Grey's policy and asserted the duty to secure peace at the earliest possible moment. A majority of the Parliamentary Party objected to MacDonald's proposal to speak in the House of Commons on the lines of this resolution, and he thereupon resigned his Chairmanship. The work of leader was handed over to Arthur Henderson (who had succeeded MacDonald as Party Secretary in 1911), and he was subsequently elected Chairman 'for the war period'.

In May of 1915, when Asquith formed the first Coalition, he invited Labour participation. It is of some interest and importance to note that Henderson first approached the National Executive of the Party and secured its approval of such participation and of his own entry into the Cabinet. Asquith's invitation was then rejected by the Parliamentary Party, by a small majority, but was subsequently accepted by majority vote at a joint meeting of the two bodies. Henderson thereupon accepted a seat in the Cabinet, and two other Labour representatives took subordinate offices. The Labour Party thus relinquished its position of independence in face of the national emergency, although its decision was not sanctioned by a Party Conference until January 1916. With Henderson in the Coalition Cabinet, John Hodge became acting Chairman of the Parliamentary Party, and was later succeeded in that capacity by George Wardle. Henderson retained the Party Secretaryship. His position was curious, and often difficult, particularly in relation to the conscription issue. On that question the Trades Union Congress passed a resolution opposing, while a joint meeting of the Party's National Executive and the Parliamentary Party decided that the Labour Ministers should withdraw from the Government. Asquith, however, secured withdrawal of the resignations pending a decision by the Party's Annual Conference. That conference declared its opposition to conscription by a large majority, but at the same time endorsed the decision to enter the Coalition Government and instructed Henderson to remain in the Cabinet. Henderson thus had to share the responsibility for a policy repudiated by his own Party. When Lloyd George formed his administration in December 1916, he offered the Labour Party much increased representation. But it was only after a joint meeting of the National Executive and the Parliamentary Party with the new Premier that the decision was taken by a small majority to accept the offer, though the next Party Conference endorsed the decision emphatically. Henderson entered the small War Cabinet, and continued to retain the Party Secretaryship.

The strong minority opposition to these decisions comprised, or came to comprise, many different elements. The shorthand description of it as an 'anti-war' minority is in some ways very misleading. It was partly pacifist, the pacifist elements varying from those who were opposed to all war to those who, for one reason or another, were opposed to the particular war, and those who were in favour of trying to bring the war to an end by means of diplomatic negotiations. It included many who, while not opposed to the prosecution of the war, disagreed with the attitude and actions of the Labour Party majority; and the number of such people increased as the strains of the war were prolonged and intensified. The minority, however, also included militant revolutionaries.

The leadership of this Labour minority was largely provided, especially on its pacifist side, by the most influential of the Socialist societies, the Independent Labour Party, which, under Keir

Hardie's leadership, had been primarily instrumental in the formation of the Labour Party. In the I.L.P. the outstanding personalities (particularly after Hardie's death in August 1915) were
MacDonald and Philip Snowden. MacDonald's position has a
special interest and importance. To Snowden, a pacifist of uncompromisingly doctrinaire convictions, it was far from satisfactory. While taking the view that the war effort must be supported, MacDonald's efforts were directed (1) to making clear
what he considered to be the causes of the war, (2) to insistence
upon the need for, and the conditions of, a just and lasting peace,
(3) to the promotion of such a peace by diplomatic negotiations and
(4) the maintenance of civil liberties. In the public mind, however,
MacDonald was identified with the anti-war extremists of the
I.L.P. and other bodies. He was subjected to the most persistent
and violent abuse, and because of his position and activities
became the chief target of the self-appointed 'patriots' in the press.
One consequence of this was that he became the idol of considerable rank-and-file 'Left' elements in the Labour and Socialist
movement, ceasing for the time being to be for them a mistrusted
moderate. In fact, although exercising a potent influence within the
I.L.P., MacDonald worked chiefly during the war with a group of
people many of whom were not, certainly at that time, Labour or
Socialist, and who formed, with him, two actively influential
bodies, the Union of Democratic Control and the National Council
for the Protection of Civil Liberties.

Labour's internal war-time dissensions, acute though they often
were, did not lead to the break-up of the Party: on the contrary,
the Party emerged strengthened and relatively united. There were
many reasons for that; but perhaps the basic explanation is to be
found in the Party's structure, though the restraint and far-
sightedness of the more influential leaders on both sides played an
essential part. The Party was, as it still remains, a federal organization. It was based upon the 'Labour Alliance', an alliance between Trade Unions and Socialist societies. Prior to 1918, the
federation consisted almost exclusively of such bodies. There were
few local Labour Parties, and no effective individual membership
of the Labour Party as such. The Trade Unions, then as now,
were financially and numerically the dominant partners in the
Labour alliance. If substantially united on any issue, they were, as
they still are, in a position either to assert effective control over the

Party or to break it. That fact is particularly relevant to the 1931 crisis. The position resulting from it has had, as it continues to have, both advantages and disadvantages for the Labour Party. The basic interests of the Trade Unions are of course industrial and not directly political. On the other hand, the leadership of the Parliamentary Labour Party (and therefore of Labour Governments) has been drawn mainly from non-Trade Union elements, though partly from Trade Unionists who none the less have become, or tend to become, immersed in the political side of the Labour movement. The dichotomy between the industrial and political leadership of that movement has been a permanent factor in the situation. Conflict between them has usually been latent rather than open, and has assumed different forms at different times. On occasions the Trade Unions and the industrial leaders have appeared to be predominantly 'on the Left'; in other phases they have operated as a moderating, restraining force. The Parliamentary leadership has been severely handicapped by the independent actions of the Trade Unions or by the actual or potential revolt of the Trade Unions against its policies. At the same time the Trade Unions have provided a solid, stable foundation for the Labour Party in times of acute internal dissensions. That was so during the First War. The Trade Unions gave the Party an underlying unity absent in the case of the Liberals, although there was the danger that they might dissolve the alliance with the Socialist societies and form a new Trade Union Labour Party. And the war itself gave a great impetus to Trade Union organization, thus providing a potentially much stronger basis for the Labour Party.

The disruption of the Liberal Party, moreover, gave Labour the opportunity of rallying to its support the full strength of Labour and Socialist opinion in the country. And, while the Labour majority temporarily turned to collaboration with the Coalition Governments, the Labour minority entered into close association with like-minded Liberals and Radicals. This association was to prove in large measure enduring. Important accessions of strength came to Labour from the pacifist wing of the Liberal Party. In this respect, too, the federal structure of the Labour Party helped. The so-called 'anti-war' Liberals and Radicals would have found effective co-operation difficult and even undesirable with a Labour Party based entirely upon individual membership and controlled

by a 'pro-War' majority. But they were able to work with the
I.L.P., and to join it in increasing numbers.

None the less, the differences within the Labour Party, often
very sharp, as in regard to compulsory military service, and still
more so in regard to the decision to enter Lloyd George's Government, might well have led to a definite split and a breakdown of the
'Labour Alliance', had it not been for the moderating influence of
some of the leading personalities involved. In this connection,
three men were outstanding: Arthur Henderson, Party Secretary
whether in or out of the Cabinet, and concerned as always with the
maintenance of the Party's cohesion; MacDonald, who retained
his Treasurership of the Party throughout, and exercised a potent
restraining influence over the hot-heads within the I.L.P.; and the
Railwaymen's leader, J. H. Thomas, who, despite his strong support of the war, refused a seat in the Lloyd George Coalition, and
showed himself one of the most courageous defenders of civil
liberties during the war period and a staunch opponent of all
attempts to drive the minority out of the Party. Notwithstanding
the emotions often aroused, the two wings of the Party continued
to work together in conducting party business and a wide range of
war-time activities. And, as time went on and attention became
increasingly directed towards the problems of peace, the distance
separating the two main sections lessened. A turning-point
occurred when Henderson resigned from the War Cabinet in the
summer of 1917 on the question of the proposed International
Socialist Conference at Stockholm and devoted himself to Party
reorganization. At the end of that year the Labour Party was able
to present an agreed Memorandum on War Aims. Early in 1918,
it adopted its new constitution, largely the joint work of Henderson
and MacDonald. Its chief features were (1) the strengthening of
the position of the Trade Unions by giving them a controlling
voice in the selection of all members of the National Executive, and
(2) the decision to provide for constituency Labour Parties and
individual membership of the Party. Though the full effects of this
latter decision were not felt for some years to come, it involved a
relative weakening of the influence of the I.L.P., a process also
promoted by the drafting of *Labour and the New Social Order*, a
policy declaration which committed the Party for the first time to
explicit Socialist objectives and which was endorsed by the Party
Conference in June of 1918.

When the Party was confronted, after the signing of the Armistice, by an imminent General Election, the majority of the Parliamentary Party, led by J. R. Clynes, favoured continued participation in Lloyd George's Government until peace was signed. However, at the special Party Conference on November 14, 1918, the recommendation of the National Executive that the Party should resume its independence and withdraw its members from the Government was carried by a more than two-to-one majority. Clynes and most of his supporters accepted the situation; and the Labour Party entered the General Election campaign substantially united, in marked contrast to the shattered Liberal Party. None the less, the degree of unity in the Labour ranks must not be exaggerated. Four Labour Ministers (including two former Chairmen of the Party, Wardle and Barnes) fought the election as Government-supported candidates; the ultra-patriotic Labour elements formed an organization known as the National Democratic Party which operated as part of the Government combination; and the war-time cleavage in the party was reflected by the wide variations in the nature of the campaigns of the 363 candidates who, by a great effort, were nominated.

THE GENERAL ELECTION OF 1918

The decision of the Conservative Party to continue its support of a Coalition Government under Lloyd George's leadership was doubtless partly motivated by a recognition of the Premier's tremendous personal prestige at the close of hostilities, but it was also due to a realization on the part of the Conservative Leader, Bonar Law, and his more far-seeing associates, that the profound change in circumstances demanded far-reaching adjustments in their Party's organization and policy. In their view, the difficult problems arising out of the war could best be solved by continuance of the Coalition, so that the requisite reforms might be carried through, as Bonar Law himself put it, 'in a way as little revolutionary as possible.' Moreover, there was the chance, and the hope, that Lloyd George and his Liberal colleagues would come to work with the Conservatives just as Joseph Chamberlain and the Liberal and Radical Unionists had done after their breach with Gladstone over the Irish question. At the same time, Bonar Law was concerned not to allow participation in the Coalition to lead to a split in the Conservative ranks.

Any temptation to discuss at length the General Election of December 1918 must be resisted, but two important points require attention. The 'coupon' feature of the Election has been customarily distorted in subsequent comment. Lloyd George and Bonar Law, as the two Coalition leaders, were fully entitled to send a letter of endorsement to those candidates whom they regarded as supporters of their Government. They have been heavily attacked for denying this endorsement to the Asquithian Liberals; but the latter were in fact in opposition to the Lloyd George–Bonar Law administration; indeed, 'opposition' may well be considered too mild a description of their attitude. In a somewhat similar fashion, the electoral arrangements on the Government side have been condemned on the ground that the Conservatives drove a hard bargain with Lloyd George and secured a three-to-one majority of the Government candidatures. This was not, however, the result of Conservative pressure. It was partly due to the fact that the bulk of the Government's supporters seeking re-election were Conservatives, and partly to the fact that the Lloyd George Liberals, with an improvised organization and much Liberal opposition in the constituencies, could not find new candidates in greater numbers. Even so, the Conservative organization met with considerable difficulties (usually but not always overcome) in its attempts to give such candidates a clear field.

The result of the Election was a victory for the Coalition, overwhelming in terms of seats and decisive in terms of votes. The Independent or Asquithian Liberals met with a crushing defeat. Since the Sinn Feiners absented themselves from the new House of Commons, the 59 Labour members constituted numerically the chief opposition group and, successfully asserting their claim, became, prematurely, the official Opposition. The Parliamentary Labour Party in the 1918–22 Parliament was, however, inadequately representative of the party in the country, being drawn for by far the greater part from the 'pro-War' Trade Union elements. The principal leaders of the Party had nearly all been badly beaten. A Scottish miners' official, William Adamson, became Chairman, and thus Leader, of the Party. He proved mediocre and ineffective. The chief figures were J. R. Clynes, who succeeded Adamson in 1921, and J. H. Thomas. Henderson, who re-entered the House at a by-election in August 1919, did not resume the leadership, concentrating upon his work as Party Secretary.

PARLIAMENT OR REVOLUTION

During the immediate post-war years, the Labour movement passed through a stormy and testing phase. Nothing less was at stake than the future of British parliamentary democracy. Those on the Labour side who stood for parliamentary action were engaged in a stern fight, and one which was waged on many fronts, ideological as well as organizational, international as well as national.

Three powerful tendencies merged in the revolutionary or anti-parliamentary trend. One was the syndicalist influence, a survival from the pre-war period, with its emphasis upon direct industrial action for political ends; the second was the influence of the Russian Revolutions; and the third was the reaction to Labour's parliamentary weakness. Political activity and controversy was concentrated, to a far greater extent than is customary, outside Parliament. For the most part, the apparent sympathy displayed in Labour circles with the Soviet Government was a reaction to the attacks made upon that Government by Labour's domestic opponents, a disinclination to be too critical of a regime which, in spite of its methods, proclaimed itself and was condemned for being 'Socialist', and, above all, a refusal to support either the continuance or renewal of military operations anywhere, but least of all in Eastern Europe. None the less, the rejection of Soviet Communism was not a foregone conclusion, and a prolonged, many-sided struggle ensued.

The Communist Party of Great Britain was formed in July 1920. It applied at once for affiliation to the Labour Party; the first of many applications, all of which had considerable backing but all of which were to be turned down. The desire to re-establish a unified International Socialist organization also provided opportunities for the Communists and their sympathizers. The details of the struggle must not detain us, but two points have special import-ance. First, the alleged association of the Labour Party with the Bolsheviks, for which some Left-Wing elements provided plaus-ible though wholly inadequate justification, was persistently ex-ploited by Labour's opponents. Secondly, the outstanding oppon-ent of the Communist dictatorship and the most effective defender of parliamentary democracy, both theoretically and practically, was MacDonald. Alike in this country and in the international

Socialist movement, he played the leading part, ably supported by pen and speech by Snowden, and staunchly on the organizational side by Henderson.

After a period of unprecedented industrial unrest, culminating for the time being in the abandonment of a threatened General Strike and the collapse of the famous 'Triple Alliance' in the spring of 1921, and a succession of defeats sustained by the industrial side, the pendulum in the Labour movement swung back in favour of orthodox political action once again. It may be noted also that these years of the Coalition Government were the great days of the I.L.P., reinforced by Radical elements, not yet rendered redundant by the growth of the constituency Labour parties, and still effectively controlled, despite internal differences, by the moderates under the leadership of MacDonald and Snowden.

THE FALL OF THE COALITION

A recent historian has written that when the Lloyd George Coalition fell in mid-October 1922, there ended

> the reign of the great ones, the giants of the Edwardian era and of the war, and the rule of the pygmies, of the 'second-class brains' began, to continue until 1940.[1]

It is a strange comment, but no stranger than many of a similar kind; and it is certainly true that some of the Coalition leaders regarded themselves as 'giants' or as 'first-class brains', and those who eventually displaced them as 'members of the second eleven' or as 'unfit to govern', to use two well-known phrases coined by Churchill. Yet the fact remains that in less than four years the 'giants' fell from power so discredited that their leader was never to attain office again, and the ideas developed by some of his chief colleagues for a great permanent Centre Party or an anti-Labour coalition received a decisive check. Even if the Coalition leaders' valuation of themselves, and the fashionable estimate of them by so many present-day intellectuals, be accepted, it must none the less be pointed out that these 'first-class brains', despite the considerable achievements with which they can legitimately be credited, signally failed in their main task, that of conducting the government of the country in conformity with the requirements of parliamentary democracy. A. W. Baldwin has quoted a letter of his

[1] Mowat, op. cit. p. 142.

father's about the political situation in 1919 and 1920 in which the future Conservative leader wrote:

> The bitterness in the country was of the devil; no one in the higher political world seemed to realize it or give it a thought. One thing was clear to me, that under the then government which was Lloyd George, F. E. Smith and Winston, buttressed by the respectability of Balfour and Austen Chamberlain, things would get rapidly worse, until you might pass quickly into a condition little short of revolution. I felt that it was essential to break up that government, but it looked impregnable.[1]

That passage contains an important clue to an understanding of British politics during this period.

The collapse of Lloyd George's Coalition was brought about by a Conservative revolt. Though the attitude of the so-called 'Die-Hards' was a contributory factor of importance, the decisive influence was exerted by the emerging moderate leaders, and by Bonar Law, whose main preoccupation was the preservation of Conservative unity. It was part of a much wider public reaction against the character and policies of the Government, and especially against the Premier's own methods, but the detailed causes of the revolt need not detain us. The resulting fall of the Coalition marks an important turning-point in party politics. From that standpoint, the great question was whether or not the Coalition could be transformed into a single party in opposition to an advancing Labour Party now committed to Socialism; whether or not the temporary alliance of Conservatives and Liberals in the Coalition could be made permanent and extended. Such a development was agreeable to Lloyd George, ardently advocated by Churchill, and favourably regarded by the chief Conservative leaders, especially by Austen Chamberlain (who in March 1921 succeeded Bonar Law as Leader of the House of Commons and of the Conservative Party), Birkenhead (F. E. Smith) and Balfour. When, despite but largely in consequence of mounting evidence that Conservatives desired to resume their independence, the Coalition leaders decided in the autumn of 1922 to seek a dissolution of Parliament and to go to the country as a Coalition, they were decisively defeated at the famous Carlton Club meeting of Conservative M.P.s which they had themselves summoned. The opposition to them was led by

[1] A. W. Baldwin, op. cit. p. 327.

Stanley Baldwin and by most of the Junior Ministers, but received the last minute backing of Lord Curzon, and, more decisively, that of Bonar Law, to whom the main consideration undoubtedly was a fear lest the Conservative Party should be hopelessly and permanently split if the Coalition were to continue. By rather more than two to one, the Conservative M.P.s decided to fight the next Election as an independent party. Lloyd George thereupon resigned; Austen Chamberlain renounced the Conservative leadership; Bonar Law was elected in his place and accepted the task of forming a purely Conservative Government and seeking the support of the electorate for it.

THE 1922 AND 1923 ELECTIONS

The hopes of those who sought to confront the Labour Party with a great Conservative-Liberal alliance were thus shattered. For another decade at least there was to be what came to be called a three-party system. In reality the position was much more complicated than that phrase would suggest; and the country was to have the unpalatable experience of three General Elections in less than three years before governmental stability was temporarily achieved. Even then the so-called three-party system persisted. Instead of any formal merger of Conservative and Liberal elements into a single Centre Party, what was to happen was the consolidation and modernization of the Conservative Party. Under Baldwin's leadership, that Party was transformed into a broadly-based party pursuing a moderate and progressive policy, increasingly attracting Liberal and even Labour support, without losing the backing of the Right Wing minority elements, however troublesome the latter might be.

Conservative unity was not speedily restored. The evicted and enraged 'first-class brains' at once went into vigorous and confident action against the new Government; and at the General Election of November 1922 Bonar Law was opposed by these dissident Conservative Coalitionists, by the Lloyd George or National Liberals, by the Asquithian Liberals, overjoyed at the fall of Lloyd George but fighting independently, and by the more formidable Labour Party, itself a kind of coalition of extremely divergent elements. The keynote of Bonar Law's campaign was, in his own words, 'tranquillity and freedom from adventures and commitments both at home and abroad.' During the contest he gave a pledge, which was to prove important, that he would make no change in the fiscal system until he had made a second appeal to the nation.

The outcome of this extremely confused election was a working Conservative majority in the House of Commons of about 80; but in terms of votes the Conservatives were in a very considerable minority. The two sections of the divided Liberals came back in almost equal strength one to the other; and their total vote in the country was approximately the same as that cast for the Labour Party. But it was the advance of the latter which provided the most significant feature of the results. Labour's strength in the House rose to 138; MacDonald, Snowden, and most of the other 'anti-war' leaders were returned, together with notable Pacifist and Radical recruits; and the I.L.P. was strongly represented. Attracting the greatest stir were the newcomers from Scotland, among whom were those militant Left-Wing personalities who became known as the 'Clyde Group', led by an able Roman Catholic business man, John Wheatley, and by James Maxton, a charming man and an artist on the platform, but hopelessly lacking in the requisite qualities of leadership.

At the first meeting of the Parliamentary Labour Party after the election, MacDonald was elected Chairman and Leader. He had a small majority over Clynes, who had held the position in the preceding year; and the suggestion has frequently been made in later years that MacDonald owed his election to a mistaken assumption that he was a man of the Left on the part of the Clydesiders who were among those who voted for him. But the latter group's support of MacDonald, like that of the bulk of the new Labour M.P.s, is easily explicable on other grounds. It would have been surprising indeed if the 'Left' had preferred Clynes, in view of his record during the war and his support of the Coalition Government down to the very last moment. Moreover, the preference for MacDonald was a natural recognition of his obviously superior abilities. The large vote for Clynes was basically a 'loyalty' vote on the part of those M.P.s who had been in the previous Parliament, although to some extent an expression of narrow Trade Unionist sentiment.

With an assured majority, the new Conservative Government might well have continued in office for several years. That, however, did not happen. Bonar Law was compelled to retire after a Premiership of little more than six months, and died some five months later. Stanley Baldwin was selected as his successor in preference to Lord Curzon. The controversy which still persists concerning the details of his selection can be ignored. The reasons for it are plain enough. Curzon's personality and temperament were unsuited to the changed political conditions, and his appointment would probably have proved fatal to his party. Most of his ministerial colleagues were opposed to his selection, and the dissident Coalitionists whom it was hoped to bring back into the fold would have found it even more objectionable. The fact that Curzon was a peer provided a convenient excuse for passing him over.

Relatively unknown to the general public at the time of his appointment, Baldwin rapidly established his authority in the House of Commons. But, in less than eight months he was out of office and the first Labour Government had been installed. Baldwin's motives in resorting to a dissolution of Parliament in November of 1923 have been much discussed. The decisive consideration, in all probability, was his desire to secure release from Bonar Law's pledge. In his view, the unemployment problem could only be dealt with satisfactorily by a protective tariff, and for that a mandate from the electorate was required. Other considerations undoubtedly played their part. By raising the issue of protection, the danger of a revival of the Conservative-Liberal Coalition would be removed, a reconciliation could be effected with Austen Chamberlain and the dissentient Conservatives, and, if Liberal reunion were also promoted, so much the better, since such a development might check Labour's advance.

Although Baldwin at once secured the backing of Austen Chamberlain and his associates, the Conservatives were by no means all in favour of a protectionist policy. Still less was there agreement about the precise nature of any tariff proposals. The actual proposals presented to the electorate were general and ambiguous: the Conservative Free Traders acquiesced with great reluctance, the ardent Protectionists with anxiety. Baldwin had little wholehearted or effective press backing. The newspapers controlled by Lords Beaverbrook and Rothermere, though claiming to be archprotectionist, devoted themselves to attacks upon Baldwin. Rothermere himself even reached the point of urging that the Liberals should be supported and Free Trade given another chance. The bitter opposition to Baldwin of these Press Lords was to be one of the central political facts during the following decade and a half.

Baldwin's decision led to an immediate reunion, for election purposes, of the two parts into which the Liberal Party had been so bitterly divided; and to an energetic campaign on the old Free Trade basis. Churchill was one of the first to rally to the cause, and Lloyd George agreed to serve under Asquith's leadership. Liberals, indeed, were jubilant and hopeful that they might at least recover to the point of being able to supplant Labour as the official Opposition. The protectionist issue was an embarrassment to the Labour Party, which consequently sought to represent that issue as a diversion, and to conduct its electoral campaign on the widest possible front, distinguishing itself as far as possible from the Liberals, and concerned above all else to prevent any Liberal revival and to promote that Party's destruction. The assumption, common to both Right and Left in the Labour Party, that the road to political power lay through the elimination of the Liberal Party was another cardinal feature of the political situation in these years.

In terms of votes the General Election of 1923 showed remarkably little change; but in terms of seats, owing to the vagaries of our electoral system, the transformation was striking. The Conservatives found themselves in a minority of nearly 100, although, with 258 seats, still the largest single party. Labour held 191 seats; the Liberals 159. The resulting Parliamentary situation was unprecedented, and the quite unexpected outcome of the Election was a Labour Government. The great Liberal effort had failed as against Labour. On the other hand, the considerable successes of the Liberals as against the Conservatives placed the former in an unhappy situation. The circumstances of the Election and the clash of personalities barred any prospect of a Conservative-Liberal Coalition; and, although Baldwin, quite properly, did not resign until defeated in the new House of Commons, there was no real alternative to giving Labour the opportunity of forming a Government. Nor for the Labour Party was there any practical alternative to acceptance of the opportunity. With the full consent of his colleagues, MacDonald undertook what Lord Stamfordham, the King's Secretary, described as 'what we must all admit will be a task of almost incalculable magnitude'.

The First Labour Government

MacDonald had always thought that Labour's first chance of Government would come to it as a minority; but no one had envisaged that the opportunity would come so soon or that when it

came Labour would not be the largest single party and would not
have the support of even a third of the electorate. No doubt many
on the Labour side would have preferred a Conservative-Liberal
coalition, but there was general agreement that Labour had to take
office, and general agreement also that no alliance with the Liberals
should be entered into. No such concensus of opinion existed,
however, about the line a Labour minority government should
pursue. A substantial minority wanted Labour to take office with
the sole purpose of producing a full socialist programme and so
inviting immediate defeat and another appeal to the country. The
attitude so expressed was to be persisted in, and to gather strength
as the first Labour Government proceeded on its difficult path.
MacDonald and his leading colleagues, on the other hand, decisively rejected this notion of 'riding for a fall'. In his and their
opinion, it would have been a fatuous gesture to go in for the sake
of coming out. It would have been to throw away the chance of
demonstrating to the electorate that the Labour Party was capable
of governing the country and willing to put the national interests
above narrow party considerations. It would have destroyed the
prospect of gaining the confidence of the predominantly non-
Socialist public; and to achieve that confidence was, from the party
standpoint, the primary and all-important task. The only practicable line, in the view of the party leaders, was to try to administer
the nation's affairs in a moderate and responsible manner. Not
unnaturally, such a line was highly repugnant to the Left Wing and
to Socialist doctrinaires in general. This fact, combined with the
circumstances in which MacDonald took office, the weakness of
his support in the House of Commons and the country, the inadequacy of his resources in terms of personnel, and the almost
total lack in his Party of previous governmental experience, made
the task exceptionally difficult. Indeed, the formation of the first
Labour Government was 'a great adventure', even, as MacDonald
is said to have described it, 'an insane miracle'.

Though brief, the experiment lasted much longer than had been
anticipated; and its effects upon British politics were far-reaching.
When finally defeated in the House of Commons early in October
1924 on a question of confidence, MacDonald claimed, modestly
but justly, that the Labour Party had 'shown the country that they
have the capacity to govern in an equal degree with the other
Parties in the House', and that they had 'left the international

c

situation in a more favourable position than that which they in-
herited'.[1] The first Labour Government was in fact more successful and impressive in its external than in its home policy. Combin-
ing the arduous duties of Foreign Secretary with those of the
Premiership, MacDonald greatly enhanced his personal reputation
and that of his Government. As Chancellor of the Exchequer,
Philip Snowden also created an excellent impression upon the
general public. The Government's chief political troubles came
from within the Labour movement itself; for neither the Socialist
militants nor the pacifist elements proved willing to accept — if,
indeed, they grasped — the conditions of parliamentary government, still less those of a minority government. And it is difficult
to-day to recapture the atmosphere in which the Government's
conformity to traditional constitutional forms and procedures outraged and excited so many of the faithful.

The circumstances in which this first Labour administration was
defeated in the Commons and in which the consequential General
Election was contested aroused much subsequent controversy.
Considerations of space forbid any detailed treatment of them. In
the Election of October 1924, the Conservatives won an overwhelming majority of seats and proceeded to govern for four-and-a-
half years, but they had obtained considerably less than fifty per
cent of the votes cast. The Labour Party's representation fell from
191 to 151, but the Party's vote was up by well over a million. The
Liberals, on the other hand, met with a crushing disaster, their
numbers being reduced to 40, and their popular vote falling by
more than 1¼ millions. Because of its most sensational incident,
this Election has come to be known as the 'Red Letter' election,
and, following many precedents and foreshadowing others, the
results have frequently been attributed to a successful stunt, or
scare. But had there been no Zinoviev or 'Red' Letter, no proposed
Anglo-Russian Treaties, no Red scare or Russian Bolshevik issue,
and had Labour's opponents presented the unusual spectacle of
complete electioneering rectitude, the outcome would not in all
probability have been very different from what it was. The basic
explanation is that the coming into existence of a Labour Government led larger numbers of electors to view the real issue as one
between the Labour and Conservative Parties. This process was
accelerated by the reduction in the number of triangular contests:

[1] Letter to the King, quoted by Nicolson, op. cit., p. 401.

for there was a very considerable fall in the number of Liberal candidatures, a fall which reflected the embarrassing position of the Liberal Party and the deterioration in its fortunes during the year. The extent of the Conservative triumph was due to the Liberal eclipse. For the time being the larger part of the Liberal vote went Conservative rather than Labour, and conspicuously so in those areas where Labour had scored its earlier successes.

THE CONSERVATIVE GOVERNMENT, 1924–29

Baldwin's new administration included not only the leading Conservative ex-Coalitionists, with Austen Chamberlain at the Foreign Office, but also, to the general surprise, Churchill, as Chancellor of the Exchequer. But, during the following years, it was the Premier himself whose personality and outlook gave to the Ministry its distinguishing characteristics. The strength of his position came essentially from the fact that he inspired and merited trust. Seldom if ever has a party leader been so respected by his political opponents of all shades of opinion. A great House of Commons man, his hold over that assembly has scarcely been paralleled, while as a speaker in the country he achieved great popularity and influence. In politics, Baldwin's chief preoccupation was to improve industrial and social relations. Like MacDonald on the other side, he consistently sought to guide his Party into the path of moderation and to keep it there. Both leaders were often checked and even set back from time to time; but their complementary contributions in this all-important respect were of lasting importance. The almost general acceptance of the methods of parliamentary democracy, and the much wider appreciation of what they in practice involve, owe much to the two outstanding statesmen of the inter-war years. Nowadays this evolution is taken so much for granted that the debt to them is seldom acknowledged.

In the period immediately following the 1924 Election, the Labour movement experienced one of those deviations to the Left which have often been the response to electoral disappointment. This development, however, was much more pronounced on the Trade Union side than on the political side. It is true that there was renewed Left-Wing criticism of the minority government experiment. This was accompanied by criticism of MacDonald's leadership, more particularly on account of his alleged ineptitude in dealing with the Zinoviev Letter.[1] But no serious challenge to MacDonald's leadership materialized; and, at the Labour Party Conference in 1925, Ernest Bevin's attempt to commit the Party never again to take office whilst having only a minority of the seats in the House of Commons was decisively defeated. On the political side, in fact, Labour was soon moving rightwards. Things were different on the industrial side. That was largely due to the industrial situation, in which the Unions were waging a stern defensive struggle. But there were other important factors. Influential posts in the Trade Union movement were occupied for the time being by Left-Wingers like A. J. Cook (the Miners' Secretary), A. A. Purcell and John Bromley. There was a swing back from parliamentary to direct industrial action, to which men like Bevin still largely pinned their faith. The leftward trend was also promoted by the Communist-inspired, and afterwards Communist-dominated, National Minority Movement.

The threat of serious industrial unrest confronted the new Government from the outset. In March 1925, by a courageous act of leadership, Baldwin sought to reduce the tension. Imposing his will on a largely reluctant Cabinet, he secured the withdrawal of a bill the purpose of which (to restrict contributions to the political funds of a Trade Union to those of its members who specifically consented to contribute) he and his party approved, but to which the Labour movement strongly objected. Rightly described by his biographer as by universal consent one of the few masterpieces of Parliamentary eloquence in modern times, Baldwin's speech on that occasion made a lasting impression upon Parliament and the country, not least in the ranks of his political opponents. Yet, in little over a year, there occurred the dramatic event of the General Strike, and in 1927 the Trade Disputes and Trade Unions Act embraced the proposal which Baldwin had induced his party to abandon in March 1925.

It was at the end of April 1925 that Churchill announced the return to the Gold Standard at the pre-war parity of exchange. This marked the achievement of a goal to which British policy had been directed ever since the conclusion of hostilities, and an

---

[1] The publication of this Letter and of the Foreign Office Note of protest placed MacDonald in an extremely embarrassing position. Readers who care to examine this incident will experience difficulty in understanding how MacDonald could have dealt with the resulting situation differently, and still greater difficulty in ascertaining what his detractors thought he ought to have done.

important step towards the restoration of international monetary stability and economic recovery. Approved by the bulk of expert opinion, and widely welcomed both at home and abroad, the return to gold was in later years to be severely censured. At the time criticism was concentrated on the parity at which the return was made, and its soundness or otherwise is still a subject of controversy. It can be said, however, that the adverse effects forecast by the critics did not materialize during the next five years or so, except perhaps in the case of the coal industry. In that particular instance, moreover, the difficulties which developed were certainly not due, either exclusively or mainly, to the return to gold.

The General Strike of 1926 has been justly described[1] as an interruption, but an interruption only, of the even tenor of Baldwin's Government and the course of economic recovery. The occasion of it arose from the lamentable condition of the coal industry, the deflationary pressure upon the miners' wages and hours of labour, and the unyielding obstinacy both of the coal owners and the miners' leaders. From one standpoint the Strike may be viewed as the belated culmination of the syndicalist-direct-actionist trend of the years immediately preceding and following the First War; and it may well be that trial and failure were needed to deprive the idea of the General Strike as a political instrument of the attraction it had long had for militant elements in the Labour movement. No doubt such elements hoped that the Strike might be turned into some sort of revolutionary movement. The great masses of the strikers, on the other hand, viewed their action simply as support of the miners in an industrial dispute and indirect defence of their own living standards. But, however unintentionally, the Strike was a challenge to parliamentary government. That any such action was bound to be so had long been argued by MacDonald, Snowden, and the other theoretical critics of Syndicalism, and by J. H. Thomas and other Trade Union leaders. The Government were equally bound to meet the challenge, and by 1926 had made adequate preparations for such a contingency. The majority of the General Council of the T.U.C. had persistently sought to avert a development which they viewed without the slightest enthusiasm; and when the unwanted Strike came their overriding object and desire was to bring it to an end at the earliest possible moment.

The General Strike and its shorter-run political consequences

[1] Mowat, op. cit., p. 284.

were a set-back to Baldwin's policy. On both sides the political leaders had to temporize with and partially to give way to their respective party militants. At the critical stage, the majority opinion in the Cabinet undoubtedly was that the challenge of a General Strike would have to be faced sooner or later and had better be met without further delay. And, although the rapid collapse of the Strike greatly increased the Government's prestige, Baldwin was unable to resist the widespread demands for legislative action to prevent any repetition of the experience. Nor could he himself repeat his gesture of March 1925 and refrain from dealing with the conditions under which the Trade Unions raised their political funds. In this respect the Government's action could very plausibly be represented as a piece of partisan vindictiveness, and it certainly incurred the enduring resentment of the Trade Unions and the Labour Party machine, though the general public treated the matter with indifference. But, despite this grievance, and the long-drawn-out struggle in the coalfields, Baldwin's general line was resumed and met with considerable success. Reactions on the Labour side helped greatly.

During the Strike, Labour's political leadership was temporarily thrust into the background. All that MacDonald and his associates could do was quietly to exert their influence on the side of industrial peace. But the effect of the Strike failure on the Labour movement was to turn it decisively away from industrial to political action once again, with MacDonald and the moderates once more in the ascendant. The predominant attitude in Trade Union circles became 'Never Again'; and the industrial and political wings were brought into substantial harmony for the time being. In 1927 and 1928 the rightward trend in the Trade Union movement became as pronounced as that in the Labour Party.

The I.L.P., however, continued to move left, and in so doing broke completely with its former leaders and began rapidly to decline. The process had begun in 1925 with the gradual formulation of what came to be known as the 'Living Wage' policy for achieving 'Socialism in Our Time'.[1] This programme was accept-

---

[1] Largely the work of E. F. Wise, a salaried official of the Russian Co-operative movement, H. N. Brailsford, the editor of the I.L.P. weekly, the *New Leader*, and J. A. Hobson, this policy aimed to secure a living wage for all by law, with state-provided family allowances, compulsory reorganization of industries unable to meet their new obligations, and nationalization of all key industries.

able neither to the Trade Unions nor the Labour Party leadership nor to Fabian planners like the Webbs. In October 1925 Mac-Donald's objections to it led to his removal from the editorship of the *Socialist Review* which he had conducted with such distinction for many years on behalf of the I.L.P. Partly as a result of this Clifford Allen (afterwards Lord Allen of Hurtwood) resigned the I.L.P. Chairmanship; and after a brief period during which the veteran F. W. Jowett was acting Chairman, the I.L.P. made the fatal mistake of electing James Maxton. If not the beginning of the end for the I.L.P., that was a great step forward towards the end. In 1927, the I.L.P. refused to choose MacDonald as one of its delegates to the Labour Party Conference or to nominate him for the Treasurership, as it had always done previously. For the time being MacDonald retained his I.L.P. membership. Snowden, however, resigned. The breach widened in 1928. When, as a result of discussions held at the invitation of Sir Alfred Mond (afterwards Lord Melchett) and a group of big employers with the T.U.C. General Council, proposals for improving industrial relations were presented, Maxton joined with A. J. Cook in issuing a manifesto denouncing 'class-collaboration' and demanding 'unceasing war against capitalism'. Maxton secured I.L.P. endorsement of his action and retained the Chairmanship. He also obtained a decision which required all I.L.P. candidates to give a pledge to carry out, if elected, the decisions of the I.L.P. conference. This decision accelerated the end of the I.L.P. as an effective force, since it implied the establishment within the Labour Party of a Party having first claim upon the allegiance of its members, a position which the Labour Party could not tolerate, and which the great majority of I.L.P. candidates and M.P.s were not prepared to accept.

In preparation for the impending General Election, the Labour Party prepared and adopted a revised statement of its long-term policy. This document, *Labour and the Nation*, was not an election programme, but a statement of aims and principles, designed partly as a response to Left-Wing activities but also to meet the renewed challenge of the Liberal Party, now under Lloyd George's energetic leadership. Asquith, who had lost his seat at the 1924 election, retired to the House of Lords in the following year. Differences of view with Lloyd George about the General Strike led to the latter's departure from the so-called Liberal 'Shadow

Cabinet'. Owing to ill-health, however, Asquith resigned the party leadership in October 1926. He was succeeded by Lloyd George, a situation highly uncongenial to the Asquithians, and one which some of them from the outset refused to accept. Walter Runciman led a small group of Radicals in opposition to Lloyd George. The Party's prospects improved in the course of 1927. The influence of Sir Herbert Samuel, who had been out of the country as High Commissioner for Palestine, and was relatively detached, was exerted on the side of unity. Lloyd George offered to finance Party candidates out of the fund which he controlled; and it was decided to put 500 candidates in the field at the next Election. Although Lord Grey and other disgruntled Asquithians formed a Liberal Council of their own, there developed a much improved measure of unity in the Liberal ranks, and, primarily owing to Lloyd George's own drive, tremendous political activity. Particularly important were the series of inquiries and policy reports which were issued, notably *Britain's Industrial Future*. These led up to the Liberal Election programme, *We Can Conquer Unemployment*, the essential feature of which was a large deficit-financed public works programme. Under Lloyd George's inspiration, the Liberals were to make their last great bid to recover their status in the country and political power.

The leadership of the Conservative Party is customarily much in advance of its rank-and-file. In Baldwin's case this was conspicuously so. Whether in social and domestic affairs, or in imperial and international affairs, the Premier was well to the left of his party. His Government's record of useful social legislation was second to none in the inter-war years. For this the main credit goes to Neville Chamberlain who, as Minister of Health, carried through a very extensive legislative programme, the chief feature of which was the Local Government Act of 1929, although the Widows' and Old Age Contributory Pensions Act was in its way of parallel importance. At the Exchequer, Churchill played a major contributory part in the Government's progressive policies, but in the sphere of external relations there were signs of his disagreement with the prevailing trends.

In the period following the General Strike, economic conditions improved considerably; employment as a whole continued to expand; unemployment fell in 1927, and after a rise in the following year, declined again. But, in the closing stages of the Baldwin administration, there is no doubt that its position weakened, despite the Premier's personal prestige and the partial economic recovery. On the Conservative side divergencies of view existed or arose on a wide range of issues. That was notably so in regard to House of Lords Reform (a scheme for which had to be abandoned), on Disarmament, on India, and about tariffs as a means of reducing unemployment, the major domestic problem. The foreign policy of the Government met with increasing criticism, notwithstanding the apparent success of Austen Chamberlain's co-operative work with France and Germany following upon the conclusion of the Locarno Agreements. That was partly due to the worsening of relations with Russia and to difficulties and incidents in the Far East, but mainly to the lack of progress in regard to Disarmament. In the sphere of external relations, public interest and enthusiasm were concentrated on this issue. Chamberlain was subjected to widespread attacks for his allegedly pro-French attitude. The Liberal press, with Lloyd George himself actively contributing, was memorably and bitterly violent in criticism of France, and in denunciation of Chamberlain's attempt to effect a compromise between the British and French views on Disarmament. In the summer of 1927, moreover, a three-power conference on Naval Disarmament (between Great Britain, the U.S.A. and Japan) failed completely because of the conflicting British and American views; and the failure provided the occasion for Lord Cecil's resignation from the Government. Lack of zeal in the cause of Disarmament, and Churchill's alleged influence in that regard, were major counts in the indictment of the Government presented by both Oppositions.

CHAPTER II

THE BACKGROUND (2)

THE SECOND LABOUR GOVERNMENT

The General Election of May 1929 brought to an end the temporary phase of governmental stability. It was a three-party contest in the full sense. Each party presented 500 candidates or more; and, although the campaign was uneventful, there was a high poll in an electorate increased by over 7 millions (largely as a result of the extension of the franchise to women between the ages of 21 and 30). Baldwin's confident reliance upon his Government's record and the slogan 'Safety First' proved in the outcome to have been misplaced. The Conservatives, with a total vote of well over 8¾ millions, obtained only 260 seats. Labour, with a lower popular vote, under 8½ millions, secured 288. The Liberal Party, although polling more than 5¼ million votes, was grossly under-represented in the new House, holding only 59 seats. The last full-scale Liberal challenge, as it was to prove to be, had failed. Despite the discrepancy between votes and seats, the result was a bitter disappointment to the Liberals. Yet the strength of Liberalism, particularly as against Labour, in wide areas of the country, must be borne in mind.

Labour, however, had come near getting a majority, and for the first time was the largest single party in the House of Commons, though not in the country. This time Baldwin did not delay his resignation, and on June 5, 1929, MacDonald accepted the task of forming a second Labour Government. The Labour Party leaders were entirely in accord about taking office again. Much more obviously than in 1924 there was no practicable alternative, save a formal coalition with the Liberals, and for that no support was for the time being forthcoming. The composition of the new Government was settled by MacDonald in close consultation with Henderson, Snowden, Thomas and Clynes. These men constituted the so-called 'Big Five' of the second Labour administration, although in its later stages Clynes's place was increasingly taken by William Graham, who became President of the Board of Trade in the new Government. The Cabinet (numbering 19 at the outset) was almost exclusively moderate or Right Wing; the only representative of the Left being George Lansbury, as First Commissioner of Works. Personnel difficulties, though not so acute as in 1924, again arose in regard both to the House of Lords and the Law Officers. In the former case the situation was met for the time being by Sidney Webb's acceptance of a peerage — which caused Beatrice much subsequent worry — as Lord Passfield, in charge of the Dominions and Colonies; and by the elevation of Brigadier C. B. Thomson, who, as Lord Thomson, became Secretary of State for Air. As to the Law offices, an Attorney-General was found in Sir William Jowitt (later Earl Jowitt), who had been elected as a Liberal, but promptly joined the Labour Party, sought re-election, and was returned by a large majority. The new Solicitor-General, Sir Stafford Cripps, was outside Parliament, and had to wait until early in 1931 before obtaining a seat, after much difficulty, at Bristol. The Lord Advocate, Craigie Aitchison, a Liberal, was a little more fortunate, obtaining a seat in the House of Commons in the following November as Labour member for Kilmarnock; but the Solicitor-General for Scotland, a non-party appointment in this instance, never entered the House.

The major difficulties in forming the new Government, however, related to the Foreign Office. These difficulties strained the relations between the 'Big Five' and had lasting effects. They sprang from Arthur Henderson's determination to have the Foreign Secretaryship. MacDonald, whose primary interest was in external affairs, and who intended again to play an active role in this sphere, naturally desired that the Foreign Office should be in the hands of someone with whom he could work harmoniously. His candidate for the post, therefore, was J. H. Thomas. Henderson strongly objected. MacDonald suggested that Henderson should take charge of employment policy with the post of Lord Privy Seal. Henderson refused, and threatened to decline office altogether. MacDonald then proposed that he should take the Foreign Office himself for a time in addition to the Premiership. Henderson was equally opposed to that. Sir Harold Nicolson has provided us with the evidence that at one stage MacDonald offered to give up the Premiership in order to take the Foreign Office, but that proved

generally unacceptable to his colleagues.[1] On the assumption that
MacDonald was to be Foreign Secretary as well as Premier, J. H.
Thomas had agreed to take the Dominions Office, only to find that
Henderson persisted in his attitude. It was then, reluctantly, that
Thomas accepted the post of Lord Privy Seal and the onerous task
of directing employment policy. MacDonald gave way to what
Snowden described as Henderson's 'stubborn pertinacity'; but,
although Henderson became Foreign Secretary, MacDonald retained certain important aspects of foreign policy, notably Anglo-
American relations, under his own control, and exercised active
supervision over the general conduct of external relations. There
can be no doubt that this episode, and its outcome, seriously prejudiced personal relations, never good, within the inner circle of
the Labour Government.[2]

So varied, and so often contradictory, are the assessments of the
leading personalities in this Government that one hesitates to ven-
ture upon any discussion of the subject. More especially is this the
case with the Prime Minister himself. It would be no exaggeration
to say that it has become fashionable to represent him as a sort of
half-wit. 'Woolly' and 'senile' are favourite adjectives. Many of our
brighter young men are content to quote, out of its context,

---

[1] Op. cit., p. 435.

[2] Mowat (op. cit., pp. 353–4) does not bring out Henderson's refusal to accept
any post other than that of Foreign Secretary; makes no allusion to Nicolson's
disclosure; and writes, with obvious inconsistency, that Thomas 'had apparently
been captivated by the opportunities open to the man who would meet the great
challenge of unemployment'. R. T. McKenzie (op. cit., p. 316, footnote) refers
his readers to Snowden 'for a description of the rather acrimonious discussions
between MacDonald and his colleagues on the subject of Cabinet making', and
also to passages in Dalton's reminiscences. He has nothing to say about Henderson's attitude, although this is assuredly relevant to his discussion of the Prime
Minister's freedom in the appointment of Ministers. And it may be pointed out
that there is no reference in Snowden to acrimony between MacDonald and his
colleagues; the acrimony was between Henderson and Thomas.

An example of the tricks which memory plays is provided in Sir Arthur
(afterwards Lord) Salter's *Personality in Politics* (pp. 58–9). Writing of Mac-
Donald's first Labour Government in 1924, he says: 'MacDonald's Foreign
Minister was Arthur Henderson, organizer and controller of the party machine,
already a not negligible rival. Jealous by temperament, MacDonald increasingly
acted as if, like several preceding Prime Ministers, he was also his own Foreign
Secretary, with Henderson rather a Minister for Geneva. He developed the
idea (and did not conceal it) that major foreign policy usually went wrong if he
did not handle it himself. This jealousy and distrust led to serious rivalry in the
Cabinet, substantially affected foreign policy, and contributed to the causes of
the break up of the party seven years later.' Henderson, of course, was not
Foreign Minister in the 1924 Government. MacDonald was Foreign Minister
as well as Premier. Henderson was Home Secretary, although he was one of the
Government delegation at Geneva.

Churchill's phrase about the 'boneless wonder'.[1] MacDonald, like
so many other Premiers, is charged with 'vanity' and 'aloofness'.
It would be intolerably tedious to enumerate the denigratory
epithets so extensively employed. In these circumstances, it is
desirable, and even necessary, to make some points about this
remarkable man, the drama of whose political career is unparalleled
in our modern history. In doing so, it will be best to rely upon the
judgments and words of his political opponents and critics. That
MacDonald towered above his colleagues in the Labour Party as a
parliamentarian and statesman even his bitterest enemies have
often been compelled, however reluctantly, to concede. 'He was
the nearest to a Gladstone British Labour has had.' More than any
other individual, he was the architect of the Labour Party's fortunes. MacDonald, it has been said, had 'a consummate political
skill, captivating personal charm, magnificent gifts of oratory, and
a fine presence'. With notable unanimity, contemporary statesmen
and politicians of all parties have singled out as his most striking
characteristic his indomitable courage, physical as well as moral
and political. Almost equally appreciated were his patience and his
readiness to take long views. Though much accused in certain
circles of over-fondness for 'society', he had 'a capacity for the
simple pleasures of human intercourse with men of all stations of
life and of all trades'. 'With the miner or the railwayman as a man,'
he was always at home: 'It was the source of his power over vast
working-class audiences.' MacDonald's interests were wide. He
had travelled more extensively than any of our Prime Ministers
before him, and his knowledge of the affairs and personalities of
other countries was quite unrivalled. As a subsequent Prime
Minister was to say of him, no British statesman of his time had
a wider personal knowledge of international figures. By general
consent, MacDonald had an extraordinary gift for chairmanship.
Haldane noted the fact at the first meeting of the first Labour
Cabinet; his colleagues at the end of his career were to comment
frequently upon it; and in the same capacity he was remarkably
successful at international conferences. Closely connected was his

---

[1] There are signs of a change. A. J. P. Taylor, in his 1956 Ford Lectures
refers to MacDonald as 'a man whom the preparation of these lectures made me
rate more highly, *to my surprise and even regret*'. (Author's italics.) And again,
'MacDonald is often regarded as an empty rhetorician, but he seems in retrospect — despite his style of utterance — the only realist among all the Dis-
senters.' (*The Trouble Makers*, pp. 95 and 144)

skill as a negotiator: his diplomatic methods were conciliatory and informal in a most unusual degree, without lack of either firmness or adroitness.[1] As a thinker and writer, MacDonald's influence upon the development of democratic socialism in this country was second to none; although to-day those in the Labour Party who are most indebted to him apparently find it politically inconvenient to acknowledge their debt, and others, because of the reactions to the 1931 crisis, are often scarcely aware of it.[2] MacDonald has been described as possibly the best-read Prime Minister (Balfour only excepted) that we have had in this country. He had an encyclopaedic knowledge of the English and Scottish writers on history, philosophy, theology, and politics, especially during the seventeenth and eighteenth centuries. At the same time he took an interest in science, in music, and in painting, keeping abreast of developments in them all. It has been doubted whether Britain has ever had a Premier 'to whom artists and architects looked in art matters of national import with more confidence that here was a man who knew how they felt and that it mattered'. Most of MacDonald's writing was done as a journalist and pamphleteer under pressure, but 'he might have become a remarkable prose-writer, had he given time and thought to it'. Even as it was, his major and more leisurely works reveal, particularly on the more narrowly political side, what a French biographer described as an almost Latin clarity and precision; and certain of his other writings, notably his memoir of his wife and his 1922 travel sketches, attracted much favourable comment on account of the high level of style attained. Something will have to be said in the following pages about MacDonald's alleged defects of character and their political consequences, but in this respect it would be relevant to quote the *Manchester Guardian* verdict that the bases of his character were 'integrity verging on austerity, "plain living and high thinking", intense industry, tireless self-improvement, constant preoccupation with the public good'.

Intellectually, and from the standpoint of political capacity, MacDonald's only serious rival among his colleagues was Philip Snowden. The latter, however, was never a dangerous challenger

---

[1] In this connection, reference may be made to the impressions of Labour's first Premier and first Foreign Secretary recorded by our Ambassador in Berlin, Lord d'Abernon.

[2] In a publication entitled *Recent Socialist Thinking*, the present leader of the Labour Party, Mr H. T. N. Gaitskell, while discussing many of MacDonald's contemporaries, makes no allusion whatever to MacDonald himself.

for the leadership of the Labour Party, although he might have succeeded to the leadership had there been a vacancy in the mid-twenties. Despite his ability, his conspicuous courage, and his determination, Snowden had important limitations. His interests were relatively narrow; he lacked flexibility; and, although at bottom a most kindly warm-hearted man, he often displayed a bitterness in controversy and a talent for invective, probably accentuated by if not due to the physical disability over which he in other respects triumphed so notably. Although his general attitude towards politics was close to MacDonald's, his approach was more doctrinaire, his methods more direct, and by the 'thirties he had become more rigid in his outlook and views, largely in reaction to what he considered, not without substantial justification, to be the follies and stupidities of the Left-Wing elements in the Labour movement. His relations with the Trade Union elements were not good; and with MacDonald there was a conflict of temperament which made him mistrustful and critical of the latter's leadership.

The remaining members of Labour's 'Inner Cabinet' all entered politics from the Trade Union side; and both Clynes and Thomas remained Union officials. Arthur Henderson, although he had for many years devoted himself to the political side of the Labour Movement, retained close associations with the Trade Unions, and was always conscious, not only of their interests, but also of their basic organizational importance within the Labour Party. Secretary of the Party from 1911 onwards, Henderson was a strong and unwavering supporter of the 'Labour Alliance'; and that was one aspect only of his constant preoccupation with the maintenance of party unity. He may well be regarded as the outstanding example of the Trade Unionist turned politician; representative of the best of them, with more than the usual complement of qualities and abilities, but with not a few of the characteristic limitations. Henderson had come to accept Socialism belatedly, drifting into it along with the Labour Party, and he always remained essentially a Labourite rather than a Socialist. He was primarily a Party manager, and never relinquished his work as such when serving either in the Coalition or Labour Governments; even when functioning in the arduous capacity of Foreign Secretary. But he was much more than controller of the party machine. His experience in governmental office was considerable, and in the international Labour and Socialist movement still more so. As we have noted, Henderson had been Leader of the Labour Party in the earlier phase of the 1914–18 War, but it is well-established that he neither sought nor wished to retain or resume the party leadership. He fully recognized MacDonald's superior qualifications; and the partnership between the two men over a long period of years, notwithstanding their strikingly dissimilar temperaments and interests, their consequential lack of intimacy, and mutually critical reactions, was a major factor in Labour's advance. Never an effective Parliamentarian, Henderson was staunch, solid, astute, and the dominant figure in the party machine.

Clynes, too, had been Leader of the Party for a brief period in 1921–22, and, also like Henderson, had had a good deal of governmental experience. A relatively colourless and less weighty personality, undistinguished in office and ineffective in the House of Commons, Clynes was none the less influential on account of his Trade Union connections and his position as one of the senior members of the Party. J. H. Thomas, on the other hand, was a particularly colourful, indeed exuberant, personality. The National Union of Railwaymen was in large measure his creation, and as its general secretary he proved not only a clever and successful negotiator but also a born leader of men. Without intellectual interests, and often creating the impression of vulgarity, mixing breezily with people of all sections of society, Thomas was regarded with exasperated enmity by the Socialist intellectuals and with hatred by the Left Wing of the Party. Energetic, widely popular, and a most effective debater, Thomas was, perhaps, MacDonald's chief adjutant on the Trade Union side; and, in the leading circles of the Party, where, as in other Parties, personal loyalties were conspicuous by their absence, Thomas was the one man upon whom MacDonald could with complete confidence rely.

BALDWIN AND THE CONSERVATIVE PARTY

The political situation in the two years of the second Labour Government was one of unusual complexity. It became more and more confused as the months went by. Each of the three parties suffered from grave internal dissensions. Each, wrote Beatrice Webb early in 1931, had its bitterest enemies among its own members or ci-devant members.[1]

On the Conservative side, a prolonged and determined effort was

[1] Diary, March 12, 1931.

made to remove Baldwin from the leadership. The most active part in the campaign against him was played by the two press Lords, Beaverbrook and Rothermere, whose newspapers pursued Baldwin with unprecedented and almost unremitting virulence. It is impossible to enter into the details and successive phases of the struggle. Those were the days of Beaverbrook's crusade for Empire Free Trade, and of complex differences within the Conservative ranks about protection, especially in regard to food taxes. Conservatives were divided also about disarmament, and more particularly about the London Naval Treaty of 1930, one of MacDonald's outstanding successes during this second Labour Government. There was, perhaps, an even deeper cleavage about India, another problem which dominated this period. In November 1925 Baldwin had appointed as Viceroy of India one of his closest political associates and personal friends, Edward Wood (created Lord Irwin, and who afterwards succeeded his father as Lord Halifax). Two years later he anticipated the provisions of the India Reform Act of 1919 by one year, and appointed the Royal Commission provided for by that Act to enquire into its working. On October 30, 1929, the Viceroy made a statement on behalf of the new Government, 'that the natural issue of India's constitutional progress . . . is the attainment of Dominion status.' Baldwin approved: Churchill and others disapproved strongly. Despite the Congress Party's dissatisfaction, and Gandhi's campaign of civil disobedience, his arrest and that of the Nehrus, the Labour Government pursued its policy of conciliation, and summoned a Round Table Conference in London (November 12, 1930). This Conference was boycotted by Congress, but sufficient progress was made under MacDonald's chairmanship to justify further consultations with representative Indians before a new constitution was framed. Baldwin was emphatic in his support of the Labour Government on this issue; and it was on this issue that Churchill, on January 27, 1931, withdrew from the so-called Conservative 'Shadow Cabinet'. A second Round Table Conference was fixed for September 7, 1931. By early March of that year Irwin had reached an agreement with Gandhi by which civil disobedience was called off and Gandhi accepted the invitation to attend the Conference in London. The imminence of this important Conference was one of the major factors in the situation at the time of the political crisis of that autumn; and, in this connection, the substantial identity of views between MacDonald and Baldwin,

D

and the fierce opposition of Churchill to those views, must be kept in mind.

Reverting to the question of the Conservative leadership, criticism of Baldwin reached such heights that, at the beginning of March 1931, he came very near a decision to retire. At the last moment he changed his mind and fought back with great effect during a famous by-election at St. George's, Westminster. The contest was between Sir Ernest Petter (an anti-Baldwin Conservative) and Alfred Duff Cooper (afterwards Viscount Norwich). Cooper won with 17,242 votes against Petter's 11,532. It was in the course of this campaign that Baldwin made his striking denunciation of the Beaverbrook and Rothermere papers and their proprietors; for which he earned their enduring hatred, and the increased respect of wide sections of the general public. To Baldwin, 1931 was always 'the year when my party tried to get rid of me'. His great prestige in the House of Commons and his popularity in the country might have failed to pull him through had it not been for the honourable conduct of Neville Chamberlain, his destined successor, who would certainly not have been sorry to see him go. However, by the time the crisis came in the late summer of 1931 the worst phase of Conservative disunity had passed, and Baldwin's position had been much strengthened.

LIBERAL DISSENSIONS

In the Liberal camp old feuds had only been patched up — scarcely even that. Although Asquith had died in 1928, Asquithians were still there to whom the leadership of Lloyd George, with the financial resources under his control, was intolerable. By the beginning of 1930, Lord Grey and his Liberal Council were taking their own course. Fresh causes of dissension soon arose. The policy of supporting a minority Labour Government imposed increasingly severe strains. The trend of economic developments imperilled the very Ark of the Covenant, Free Trade. Prominent Liberals outside Parliament, like J. M. Keynes, and inside Parliament, like Sir John Simon, became favourably disposed to a tariff. Towards the end of 1930 a new and definite breach occurred within the Liberal ranks: Sir Robert Hutchison (afterwards Lord Hutchison of Montrose), the Liberal Chief Whip, resigned his office; and in June of 1931 joined with Simon and Ernest Brown in formally repudiating the party whip. Sir Herbert Samuel, who strove to keep the party to-

gether, has described the experience of the 1929–31 Parliament in
these terms:

> Our weekly meetings were not happy occasions. About a third of our
> body, including some of the leading figures — Simon, Runciman and
> Donald Maclean — were profoundly distrustful of Lloyd George.
> Another third, including the Welsh members, were definitely his
> adherents. The remainder, of whom I was one, tried to keep the party
> together.... Presiding ... during Lloyd George's occasional absences
> was sometimes a heart-breaking experience. Not seldom, when the
> course to be taken in the House on some pending question was
> decided upon after full discussion, it would be found nevertheless that
> one section of the party voted in the 'Aye' lobby, another in the 'No'
> lobby, and a third abstained.

THE GOVERNMENT AND THE PARTY

The second Labour Government, like the first, was confronted
by the special conditions of its minority position in the House of
Commons and of its still weaker position in the country. From the
party standpoint, the main objective, clearly grasped by Mac-
Donald and his leading colleagues, less clearly by others, was to
establish the Labour Party as one of the two main parties in the
State. That involved willingness to undertake the full responsibilities of government, and to work the system as they found it.
Though substantially stronger than in 1924, the Party faced a political situation which was essentially the same. But, adding enor-
mously to difficulties already great, the formation of the new
Government coincided with the beginnings of the world economic
depression.

To many elements in the Labour movement, the situation was
irksome from the outset: to some it was definitely repugnant. In the
I.L.P., as already noted, the Left had obtained control, and before
1929 the breach with the old leaders, MacDonald and Snowden,
was complete. Shortly afterwards, on the death of John Wheatley,
the I.L.P. came definitely under Maxton's direction and moved
decisively towards a breach with the Labour Party itself. Throughout the 1929–31 Parliament, the I.L.P. group (in Sidney Webb's
words) 'took up an attitude of extreme hostility and perpetual
"nagging", leading to frequent flat rebellion in the House of Commons'. On several occasions the Government would have been defeated had the Conservatives supported Left-Wing revolts in the
division lobbies.

Much more important, however, than the attitude of the I.L.P., especially when the crisis came, was that of the General Council of the Trades Union Congress. As we have seen, influential elements in the Trade Union movement had for long pinned their faith to direct industrial action. The General Strike of 1926 suddenly revealed to them the grave political implications and dangers. By 1929, the General Council was developing a new technique, under the guidance of its two outstanding personalities, Ernest Bevin and W. M. (now Lord) Citrine, the General Secretary. The aim was to exercise effective control over the Labour Party (and any Labour Government) from outside, exploiting the organizational and financial power of the Trade Unions, potentially decisive, within the Party itself. Bevin, it has already been noted, had vainly sought to commit the Labour Party against taking office again as a Minority Government. To him, the Party was essentially a political instrument of the Trade Union movement, and as such subordinate. Dictatorial in spirit, conscious of power, and blatant in his expressions of that consciousness, Bevin was to prove a serious embarrassment and a growing menace to Labour's political leadership. His personal detestation of both MacDonald and Snowden worsened the situation; but for Parliamentarians as such he displayed scarcely concealed contempt. From the outset of the second Labour Government, the General Council adopted what Webb described as an attitude of 'aggressive independence' and made 'an arrogant claim' to prior consultation on all Cabinet projects which, in the Council's opinion, affected Trade Union interests.

THE GATHERING DEPRESSION

The Government's handling of external affairs met with widespread approval. The fact is of importance in regard to the 1931 crisis only because it greatly enhanced the reputations of the three leading figures in the Ministry, MacDonald, Snowden and Henderson. Snowden's firm and successful insistence upon equitable financial treatment for his country at the Hague Reparations Conference in August 1929 made him for the time being the idol of the press and the general public. MacDonald's conduct of Anglo-American relations, of the London Naval Conference in 1930, of the Imperial Conference, and later in the year of the first Indian Round Table Conference, added much to his already high prestige as a diplomatist. Strikingly successful, in particular, was his visit to the United

States in the autumn of 1929. 'A feat of endurance and a triumph in political activities,' wrote Beatrice Webb.[1] His speeches, afterwards published, were (wrote the *Manchester Guardian*) of 'exceptional merit, both for form and matter, and, being nearly all extempore, were really a wonderful tour de force. Their tact, vigour, and manly diplomacy could scarcely be overpraised.' Henderson's general work at the Foreign Office, and particularly his efforts at Geneva to strengthen 'the constructive machinery of peace' through the League of Nations, was enthusiastically endorsed by the bulk of Labour and Liberal, and much Conservative, opinion. Although, during the course of 1930, the international situation markedly deteriorated, the external policies of the Government aroused no serious criticism, save from the Conservative Right Wing (chiefly in regard to India and Egypt), and, as always, from the extreme Left.

It was in the sphere of trade, employment and finance that the trouble came. In this respect, the second Labour Government was singularly unlucky. Unemployment had been the most prominent issue at the General Election. Lloyd George and the Liberal Party had made the running with a policy of large-scale expenditure on public works; but Labour had also fought largely on this issue, and had pressed its traditional demand for 'work or maintenance'. But, before Parliament reassembled at the end of October 1929, the American boom had collapsed. The effects soon began to be felt; and the Government found itself confronted, not only by those industries which were chronically depressed, but also by a worldwide slump which it was powerless by itself to control. The resulting situation was one bound immensely to increase the Government's difficulties with its own followers as well as (or even more than) with its political opponents.

The familiar story of the world economic depression and the accompanying and contributing political uncertainties, which were together to lead to the widespread financial crises and political upheavals of 1931, cannot be recounted here. Suffice it to say for the moment that the number of registered unemployed in this country, which in June 1929 was 1,122,700, had risen by the summer of 1930 to well over the 2 million mark; the export trades were shrinking to an alarming extent, revenue falling, and the costs of maintaining the unemployed rising rapidly, partly owing to higher rates and

[1] *Beatrice Webb's Diaries 1924–1932*, p. 223.

more generous conditions of benefit. The deterioration in our balance of payments with the external world created growing anxiety in responsible quarters about the position of sterling. In these circumstances, the unemployment question came to overshadow everything else; and the Government was subjected to a barrage of criticism, conflicting advice, and mutually incompatible remedies, mostly based on the assumption that the problem was essentially a domestic one, and, therefore, within its control. The Liberals urged the implementation of their public works programme, which, of course, involved heavy expenditure. In Labour's own ranks, pressure of the same kind was strong, but even stronger was the demand for 'maintenance' of the unemployed at higher levels. On the Conservative side, as there has already been occasion to note, a many-sided campaign developed for protective tariffs. Indeed, this demand for protection of British industry was, by the summer of 1930, attracting growing support outside the Conservative ranks in quarters previously devoted to Free Trade.

As the Minister responsible for the co-ordination of employment schemes, J. H. Thomas had been allotted three Ministerial associates: George Lansbury (the First Commissioner of Works), Sir Oswald Mosley (who was Chancellor of the Duchy of Lancaster without a seat in the Cabinet), and Thomas Johnston (then Under-Secretary of State for Scotland). Neither from the standpoint of personal relations nor from that of policy did this arrangement function satisfactorily. Thomas himself worked energetically at his task and in complete harmony with Snowden, the Chancellor of the Exchequer; but the deepening trade depression swamped the results of his efforts, and he was subjected to violent and increasing criticism from all sides. Much controversy developed about the effect of public works upon employment; but, in accordance with the views prevalent among the financial experts, and endorsed by the Treasury and the Chancellor, schemes were limited by considerations of economic soundness, and pressure for expenditure regardless of such considerations was resisted.

Early in 1930, Mosley drafted proposals for dealing with the unemployment situation which set aside such limitations, and in other respects were a challenge both to orthodox views and to Government policy. His Memorandum, given general support by both Lansbury and Johnston, was submitted to the Cabinet without any prior consultations with Thomas. It was definitely rejected in May, and on the 21st of that month Mosley resigned. At a special meeting of the Parliamentary Labour Party, summoned at his request, Mosley presented the proposals embodied in his Memorandum, and might well have received considerable backing had he not insisted on pressing his motion of censure to a division. Beaten by 202 votes to 29, he embarked upon an energetic personal campaign in the country; and for the next nine or ten months he was the active leader of the Left Wing of the Labour movement. In October 1930, his supporters were only narrowly defeated at the Llandudno Conference of the Labour Party, and he himself was elected to the National Executive. That Conference, however, was (in Beatrice Webb's words) an 'oratorical triumph' for MacDonald. Mosley seriously miscalculated his strength. In December 1930 he published a Manifesto, which had the backing of A. J. Cook, and had been drafted in collaboration with John Strachey, Aneurin Bevan and W. J. Brown. Seventeen M.P.s signed this Manifesto. In February 1931 Mosley took the decisive step. Issuing an extended version of his Manifesto, he announced the formation of the 'New Party'. Only four M.P.s joined him; one was his wife; Strachey was another. All were promptly (March 10) expelled from the Labour Party. Strachey, it may be noted, soon left the new organization.

THE PARLIAMENTARY SITUATION AND PARTY CO-OPERATION

Although there was to be no major reconstruction of the Government during its term of office, some changes of importance occurred. On June 6, 1930, Thomas relinquished his post as Lord Privy Seal and became Dominions Secretary, Passfield retaining the Colonies. The post vacated by Thomas was given to Vernon Hartshorn, who, however, was not entrusted with the direction of employment policy. At the Ministry of Agriculture, Dr Christopher (afterwards Lord) Addison replaced Noel Buxton, who received a peerage. The Cabinet now numbered twenty. Outside the Cabinet, the vacancy in the Chancellorship of the Duchy caused by Mosley's resignation was filled by Clement Attlee. After the tragic death of Lord Thomson in October 1930, Lord Amulree became Secretary of State for Air. Early in March of 1931, Sir Charles Trevelyan, the President of the Board of Education, who appears to have become increasingly dissatisfied with the Government's general policy, re-

signed, and his place was taken by H. B. Lees Smith. At the same
time, Herbert Morrison, the Minister of Transport, was brought
into the Cabinet, which consequently numbered twenty-one, the
figure at which it stood when the crisis came. The death of Vernon
Hartshorn that same month led to the only other Cabinet change.
His successor as Lord Privy Seal was Thomas Johnston.

When J. H. Thomas went to the Dominions office in the summer
of 1930, his special responsibilities in connection with unemployment were not transferred to his successor at the Privy Seal office.
MacDonald himself assumed responsibility for supervising the
efforts of the departments to provide employment; and at the same
time sought the co-operation of the other parties in dealing with
the problem.

Opposition to any form of collaboration with other parties (save
the Communist Party) has always been a cardinal feature of the
attitude of Labour's Left Wing. A minority government, however,
dependent upon the support of another party or other parties for
its necessary majority in the House of Commons, is bound, if it is
to endure, to enter into some form of collaboration, some kind of
informal coalition. And that, despite its original decision to the
contrary, is what happened with the second Labour Government.

At the very outset, in his first speech to the new Parliament in
1929, MacDonald had referred to the very serious problems confronting the country, and had said:

> I wonder how far it is possible, without in any way abandoning any of
> our party positions . . . to consider ourselves more as a Council of
> State and less as arrayed regiments facing each other in battle . . . so
> far as we are concerned, co-operation will be welcomed . . . so that by
> putting our ideas into a common pool we can bring out . . . legislation
> and administration that will be of substantial benefit for the nation as
> a whole.

After the crisis of 1931, as will be seen, this utterance was to be recalled and given a wholly exaggerated significance. MacDonald,
however, was expressing something like a hope that the major
problems of the day might be lifted above the party struggle. The
hope, in so far as it was one, was not entirely disappointed. On the
Indian problem, for example, there was effective co-operation, despite the attitude of Churchill and the Conservative Right Wing.
A parallel development took place in regard to 'disarmament', not-

withstanding opposition from the same quarters and from the strict pacifists. The Three-Party Committee of the Committee of Imperial Defence set up by MacDonald in March of 1931 'to advise as to the policy to be adopted at the forthcoming Disarmament Conference' has been described by Lord Templewood as 'a remarkable example of inter-party co-operation on a vital question of Imperial policy'. Templewood points out that this three-party committee reached agreement on its recommendations, the chief of which was: 'Any further reduction of British armaments could only be undertaken as part of an international agreement containing comparable reductions by other Powers, and after taking into account the particular obligations and dangers of each country.' The recommendations, as Templewood says, were the basis of MacDonald's speech on June 29, 1931, when the only dissentient voice was Churchill's; and the basis also of the National Government's policy at the Disarmament Conference. He adds: 'The debate in June 1931 had shown the general agreement between the Opposition and the Government. By July 1932, however, the political atmosphere had changed after the fall of the Labour Government, and the unanimity that had been the outstanding feature of the 1931 debates had finally disappeared.'[1]

In regard to domestic affairs, however, the story was very different. The Government itself was seriously hampered in this respect not only by its Left-Wing critics but also by the prevailing mood of the Labour rank-and-file generally. The Conservative leadership, severely challenged, laboured under parallel handicaps. The Government was engaged in a continuous struggle on two fronts complicated by the uncertainty of its relations with the Liberals and by the astute tactics of Lloyd George. One has only to reread, for example, the debates on economy and unemployment insurance in February 1931 to appreciate the strength of partisan feeling and the informal combination of the militants on both sides against any kind of co-operation or compromise by their respective leaders. But, despite the difficulties, the Government sought to secure the collaboration called for both by the facts of the parliamentary situation and by the nature of the problems arising from the economic depression. In May 1930, confronted by repeated Conservative and Liberal attacks on the Government's unemployment policy, MacDonald suggested that the three parties should co-operate in a

[1] Op. cit., pp. 117–19.

committee of inquiry on the problem; and in June he formally proposed a three-party conference. The Conservatives refused. Baldwin was then in no position to accept the invitation: the tariff issue, Conservative dissensions about it, and the instability of his position as Leader, were insuperable bars. Lloyd George, on the other hand, accepted on behalf of the Liberals; and discussions began at once. The Liberals were represented by Lloyd George, Lord Lothian and Seebohm Rowntree; MacDonald, Snowden and Vernon Hartshorn attending for the Government.

From that time onwards regular discussions proceeded between the Government and Liberal Party representatives. This development clearly aroused no dissension within the Cabinet. Snowden approved; while Henderson's biographer assigns to him the main credit for the new arrangements. Even Lansbury favoured them: indeed, according to his biographer,[1] he appealed privately to Lloyd George in February 1931 to come with his supporters into the Labour Party, apparently envisaging Lloyd George himself as Vice-Premier. The attitude of the main body of Liberals in the House of Commons became more friendly towards the Government; although that very fact provoked further Liberal dissensions. The collaboration thus inaugurated assumed a wider basis in the closing months of 1930. Late in September of that year, Lloyd George made further support of the Government dependent upon an understanding that a measure for electoral reform would be introduced and passed. An all-party committee, under an ex-Speaker, Lord Ullswater, appointed in December 1929 to discuss the matter, had by July 1930 completely failed to reach any agreement. Its Labour members had opposed any major change, while the Conservatives and Liberals had favoured a system of Proportional Representation. The Liberals, however, had expressed a willingness to consider the adoption of the Alternative Vote system. After Lloyd George's intimation, consultations took place between Government representatives (Henderson, Snowden and Lord Arnold) and the Liberals (Samuel, Ramsay Muir and Sir Archibald Sinclair[2]). Agreement was reached on the compromise basis of the. Alternative Vote. Thenceforward the main body of the Liberals were prepared, and indeed anxious, to keep the Labour Government in office until the electoral reform bill was passed, and that, in

[1] Op. cit., p. 265.
[2] Now Lord Thurso.

view of the probable attitude of the House of Lords, was likely to
take another two years.

THE ONSET OF THE FINANCIAL CRISIS

Meanwhile the world economic situation steadily worsened, and
with its deterioration came ominous political repercussions, notably
in Germany. In this country, the number of registered unemployed
rose before the end of 1930 to over the $2\frac{1}{2}$ million mark. Here, as
elsewhere, serious Budgetary problems loomed ahead. Evidence
accumulated of a developing lack of confidence abroad in our financial position and in the policy of the Government. A withdrawal of
funds from London began. Demands arose for drastic reduction of
national expenditure. Increasing criticism was directed at the growing burden of payments to the unemployed. In that respect the
Labour Government was in a position of peculiar difficulty. It had
been, and remained, under constant pressure and attack from its
Left Wing on account of the alleged inadequacy of provision for
the unemployed. The Minister of Labour, Miss Margaret Bondfield, was criticized even more bitterly, and just as unfairly, as
Thomas. One of the Government's first measures, however, after
taking office, had been to secure amendments to the Unemployment Insurance Act. Rates of benefit were increased, and the condition of 'genuinely seeking work' abolished. At the same time the
cost of 'transitional benefit', i.e. the benefit continued after the
expiry of insurance rights, was transferred from the Insurance Fund
to the Exchequer. This measure had been passed only after a
struggle with the Trade Union section of the Labour Party, which
asked for still higher rates, and in spite of the irreconcilable opposition of the Left Wing. In the House of Commons on February 18,
1931, in one of his many irresponsible speeches during this period,
Churchill reproved the Labour extremists for their ingratitude to
the Government, whose members, he said, could

> truly and honestly proclaim . . . that by every device and by every
> dodge, by every shift and, almost, by every turpitude, they have
> managed to keep on paying for the longest time in the loosest fashion
> the largest doles to the largest number.

With the growth in the numbers of the unemployed, the burden
on the Exchequer in respect of transitional benefit became increasingly onerous; and at the same time the borrowing powers of the

Insurance Fund had to be extended. The Government at first attempted to deal with the problem by a three-party committee. As Snowden said on February 11, 1931, 'we wanted to refer this to a Council of State, and I agree that this is a matter which no one Government can settle.' This Three-Party Committee proved fruitless. It was wound up, in circumstances which led to some recrimination, when the Government referred the whole matter to a Royal Commission, under the Chairmanship of Judge Holman Gregory, towards the end of 1930.

The Unemployment Insurance Fund was heavily in debt and running further into debt at the rate of £40 million a year. On January 29, 1931, the Treasury representative, Sir Richard Hopkins, gave evidence before the Royal Commission. In the Memorandum he submitted it was said that

> continued State borrowing on the present vast scale without adequate provision for repayment by the fund would quickly call in question the stability of the British financial system. The State has every year to borrow large sums for various productive purposes. This additional borrowing — for purposes other than productive — is now on a scale which in substance obliterates the effect of the Sinking Fund. Apart from the impairment of Government credit which such operations inevitably involve these vast Treasury loans are coming to represent in effect State borrowing to relieve current State obligations at the expense of the future and this is the ordinary and well-recognized sign of an unbalanced Budget.

This Treasury evidence provided a strong basis for Conservative and Liberal criticisms of Government policy. It also gave rise to resentment in Labour circles, a resentment by no means confined to the extreme Left. In these circles there was at the outset considerable criticism of the Treasury officials; but Snowden quickly made it clear that the Hopkins Memorandum had been submitted to and approved by him. After the crisis, Webb was to contend that the statement should not have been made, or at any rate made public, without the approval of the Cabinet.

THE MAY COMMITTEE

The Government's position appeared extremely precarious from the beginning of the year 1931. Few expected it to survive, and political possibilities of considerable variety were canvassed. A series of important debates occurred towards the middle of February. On February 11, the Government had to meet a Conservative motion of censure on its policy in regard to public expenditure. To this the Liberals submitted an amendment demanding the appointment of 'a small and independent Committee to make representations to Mr Chancellor of the Exchequer for effecting forthwith all practical and legitimate reductions in the national expenditure consistent with the efficiency of the services'. On behalf of the Government, Snowden accepted the Liberal amendment, which was carried by 468 votes to 21. The minority consisted of Labour back-benchers, mostly Left-Wing representatives. The outstanding feature of this debate was the Chancellor's pronouncement on the gravity of the financial situation:

> I say with all the seriousness I can command that the national position is so grave that drastic and disagreeable measures will have to be taken if Budget equilibrium is to be maintained and if industrial progress is to be made.

Addressing himself particularly to the Labour members, Snowden urged the necessity of temporary sacrifices in order to make future progress possible. That there would be a heavy deficit at the end of the year was no secret:

> No Budget in the world could stand such an excessive strain as that which has been placed upon it by the increase of unemployment during the last 12 months.

The Conservative spokesman, Sir Laming Worthington-Evans, had quoted a statement made by Sir Richard Hopkins in his evidence before the Royal Commission on Unemployment Insurance. This statement emphasized that foreign observers were bound to pass an adverse judgment on our Budgetary situation, a fact which had to be continuously borne in mind in view of our wide international connections. Worthington-Evans had gone on to refer to the withdrawal of funds from London. Snowden agreed that this was 'the vulnerable spot in our position':

> It is quite true . . . that if there were well grounded fears that this country's budgeting was not sound, then it might have disastrous consequences, and very disastrous consequences, which would have their repercussions abroad. It is quite true that other countries are watching, and we must maintain our financial reputation. That we can do. Our position is fundamentally sound, sounder than that of any

other country in the world, and all that is required is an effort to get
over the present temporary crisis, and that can be done without any
very great efforts. It will involve some temporary sacrifices from all,
and those best able to bear them will have to make the largest sacrifices. In the general sacrifice, the Members of the Cabinet are prepared to make their substantial contribution.

Snowden ended with an appeal for all-party co-operation:

As I have said before, this is a problem which no one party can solve,
but the country and the House of Commons must realize the gravity
of the position. Instead of party bickering, which we can resume later,
we must unite in a common effort to take effective measures to overcome our temporary difficulties and to restore our former prosperity.

The debate foreshadowed much of what was to come. The
official spokesmen of all three parties urged co-operation. Worthington-Evans pleaded that the House should act as a Council of
State. Snowden, as already noted, used the same expression in a
particular context, and twice insisted that the task ahead was too
big for any one party. Sir Donald Maclean, for the Liberals, alluded
to the phrase, and offered his party's hearty co-operation in any
practical scheme. There was some rank-and-file Conservative and
Liberal endorsement of the desire to get away from party bickering.
But partisan controversy largely dominated the discussion; it had
occupied most of the Chancellor's own speech; and the prospect of
party co-operation was highly unwelcome to the militants on both
sides of the House. Moreover, Snowden's warning and plea received no effective backing from the Labour benches; indeed, they
created alarm or anxiety on the Government side. Significantly,
Noel Baker maintained that expenditure on unemployment insurance was immensely in the national interest, and William Graham,
the President of the Board of Trade, opposed any attack either
upon the rates of unemployment benefit or upon the social services. Left-Wing spokesmen were at once up in arms. E. F. Wise
announced 'the very greatest apprehension and opposition' to what
he feared was a surrender on the part of the Government. W. J.
Brown delivered an unqualified attack on Snowden's speech on the
ground that 'it prepares the mind of this House for the sacrifice of
the unemployed man and woman', and provided 'the plainest possible intimation' that the Government was becoming 'the humble
custodian of the capitalist interest which we were sent here to

destroy'. Brown's utterance was warmly welcomed by Robert
Boothby from the other extreme. Boothby sneered at the talk of a
Council of State, and hoped that the House had heard the last of it,
maintaining that the Conservative Opposition's objective was to
turn out the Government at the first possible moment. 'Therefore,
for goodness sake do not let us have any more nonsense on the subject of a Council of State.' In more responsible Opposition circles,
there was openly expressed mistrust at the alleged collusion between the official elements in the Labour and Liberal parties and
what Sir Hilton Young described as the 'sham fight' between them.
That mistrust was confirmed by the proceedings in the House on
the following days, when a Liberal motion on unemployment was
accepted by the Government, and a measure had to be passed still
further increasing the borrowing powers of the Unemployment Insurance Fund and the Exchequer contribution to the cost of transitional benefit. Political intrigues and rumours of such intrigues
were rife during this period. It is indicative of the confused situation that while both Churchill and Ormsby-Gore accused Lloyd
George of scheming to secure power with the aid of the Labour
Left, Lloyd George attacked Churchill as Lord Rothermere's
nominee for the leadership of the Conservative Party.

Snowden did not confine his warning to the House of Commons.
He repeated it in sterner terms at a specially summoned meeting of
the Parliamentary Labour Party, but again without eliciting any
open support.

The Committee agreed to on February 11, 1931, was appointed
by Snowden in consultation with the three parties. It was composed
of a Chairman and six members, two suggested by each party. The
Chairman selected was Sir George May,[1] who had then recently
retired from his position as secretary of the Prudential Assurance
Company.

THE BUDGET OF 1931

The Chancellor of the Exchequer himself was taken seriously ill
three weeks later. A severe operation kept him away from the
House of Commons until he presented his Budget on April 27.
Later on this Budget was much criticized on account of its mild-
ness, particularly in view of the grave warning Snowden had given
in February. The Chancellor balanced his Budget by various exped-

[1] Later Lord May.

ients without imposing any increased taxation, apart from raising the petrol duty. Avowedly, however, it was a stop-gap Budget. Snowden was awaiting the reports of Sir George May's Economy Committee and of the Royal Commission on Unemployment Insurance; and he was afterwards to explain that he expected a supplementary Budget would become necessary in the autumn.[1] His previous warnings had been very badly received within the Labour Party; and his view was that it would have been quite impossible then to persuade the House of Commons to agree to drastic reductions in expenditure and to heavy additional taxation.[2] It must also be understood that, at the end of April 1931, the financial situation, although serious and potentially dangerous, was not one calling for emergency action. It had not greatly changed during the previous two months.

Controversy about the Budget at the time arose out of Snowden's scheme for the taxation of land values. By a complex series of circumstances which need not concern us here it led for the time being to extremely strained relations between Snowden himself and the Liberals. The breach, however, was brief; and Governmental-Liberal co-operation on other matters was scarcely inter-

---

[1] *An Autobiography*, II, p. 904.
[2] Replying to a personal attack by Attlee in the House of Commons on October 2, 1931, Snowden said: 'In the earlier part of his speech the hon. Member complained that I did not deal with the financial position of the country in my Budget last April. He complained about the Economy Committee. The hon. Member helped to set up the Economy Committee, and with the exception of fewer than 20 every member of the Labour Party voted for the setting up of that Committee. I put before the House of Commons and the country last February a statement of the financial position. I never received one word of public support for the position I put forward from any Member of the then Government which is now in opposition; not one. I not only put the position before the House of Commons, but I addressed a special meeting of the Labour party, and in what I expected would be the secrecy of that meeting — secrecy which was afterwards betrayed — I spoke much more frankly than I had spoken to the House of Commons. What support did I get there? I got none. . . . The hon. Member repeated to-day what had been said by other speakers in the course of the Debate. He said that I ought to have done something in the Budget of last April. (Hon. Members: So you ought.) Why did not you make that criticism then? The answer to that is quite clear, and I think it will penetrate the brains of hon. Members opposite. I said then, and I repeated later, that the economies which were necessary could never be carried through this House merely on the support of a minority Government. If hon. Members will do me the fairness of reading my speeches, they will see that over and over again I said that the enforcement of economies was such an unpopular thing that they could only be carried through either by a united House of Commons or by a large majority of the House of Commons. We had to wait for the report of the Economy Committee, for the report of a Committee set up by hon. Members opposite, and as soon as that report was received we acted upon it.'

rupted. It was based partly upon the electoral reform bill, although that measure soon encountered difficulties and aroused not the slightest enthusiasm on the Labour side. The more important basis, however, albeit a somewhat unsure one, was provided by the Free Trade issue.

THE TARIFF AGITATION

Throughout the early months of 1931 the movement of opinion in favour of a tariff gathered increasing impetus. Churchill, previously an ardent Free Trader, became a convert. Apart from Conservative agitation, and demands from industrial and commercial interests, important sections of Liberal and Labour opinion were moving in the same direction. The proposal for a 10 per cent general revenue tariff, made by J. M. Keynes in March, aroused bitter controversy in the Liberal camp and among economists. Other prominent Liberals, including Reginald McKenna (Chairman of the Midland Bank Ltd), Sir Josiah Stamp (a Director of the Bank of England), and Sir John Simon, were prepared to consider fiscal changes. Mosley's New Party included protection in its programme. More significantly, the Trades Union Congress was becoming more favourably disposed to a tariff, and there were elements in the Government itself which were also sympathetically inclined.

In these circumstances, supporters of Free Trade rallied in its defence. The Chancellor's wife was particularly active in bringing them together, irrespective of party considerations.[1] At one of the regular discussions between the representatives of the Government and the Liberal Party, Lloyd George proposed wider co-operation between them and a joint campaign in defence of Free Trade. At subsequent meetings the discussions on the subject were pursued, and the formulation of plans for the campaign was proceeding when the crisis came at the end of July.

For an understanding of that crisis, it is essential to realize that in the previous months the Government had entered into closer co-operation with the official Liberal Party, and that the basis of this more effective association was opposition to a tariff. The Government's position in the House of Commons was strengthened by the alliance with the main section of the Liberals. There was even the possibility of a Labour-Liberal Coalition Government.

[1] Snowden, op. cit., II, p. 922.

E

That there was some discussion of such a project towards the end of July is plain.[1] It was, indeed, a more feasible proposition than that of a National or All-Party Government which was being discussed in many quarters during this period.

The Cabinet and the House of Lords

Apart from such possibilities, there was considerable discussion, and no little intrigue, during the early summer months of 1931 about the reconstruction of the Cabinet itself. The main problem of personnel confronting the Prime Minister at this time was that of the Leadership of the Labour Party in the House of Lords. Combined with that was the weakness of Labour representation in that assembly. But the problem of the House of Lords became to some extent entangled with the vexed question of the Foreign Secretaryship and other possible Governmental changes.

Lord Parmoor, who had been Leader in the Lords since the formation of the Government, was temporarily incapacitated in March 1931 and wished to retire, a desire which he formally expressed later in the summer. Snowden's serious illness in the same month of March raised the question of his possible retirement also. It was then (according to Beatrice Webb[2]) that he told Lord Passfield of his decision not to contest his seat at the next Election, and also that he might go to the House of Lords before the Labour Government came to an end. Anxious to retire from office himself, Passfield welcomed this prospect, and suggested to Snowden that the latter should succeed him as Colonial Secretary — a suggestion which, again according to Beatrice Webb, Snowden found acceptable. The Chancellor, however, recovered from his illness, and presented his Budget at the end of April. From then onwards, Snowden afterwards stated,[3] there was a sustained press campaign against him inspired by elements within the Labour Party; and, according to the same source, simultaneous intrigues to supplant MacDonald by Henderson. Snowden was also to assert that Thomas was pressing MacDonald to give him the Chancellorship when it became vacant.

In May, at one of the weekly meetings of the 'Big Five' of the Government — meetings held to discuss informally the general

---

[1] See, e.g., Frank Owen, *Tempestuous Journey*, p. 717.
[2] Op. cit., p. 269.
[3] Op. cit., II, p. 924.

Parliamentary and Party position — Henderson announced (according to Snowden[1]) that, on account of the state of his health, he wished to go to the House of Lords, a step strongly opposed by the others. In the following week, Henderson again raised the matter, and it became clear that he desired to succeed Parmoor as Leader of the Party in the House of Lords. His contention that he found the strain of the House of Commons too great did not impress Snowden, nor apparently any of the others. In the course of the subsequent discussion on that occasion, Snowden told his four colleagues of his intention to retire from the House of Commons at the end of the existing Parliament. According to him,[2] Lord Passfield and Mrs Webb visited him shortly afterwards, and pressed him to retire from the Chancellorship and to go to the House of Lords as Leader of the Party there and as Colonial Secretary. Snowden, however, was anxious to remain Chancellor for the time being, and, in particular, to carry through a major conversion operation in order to reduce the burden of the National Debt.

Towards the end of May, Passfield wrote to MacDonald pleading for retirement, and insisting that he must be released from office by the following October. He suggested Snowden, and alternatively Lord Ponsonby, as his successor at the Colonial Office. MacDonald replied expressing his sorrow, and promising to consider the whole business of Cabinet reconstruction. Some six weeks later (July 14), the Prime Minister wrote a letter of birthday greetings to Passfield, in the course of which he said:

> As you know, I am in a most awful difficulty about the House of Lords. You may think that I have been doing nothing, but as a matter of fact I have been working at it for week-end after week-end, and am in a complete dead end. We have not the material in our Party that we ought to have. The solution will have to come, I am afraid, by moves which will surprise all of you. I am still working at it however.

After the crisis, this passage, with the first sentence omitted, was to be given a curious interpretation by the Webbs, and was to be publicized by others to whom it was communicated, in support of a theory that MacDonald had long planned to place himself at the head of a National Government.[3]

---

[1] Op. cit., II, p. 925.
[2] Op. cit., p. 927.
[3] See below, Appendix V, pp. 409–412.

The World Financial Crisis

With the collapse of the most important Austrian Bank, the Credit-Anstalt, on May 11, 1931, there began that succession of bank failures and financial panics which led in mid-July to a serious development of the run on sterling. By the end of May, the German banks were dangerously involved, and the ensuing financial crisis in that country, complicated by political difficulties, both internal and international, was the main preoccupation of the British Government and banking authorities throughout the months of June and July.

In the meantime the position of sterling weakened. The German crisis would in any event have had adverse repercussions in London, but its effects were much intensified by the widespread and growing lack of confidence in British finance. A distinguished economist later described the situation in these terms:

> For years, Continental opinion had been coming to the view that the British system was dying of ossification. The inflexibility of the wage-level, the drain on the Government finances of the colossal expenditure on unemployment relief, the incessant propaganda for cheap money, were widely noted. Englishmen travelling on the Continent in those years speedily became aware that, from the European point of view, these were the conspicuous features of the economic position of Great Britain. Rightly or wrongly, the Continent had come to the conclusion that if serious strain were to occur the adjustments necessary to remain on the Gold Standard would not be made.[1]

Foreign apprehensions were increased by the publication on June 4 of an interim report by the Royal Commission on Unemployment Insurance and by the political reactions in this country to its recommendations. The report presented the facts about the inadequacy and indebtedness of the Insurance Fund: it proposed increased contributions, reductions in the rates of benefit, and the tightening up of qualifying conditions. Disapproval in Labour ranks was widespread and vigorously expressed. No party urged the implementation of the proposals. Governmental action was confined to introducing and eventually passing, in spite of bitter opposition from the I.L.P. group and other Labour back-benchers, and from Mosley's New Party, a measure correcting some anomalies in the system. Before taking or proposing any further steps,

[1] L. Robbins, *The Great Depression*, pp. 93–4.

the Government awaited the Commission's final report and that of Sir George May's Economy Committee.

With the breakdown of the German banking system on July 14, and the failure of the London Conference of Ministers on the 20th, the sterling situation entered upon a graver phase. By July 22 the Bank of England had lost £22 million of gold; and next day the bank rate was raised from 2½ to 3½ per cent. A week later, the drain continuing, the rate was raised to 4½ per cent. On Saturday, August 1, the Bank announced that credits had been obtained from the Federal Reserve Bank of New York and the Bank of France to the combined value of £50 million. At the same time the Fiduciary Issue was increased by £15 million. These measures failed to restore confidence. They would probably have failed to do so in any event, but might conceivably have met with some success had it not been for the publication, almost simultaneously with the announcement of the credits, of the May Committee's report.

CHAPTER III

THE MAY REPORT AND PARTY CO-OPERATION

On July 28, *The Times* had stated that the Report of the May Economy Committee would be published on Friday, the 31st; and on the 29th that Ministers had already received copies. In the House of Commons on July 30 the Chancellor of the Exchequer, replying to a non-partisan speech from Neville Chamberlain, and by previous agreement with him,[1] announced that the Report of the May Committee had been received; that it would be published next day; and that it would come as a shock to the country. Snowden emphasized the responsibility of all parties for dealing with the crisis, and said that no Government, especially one which did not command a majority of its own, could expect to carry through drastic reductions of expenditure without the co-operation of all other parties. The House of Commons adjourned for the summer recess next day (July 31), and later that same day the May Committee's Report was published.

Before dealing with the recommendations of that Report, it is desirable to examine more thoroughly the matter of co-operation between the political parties. After the formation of the National Government, it was frequently to be suggested that such a development had long been premeditated, and, indeed, consciously planned. Any basis for the suggestion is slender in the extreme.

It is important, first of all, to distinguish between the co-opera-

[1] According to Snowden's autobiography (II, p. 929), 'Mr Neville Chamberlain came into my room and said that he intended next day in the debate on the adjournment to speak upon the situation, but he was very anxious to say nothing which would have a disturbing effect. He was well aware of the actual financial situation, and he would make a non-partisan speech and would avoid putting any questions to me which might place me in an embarrassing position. He was anxious to be helpful, and he thought it might be well if I could make a reply to him which would impress the country with the gravity of the situation without causing a panic. I gave him a full account of the information in my possession. We agreed upon the general line that he would take in his speech, and I promised to follow with a speech which would raise the discussion above Party controversy.'

tion of parties in government (that is, any form of coalition government) and co-operation of the Government party or parties with
the Opposition party or parties. It has already been pointed out
that a so-called minority Government (like the first and second
Labour Governments) is necessarily a Government based upon
co-operation (formal or informal) between the Government party
and another party (or other parties). Informal party co-operation,
of course, can and very frequently does take place, whether or not
the Government is a minority Government: indeed, it must always
be present in some degree under a parliamentary system.

In the second place, distinctions need to be drawn between the
various kinds of coalition government. There may be (1) coalition
of two or more parties in government; or (2) coalition of all the
major parties; or (3) government composed of persons drawn from
all the major parties. Only (2) and (3) can legitimately be described
as 'National Governments': indeed, some would hold that the
designation is properly applied only to (2), unless, in the case of (3),
no major party is in opposition. Only as a result of loose use of the
term 'National Government' has it been possible for commentators
plausibly to suggest, or make the charge, that the National Government of August 1931 had been planned in advance. In seeking to
establish such a contention, many have thought it sufficient to point
out that this newspaper or that publicist or the other politician
talked of a possible National Government in the earlier months of
1931, or even before.

It is true, of course, that the idea of a National Government, in
the sense of an all-party Government, had been frequently mooted.
It is also true that the politicians of all parties had had this possible
expedient in their minds. No inside information revealed, or gossip
recalled, after the crisis is required in order to establish that fact. A
National Government of that kind is plainly a possibility when a
critical situation develops and drastic unpopular measures are considered requisite. It is even more likely when the existing Government is a minority Government; and its likelihood is still greater
if the measures contemplated are particularly repugnant to the
Government's own party supporters. Politicians in all camps would
have been strangely obtuse if the notion of an all-party administration had never occurred to them and had never received their consideration. And that some of them had contemplated the possibility was a matter of public record before the final crisis came.

Baldwin, for example, had rejected the idea, and given his reasons, in a speech at Hull on July 17. But what he rejected, and what alone was being advocated in some quarters and being discussed or thought about in others, was a Coalition Government of all three major parties, that is to say, a Government in which all three parties officially participated. In his speech to the Trades Union Congress at Bristol on September 9, 1931, Arthur Henderson himself was to concede that the formation of such a Government might well have been seriously considered by the Labour Government and the Labour movement in the previous July.[1]

In so far as it was then considered, the idea was promptly dismissed. In July of 1931 an all-party coalition was not a practicable proposition. Baldwin, in the speech already referred to, stated the main difficulty on the Conservative side. He was prepared, he said, to co-operate only with those who were willing to accept tariffs. Discussing the matter editorially on July 18, *The Times* described as 'wholly impracticable' any coalition between the three political parties upon a national policy, because the existing alliance between the official Liberal and Labour parties had been expressly founded to resist protection. While the Conservatives were not prepared to enter a three-party Government lest it should tie their hands with regard to tariffs (quite apart from Baldwin's strong aversion to the idea of any coalition), the main body of the Liberals was at least equally hostile, precisely because of the tariff issue, to any combination with the Conservatives; and their attitude was fully shared by the Chancellor of the Exchequer and other Free Traders in the Labour Government. Furthermore, an all-party

---

[1] Henderson said: 'On my return I was informed that whilst I was in Paris the question of a National Government had been the subject of conversation. (A Voice: 'Shame') 'I am not so sure that there was very much shame in it, because, as I have said before, if this situation is all that we have been told, if in its magnitude, if in its possible consequences, if in its urgency it was such as has been described, I have no hesitation in saying that I would have preferred that the idea of a National Government had been seriously considered and approached in the proper way. . . . I would have preferred to have come to a specially convened Labour Conference. I would have preferred to have gone and looked into the faces of the Parliamentary Party . . . and to allow them to have said to us: "Friends, you have put before us a very serious situation. Much as we dislike it, much as it is contrary to every expectation we ever formed, we believe that for the time being, until we can get international finance as well as national finance placed upon a better basis, it would be well to give you consent to join in this move, but we hope it will be of the shortest possible period." I say I would have preferred, much as I might have disliked it, that method of approach to the question of a National Government rather than it should have been left to the eleventh hour and the fifty-ninth minute.'

coalition (or for that matter any form of coalition) was highly repugnant to the great majority of the Labour Party.

Snowden's invitation to the Opposition parties to co-operate was
a very different proposition. He has himself related (amusingly
enough in view of the countenance he gave, on similar but even
more slender grounds, to the theory of a deep-laid plot on Mac-
Donald's part) that his remarks on July 30 were regarded in many
quarters 'as an invitation to form a National Government to tide
over the financial crisis', though such an idea was not in his mind.
Snowden was certainly not appealing for an all-party coalition. The
co-operation which he asked for, and considered imperative, was
that the other parties should not oppose in a partisan spirit the
proposals which the Government would have to submit, but
should, if necessary, actively support them.

In any event, no measures the minority Labour Government
might decide upon could be carried against the joint opposition of
the other parties; and to refrain from taking such measures as the
other parties might consider necessary would also involve the
Government in certain defeat. But, if there was to be that all-party
co-operation which the Chancellor asked for, then, plainly enough,
the Government's proposals would have to prove acceptable to the
other parties. And that clearly implied preliminary conversations
between the representatives of the three parties. The duty of formu-
lating proposals, however, rested upon the Government, who would
remain fully responsible for submitting them eventually to Parliament.

In the circumstances which had arisen at the beginning of
August 1931, the Labour Cabinet were agreed about seeking the
co-operation of the other political parties. They were to remain so
in the following weeks. Their attitude was vigorously expressed by
Clynes, the Home Secretary, and one of the 'Big Five' of the
Government, in a speech at Brighton on August 14:

> Parties must act co-operatively when the nation is faced with a finan-
> cial crisis or a crisis of any other kind. The country has the right not
> merely to seek but to expect and to demand co-operation on the part
> of the three great political parties.[1]

[1] *The Times*, August 15. The worthlessness of Clynes's *Memoirs* may be illustrated by the following passage (p. 195): 'Mr Baldwin and Mr Neville Chamberlain visited the Prime Minister, giving a theatrical air of coming catastrophe.
Some of us now began to feel very uneasy at all this parleying with the other
Party. . . .' The visit of the two Conservative leaders to the Prime Minister was
on August 13, the day before Clynes's Brighton speech.

After the break-up of the Government, Henderson was to state in the House of Commons (September 8) about seeking the co-operation of the other parties: 'I must say that we were all agreed that that course should be followed.'

The desirability of seeking the continuous co-operation of the other political parties rested on the ground, to use Snowden's words,

> that it would be impossible for a minority government to carry proposals for the drastic reduction of expenditure if the Opposition were to pursue Party tactics and to endeavour to make Party capital out of unpopular proposals.[1]

The problem is one which frequently recurs, whether or not the Government of the day has a party majority of its own. If, for example, a Government be confronted with the unpopular task of rearmament, it will be greatly hampered, and perhaps prevented from carrying out its task, should the Opposition exploit the situation for partisan electoral advantage. Samuel was to make the point in the House of Commons on September 14, 1931, in terms which deserve quotation:

> The late Government (i.e. the Labour Government) were entitled to say that a task so unpopular and so unpalatable as that of effecting great economies of this nature could not be carried out by any one party alone, and they were entitled to ask and to know what would be the attitude of the other two parties in the House of Commons if these proposals were made. They were entitled to know that if they undertook what was really a national duty in a bold spirit their political opponents would not seize the opportunity to make party capital out of the position, to leave them with the responsibility for the proposals they had made, and to denounce them in Parliament and the constituencies for having made harsh and avoidable attacks upon the standard of life of the people.

The Conservatives and Liberals, owing to the same fear of partisan exploitation of unpopular measures, greatly preferred that the situation should be dealt with by the Labour Government than that they should undertake the political risks involved. They were to give repeated assurances of their readiness to support the Government in taking such measures as might be necessary; and

[1] Op. cit., II, p. 932.

there is no ground for any suggestion that they sought to bring down the Labour Government on this issue, still less to compel the formation of a coalition or all-party Government. Writing on August 16, after being informed of the Government's intention to balance the Budget on the basis of equality of sacrifice, Neville Chamberlain said: '. . . to secure such a measure of relief, and to do it through a Socialist Government, seems to me so important in the national interest that we must give it our support, provided the proposals for equal sacrifice do not imperil British credit, or too brazenly affront ordinary rules of justice and fair play. And I don't think they will do either.'[1]

The Report of Sir George May's Committee certainly came as a general shock. It was estimated that by April 1932 the Budgetary deficit would be £120 million. The Committee's recommendations, from most of which its two Labour members dissented, were that £24 million should be found by new taxation, and that expenditure should be cut down by £96 million. The economies were to be made by reducing official salaries, the salaries of civil servants and teachers, servicemen's pay, and unemployment expenditures — the last-mentioned by £66½ million, including a 20 per cent reduction in the rates of benefit. The Labour members, in their minority report, rejected all the recommendations affecting unemployment insurance. The May Report has been aptly described as alarming to the foreigner and provocative to the Government's supporters.

Snowden had promised to inform the House of Commons of the Government's proposals when Parliament reassembled in October. After the debate on July 30, the Cabinet met and appointed a sub-committee to consider the May Report and to submit proposals to the Cabinet in the following September. The sub-committee, which came to be known as the Cabinet Economy Committee, consisted of five members: the Prime Minister as Chairman, Snowden, Henderson, Thomas and Graham. The Government departments concerned were immediately instructed to examine the May Committee's recommendations and to submit their reports before August 18, so that the latter could be considered by the members of the Cabinet Economy Committee before they met. Their first meeting was fixed for August 25.

Serious though the financial situation was, it had not then become

[1] Quoted by Keith Feiling, op. cit., p. 191.

urgently grave. Most members of the Government and other politicians dispersed for their summer holidays; although the Chancellor of the Exchequer himself remained at his home and in close touch with the Treasury and the Bank of England.

CHAPTER IV

THE CABINET ECONOMY
COMMITTEE

W ithin less than a week of Parliament's adjournment, the position began rapidly to worsen. Withdrawals of foreign balances from London were resumed at a heavy and daily increasing rate. The temporary credit of £50 million supplied half by the Bank of France and half by the Federal Reserve Bank of New York was quickly being used up. There was danger of Britain being forced off the Gold Standard, with rapid depreciation of sterling, great rise in prices, serious commercial dislocation, and the prospect of greatly aggravated unemployment. The root cause, of course, was the developing international crisis. The special contributory factor affecting Great Britain was lack of confidence in America and in parts of Europe, arising from a belief that our budgetary position was unsound, particularly because of the state of the Unemployment Insurance Fund. This belief had been much strengthened, though not of course created, by the publication of the May Committee's Report, which undoubtedly had a seriously adverse effect upon foreign opinion.

Apprised of the heavy foreign withdrawals, Snowden communicated the facts of the situation to the Prime Minister at Lossiemouth, suggesting that the Cabinet Economy Committee should be called together as soon as possible.[1] MacDonald returned to London, arriving at King's Cross early on the morning of August 11. During the course of the morning he saw Sir Clive (afterwards Lord) Wigram, the King's private secretary, but no information is available about the interview. The King went to Sandringham on

---

[1] According to Snowden (op. cit., II, p. 936), he communicated with Mac-Donald on August 7, and MacDonald returned to London at once, travelling overnight. MacDonald, however, travelled back on the night of August 10–11: he had been visiting Stimson, the American Secretary of State, in Sutherland, from August 6 to August 9, returning to Lossiemouth on the 9th (*The Times*, August 7 and August 10–12).

that day. From 11 a.m. until 5 p.m., apart from a luncheon interval, MacDonald and Snowden were in conference, and during the period, according to Snowden, were in consultation with 'a number of representative bankers'. The expression 'representative bankers' was also used in *The Times* report on August 12.

Information about this consultation with the bankers is derived largely from Neville Chamberlain's biography (pp. 190–1). In a communication to Sir Philip Cunliffe-Lister (now Viscount Swinton), Chamberlain wrote, first, that the credits were rapidly disappearing, and that enquiries in Paris and New York showed that there was no chance of a loan in either quarter. From other sources, it is understood that the bankers warned the Prime Minister and the Chancellor of the Exchequer of the possibility that the Government itself would have to borrow £80 million in order to avert a moratorium, since the Bank of England's own credit was being so quickly exhausted. Chamberlain's letter to Cunliffe-Lister (dated August 15) proceeded in these terms:

> In these circumstances the Bankers, i.e. the Deputy Governor and Peacock, went to R.M. and told him plainly (1) that we were on the edge of the precipice and, unless the situation changed radically, we should be over it directly, (2) that the cause of the trouble was not financial but political, and lay in the complete want of confidence in H.M.G. existing among foreigners, (3) that the remedy was in the hands of the Government alone. . . .

The 'representative bankers', therefore, either were or included 'the Bank of England's representatives'; and the latter, as is known from other sources, were Sir Ernest Harvey, the Deputy Governor, and Mr (afterwards Sir) Edward Peacock, a Director. The point is of some importance, because, after the crisis, at least one ex-Minister, Lansbury, denounced what he described as the sinister influence of Montagu Norman (later Lord Norman), the Governor of the Bank; and much criticism has been directed against the Governor in connection with the crisis. No doubt the policy pursued by the Bank had the Governor's approval; but it should be noted that Norman was ill, almost immediately went abroad, and was absent during the crisis.[1]

[1] Norman had collapsed on July 29, and was virtually out of action during the following fortnight. On August 15 he sailed to Canada for a complete rest, and the Bank issued the following statement: 'The Governor of the Bank of England has been indisposed as the result of the exceptional strain to which he has been

Chamberlain, apparently, did not specifically tell his correspondent that the above-quoted warning of the bankers was delivered to the Prime Minister and Snowden on August 11, but a further paragraph in the communication seems to make it clear that it was given on that day. Chamberlain proceeded:

> As they (i.e. the Bankers) were still in serious doubt as to whether any action would be taken, they asked to be allowed to put the facts before the other parties. R.M. assented, and it was in response to a message from the Deputy Governor that I went to London. . . .

And his biographer states that 'On August 11, he was called to London, where he found MacDonald and Snowden in touch with Baldwin, Samuel, and the Bank'.

This might suggest that Chamberlain returned to London on August 11, and also that Baldwin and Samuel were both there on that day. That, of course, was not so. Chamberlain was on holiday in Perthshire when he received his communication from the Deputy Governor. On August 13, *The Times* reported that he had decided on the previous day to cut his holiday short, had left Scotland by a night train, and would be back in London 'this morning'. Since Samuel (according to *The Times*, August 14) returned to London on the night of August 12, and Baldwin arrived back there from France early on the morning of August 13, as did Chamberlain from Scotland, and none of them saw the Prime Minister until August 13, it is clear that Chamberlain's biographer means that Chamberlain was called back to London on August 11, and found there whatever he did find on his arrival on August 13. That Chamberlain was 'called' to London is perhaps a little doubtful: what is clear is that, because of the information he had received, he decided that it was his duty to return. It may be noted (the point is of some importance) that on August 14 *The Times* reported that neither Baldwin nor Chamberlain had been invited to return to London by the Prime Minister, but had both independently decided to do so 'on information which reached them from the City of London'. Snowden's assertion[1] that MacDonald asked

---

subjected during recent months. Acting on medical advice, he has had to abandon all work for the present, and has gone abroad for rest and change. He has been assured that a period of complete quiet and entire freedom from work should be sufficient to enable him to resume his full normal duties at the Bank.' The newspapers reported that Montagu Norman returned to this country on September 23.

[1] Op. cit., II, p. 937.

Baldwin, Chamberlain and Samuel to return appears to be in-accurate. There is no evidence that MacDonald himself communi-cated with the three leaders. He may possibly have known that the Deputy Governor intended to ask them to return; or he may have thought it probable that they would return on being informed of the situation. In his *Memoirs*[1] Samuel says that, while staying in Norfolk, he received a telegram asking him to come to the Bank of England on a matter of importance. On doing so, he was received by the Deputy Governor and told of the situation. Samuel adds: 'The Government thought that the leaders of parties in the House of Commons should be made aware of the position.' It is probable, therefore, that Baldwin and Chamberlain received similar requests from the Bank to come to London; but this is not certain, partic-ularly since the one was in Aix and the other in Perthshire.

Either immediately upon receiving Snowden's original com-munication at Lossiemouth (as Snowden states), or after the con-ference with the Bank of England officials on August 11 (as Nicol-son says), the Prime Minister summoned the other members of the Cabinet Economy Committee urgently to London. On August 12, *The Times* reported that it had been agreed to hold the first meeting of the Committee at 4 p.m. that day, to resume on the following (Thursday) morning, and to hold a further meeting on Monday, August 17.

It is important to realize that from the moment of its publication there was bitter hostility in Labour ranks towards the May Com-mittee's Report. From the outset it was clear that the Government could not be sure of retaining the support of the majority of its own Party in the House of Commons if it attempted to carry through the Committee's recommendations. This same fact constituted an-other major difficulty in the way of the formation of an all-party Government, had that been contemplated. On August 1 *The Times* wrote, near-prophetically, that any kind of National Government, if it were to succeed in enforcing economy, would sooner or later find itself exposed to the attacks of a united Socialist Party, 'some asserting that they had always fought attacks upon the working classes and others that they had only yielded to *force majeure* in a situation which no longer existed.' *The Times* drew the conclusion that any kind of National Government would become impossible if Labour hostility to the May Report persisted. Since that hostility

[1] Pp. 201–2.

was intensified in the following days, and was expressed by considerable sections of the Labour Movement, *The Times*, on August 10, ruled out altogether the suggestion of a National Government. And it was generally taken for granted that any drastic action by the Government would encounter fierce opposition from the Left Wing of the Labour Party.

The first meeting of the Cabinet Economy Committee was held at 4 p.m. on Wednesday, August 12. At 7 p.m. the Committee adjourned until the following morning. No detailed account of this first meeting was given by Snowden in his autobiography; nor has any account been published subsequently. In the interval between the change of Government and the reassembly of Parliament, however, two documents were compiled from the recollections of the ex-Ministers and revised by them in a series of mutual consultations. The first of these related to the proceedings of the Cabinet Economy Committee. Drafted by Graham, it constitutes a record agreed upon by himself and Henderson, the two ex-Ministers concerned. The other, drafted by Greenwood, related to the subsequent Cabinet proceedings. In the following pages, the one will be referred to as 'the Graham Memorandum', and the other as 'the ex-Ministers' Memorandum'.

In the Graham Memorandum, and also in some comments made by Sidney Webb (Lord Passfield), it is stated that at the first meeting of the Committee at least two members (presumably Henderson and Graham) were surprised (or 'somewhat surprised' — there may be much virtue in the 'somewhat') to learn that the Prime Minister and Chancellor had already been in 'informal conversation' (or had 'already begun secret consultations') with the Opposition leaders. Since the Opposition leaders had been far away from London, and were still out of London on the evening of August 12 when the Committee met, and since neither MacDonald nor Snowden had communicated with them directly, the only possible basis for the suggestion would appear to be that the Prime Minister informed the Committee that he had agreed to the Opposition leaders being told of the situation by the Bank of England's representatives. The expression 'secret consultations' is particularly indefensible. If the reference, however inaccurately made to a period prior to the meeting on August 12, should be intended to apply to the subsequent conversations with the Opposition leaders, it must be pointed out that no secret was made of those necessarily 'secret'

F

discussions. Not only were they authorized, first by the Cabinet Economy Committee, and afterwards by the full Cabinet, but the newspapers reported the times and duration of the three-party conferences.

It is understood that at this first meeting of the Cabinet Economy Committee, the Chancellor of the Exchequer informed the members that the estimated deficit for the financial year 1932–33 was £170 million, and not the May Committee's figure of £120 million.

The Committee met a second time on Thursday, August 13, at 11 a.m., and adjourned at luncheon time until the following Monday. The full Cabinet was summoned for the subsequent Wednesday. The Committee issued a statement that the Government would balance the Budget, on the basis of equality of sacrifice for all concerned.

Prior to the Committee meeting on August 13, Samuel, who had returned to London during the course of the previous evening, called to see MacDonald. According to *The Times* (August 14), Baldwin and Chamberlain reached London almost simultaneously on the morning of the 13th: they conferred together at Baldwin's house, and also saw Sir Robert Horne and a number of leading bankers. *The Times* also reported that as soon as the Prime Minister heard of Baldwin's arrival in London, he invited him and Chamberlain to come to Downing Street. The two Conservative leaders at once accepted the invitation; arrived at Downing Street at 2 p.m.; and were with MacDonald and Snowden for about half an hour.

The interviews with Samuel in the morning and with the two Conservative leaders in the afternoon of August 13 were the first of the consultations during the crisis between the leaders of the three parties. These first meetings were very brief. It is clear from Chamberlain's account (in the letter to Cunliffe-Lister) that the Prime Minister and the Chancellor only explained in general terms the financial situation and the Government's intentions with regard to balancing the Budget.

Samuel's account in his *Memoirs* (p. 202) appears to be in some respects inaccurate and a little misleading. 'On August 13th,' he wrote, 'MacDonald and Snowden had a conversation with Baldwin, who had come back from Aix-les-Bains, and Neville Chamberlain; and afterwards with myself.' Samuel had in fact seen MacDonald first. 'We were told in outline the facts as they then stood: the Budget deficit for the current year would be £40 million, and was estimated for the next year at no less than £170 million.' This last figure may have been given to Samuel, but it was not apparently given to the Conservative leaders at this first interview: according to Chamberlain, they were told that the situation was worse than indicated by the May Committee, but no actual figure was given. Samuel's account proceeded: 'The Government and its advisers were agreed that drastic economies in expenditure, and equally drastic increases in taxation, were indispensable: only in that way could the Budget be balanced. And only if it were balanced could confidence in the £ sterling be restored and the crisis overcome. The Ministers communicated to us the measures they proposed to present to their colleagues.' The last sentence may convey a misleading impression, because Chamberlain's statement clearly shows that no details of proposed measures were given on this occasion to the Conservative leaders, whatever information may have been given to Samuel.

According to Snowden, the Opposition leaders all showed a willingness to be helpful and promised to be available for any further conversations. Since the Cabinet Economy Committee had not then completed their discussions, the representatives of the Government had no definite proposals to place before the Opposition leaders. They were not in a position, therefore, to ask for the co-operation of the other parties; and, according to *The Times* (August 14), the Prime Minister did not ask for any such co-operation. *The Times* commented:

> Mr MacDonald recognizes fully that it is the duty of the Cabinet to take the full responsibility for any scheme which is presented to Parliament, though, naturally, it would be of considerable assistance to him if he knew in advance that he could rely on the support of both the Conservative and Liberal parties. It is taken for granted, accordingly, that there will be a continuation of the conferences which began yesterday. The Conservatives recognize that the Government are in an extremely difficult position, largely owing to the campaign which is already being waged in some Labour quarters against the May Report.[1]

[1] Mowat has written (op. cit., p. 386) that the meetings with the Opposition leaders on August 13 were 'rather premature', but, he adds, 'they set the pattern for the future: consultations which compromised the Cabinet's decisions, and which were attended and reported upon by two members only.' Such elucidation as he provides later is discussed below.

Plainly, sufficient progress had been made in the discussions of the Cabinet Economy Committee on August 13 to warrant adjournment until the following Monday at 4 p.m. Ministers and Opposition leaders dispersed again for the week-end. MacDonald and Chamberlain returned to Scotland that night, both having arranged to be back in London on the Monday. Baldwin left for Aix-les-Bains, and *The Times* reported (August 14) that he would stay there for the time being unless Chamberlain considered his presence in London necessary. Chamberlain, of course, was his Party's principal spokesman on financial matters.[1]

During the week-end MacDonald and Snowden both made statements to a representative of the *Daily Herald*. Both stressed the seriousness of the situation and the need for drastic economies: at the same time they both urged that there was no occasion for panic and that the financial position of the country was fundamentally sound. MacDonald gave a message to the Labour Party members in the following terms:

> I ask them to remember that we are grappling with this situation with all our ideals unchanged. We have not changed our policy. We are simply compelled to devise special measures to meet the temporary difficulties. Of course we shall have our critics. In fact we can already make the speeches that they will deliver. But the critics, like anybody else, will have to face facts and deal honestly with the interests of the country.

He added an appeal for special sympathy with Snowden:

> The nation ought to be aware of the grievous burden which rests upon the shoulders of the Chancellor; and it ought to give him the confidence to which he is so thoroughly entitled in his arduous task.

Snowden, in the course of his interview, said:

> While a National Government is out of the question, the situation calls for the co-operation of all parties in the House of Commons, because a Government — and especially a Government without a major-

---

[1] At this stage, Mowat accuses *The Times* of having done much 'to build up the crisis (and discourage the foreign creditor)'. In support of the charge, he quotes a passage from the editorial on August 12 which is simply a legitimate warning of the danger involved in any delay in reaching a decision. Mowat adds that *The Times* did not improve matters 'by propagating, by means of denying them, tendentious reports of a Cabinet split (which had not yet begun)'. This is surely most unfair to *The Times*, which made one straightforward denial of such reports, pointing out that the Cabinet had not even met; a legitimate and even desirable denial.

ity — cannot carry through economy proposals of this kind and be attacked afterwards for doing so. It is the responsibility of the Government to submit its proposals to the House of Commons, but the responsibility for carrying out those proposals must rest with the whole House, so that no Party can go to the country and make Party capital out of what may be unpopular in certain quarters.

As arranged, the Cabinet Economy Committee met again on Monday, August 17; and a further long meeting was held on the 18th. Its proposals were submitted to the full Cabinet for consideration on Wednesday, August 19.

When Parliament met after the change of Government, controversies of much bitterness arose concerning the proceedings of both the Cabinet Economy Committee and the Cabinet itself. Commenting on them, Baldwin quoted someone else's remark that:

The longer he had been in public life, the less he was struck by the diversity of testimony than he was by the many-sidedness of truth.

As has been pointed out in regard to its first meeting, no detailed record of the Committee's discussions is available to the general public. The Graham Memorandum, drawn up for the use of ex-Ministers, is not a stage-by-stage record, and does not make it possible to say definitely when and in what order particular topics were discussed. Certain points, however, are well-established.

The Committee had before it at the outset a set of proposals drawn up by the Treasury; substantially in line with the May Committee's recommendations but by no means identical with them, the general plan providing for approximately as much to be raised by fresh taxation as was to be saved by economies. The Committee concentrated its attention upon the proposals for reducing expenditure. At an early stage in his first speech when Parliament met on September 8 after the change of Government, Henderson said (incidentally beginning the process of public disclosure of Cabinet discussions which was to be the subject of so much criticism) that he had at once objected to this approach. Henderson apparently desired that attention should first be given to methods of raising additional revenue. It is clear, however, that his objection was not seriously pressed.[1] The work of the Committee was based on the assumption that approximately half of the estimated deficit would have to be met by additional taxation; and during its proceedings

[1] See J. H. Thomas, House of Commons, September 11, 1931.

the Chancellor of the Exchequer indicated the general lines upon which he would propose to find the increased revenue, although, of course, any detailed proposals would have to be reserved in the usual way for a Budget statement.

The economy proposals put before the full Cabinet as a result of the Committee's deliberations were 'only tentative proposals for consideration.' That is Snowden's description of them; and there has never been any doubt on that point. They were not presented in the form of definite recommendations. The Committee, plainly, did not envisage its task as that of reaching decisions which in effect would be final, but as a preliminary survey for the guidance of the Cabinet in taking final decisions.

After the change of Government, many (if not all) of the ex-Ministers were to contend that they had consistently refused, during the Cabinet discussions, to commit themselves to anything until they had seen 'the complete picture' (an expression of Henderson's which became by repetition a familiar feature of the controversy). This contention will receive examination. For the moment, the important point is that Henderson, in his speech on September 8, stated that 'even in the early stages' (i.e. presumably, in the Cabinet Economy Committee) he had 'reserved his decision' until he had seen 'the complete picture'. But, so far as the Committee is concerned, it was generally accepted that the economy proposals were not to be put before the Cabinet as specific recommendations.

The members of the Committee, therefore, were uncommitted to any particular proposal for the reduction of expenditure. This fact was to be used by Henderson and Graham (and the same argument was to be advanced in regard to the Cabinet's proceedings also) to support a contention that the members of the Committee were uncommitted to anything at all. But the Committee certainly took one decision. They decided to submit a set of economy proposals to the Cabinet for the latter's consideration. And for that decision the members of the Committee were collectively responsible; Henderson and Graham as responsible as the other three. To the argument that the admittedly tentative nature of the proposals justified members of the Committee in rejecting all of the proposals at a later stage, the obvious answer was that such action rendered the whole process of considering and submitting economy proposals a sheer waste of time, unless, indeed, those concerned were prepared to propose alternative economies. Anyhow, the argument was double-edged, even though only one edge of it has been widely used in subsequent controversy. For, while the Committee members were uncommitted to the inclusion of any particular proposal in the final economy scheme, they were similarly uncommitted to the exclusion of any particular proposal.

The point is important in regard to the proposal for a reduction in the standard rates of unemployment insurance benefit. The May Committee, as already noted, had proposed a 20 per cent cut in those rates. The Treasury suggestions under consideration by the Cabinet Economy Committee included a 10 per cent cut. The economy proposals presented by the latter Committee to the full Cabinet did not include any cut in the standard rates. There is no question about that. It has been agreed by all concerned. Snowden stated the fact in his autobiography. It was also pointed out by Samuel (on MacDonald's authority) in his important speech in the House of Commons on September 14, 1931.

But, while Henderson and Graham are said to have taken up the position that they could not under any circumstances agree to a cut in the rates of unemployment insurance benefit, it is clear that the Cabinet Economy Committee came to no definite decision on the matter. It is also clear that other proposals, about which also no definite decision was reached, were discussed by the Committee as possible alternatives to a cut in the rates of benefit. That applies, for example, to the proposal for a revenue tariff. In the Graham Memorandum already alluded to, it is stated that, although all the members of the Committee, with the possible exception of Thomas, were opposed to such a tariff in principle, all of them, except Snowden, preferred it to a cut in the rates of unemployment insurance benefit or anything of that kind. There is no doubt at all that the members of the Committee held divergent views on several important issues, and expressed them with varying degrees of decisiveness; and that, as a consequence, the matters concerned were not included in the tentative proposals submitted for the Cabinet's consideration. Two major controversial issues were thus excluded for the time being, (1) the suggested 10 per cent cut in unemployment benefit rates, and (2) the proposal for a revenue tariff. There was nothing to bar either of these issues from being raised in the full Cabinet by members of the Committee themselves. Both were to be raised; the second by Henderson and Graham.

The proposals drawn up in these circumstances by the Cabinet Economy Committee, and put before the Cabinet at its first meeting on August 19, estimated the deficit at £170 million, to be met to the extent of £78,575,000 by suggested economies. The list of economies presented for consideration, as given by Nicolson (p. 457), was as follows:

Unemployment Benefit	-			£48,500,000
Teachers' Salaries	-		-	11,400,000
Service Pay	-	-	-	9,000,000
Police Pay	-	-	-	500,000
Roads	-	-	-	7,800,000
Other economies	-		-	5,350,000

The figure of £48½ million in respect of unemployment benefit was divided into two parts. It was proposed to reduce the cost of unemployment insurance by £28½ million (£15 million by increased contributions, £8 million by reduction in benefit period to 26 weeks, £2½ million by a special deduction from the benefit paid to all unemployed persons, and £3 million by removal of anomalies). The remaining £20 million represented a reduction of the Exchequer contribution to transitional benefit. The position in regard to transitional benefit appears to have been left rather vague. It is known, however, that the Committee agreed to the proposal that there should be some form of means test.[1]

One further decision was taken at, or as a consequence of the deliberations of, the Cabinet Economy Committee. *The Times* reported on Monday, August 17, that the Consultative Committee of the Parliamentary Labour Party had been summoned for 11 a.m. on the following Thursday (August 20), and that at 3 p.m. on the same day a joint meeting of the General Council of the Trades Union Congress and the National Executive of the Labour Party would be held 'to discuss the national financial situation'. It was understood that the Prime Minister and some of his colleagues on the Economy Committee would attend. According to statements

---

[1] On October 21, in his reply to Graham's election broadcast, Snowden gave the figure of proposed savings on unemployment as £43½ million instead of £48½ million. The discrepancy is explained by his inclusion of £10 million instead of £15 million in respect of increased contributions. Snowden omitted the £5 million of increased contributions which the State would be called upon to pay. It may be noted that, in Snowden's view, the £10 million increased contributions to be paid by employers and workers was not strictly an economy at all.

subsequently made by Henderson, he asked on more than one occasion that the members of the Party should be called together in order that the situation might be reported to them. It is confirmed (from sources closely associated with Henderson) that the Foreign Secretary, on the second occasion, urged the importance of getting the support of the three committees of the Labour Movement (the General Council of the T.U.C., the National Executive of the Labour Party, and the Consultative Committee of the Parliamentary Labour Party). According to Snowden,[1] the decision of the Cabinet Economy Committee to meet the three Labour executives on August 20 was made at Henderson's suggestion. Snowden said that he attended the meeting with great reluctance, since he had never recognized the right of the T.U.C. Council to be consulted on matters of Cabinet policy, and only consented to go because representatives of the Party Executive and of the Parliamentary Labour Party would also be present.

[1] Op. cit., II, pp. 940–1.

CHAPTER V

THE CABINET AND A REVENUE TARIFF

On August 19 the Cabinet met at 11 a.m. and sat for a total of nearly nine hours, with brief intervals for luncheon and dinner, the meeting ending at 10.25 p.m. In regard to these long Cabinet sessions (as in regard to the subsequent Cabinet meetings) no authoritative detailed record has been published, although a considerable amount of information became available after the change of Government, and further information has been forthcoming subsequently from other sources, in addition to that contained in the ex-Ministers' Memorandum already referred to. The position, however, is that many points about the Cabinet proceedings are agreed and others fairly well established.

Cabinet discussions proceeded on the basis of the Economy Committee's tentative proposals and a verbal report of its proceedings given by the Chancellor of the Exchequer. The ground covered appears to have been comprehensively wide. When the Cabinet adjourned that night, it had not agreed upon a definite set of proposals; and the duration of its sessions, combined with the absence of information, led *The Times* next day to describe the situation as 'disquieting'. The fact that no final decisions had been arrived at was particularly awkward in view of the meetings which had been arranged and announced for the following day. These included a three-party conference, to which the Cabinet had agreed, and the consultations with the three Labour executives. The consequential difficulties gave rise to much misunderstanding and subsequent controversy.

None the less, the Cabinet had made considerable progress. Agreement had been provisionally reached on economies amounting to £56,250,000. This figure included £22 million in respect of unemployment insurance. The proposal which had been submitted to save £20 million on transitional benefit was left over for further consideration, the matter being referred to a sub-committee of four (Greenwood, Graham, Johnston and Miss Bondfield). Other important issues were deferred. They included the questions of debt conversion and reduction of the amount allocated to debt remission through the Sinking Fund. The *Daily Herald* next morning stated, moreover, that 'a debate on a temporary tariff for revenue purposes was adjourned'.

The revenue tariff proposal gave rise to acute disagreements within the Cabinet, and was eventually abandoned on August 21. In the absence of any detailed chronicle of the course of the discussions, it will be convenient to deal with the matter at this stage of the narrative. After the change of Government, and during the subsequent Election, controversy about it became embittered. It was then contended that those who had supported a revenue tariff had done so (with one or two possible exceptions) only as a preferable alternative to a reduction in the rates of unemployment benefit or to other proposed economies. This, no doubt, was substantially true, but did not suffice to dispose of the criticisms made by the opponents of a tariff.

It has already been emphasized that opinion in the country generally had been moving in favour of a tariff. In Trade Union circles, concerned with the maintenance of wage rates, the idea had been gaining ground. On August 18 the *Daily Herald* quoted a statement made by a 'prominent' Trade Union leader that: 'If we are to choose between extensive sacrifices by those least able to bear them and a temporary 10 per cent tariff for revenue purposes, I and some of my friends will plump for the latter.' Next day (August 19), under the headline: 'Revenue Tariff. Decision To-day', the *Herald* announced that among the proposals to be laid before the Cabinet for discussion would be:

A 10 per cent tariff for revenue purposes. Temporary suspension of the sinking fund. A special Tax on fixed interest bearing securities. Increased contributions to unemployment insurance, with or without reductions of benefit, but coupled with administrative changes to prevent proved abuses. Voluntary conversion of War Loan to a lower rate of interest.

The *Herald* added:

The proposal for a revenue tariff will receive support from Ministers who have hitherto been rigid free-traders. A 10 per cent tariff on retained manufactures, including those imported partly finished, would yield £20,000,000. A further 10 per cent on food at present untaxed ought to yield about £25,000,000.

When, on August 19, Snowden gave to the Cabinet his verbal report about the Economy Committee's proceedings, he made no reference to the subject; and Henderson at once drew attention to the omission. The Prime Minister then explained that there was a division of opinion in the Committee on this matter. None the less, the point was pressed, and it is clear that a prolonged discussion ensued. That was known to the general public at the time. The *Daily Herald*, as we have seen, reported the adjournment of the debate on the subject. The *Daily Express* went so far as to write of a 'Cabinet All-Day Tariff Battle'. Snowden, in his unyielding hostility to the proposal, was said by this paper to have had his 'back to the wall', having been deserted by Graham and opposed by Henderson. 'It is quite understandable', added the *Express*, 'that in such a setting Mr Ramsay MacDonald has sought to guide rather than dominate.'

Although the available evidence is not absolutely conclusive, it was probably on this occasion that the Cabinet 'voted' on the revenue tariff issue. Beatrice Webb's diary entry (4 a.m., August 22) appears to refer to the Cabinet sessions on the 19th in writing that the free traders were beaten over the revenue tariff on manufactured goods (there were only five of them in addition to Snowden, the names given being those of Lees-Smith, Benn, Parmoor, Alexander, and Sidney Webb himself), and describing the defeat as 'an humiliation for Philip Snowden'.[1] The ex-Ministers' Memorandum is reticent on the subject, but speaks of 'a considerable majority' prepared, on August 19, to agree to a revenue tariff.

The matter was debated at length by the General Council of the Trades Union Congress during its discussions next day (August 20); and, although no decision was taken by that body (on grounds of procedure), it is probable that the majority of the General Council were favourably disposed. The Council's views on this and other matters were brought to the attention of the Cabinet that night (see pp. 96-8 below).

References were made in the press at the time to the Cabinet divisions on the subject. The official Labour organ disclosed that fifteen members of the Cabinet had voted for a revenue tariff on

---

[1] *Beatrice Webb's Diaries 1924-1932*, p. 280.

manufactured goods, and that some of them had supported its application to food and raw materials. The *Daily Express* (August 22) stated that fifteen members of the Cabinet were willing to support a tariff policy as an alternative to further cuts, while there were five 'unalterable Free Traders', headed by Snowden. This paper added, however, that the Government, if they were to secure and retain Liberal support, would have to give unequivocal assurances that tariffs would not be included in their proposals. And on that same day (August 22) the *Daily Herald* stated baldly that the Cabinet had turned down the revenue tariff. Beatrice Webb's diary entry, made that day after Webb's return home, recorded that the Cabinet were now unanimous against tariffs. The ex-Ministers' Memorandum merely states: 'The question of the revenue tariff was no longer pressed.'

On the day Parliament reassembled after the change of Government (September 8), Churchill alluded in his speech to the press disclosures:

> Three-quarters of the late Labour Cabinet, lifelong Free Traders, or at any rate a very large proportion, were prepared, we are told, in this crisis to adopt or approve a tariff for revenue, which, since it would have had no countervailing excise, would unquestionably be the establishment of a general protective tariff.

Two days later (September 10), addressing the Trades Union Congress at Bristol, Henderson described his attitude during the Cabinet discussions. He said:

> I am further going to make a little confession to you. I went on to say, if I am faced — and I claim to be as strong a Free Trader as any who were there — if I am faced with a large cut from the payments given to the unemployed and a 10 per cent revenue tariff, as an emergency, as an expedient, the revenue accruing therefrom to be assigned to unemployment purposes, I am going to try the value of that experiment.

According to the report of this speech in *The Times*, Henderson had actually said 20 per cent, but it was stated that the newspaper had been officially requested to intimate his wish to correct the figure to 10 per cent. The *Daily Herald's* report gave 10 per cent, and stated: 'Mr Henderson actually spoke of a 20 per cent revenue tariff, but it was explained on his behalf by Mr Arthur Hayday, the Chairman, at the close of the speech, that this was a slip. 10 per cent was meant.'

Snowden alluded to this Bristol utterance in the House of Commons on October 2. Henderson (said the Chancellor)

> said that he was in favour, under certain conditions, of a revenue tariff. He was not quite sure whether he was in favour of a 20 per cent or a 10 per cent tariff, but at any rate he was in favour of a tariff, and we have been told by the official organ of the Labour Party — the figures were given in that organ — that 15 out of 20 of the members of the late Cabinet voted for a revenue tariff. I believe the statement was further made that a number of them were in favour of a whole-hog policy, including the taxation of food and of raw materials.

It will be noted that Snowden made no disclosure of his own, confining himself to disclosures already made by Henderson and the *Daily Herald*.

Further light was thrown on this matter during the General Election campaign. The exchanges which then took place, besides being important in themselves, admirably illustrate the nature of the general controversy about the Cabinet discussions.

In a letter to National Labour candidates, published on October 17, Snowden wrote of the signatories of the Labour Party's election manifesto in the following terms:

> They are now professing to be opposed to tariffs. This is the crowning act of their attempt to delude the electors. The very men who have issued the Labour Party appeal against tariffs proposed and voted in the late Labour Cabinet for the immediate imposition of tariffs! What can be said of the political honesty of men who play fast and loose with principles for the sake of party advantage?

Henderson referred to this charge in a speech at Accrington on October 19, and replied:

> Mr Snowden knows quite well that this is a travesty of the fact. He knows quite well that there was only one reason why we ever gave any consideration to the proposal of a temporary revenue tariff. It was because of his determination to balance the Budget by cutting down unemployment benefits and social services and our desire to find some alternative.
>
> There never was any question of a majority of my colleagues committing themselves to the principle of tariffs. It was simply a question of the lesser of two evils. Faced with the impossible proposition of refusing out-of-work benefits, a revenue tariff seemed to some of us a less disagreeable alternative.

Mr Snowden says we proposed the revenue tariff. That is not a fact. None of the signatories in the Labour party manifesto made this proposal. The idea was brought forward by a member of the present Government.[1]

Henderson then repeated, in almost the same words, his already-quoted statement to the Trades Union Congress, and went on:

It is obvious that what we were doing was making a supreme effort to prevent unemployment cuts.

Why did we not proceed with the revenue tariff? It was unanimously decided to drop the whole idea. We dropped the idea because at that point a tentative proposal to balance the Budget did not include any cuts in the unemployed benefit rates.

We have got to remember that the situation was changing from day to day. Mr Snowden evidently wants to commit his old colleagues to every tentative suggestion that was made in those long and complicated conversations.

Why does he not apply the same standards to the Prime Minister? Mr MacDonald is included among three others who supported the tentative revenue tariff against Mr Snowden.[2] Why does not Mr Snowden criticize the Prime Minister for not definitely including a revenue tariff in his election manifesto?

On the same evening (October 19), Snowden was delivering his famous election broadcast, in the course of which he said:

A month ago the Trades Union Council was preparing a tariff policy. When the General Election became imminent they dropped that in order to pose as an anti-tariff party.

Mr Henderson is quoted in the *Daily Herald* this morning as having said that if he were faced with a large cut in unemployment pay or a 20 per cent revenue tariff as an emergency expedient he was going to try the value of that expedient. Now he is denouncing tariffs as an expedient to raise prices and lower wages. He was prepared a month ago to raise the cost of living to the unemployed and to all employed workers by 20 per cent rather than adopt the straightforward course

---

[1] J. H. Thomas, speaking at Derby next day (October 20), admitted that he was the Minister indicated by Henderson who had proposed a revenue tariff. It is clear, however, that this must have occurred in the Cabinet Economy Committee, not in the Cabinet itself. Snowden's reference had been to the latter. Thomas added: 'But it was equally true that Mr Henderson and 15 others had voted for it.'

[2] This again makes it plain that Henderson was speaking, not of the Cabinet, but of the Cabinet Economy Committee. The form of his allusion to MacDonald suggests that he was basing it upon the Graham Memorandum's statement about the tariff discussion in the Economy Committee (p. 71 above).

of reducing the benefits by 10 per cent. This is the party which Mr Lloyd George recommends the electors to support as a sound free trade party.[1]

On the following day (October 20) an article by Snowden appeared in the *Daily Mail*, and was reproduced next day in other papers. In this article, his comments on this particular issue were as follows:

They (i.e. 'the present Labour leaders') are now trying to wriggle out of their proposal to impose a revenue tariff. But unfortunately for them we have Mr Henderson's specific statement to the Trades Union Congress that he was prepared to try this 'expedient'. No amount of equivocation and denial can alter the fact recorded in the official organ of the party that 15 members of the Cabinet voted for a revenue tariff.

That night (October 20) Graham delivered his election broadcast, in the course of which he said:

The Chancellor of the Exchequer has stated in writing that the very men who have issued the Labour Party appeal against tariffs proposed and voted in the late Labour Cabinet for the immediate imposition of tariffs. That statement is untrue. At no time during its two years of office did the Labour Cabinet ever decide to support protectionist tariffs. The simple facts are that at one stage during the emergency discussions of August the Prime Minister and the Chancellor of the Exchequer were insisting on the reduction in the rate of unemployment insurance benefit. Innumerable alternative proposals were pressed upon them. In particular many members of the Cabinet indicated that if they had to choose between a cut in the rate of unemployment benefit and a small revenue tariff they would sooner have the revenue proposal; but they also insisted that there was no need whatever to be confronted with such a choice. A little later the Prime Minister and the Chancellor of the Exchequer appeared to be willing to consider other proposals. At that point all further reference to a revenue tariff was abandoned. You will see therefore that there was not the slightest foundation for the statement that the Labour Government was committed to protectionist tariffs.

Graham's phrases, 'at one stage', 'a little later', and 'at that point', were studiously vague. The qualification of the word 'tariffs'

[1] The *Daily Herald* that morning (October 19) had reproduced the passage from Henderson's Bristol speech with its original reference to 20 per cent. Snowden, like the *Herald*, ignored, or forgot, Henderson's subsequent correction of the figure to 10 per cent.

by the adjective 'protectionist' in the two emphatic denials may also be noted, as it was at the time. The denials themselves were irrelevant. No one had suggested that the Labour Government had ever decided or been committed to tariffs, 'protectionist' or otherwise. But the clear implication of the denials was that no vote had been taken in the Cabinet on the tariff issue. That was the implication, though there was no assertion to that effect. Graham could not go so far as to make such an assertion. The suggestions that the Prime Minister and the Chancellor 'appeared to be willing to consider other proposals' (as alternatives to a reduction in the rate of unemployment insurance benefit or a revenue tariff) only 'a little later' than 'at one stage', and that the idea of a revenue tariff was then completely abandoned, were extremely confusing. Did the 'stage' occur during the proceedings of the Cabinet Economy Committee, or was it during the sessions of the Cabinet? Was 'a little later' before or after the full Cabinet sessions began? Graham well knew (and insisted on other occasions) that neither the proposal to cut the rate of benefit nor the proposal for a revenue tariff was included in the tentative economy scheme presented by the Cabinet Economy Committee to the Cabinet itself. The Prime Minister and the Chancellor were clearly 'willing to consider other proposals' at that stage. And it is a well-established fact that, so far from the idea of a revenue tariff having then been abandoned, the subject was almost immediately raised again when the full Cabinet met, by Henderson, and pressed in the subsequent discussion by Graham himself. Graham did not point out that the Prime Minister was one of 'the many members of the Cabinet' who preferred a revenue tariff to a cut in the rate of unemployment benefit. That this was the Prime Minister's attitude during the proceedings of the Cabinet Economy Committee was pointed out, as already noted, in the record of those proceedings drawn up by Graham for the guidance of ex-Ministers.

Snowden promptly (October 21) issued a statement attacking what he described as 'several grossly inaccurate statements' in Graham's broadcast. The third of these was 'that he and his colleagues did not vote in the Labour Cabinet for the immediate imposition of tariffs'. On this Snowden wrote:

Mr Graham says there was no decision by the Labour Cabinet to impose a tariff for revenue as an alternative to a reduction of 10 per cent in unemployed pay. Again he is quite wrong. I do not remember who

G

first raised this question, but I do know that Mr Graham and Mr Henderson were its strongest supporters. Mr Graham put the case for the tariff. He told us a tax of 10 per cent on imported manufactured and semi-manufactured goods would raise £25,000,000 a year, and a tax on all imports £60,000,000 a year.

We took two votes. The first was whether we should adopt the proposal of a 10 per cent tax on manufactured and semi-manufatured imports. Fifteen members, including Mr Graham, voted for that, and five against. Then the question of a duty on all imports was put, including food and raw materials. Mr Graham and four others voted for that, and 15 against. It was only after these votes, when it was seen that we could not get unanimity, that the proposal was dropped, because, as Mr Henderson put it, if it had been persisted with it would have broken up the Cabinet.

Mr Graham in his broadcast talk was very careful to say that the Cabinet had not discussed a 'Protectionist' tariff. Quite true. They called it a 'revenue' tariff. But Mr Graham had better explain the difference in the effect of a 10 per cent 'revenue' tariff and a 10 per cent 'Protectionist' tariff. He told his hearers that a tariff raises prices to the consumers by more than the amount of the duty. So Mr Graham on his own admission was prepared to raise the cost of living to everybody, including the unemployed, by more than 10 per cent. This was a back-door method of reducing the pay of the unemployed because he and his colleagues were afraid to do it in a straightforward, honest way. Every fact I have given in this statement could be proved from the records.

On this occasion, it will be noted, Snowden went beyond what others had previously disclosed, providing certain further details. No refutation of Snowden's assertions about the two Cabinet votes has ever appeared, although he was much criticized for making them. They were not denied in the subsequent stages of the election controversy on the subject. Confirmatory evidence of a vote (in the Cabinet sense of the term at any rate) is provided in the passage quoted above from Beatrice Webb's diary.

A reply to Snowden came in a *Manchester Guardian* interview with Arthur Greenwood, who said, on the tariff issue:

Mr Snowden attributes the authorship of the proposal for a 10 per cent revenue tariff on manufactured articles to Mr Arthur Henderson and Mr Graham. I fancy its strongest advocate was Mr. Thomas, and I understand that in the Economy Committee of five every member, with the exception of Mr Snowden, and including the Prime Min-

ister, agreed that of the two alternatives — a cut of the benefit or a
revenue tariff — the latter was preferable.

No decision was ever taken on the tariff issue on its merits. It was
discussed in relation to unemployment insurance benefit. It is true
that a big majority of the Cabinet would have reluctantly accepted the
tariff rather than betray the unemployed. The matter was subsequently dropped, not because it would have broken the Government
to have finally accepted it, but because the majority believed that
other methods could be found to maintain existing rates of unemployment insurance benefit. It was suggested, for example, that the Sinking Fund should be suspended for the time. Mr Snowden was then
implacably opposed to this suggestion, but his new Liberal colleagues
appear to have persuaded him of its wisdom. Proposals were also put
forward to repeal wholly or in part the Derating Act, which is costing
the Exchequer £30,000,000 a year.

I cannot understand Mr Snowden's statement that a decision was
taken on the tariff question. If the Cabinet had made a decision, then
why was it never put to the leaders of the political parties and to the
bankers, and why did Mr Snowden, as the high priest of all the fiscal
purists, not resign?

There is a little more to be said on this issue. A double ambiguity is involved in the word 'decision' as used by both Snowden
and Greenwood. In the first place, when the propositions were
voted upon, the Cabinet were not necessarily deciding finally
whether or not a tariff should form part of a completed scheme.
Secondly, a vote in Cabinet (whether formal or informal) does not
necessarily imply or lead to a decision in accordance with the
majority view. Whether or not in such circumstances the majority
view is accepted as the decision of the Cabinet depends either upon
the willingness of the minority to acquiesce or upon that of the
majority to proceed without the minority, that is to say, to carry on
despite the resignations of the dissenting members. If the minority
is not prepared to accept the verdict, and the majority is not prepared to proceed without the minority, the decision of the Cabinet
can only be to drop the proposition, at any rate for the time being,
unless it decides to give up altogether. In this particular instance,
it is not known whether or not the members of the minority
threatened to resign rather than acquiesce. In all probability they
did not, because there was no need to do so, for the whole Cabinet
must have been conscious that resignations would follow if the
tariff proposal were persisted in. There can scarcely be any doubt that

the Chancellor of the Exchequer would have resigned in that eventuality: hence Greenwood's final debating question. It is equally
plain that the Cabinet could not have survived, in the circumstances then existing, without Snowden; and the latter would probably have been accompanied by other important Ministers.

These factors alone would have sufficed to bring about the abandonment of the tariff proposal. But there was another reason, and
one at least equally decisive. That was the known opposition to a
tariff of the official Liberal Party. It was this fact with which, apparently, MacDonald clinched the matter in the Cabinet.[1] And, in the
circumstances, it seems unlikely that the Cabinet discussions on
the subject reached a point at which the break-up of the Cabinet
would have appeared imminent.

[1] Nicolson, op. cit., p. 457.

CHAPTER VI

THURSDAY, AUGUST 20

THE FIRST THREE-PARTY CONFERENCE

Summoned by the Prime Minister in accordance with the Cabinet's decision, the first conference with the Opposition leaders took place at 10 a.m. on August 20. The Liberals were represented by Sir Herbert Samuel and Sir Donald Maclean; the Conservatives by Mr Neville Chamberlain and Sir Samuel Hoare. The last-named had been selected as his associate by Chamberlain, acting under a general authority from Baldwin, who was still at Aix. According to Lord Templewood's account, J. H. Thomas was present, as well as MacDonald and Snowden, on behalf of the Government. Snowden makes no reference to Thomas's presence.

The Opposition leaders were informed for the first time (certainly so far as the Conservatives were concerned) that the estimated deficit was £170 million. They were also told that the Cabinet Economy Committee were submitting tentative economy proposals amounting to £78½ million for the Cabinet's consideration, and that these did not include any proposed cut in the standard rates of unemployment allowances.

Some confusion has arisen about this first three-party conference. In his speech on September 14, 1931, Samuel said:

> We were told that the Cabinet Committee had met and had prepared certain proposals which it was intended to lay before the Cabinet, but they had not then been considered by the Cabinet.

The Cabinet, however, had met, to the knowledge of Samuel and the other Opposition leaders (and to the knowledge of the general public) for about nine hours on the previous day; and it must have been perfectly clear to all concerned that the Cabinet had been considering its Committee's suggestions. The likely — indeed, the only feasible — interpretation of Samuel's remark is that the Opposition leaders were told that the Cabinet had not concluded their consideration of the Economy Committee's tentative proposals.

Mowat has written (p. 388) that the meeting was held to tell the Opposition leaders 'the results of the Cabinet's meeting'. That may well have been an original intention, though clearly not the whole purpose, of the conference. And had the Cabinet reached agreement on a complete scheme, the results of their deliberations on the previous day could, and doubtless would, have been put before the Opposition representatives. In the circumstances, however, MacDonald and his Cabinet colleague (or colleagues) were unable to present any definite Cabinet proposals. Mowat proceeds:

> . . . but, curiously, the figure which they mentioned for proposed economies was £78 million (the figure which the Cabinet Economy Committee had discussed) and not the £56 million provisionally accepted the previous evening.

It is difficult to understand the use of the word 'curiously'. The £78½ million of proposed economies were those not only discussed by the Cabinet Economy Committee but also submitted by them for the consideration of the Cabinet as a whole. The £56¼ million provisionally accepted by the Cabinet on the previous day were not substituted for the £78½ million. They represented a partial acceptance of the Committee's proposals. The remainder of those proposals had not been rejected. The position was that they were to be further considered. It was surely legitimate, and even desirable, that the Government representatives should refrain from disclosing the precise state of the Cabinet's unfinished deliberations. Had they done otherwise, they would have incurred legitimate criticism. However, a charge made by Mowat (p. 394) that MacDonald 'compromised' his Cabinet colleagues, 'by his meetings with the Opposition leaders, and by the misleading reports of Cabinet discussions which he gave them,' apparently rests on this incident. The word 'curiously', and a later statement (see p. 106 below) that MacDonald and Snowden subsequently 'admitted' something, together constitute a suggestion of deception which is the only evidence Mowat provides in support of his charge.

Mowat then writes:

> The Opposition leaders accepted the economies of £78 million as a bold and courageous scheme, and adjourned to prepare detailed proposals for a later meeting.

This is oddly put. The Opposition leaders undoubtedly considered the Cabinet Economy Committee's tentative proposals to be bold and courageous. If, however, they had 'accepted' them as adequate, why should they have desired an adjournment in order to prepare detailed proposals? In fact, they did not seek an adjournment for that purpose. It was not their business to present detailed proposals. The Opposition leaders required the adjournment in order to consult their associates and to give further consideration to the proposals of the Cabinet Economy Committee. Despite statements which have been made suggesting otherwise, the Opposition leaders did not at this first conference on August 20 agree to recommend their respective parties to support the proposals. As Samuel said in his speech on September 14, 'The conference adjourned to allow us to give these matters consideration.'

Writing of this conference, Templewood says that Snowden 'was obviously speaking to the Cabinet brief, and made no effort to conceal his personal opinion that it did not go far enough'.[1] Chamberlain, he adds, 'at once declared that what was proposed was completely inadequate.' Chamberlain's own account, as set out in his biography,[2] is that he

stressed two points; first, that in view of the increased estimate of deficit, to produce economies less than the aggregate recommended by May[3] was wrong, and second, that if unemployment benefit were left untouched, the contemplated economies . . . would certainly be jeopardized. In effect the P.M. and Snowden gave us to understand that they quite agreed, the latter saying that if you took into account both the fall in the cost of living and the rise in the benefits, the unemployed were 36 per cent better off than in 1924.

The Joint Meeting

During and after the conference with the Opposition leaders, there was an interview between representatives of the Cabinet Economy Committee and the Consultative Committee of the Parliamentary Labour Party. This, as already noted, had been arranged for 11 a.m. In the House of Commons on September 8, Mr J. Chuter Ede read extracts from notes made by him after leaving the meeting. Seven members of the Consultative Committee were present. They were received at No. 10 Downing Street by the Prime

[1] Op. cit., p. 17.
[2] Op. cit., p. 192.
[3] The May Committee, it will be recalled, had recommended the reduction of expenditure by £96 million.

Minister, Henderson, Graham and Thomas, but MacDonald had to return at once to the conference then going on with the representatives of the other parties. Henderson explained that the deficit was much greater than the £120 million of the May Committee, and that every expedient had been examined, but no final decision reached. The Prime Minister came in at 11.30 a.m., and, from his subsequent statement, Ede 'gathered that the Conservative and Liberal Parties insisted on the cost-of-living cut in unemployment benefit'. There is little further information about this interview.[1] According to Ede, the seven members of the Consultative Committee held a brief consultation after the interview, and came to the unanimous conclusion that if the Government attempted to meet the conditions of the Opposition parties 'it was very doubtful if they would get any other votes from our party other than the lawyers'.

At 3 p.m., as arranged, the members of the Cabinet Economy Committee attended a joint meeting of the General Council of the Trades Union Congress and the National Executive of the Labour Party.[2] The General Council had met separately at 2 p.m. to determine their procedure at this gathering. At the joint meeting, the Prime Minister made a statement on the situation in very general terms; and, in response to a demand from Citrine for further information, Snowden then made a statement on the proposals under consideration by the Government.

One passage in the Chancellor's statement gave rise to much subsequent controversy. Mowat writes (p. 388):

> Economies were discussed, and an assurance given by Snowden that no reduction in unemployment allowances was proposed. Later there was controversy over this statement: what the T.U.C. took as a positive assurance implied, according to Snowden, only that no decision had yet been reached.

No exception can legitimately be taken to Mowat's reference to the later controversy; but his previous assertion about the 'assurance' begs the whole question. This matter loomed so large in public

[1] An allusion to it by Henderson, quoted below, pp. 90-1, suggested that a statement was made by the Home Secretary, Clynes, who, however, was a member neither of the Cabinet Economy Committee nor of the Consultative Committee.

[2] According to some reports, the Consultative Committee of the Parliamentary Labour Party were also present; but in this respect the reports are apparently erroneous.

argument at the time, and has so often been the subject of comment since, that it needs to be fully examined.

Snowden's autobiography (p. 941) contains the following passage:

I put before this meeting a statement of the economies on which the Cabinet had already agreed, but pointed out that at present they had not decided upon a reduction in the Unemployment allowances. That statement of mine was construed by the meeting as a definite decision of the Cabinet not to make any reduction in the Unemployment payments.

That, however, was not my intention. There was a division of opinion in the Cabinet on that question, and I did not regard the matter as having been finally closed. As a matter of fact, there was a small majority in the Cabinet favourable to a reduction in the Unemployment allowances. This was disclosed at the time in the *Daily Herald*, the organ of the Labour Party, in full detail, with the names of the Ministers who took the one view or the other. My statement to this joint Conference simply amounted to this, that at that time the Cabinet had not included any reduction of Unemployment allowances in their economy proposals, but the Cabinet did on the following days reconsider seriously the possibility of increasing the total of the economies by a 10 per cent reduction in the Unemployment benefits.[1]

On September 7, 1931, the opening day of the Trades Union Congress at Bristol, Citrine made a statement on the financial situation, in the course of which he dealt at length with the joint meeting on August 20. The main points in his account of Snowden's statement on that occasion may be summarized as follows:

(1) The Cabinet Committee had been considering a series of proposals: they had not accepted any of them: none were final, none definite;

(2) The practice of providing for unemployment by borrowing could no longer be continued: the deficit on the Insurance Fund, and the amounts necessary for transitional benefits, would have to be met out of the annual revenue;

(3) It was proposed to increase contributions by £15 million, £5 million each from the workers, the employers, and the State; and to reduce to 26 weeks the period of insurance benefit;

---

[1] The references in this passage to 'a small majority of the Cabinet' and to the *Daily Herald's* disclosures presumably relate to the Cabinet meeting on August 23, when the final breach occurred.

(4) 'These are the only two proposals we are making. There is no proposal for a cut in the amount of unemployment benefit';

(5) Reductions would have to be made in the salaries of certain classes of public and Government employees (Snowden specified teachers' salaries; the pay of servicemen and police; the salaries of Cabinet Ministers, judges, etc.);

(6) There would be a reduction of approximately £8 million on roads;

(7) Only approximately half the deficit would be covered by the proposed reductions, and consequently there would have to be increased taxation based on the principle of equality of sacrifice. Snowden 'steadfastly refused to disclose' the methods of raising the additional revenue.

The point now under examination was raised next day (September 8) by Henderson in his first speech when Parliament reassembled. He said:

The Chancellor of the Exchequer informed these two national committees — that was on the Thursday before we resigned — that cuts in the unemployment benefits were not part of our proposals. . . . I kept in mind that we had told these committees that cuts in the rates of unemployment benefit were not part of our proposals.

A little later in his speech, however, Henderson made the point in a different form, and was at once challenged. The report in *Hansard* reads as follows:

. . . I was not prepared, whatever happened, to be guilty, especially without going to the committees to whom we had said, 'There is to be no reduction in unemployment benefit.' (Interruption.) We are now told that the Chancellor of the Exchequer said nothing of the sort. May I just say that I have had the shorthand notes checked, and if the Chancellor desires it, I will to-morrow send him an extract of his own statement. What is more, there are hon. Members here and there, outside the delegation, who were there and heard the statement, and I had told my own committee, as secretary of that committee, when they were pointing out the danger of cuts in the unemployment benefit, 'You remember the statement made by the Chancellor of the Exchequer, and I stand by his statement.' What is more, there are hon. Members on this side who attended a committee — that is, the committee of this Parliamentary Party — who in the morning had a statement made to them, and the right hon. Gentleman the late Home Secretary made the deliberate statement to them that the Chancellor of the Exchequer had made, that there were no cuts in the unemployment benefit included in our proposals.[1]

Whether or not the shorthand notes reached Snowden is unknown. It is hardly likely that he asked to see them. Nor were they published; although, in the course of the subsequent election campaign, Citrine quoted a brief passage from them solely with the object of refuting the allegation of T.U.C. 'dictation' (see below, pp. 92-3). In the House of Commons on September 14, Snowden intervened in the debate in reply to a reference to his statement to the joint meeting on August 20. *Hansard* records:

> I do not think I gave them the exact figures in every case, but I gave them every one of those cuts, without the slightest protest from the right hon. Gentleman the Member for Burnley (i.e. Henderson) who was sitting within a yard of me. (Interruption.)
>
> *Miss Lawrence:* I desire to ask the Chancellor of the Exchequer whether at that meeting he did not most expressly and clearly tell us that these were matters which were under consideration, and gave us to understand that no decision of any kind had been reached?
>
> *Mr Snowden:* It is true that I gave these as matters that had been under the consideration of the Cabinet and, to use the words of the right hon. Gentleman the Member for Burnley, had been provisionally agreed upon. I should never, with the concurrence of my colleagues in the Cabinet, have made those disclosures to the meeting if I had not had the approval of the Cabinet. I understood that to be a private meeting, but I gather from what the right hon. Gentleman said in his inaugural address to the House, and from what was repeated by the Secretary to the Trade Union Congress at the conference last week, that at that private meeting they had hidden, I suppose, under the table some shorthand writer who took a verbatim note.

In a speech at Burnley on September 25 (afterwards reprinted by the Labour Party as a pamphlet, *Labour and the Crisis*), Henderson referred to the meeting on August 20, and said:

> In his speech the Chancellor said that no proposal for a reduction of Unemployment Benefit was under consideration.

In the ex-Ministers' Memorandum, the Chancellor was said to

---

[1] Clearly, the late Home Secretary (Clynes) could not have repeated in the morning the statement Snowden had made in the afternoon. Since Snowden had not then made the alleged statement, Henderson presumably meant 'afterwards made' not 'had made'. He may conceivably have meant that Clynes made a statement in the same terms as those said to have been used by Snowden afterwards; but, as will be seen, Henderson appears to have assigned Clynes's statement to the wrong occasion.

have stated 'that a cut in Unemployment Benefit was not a part of the Government's proposals'.

The shorthand note of Snowden's speech was made — so H. J. Laski told Sidney Webb — by Citrine himself, 'according to his habit', for the purpose of his own reply.[1] What purports to be a copy of it is as follows:

At the Joint Meeting of the Labour Party Executive and the T.U.C. General Council on Thursday, August 20, Mr Philip Snowden said he would indicate for them, not the definite decisions of the Cabinet, but matters they had been considering as possible economies. They knew the British position was due to the enormous drain on the Exchequer for unemployment, £130 million, and if there was an increase in the number of unemployed next year that would be much higher. They estimated that without any change the cost of transitional benefit next year would be about £40 million. They had been borrowing at the rate of £50 million a year, and next year without any change they would have to borrow £60 million. They have come to an end of borrowing, and any failure on the part of the insurance system to make itself self-supporting, any failure which had hitherto been met by borrowing, would have to be met out of current revenue. If it was £60 million next year, that would be an addition to the Budget of £60 million. A question had been asked if they had considered an increase in contributions. They had. And considered an increase which would amount to £15 million a year, £5 million of which would be contributed by the employers, and £5 million by the wage-earners and £5 million by the Treasury. And they had also considered improving the finances of the Government by limiting payments in the Unemployment Insurance Scheme to 26 weeks a year. They were the only two proposals on which they had taken a decision with regard to unemployment insurance. They had not made any reduction with regard to benefit. So much for unemployment.

This, plainly enough, was not a complete account of Snowden's speech on the occasion in question: it is an account only of his remarks on the subject of unemployment insurance. On October 22 (as reported in the *Daily Herald* next day), Citrine, addressing an election meeting at Hull, and attempting to refute Snowden's charges of T.U.C. 'dictation', was said to have 'produced the actual shorthand note of what Mr Snowden said when he and the Premier visited the T.U.C. and quoted it as follows:

[1] Lord Citrine, however, has no recollection of making the shorthand note.

No very useful purpose will probably be served by our meeting together unless you are in possession of some specific proposals.

I do not say that they have been definitely approved and accepted by the Government but they are under our consideration. We realize that any proposals have eventually to be submitted to the House of Commons.

The real cause why you have been asked to meet us is that the two Executives may be put in possession of the causes of the present financial position and at the same time see how far we can come to agreement on proposals which have been made.'

No further light is thrown by that passage on the question under discussion.

If what purports to be a record of what Snowden said about unemployment insurance be a correct record, it substantiates his version of the incident; and that may explain why it has not hitherto been published. There is a striking contrast between the passage in the reputed copy of the shorthand note:

They were the only two proposals on which they had taken a decision with regard to unemployment insurance. They had not made any reduction with regard to benefit.

and Citrine's Bristol quotation:

These are the only two proposals we are making. There is no proposal for a cut in the amount of unemployment benefit.

It is true that there is the customary ambiguity in the use of the word 'decision'; but Snowden had begun by saying that he would not be speaking of 'definite decisions' but only of matters which the Cabinet had been considering. This is confirmed (in even plainer terms) by Citrine's speech to the Trades Union Congress; and also by Miss Susan Lawrence's remark in the House of Commons on September 14. Snowden did not say that the Cabinet had not considered reduction of unemployment benefit. He did not say that no proposal for reduction of benefit was under consideration. He did not say that there was to be no reduction. What he did say was that the only two proposals concerning unemployment insurance on which the Cabinet had taken a decision (i.e. a provisional decision) were the increased contributions and the limitation to 26 weeks; and that the Cabinet 'had not made any reduction' (i.e. had not taken any similar decision) in regard to benefit. Snowden did, therefore, plainly imply that cuts in the rates of unemployment benefit were not part of the Cabinet's proposals (still not finally settled) at the time when he was speaking. He neither said nor intended to imply that such cuts had been definitely ruled out. It can well be understood that many (perhaps most) of those who listened to him interpreted his remarks genuinely, though erroneously, to mean that there were to be no reductions in the rates of benefit. But it is difficult to believe that Henderson and other Cabinet Ministers present could possibly have interpreted what Snowden said in that way.

The National Executive

After the joint meeting on August 20, the National Executive of the Labour Party and the General Council of the Trades Union Congress both held separate meetings to discuss the situation. The report of the former body for 1930–31 (pp. 3–4), after a reference to the joint meeting, 'when the Prime Minister and the Chancellor of the Exchequer reported upon the general position of affairs, indicating broadly the nature of the proposals that were under consideration, but which did not include any reduction in general unemployment benefits,' proceeds as follows:

> The National Executive Committee, having heard a further report on the position by Mr Henderson — in which, in answer to questions, he emphasized the statement of the Chancellor of the Exchequer with regard to cuts in unemployment benefits — it was agreed to leave matters in the hands of their Ministerial colleagues in the Cabinet.

Neither the Prime Minister nor the Chancellor was present at this meeting.

In his statement to the Trades Union Congress on September 7, Citrine said that the Labour Party Executive had decided to leave the whole question to the Cabinet, and added:

> I think, in common fairness to the Executive, the reasons should be considered by you for a moment. The Party Executive in point of fact was composed, to the extent of approximately half of its membership, of people who in one form or another were inside the Government, and in those circumstances you will realize the difficulty of their taking an independent decision.

On the conclusion of Citrine's speech, Stanley Hirst (then Chairman of the Labour Party) corrected what had been said:

> What happened was this. After Mr Henderson, Mr Clynes, Mr Lansbury and Mr Morrison had given us their versions of certain things

that had happened, in addition to the MacDonald and Snowden statement, bearing in mind that Mr Snowden had said there would be no
cuts in the unemployment pay, and also bearing in mind what certain
members of the Executive had said in regard to the Joint Committee
statements, we expressed our views I think just as strongly in the
Labour Party Executive meeting as the Trades Union Congress
General Council did in their meeting. I do not want the impression
to be that the Labour Party Executive simply sat down and said,
'Leave it to the Cabinet.' I think it would be a mistake to let that go.
We said in effect on the recommendation of our Secretary, Mr Arthur
Henderson, that we would leave it with those members of the Executive who were in the Cabinet to go back and do the best they could,
with the Socialistic point of view before them, to avoid any cuts in unemployment pay or cuts in wages of any description.

Citrine thanked Hirst for his explanation, saying that he could only
report what had been reported to them, which was, merely, that it
had been decided to leave the matter to the Cabinet. In regard to
Hirst's explanation, it is a little difficult to understand why, if
Snowden had said that there would be no cuts in unemployment
pay, the members of the Executive in the Cabinet should have been
asked, on Henderson's recommendation, to do their best to avoid
any such cuts.

Henderson's biographer provides confirmation of Hirst's statement. She has written:

> Henderson, who had not spoken in the joint meeting, left his col-
> leagues on the executive in no doubt as to his immovable opposition to
> any unemployment cut, or of his apprehension of the serious nature
> of the crisis. Any proposal for unemployment cuts would be stiffly
> resisted in the Cabinet, if it came up. Clear on this point, the executive
> were satisfied to leave the matter in the hands of their representatives
> in the Cabinet.[1]

It is clear, therefore, that the possibility of a proposal for 'unemployment cuts' coming up was envisaged: indeed, Henderson
and his Cabinet colleagues on the executive not only knew that it
had already come up but also that it was coming up again. That is
plain from Ede's statement quoted above, as from other sources. It
is important also to note the ambiguity so often involved in the use
of the phrases 'any unemployment cut' and 'unemployment cuts'.
Proposals for cuts in unemployment insurance payments had been

[1] Op. cit., pp. 379–80.

provisionally agreed by the Cabinet, as Snowden had told the joint meeting. Reductions in the standard rates of unemployment benefit constituted a special issue, and these alone could have been meant by the references to 'unemployment cuts' and 'any unemployment cut' in the passage just quoted.

In the ex-Ministers' Memorandum it is stated that:

> The Foreign Secretary discussed the situation with the National Executive and on the strength of the Chancellor of the Exchequer's statement that a cut in Unemployment Benefit was not a part of the Government's proposals, he gave an assurance to this effect to the Executive and was supported by the Home Secretary.[1]

In his September 8 speech, Henderson said that later in the crisis he had reminded his colleagues:

> We told these two committees — and I am the secretary of one, and have a certain measure of responsibility as such — that we were not making a cut in the unemployment benefit part of our proposals. . . .

and (as already quoted) he subsequently referred to

> the committees to whom we had said, 'There is to be no reduction in unemployment benefit.'

If any assurance was given to the Committees of the Labour Movement that the rates of benefit would not be reduced, it is plain that the assurance was given, not by Snowden, but by Henderson and his associates.

THE T.U.C. GENERAL COUNCIL

After the joint meeting, the General Council of the Trades Union Congress deliberated for four hours. only terminating its discussions shortly before 8 p.m. It was then announced that the views of the Council would be conveyed to the Cabinet by a deputation consisting of Messrs. Hayday, Citrine, Ernest Bevin, Arthur Pugh, and A. J. Walkden.

The Cabinet met at 8.30 p.m. that evening and received reports

---

[1] This seems to clear up the confusion arising from Henderson's allusion to the Home Secretary in his speech of September 8 (see pp. 90-1 above and footnote). Clynes's 'deliberate statement' was evidently made to the National Executive of the Labour Party on the afternoon of August 20, and not to the Consultative Committee of the Parliamentary Labour Party in the morning of that day.

of the conference with the Opposition leaders, of the interview with the members of the Consultative Committee of the Parliamentary Labour Party, and of the joint meeting with the National Executive of the Labour Party and the General Council of the Trades Union Congress. It was informed, therefore (and this was to be confirmed by Alexander in the House of Commons on September 8), that the £78½ million of proposed economies, submitted by the Cabinet Economy Committee for the consideration of the Cabinet as a whole, were regarded as inadequate by the Opposition leaders. At this same Cabinet meeting (terminated because of the visit of the T.U.C. deputation), a report was also received from a sub-committee on Unemployment Insurance. This sub-committee, presumably, was that appointed on the previous day to consider the problem of transitional benefit. The ex-Ministers' Memorandum, in its brief allusion to the sub-committee's report, states that, even if further adjustments (apparently those recommended by the sub-committee) were made, a sum of £19½ million would remain to be found. Nicolson (p. 457) says of the sub-committee on the transitional benefit problem that it proposed only some slight re-arrangement of contributions, producing a saving of £4 million in place of the £20 million suggested in the Cabinet Economy Committee's tentative proposals. He adds that the Prime Minister made it clear that such a saving could not be regarded as adequate. Nicolson does not indicate when this happened, and he links it with MacDonald's statement that all idea of a revenue tariff would have to be abandoned because of the attitude of the Liberal Party.

The Cabinet rose at 9.30 p.m. to enable the members of its Economy Committee to receive the deputation from the General Council of the T.U.C. In his speech to the Trades Union Congress at Bristol, Citrine said that the General Council decided that they could not subscribe to the Government's policy — that they 'must oppose the whole thing'. They agreed to make alternative proposals, which were subsequently published. These were:

(1) that the unemployment insurance contributions from worker, employer and State should be replaced by a graduated levy upon profits, incomes and earnings: a scheme put forward by the General Council to the Royal Commission on Unemployment Insurance.

(2) that there should be new taxation upon fixed interest securities and other unearned income.

(3) that the Sinking Fund should be suspended.

H

As its final 'proposal', the General Council listed the following:

> (4) The question of a Revenue Tariff was discussed, and it was agreed that a matter of such fundamental importance could not be decided by the General Council. It was felt that Congress decisions in the past precluded the General Council from pronouncing upon this matter.

It appears from Citrine's speech on the subject that it was this last issue which occupied by far the greater part of the Council's four-hour meeting, for, he said, 'we debated for several hours as to whether in the circumstances we should be justified in expressing an opinion.' It is obvious that no problem would have arisen in this respect had not the majority of the Council been favourable to a revenue tariff.

The General Council's conclusions were presented to the Cabinet Economy Committee (not to MacDonald and Snowden alone as is usually stated) by Bevin and Citrine. In his autobiography (p. 942), Snowden wrote:

> This deputation took up the attitude of opposition to practically all the economy proposals which had been explained to them. They opposed any interference with the existing terms and conditions of the Unemployment Insurance Scheme, including the limitation of statutory benefit to 26 weeks. We were told that the Trade Unions would oppose the suggested economies on teachers' salaries and pay of the men in the Fighting Services, and any suggestions for reducing expenditure on works in relief of unemployment.
>
> The only proposal to which the General Council were not completely opposed was that the salaries of Ministers and Judges should be subjected to a cut! They were of opinion that no economies were needed, and all the revenue that was necessary could be obtained by additional direct taxation and the suspension of the Sinking Fund!

Snowden replied 'to all the points they raised at some length'. According to Citrine, he said 'in effect' that the General Council did not appreciate how serious the problem was. 'Some of us', Citrine added, thought that 'two members of the Cabinet at least had made up their minds that nothing we could represent would materially alter their point of view'. Snowden, on his side, wrote:

> we had to realize that the Trade Union General Council were not prepared to play their part in the existing crisis, nor to accept even the scheme of economies which had already been provisionally agreed to by the Cabinet.

CHAPTER VII

FRIDAY, AUGUST 21

CABINET AND T.U.C.

On the following morning (August 21) the General Council of the T.U.C. met again. As a consequence, the letter set out below was sent to the Prime Minister by Citrine:

The Deputation which met the Cabinet Committee last night have presented to the General Council a report of the proceedings, copy of which I enclose for your information.

I was asked to inform you that the General Council adhere to their views as expressed to you by the Deputation, and have instructed their Economic Committee to keep in touch with the whole situation with a view to presenting a report to Congress, which, of course, will have to be done in accordance with our Constitution.

On the same day the Prime Minister replied to Citrine in the following terms:

We told you last night that we were exceedingly obliged to you and your colleagues for coming to see us and for the way you laid your views before us. I am very glad to have them in writing so that they are available for more careful study. As I said to you yesterday, however, they do not meet the pressing financial situation which the Government has been called upon to deal with; and instead of reducing expenditure they would substantially increase it.

The Cabinet met again this morning, and its Sub-Committee, whom you saw, reported what you said to it. It felt bound, however, to proceed with its examination of the scheme about which the Chancellor and myself talked to the joint meeting yesterday. It did this in the belief that if it took another course the situation would steadily worsen, and unemployment would rapidly increase — far more rapidly than we have known it even during this terrible time of depression. As you know, nothing gives me greater regret than to disagree with

99

old industrial friends, but I really personally find it absolutely impossible to overlook dread realities, as I am afraid you are doing.[1]

The terms of these letters make it clear that the General Council's deputation on the previous night were seen by all the members of the Cabinet Economy Committee and not merely by MacDonald and Snowden. That is confirmed by a statement of Citrine's in reply to questions at the Bristol Congress, when he said, 'we met the five representatives of the Cabinet Committee.'

Mowat's treatment of this episode leaves much to be desired, even allowing for the pressure on his space. He writes (p. 388): 'The General Council followed this with a four-hour meeting, as a result of which Walter Citrine and Ernest Bevin were sent to represent to the Cabinet the Council's objections to many of the proposed economies; they saw MacDonald and Snowden at 9.30 p.m., just after a Cabinet meeting, and became convinced that the ministers' minds were made up to accept, at the dictation of outside forces, proposals which the T.U.C. would find intolerable. These meetings later received great prominence, being the basis for Conservative charges that the T.U.C. had "dictated" to the Government (the obverse of Labour charges of dictation by the bankers).' The phrase 'many of the proposed economies' may well be considered an understatement. The General Council opposed 'the whole thing'. Anyhow, the passage is one-sided and inadequate. Mowat's reference to 'the dictation of outside forces' is probably derived from Citrine's statement in his Bristol speech: 'we differed materially in the degree to which we were being stampeded and driven by forces which every man in this Congress knows were in operation, and we told them plainly that if they were going to allow themselves to be dictated to, the British Trades Union Congress would not be an assenting party to it.' The charge of T.U.C. dictation was by no means confined to Conservatives; nor did Conservatives originate the charge, which came first from the Labour Cabinet itself.

The Cabinet resumed its deliberations on the morning of August 21. It sat, morning and afternoon, for a total of about five hours. A

[1] This letter (which had already been published in a report presented to the Trades Union Congress at Bristol) was read by MacDonald on October 23, during the election campaign, in a speech at Seaham Colliery, in reply to a statement by Citrine that the T.U.C. had received nothing but praise from the Prime Minister for the scheme they had submitted to the Cabinet in August.

report was given of the interview with the deputation from the General Council of the T.U.C., and the Cabinet had before it the subsequent letter from Citrine.

The complete rejection by the General Council of the policy upon which all the members of the Cabinet (however much they differed about its details) were working, was an event of far-reaching importance in the development of the crisis. Its impact upon Ministers was bound to be considerable. Nicolson has written (p. 458) that the Prime Minister returned to Downing Street after the joint meeting 'in furious despair'. Both he and Snowden may well have been in such a mood after the meeting at Downing Street that night with the General Council's deputation. A new and major complication had been introduced to a situation already complex and desperate enough. The members of the Cabinet must all have realized that they now had to meet the determined opposition of the leaders of the industrial side of the Labour Movement, in addition to the inevitably fierce hostility of all Left-Wing elements. It is more than possible, however (as Nicolson himself has suggested), that the effect upon MacDonald of the General Council's attitude was, after the initial reaction of despair, to steel his resolution. However that may have been, the Prime Minister and the Chancellor had also to reckon with the effects of that attitude upon their Cabinet colleagues, and particularly upon those more closely associated with the Trade Unions. Henderson's line at the meeting of the National Executive immediately after the joint meeting is significant in this connection; and, whatever may have been his previous doubts and objections, they were sufficiently strengthened by the developments of August 20 to give Lansbury the impression that he had 'changed his mind'.[1] The reactions of some other members of the Cabinet besides MacDonald and Snowden may be judged by Webb's comment, as recorded by Beatrice Webb in her diary for August 22:

> 'The General Council are pigs,' S. W. said, 'they won't agree to any "cuts" of Unemployment insurance benefits or salaries or wages.' They are referring their conclusions to T.U.C. meeting, Sept. 7th.[2]

The Cabinet (according to Nicolson) agreed that no Government worthy of the name could submit to dictation from an outside

---

[1] Postgate, *The Life of George Lansbury*, p. 269.
[2] Op. cit., p. 281.

body such as the T.U.C. MacDonald's letter to Citrine shows that
the Cabinet decided to proceed with its examination of the scheme
which the General Council had so emphatically rejected. The ex-
Ministers' Memorandum states that there was a long discussion on
cuts in the rates of unemployment benefit, 'but as a substantial
minority was against an alteration, the question was dropped and
other proposals considered relating to Unemployment Insurance.'
This passage is important in two respects: first, despite Snowden's
alleged statement to the joint meeting on the previous day, the
question of cuts in benefit had almost immediately 'come up' again
in the Cabinet; and secondly, cuts were opposed, not by the majority of the Cabinet, but by 'a substantial minority'. The same
Memorandum states that during later stages of the Cabinet's discussions that day, 'reference was made' to (1) raising additional
revenue, mostly by direct taxation, as a necessary condition of any
agreement; (2) the Sinking Fund; and (3) Exchequer savings which
might be made to Derating; and, finally, that the question of the
revenue tariff was no longer pressed. Beatrice Webb's diary for
August 22 provides some confirmatory evidence. The Cabinet was
said to be now unanimous against tariffs; and adhered to the 50–50
basis in regard to 'cuts' and taxes, as against the Conservative
leaders' view that only 25 per cent of the deficit should be met by
increased taxation.

CABINET PROPOSALS

The outcome of the Cabinet's deliberations that day was that,
while the economies provisionally accepted on August 19 remained
despite some adjustments, at a figure of approximately £56 million, the Cabinet as a whole were now unwilling to go further, and
were prepared to put forward proposals on that basis for eventual
submission to Parliament.

No doubt at all exists that the whole Cabinet did provisionally
accept economies of £56 million. Henderson, indeed, was to disclose the fact in his speech on September 8, and he stressed the
point repeatedly in order to show that the whole Cabinet realized
the reality and gravity of the crisis and were prepared to balance
the Budget. The economies thus provisionally accepted[1] included
a 15 per cent cut in teachers' salaries and substantial reductions in
the pay of the police, of the men in the Fighting Services, and Civil

[1] See footnote 1 on opposite page.

Servants. Immediate instructions were given to the Departmental Ministers concerned to begin negotiations in respect of these cuts. A figure of £22 million was included in regard to unemployment expenditure. £10 million of this was to come from the increased contributions of workers and employers. A further £4 million was to be obtained by a special additional levy of 2d per week on employed workers. It seems that this extra levy was 'the slight rearrangement' recommended by the Cabinet's sub-committee on Unemployment Insurance. Snowden was to assert (in his statement of October 21) that it was agreed to at Henderson's 'strong request'; and he had previously described it (in his *Daily Mail* article) as 'another of Henderson's pet schemes for following the trade union practice of a special levy for unemployment'. These two items, amounting to £14 million, were considered by Snowden as, in reality, additional taxation, not economies at all. £3 million out of the £22 million represented savings already decided upon under the Anomalies Act then recently passed; and the remaining £5 million was to be obtained by imposing a Means Test for Transitional Benefit.[2]

The position was this. The Cabinet, on August 21, substantially reaffirmed their provisional acceptance on August 19 of approxi-

---

[1] Snowden set out the details in his autobiography, as follows:

Unemployment Insurance (limitation of insurance benefit to 26 weeks, means test after that for transitional benefit, removal of 'anomalies', and increased contributions)	£22,000,000
Education (including 15 per cent reduction in teachers' salaries	10,700,000
Defence (including present reductions in pay of the Forces)	9,000,000
Roads	7,800,000
Police Pay — first year	500,000
(Second year, £1,000,000)	
Unemployment Grants	500,000
Afforestation	500,000
Agriculture	700,000
Health — Doctors	700,000
Other Economies	1,000,000
Empire Marketing Board	250,000
Colonial Development Fund	250,000
Miscellaneous (including reductions for Cabinet Ministers and others)	2,500,000
	£56,400,000

[2] It seems that the idea of transferring the recipients of transitional benefit to public assistance was abandoned because of strong opposition (see Beatrice Webb's diary, August 22, 4 a.m., op. cit., p. 280); and that it was because of this fact that the issue of reductions in the standard rates of unemployment benefit had 'come up' again.

mately £56¼ million of the economies (amounting to £78½ million) which had been submitted to them for consideration by their Economy Committee. But, whereas they had on August 19 left over for further consideration the remainder of their Committee's proposals in regard to unemployment insurance, on August 21 they dropped the whole (substantially) of those deferred proposals. And they did so because 'a substantial minority' objected, and an agreed decision to accept such proposals could not therefore be reached. There can be little doubt that the opposition had been strengthened in some degree by the attitude of the General Council of the Trades Union Congress.

In his speech on September 8, Henderson said that, the £56 million of proposed economies having been provisionally accepted, he had understood 'we would face Parliament', but, so far as he was concerned, only if 'we carried our own people with us'. According to Beatrice Webb, Parliament was to be summoned on September 14, when the Government expected to be defeated and the Conservatives to take office. ' "No resignations" urged J. R. M. and no general election till the budget is balanced. . . . He (i.e. Sidney Webb) thinks J. R. M. has behaved in all good faith over the whole business.'[1]

While the acceptance of the £56 million of economies was provisional, the abandonment of the further economies which had been suggested was also provisional; but the important difference between the position at the end of the Cabinet meetings on August 21 from that which had existed on the previous day was that the Cabinet had now provisionally completed their consideration of the proposals they were willing to place before Parliament, and, therefore, as a preliminary, before the representatives of the other political parties.

The brief account in Mowat's book (p. 388) reads as follows:

On Friday the 21st, there was another long Cabinet meeting. Agreement on economies to be proposed to Parliament was reached, the crisis was apparently over, and the members dispersed to their weekend retreats. The economies, however, still amounted to only £56 million. MacDonald and Snowden made their report to the Opposition leaders at five that afternoon; and the apple cart was upset again.

It is difficult to understand what is meant here by 'the crisis' being

---

[1] Diary, August 22, op. cit., p. 281.

'apparently over', unless the crisis is considered in terms merely of
the differences within the Cabinet which had caused the delay in
reaching a provisional decision. By general admission, moreover,
the agreement reached was provisional only. The other members
of the Cabinet, when they 'dispersed to their week-end retreats'
knew, of course, that MacDonald and Snowden were almost
immediately going to meet the Opposition leaders and place before
them the Government's proposals. It was repeatedly stated, and,
was never challenged, that the Prime Minister and the Chancellor
did so on the Cabinet's authority.

THE SECOND THREE-PARTY CONFERENCE

During the course of the Cabinet's deliberations on the 21st, the
resumption of the three-party conference was fixed for 5 p.m. In
the interim, both Liberal and Conservative leaders had conferred
with their respective colleagues, and were prepared, subject to one
important reservation, to recommend their parties to support an
economy scheme on the lines of the Cabinet Economy Committee's
tentative proposals of which they had been informed on the morning of the 20th. In his speech on September 14 in the House of
Commons, Samuel said:

> We had consultations with our political friends and the Conservative
> party representatives had similar consultations, and we were all of
> opinion that those proposals represented a very bold scheme, and a
> courageous attempt to grapple with the realities of the situation, but
> we doubted whether such a large sum of savings could be effected
> with regard to unemployment without a diminution in the scale of
> unemployment allowances, and we determined to raise this point at
> the next conference. We were prepared to give a general assurance of
> support if measures of that kind were laid before Parliament.

When the three-party conference reassembled (with the same
representatives) at 5 p.m. on August 21, the Opposition leaders
were confronted by an unexpected situation. The same speech of
Samuel's may be quoted again:

> Before any statement of our views was made on that occasion the
> Prime Minister and the Chancellor of the Exchequer told us that the
> plans which had been stated in general terms on the previous day had
> been modified by the Cabinet, and that they had accepted the whole
> of those proposals, except those relating to unemployment.

Samuel went on to state in detail the proposals in regard to un-employment expenditure which the Cabinet had provisionally ac-cepted, as already set out above. In his address to the Liberal Party meeting on August 28, after the change of Government, Samuel said that he and Maclean had gone to the conference on the 21st

> with the hope that the then Government would present adequate measures to Parliament which they would be able to support.
>
> We found, however, to our surprise and deeper regret, that so far from being willing to make any advance upon the plans that had been sketched out and the real savings that had been proposed, the Cabinet had struck out roughly one-third.

There can be no valid excuse for misunderstanding of these re-marks or of what had happened. 'The plans which had been stated in general terms on the previous day', 'the plans that had been sketched out', were of course the Cabinet Economy Committee's tentative economies of £78½ million. The Opposition leaders, while willing, after consultations, to give these proposals their general support, had not considered them in one important respect adequate, and they had determined to press that particular matter, viz.: reductions in the scale of unemployment allowances. They were, however, immediately faced by the news that the Cabinet had decided to propose economies of only £56 million, made up as already outlined above.

After writing that 'the apple cart was upset again', Mowat pro-ceeds (pp. 388–9):

> For now they (i.e. MacDonald and Snowden) admitted that the Cabi-net had modified its previous plans and accepted economies of £56 million — actually, the only figure ever accepted by the Cabinet — instead of the £78 million; and the Opposition leaders, who had come (by the testimony of Chamberlain and Samuel) to propose larger economies, especially over unemployment payments, were naturally indignant at the apparent diminution.

The implication seems to be that on the previous day MacDonald and Snowden ought to have 'admitted' something which had not then happened and was never to happen. Until August 21 the Cabinet had no 'plans', and could not therefore have 'modified' them; nor did Samuel ever say that it had done so. What it had done, but did not do until the 21st, was to modify the plans pre-sented to it for consideration by its Economy Committee.

Chamberlain's diary records that, after the information had been given by the Government spokesmen,

> We asked whether it was proposed to announce that this was the last word, and were told 'yes'. When we asked what would happen if this announcement failed to restore foreign confidence . . . Snowden replied 'the deluge'.[1]

In the changed circumstances, the Opposition leaders asked for further time for consideration, and the conference adjourned. According to *The Times*, the two Conservatives left shortly after 6.30 p.m., and the two Liberals at 7 p.m.; the arrangement being that they should all return later in the evening.

It appears that the initial reactions of the Opposition leaders led to an immediate effort to recall the other members of the Cabinet. The *Daily Herald* (August 22) reported that, to the surprise of the spectators in Downing Street, members of the Cabinet began to arrive back before the Opposition leaders left. The announcement then made that no statement would be forthcoming, together with the news that the Opposition leaders would be returning later, disclosed that a hitch had taken place. And this was confirmed, said the *Herald*, 'by the knowledge that an emergency Cabinet meeting had been called, but that owing to the short notice it had not been possible to get all the members together.' Those Cabinet Ministers who had responded to the call then left, and a special meeting was immediately summoned for 9.30 on the following morning (August 22).

After departing from Downing Street, the Opposition leaders consulted their respective colleagues. According to Samuel, the two Liberals consulted Lloyd George as well as Reading. The result of the consultations was that both party groups came to the conclusion that the Cabinet's proposals were inadequate.

THE THIRD THREE-PARTY CONFERENCE

The Opposition leaders returned to Downing Street at 9.30 p.m. Chamberlain (according to his diary) opened the conference and intimated

> (1) that if these were the final proposals . . . we should turn them out immediately the House met: (2) that before then we anticipated that the financial crash must come: (3) that we considered that it was the

[1] Feiling, op. cit., p. 192.

P.M.'s bounden duty to avoid that crash: and (4) that we were ready to give him any support in our power for that purpose, either with his present, or in a reconstructed government. Samuel followed on exactly the same lines. . . .

In his speech to the Liberal Party meeting on August 28, Samuel said:

we found it our duty to state in very friendly but definite terms that the proposals as they then stood must be regarded as inadequate, that we felt sure that Parliament would not be able to accept them; furthermore, that in our view the situation could not be allowed to drift until Parliament met after some two or three weeks, and indeed that the situation was most serious and that a solution could not be delayed even over the week-end.

Information about the response made by the Prime Minister and the Chancellor of the Exchequer is extremely scanty. Snowden gave none at all in his autobiography. Chamberlain's diary (as quoted by his biographer, pp. 192–3) records:

The P.M. began by drawing a touching picture of his own position (a thing he loves to do) . . . he did not think resignation would help. He would remain P.M. . . . invite his colleagues to support him, and tell those who would not that they might go when they liked.

The other Conservative representative, the present Lord Templewood, has an interesting passage in his reminiscences, although his picture is confused by a reference to Thomas. It reads as follows:[1]

Snowden, supported by Thomas, was obviously ready to accept Chamberlain's requirements. MacDonald, who certainly did not disagree with his two colleagues, was nervous of undertaking the responsibility of a decision that at least half his Cabinet and all the T.U.C. opposed.

So far the passage is not specifically related to the conference on the night of August 21, nor, it follows, is Thomas specifically stated to have been present on that occasion. Templewood proceeds:

Even when he implied at the last of the conferences that he was ready to break with the dissidents and carry on as best he could, it was clear to me that he felt that the task would be beyond his powers. His doubts became even more evident when, after the last meeting, he asked Chamberlain and me to talk to him alone in his upstairs sitting-

[1] Op. cit., pp. 17–18.

room. It was late in the evening, and the room was almost dark when, for many minutes, he soliloquized to us about his own troubles and the country's need of an all-party effort. His words, like the atmosphere, were obscure, but the conclusion that Chamberlain and I drew from them was the same. He had decided to resign, and to advise the King to send for the party leaders for consultations as to the next step. Having no instructions from Baldwin, we could give him no advice, least of all on the question of his resignation.

It is clear that all this relates to the late evening of August 21.

Samuel, in his *Memoirs*, has only a very brief reference, and, unfortunately, that is mis-dated (see below, Appendix II, p. 377 *et seq.*). Assigned, as it should be, to August 21 and not to August 22, the reference is:

> At the final meeting, at nine o'clock that night, the Prime Minister told us that the Cabinet deadlock could not be overcome and that he had decided to resign.

The accuracy of this statement is highly questionable. The Cabinet had not reached a state of deadlock on the evening of August 21; nor did the Prime Minister, during his conference with the Opposition leaders, definitely tell them he had decided to resign.

The position that evening was that a formal deadlock existed between the Cabinet as a whole and the Opposition parties. Unless the Prime Minister could break that deadlock, a change of Government was inevitable, either before or immediately after Parliament reassembled — and, in the circumstances, probably before that event. The Opposition leaders were aware (probably before the meetings on the 21st, and certainly during their course) of the attitude which had been taken up by the General Council of the T.U.C. They could draw their own conclusions about the likely reactions of Ministers; but it is plain that they were told that differences within the Cabinet had been responsible for the decision that day to limit the proposed economies to the figure of £56 million. That the Cabinet might soon reach a state of deadlock was clearly possible, and even likely, but, late on the night of August 21, the members of the Cabinet (other than the Prime Minister and Snowden) were not aware of the Opposition leaders' reactions to their decision.

Further information about the three-party talks late on August 21 is derived, as will be seen, from disclosures of subsequent Cabinet proceedings and the controversy resulting therefrom.

According to at least one account (the ex-Ministers' Memorandum) the Prime Minister and the Chancellor, at some time after the Cabinet meeting on August 21, also saw 'the Bankers'. Any such interview presumably took place between 7 p.m. and 9.30 p.m., that is to say, during the adjournment of the three-party conference. That provides evidence, if any be required, that both the Government representatives and the Opposition leaders were fully aware of the financial situation as it then stood and of the Bankers' views thereon. The point is important, since it does much to explain the atmosphere of gathering urgency which thenceforward prevailed. Undoubtedly also, whatever information the Prime Minister and the Chancellor received from the Bank of England's representatives only confirmed the Opposition leaders' warning that a crash would probably come before Parliament reassembled on September 14. The growing imminence of financial disaster rendered impracticable any idea that may have been entertained that the Government should face Parliament with proposals known to be unacceptable to the Opposition and so court defeat. The position from the standpoint of the Opposition leaders was stated by Samuel in his speech to the Liberal Party on August 28 in these terms:

> We came to the conclusion that the plans as they then stood must be regarded as unacceptable, that they would involve a colossal burden of new taxation, and that when they were announced, together with the decision of the other two parties which could not be withheld from public knowledge, the effect must be to precipitate a disaster. . . .

Apart, however, from the worsening and the uncertainty of the financial situation, for the Government to follow the procedure of courting an inevitable defeat would have been an act of irresponsibility which it is difficult to believe that any of the Ministers seriously contemplated. In other words, the issue really turned on whether or not the support of the Opposition parties could be obtained; and that, of course, is why the Cabinet as a whole were agreed in seeking that support. Hence the question of the Ministry's immediate resignation at once arose when the Opposition leaders declared that the proposals put before them were inadequate and would be resolutely opposed. In these circumstances, it was plainly necessary that the Cabinet should meet again as soon as possible. And, indeed, as previously noted, efforts were made to

collect the Cabinet again immediately the likely attitude of the
Opposition leaders became apparent.

Note

After the change of government, some ex-Ministers were to imply
(rather than state) that the Cabinet, on the afternoon of the 21st,
had decided to face Parliament with their proposals regardless of
the attitude which the Opposition parties might take up. It is difficult to believe that any of them could have thought that the proposals were going to be communicated to the Opposition leaders
for their information only. But Henderson (in his speech of September 8) said: 'we went away on the understanding, at any rate as I
understood it . . . that we would face Parliament. . . . We met next
morning and were told that the Prime Minister and the Chancellor
of the Exchequer had had another interview with the leaders of the
other parties, and they reported to us. . . .' — as though Henderson
had not known that the interview was going to take place. Parmoor
quoted this passage in his reminiscences, after saying that 'on going
home in the late afternoon I thought that the difficulties had been
settled'. Parmoor then added: 'In fact, on Friday evening, so far as
I then knew, no suggestion was made that the Government would
not, in the usual manner, apply to the House of Commons to sanction the raising of any additional funds required to balance the
Budget, following the ordinary constitutional procedure. It had
certainly never occurred to me that the Prime Minister would seek
to override the Labour Cabinet by making arrangements with the
leaders of the Conservative and Liberal Parties.' This last sentence
may be interpreted, of course, as a reference to the formation of the
National Government; but, if that be the correct interpretation, it
is difficult to grasp the relevance of the sentence. But it assuredly
must have occurred, even to the venerable Parmoor, that the Prime
Minister and the Chancellor were at once going to see the leaders
of the Opposition parties and submit the Cabinet's proposals to
them.

Mowat, clearly enough, has been influenced by the suggestions
that all had been finally settled, so far as the Cabinet was concerned,
when the meeting on the afternoon of August 21 terminated. His
passage, 'the crisis was apparently over, and the members dispersed to their week-end retreats,' has already been noted. On p.
390 he resumes the theme: 'It is not surprising that at the Cabinet

meeting on Saturday morning, August 22, signs of a split appeared. The members had done their work, as they thought, and gone home. Now they had been brought back again. . . .' However, the really surprising thing about this passage is the suggestion that signs of a Cabinet split appeared for the first time on the Saturday.

CHAPTER VIII

SATURDAY, AUGUST 22

THE KING

The Conservative leaders were in communication with Baldwin during the evening of August 21. On the following morning *The Times* reported that the Leader of the Opposition had left Aix for London, had reached Paris overnight, and would resume his journey that morning.

The King, as already mentioned, had been at Sandringham; and it had been announced that he would leave for Balmoral on the night of August 21. According to Morshead[1] and Nicolson, the King suggested to the Prime Minister that the visit to Scotland should be postponed. MacDonald, however, advised against postponement, on the ground that it would disturb public confidence, and thus promote the financial disaster which it was sought to avert. George V, accordingly, decided to leave for Balmoral. This, presumably, happened before the resumption of the three-party conference late on the 21st.

The King arrived at Balmoral early on the morning of the 22nd; but, in view of the gravity of the messages which reached him from London, he decided to return that evening. According to Nicolson, he had a telephone message (presumably from or through MacDonald) that his presence in London might become necessary; but the decision to return seems to have been his own.[2] The ex-Ministers' Memorandum states that the Cabinet was informed, at its meeting on the morning of August 22, that the Opposition leaders had suggested on the previous night that the Prime Minister should see the King. But, after the resumed three-party conference, late on the 21st, MacDonald would anyhow have had to inform the King of the possibility of the Government's resignation.

It is rather curiously suggested by Mowat (pp. 389–90) that the

---

[1] *D.N.B.* 1931–40, George V.
[2] Templewood, op. cit., p. 18.

return of the King and that of Baldwin, or, rather, the newspaper reports of these events, were part of a process by which the crisis was 'worked up to the highest pitch (though had the apparent settlement on Friday endured it would have subsided at once)'. Here we have another reference in Mowat to 'the apparent settlement' on the Friday afternoon. But had this apparent settlement within the Cabinet been endorsed by the representatives of the Opposition parties, it is by no means certain (or even probable) that the crisis would immediately have subsided. Mowat means, presumably, that the 'working up' of the crisis would have subsided at once. By which he presumably means (*inter alia*) that Baldwin would have remained at Aix and the King at Balmoral, or, at any rate, that the newspapers would have refrained from publishing the news that they had left or were leaving. The other elements in the 'working up' process specified by Mowat are that the newspapers reported 'rumours of splits in the Cabinet and of resignations', and also printed editorial protests against the Cabinet's delay in coming to a decision. Mowat is particularly severe on *The Times* in the last-mentioned connection. He closes with: 'On August 24, when the battle was actually over, the leader, with icy patience, was entitled "Still Waiting", and gave, with a twisted kind of loyalty, the information that the Bank of England's credits of £50 million were almost exhausted.' It would be of interest to know what Mowat means by his phrase, 'a twisted kind of loyalty.' Can it be intended as an implied criticism of *The Times* for having failed to 'work up' the crisis more effectively by publishing that information previously? It is amusing to note, in Beatrice Webb's diary for August 23, an emphasized statement by Webb that what he called 'the run on the banks by foreign financiers' had not been reported in the press.[1]

THE CABINET

When the Cabinet met at 9.30 a.m. on Saturday, August 22, the Prime Minister and the Chancellor of the Exchequer reported on the attitude of the Opposition parties and on the financial situation. A somewhat odd controversy arose later about the terms of their report on the first point, and since it attracted much attention it must be dealt with.

In his speech on September 8, Henderson said, and repeated,

[1] Op. cit., p. 282.

subsequently persisting in his statement, that the Prime Minister and the Chancellor had reported

> that the £56,000,000 of economy cuts were inadequate, and that there must be from £25,000,000 to £30,000,000 more, the bulk of which must come from the unemployed.

Samuel, interposing, said that he could not allow that statement to obtain public currency:

> It is not the case that the leaders of either of the other parties said that there must be £25,000,000 or £30,000,000 more cuts, the bulk of which must come from the unemployed, or anything like that.

Henderson, it will be noted, had not said they had; but, in repeating his point on the second occasion, had prefaced it with the remark that the Prime Minister and the Chancellor 'had had another interview with the leaders of the other parties and had reported . . .'.

Intervening before Samuel, MacDonald had asked if Henderson, 'having said so much,' would say what the figure was which had been 'presented with full authority to the leaders of the other two parties before that?' Henderson made no reply, but an answer was given by Alexander when he wound up the debate for the Labour Opposition on that occasion. Alexander first quoted from Samuel's speech on August 28 to the Liberal Party meeting. It was a passage about the three-party conference on August 20 very similar to that already quoted (p. 105 above) from Samuel's subsequent speech in the House on September 14, and was as follows:

> The Prime Minister and Mr Snowden indicated what their economy proposals were likely to be. Sir Donald Maclean and he (the Home Secretary) regarded them as in the main a bold and courageous scheme, but after consideration and consultation with others, they thought that some diminution must imperatively be made in the scale of unemployment benefit.

Alexander then pointed out that the figure which was before Samuel and his colleagues at that time (on August 20) was 'not the figure of £56,000,000', but 'a much larger figure', one 'to which we were never committed and to which we did not agree, and yet on top of that figure, we were told that we had not gone far enough, although we had been described as bold and courageous'. Alexander went on to emphasize his point that the Opposition leaders 'were demanding specific cuts upon the unemployed, not merely on top of the figure which was put forward for discussion, but on a figure of nearer £80,000,000 which was first taken by the representatives of the Cabinet in order to discuss it and to see what the figure was likely to be'. He concluded this part of his speech with these words:

> In face of that fact, I cannot see how it is necessary at all to discuss whether it was £25,000,000 or £30,000,000, or even whether in the particular case of the Home Secretary (i.e. Samuel) a figure was mentioned. The fact is that the statement of the Home Secretary to his own party, reported in *The Times*, proves the contention which was made by my right hon. Friend (i.e. Henderson) this afternoon.

Clearly, however, it did not prove Henderson's contention: and Samuel's denial was put aside, a denial made, it should be noted, not only on Samuel's own behalf but also on behalf of all the other Opposition leaders. In the concluding speech of the debate on September 14, Neville Chamberlain referred to Henderson's account, 'or what he (Henderson) said had been reported to him,' and said:

> There was no ultimatum. There was no demand for a specific increase in the economies. There never was a demand for a specific cut in unemployment benefit. Our views were put forward as suggestions, as honest expressions of opinion as to what we thought would be the steps necessary to avert the crisis.

Notwithstanding the Samuel and Chamberlain denials, and, indeed, despite the form of Henderson's original assertion, the statement inaccurately attributed to Henderson secured extensive currency. It is of some interest that the ex-Ministers' Memorandum (probably drawn up with the Parliamentary debates particularly in view) stated:

> ... the Prime Minister and the Chancellor reported. A demand was made by the Opposition leaders for further economies amounting to £25 million to £30 million (in addition to the £56 million), the bulk of which was to be found out of Unemployment Insurance. Both the Prime Minister and the Chancellor of the Exchequer made this statement.

Speaking at the Bristol Trades Union Congress two days after the debate in the House, Henderson said:

> ... I said in the House of Commons what finally decided me, at any rate, was the demand — we need not for the moment say where it

came from — we fought that out in the House — the demand that in addition to the 56 million which we all deplored, which we would have gone hurriedly away from if we could have seen the way from it — in addition to those 56 million there must be 25 or 30 more million, the bulk of which must come from the unemployed.

The explanation of this matter seems simple and obvious. Mac-Donald and Snowden clearly told the Cabinet on August 22 that the support of the Opposition parties would not be forthcoming unless the proposed economies were raised to approximately the extent mentioned, and by far the greater part of the increase found out of unemployment insurance. Their statement was accurate. Members of the Cabinet may have interpreted what was reported to them as a 'demand' by the Opposition leaders. It is conceivable that either MacDonald or Snowden, or even both of them, used the word 'demand' at one point or another. And yet, obviously enough, there was no formal demand of any kind. But, while that was so, the Opposition leaders made it plain that their parties would oppose the Government unless a certain course of action was pursued; while they did not specify in any detail what that course of action involved, they clearly indicated its general nature, viz.: greater reductions in expenditure, mainly in the sphere of unemployment insurance; and while they did not formally demand nor specifically insist upon reductions in the scale of unemployment benefits, they none the less expressed the view, and expressed it strongly, that such reductions would in all probability prove necessary. From the start, indeed, they had advanced a doubt whether the requisite economies could be made without cuts in unemployment benefit rates. The Opposition leaders presented no 'ultimatum' to the Government in the sense of saying, Do this and that or we shall turn you out. What they did was to say, and say forcibly (as Chamberlain's account shows), If you do this and fail to do that, we shall turn you out. Whether or not such a statement is legitimately described as an 'ultimatum' is perhaps a nice point; but that it amounted to an ultimatum in the everyday use of that word is plain enough.

On the second main point of their report to the Cabinet, MacDonald and Snowden told their colleagues that, owing to the rate at which funds were being withdrawn from London, a moratorium would probably be unavoidable by the following Wednesday; and that, in order to avert this, the credits of £80 million which the Government had to negotiate were urgently necessary.

At this stage it is desirable briefly to explain the position in regard to the loans or credits required. The Bank of England had exhausted its own credit in America and France. Any loans or credits had to be negotiated on behalf of the Government; and on August 13 the Bank was asked to make soundings in New York about the possibilities. The Chairman of the Federal Reserve Bank of New York, Mr George L. Harrison, responded with the suggestion that the Government should raise loans in New York and Paris of, say, £50 million each; and expressed the opinion that if an adequate economy programme was approved by Parliament such a loan would be practicable in America. The Federal Reserve Bank, however, was debarred by its charter from making loans to foreign Governments. In view of this fact, Harrison pointed out in the subsequent week that he could only give advice; and the advice he gave was that negotiations should be conducted with a consortium of New York bankers through the British Government's agents in that City, Messrs J. P. Morgan & Co. This was the procedure adopted. Thenceforward the representatives of the Federal Reserve Bank acted as advisers only. So also, of course, did Morgans, as the British Government's agents. If the large loans or credits required were to be raised or arranged, satisfactory assurances about the British financial situation had to be forthcoming. An indispensable condition was a balanced Budget. Both the proposals for effecting this, and their acceptability or otherwise to the Opposition parties, were necessarily involved.

MacDonald and Snowden told the Cabinet that it was impossible to await the reassembly of Parliament, and that a decision had to be reached without delay if a moratorium was to be avoided. It was this, apparently, which led Henderson immediately to suggest that the Government should resign. In the speech on September 8, in which he made such far-reaching disclosures of Cabinet proceedings, he said:

> But what was the remark I immediately made after the report was given on that Saturday morning — the day before we resigned, because we practically resigned on the Sunday and not on the Monday. What did I say? I said, 'Mr Prime Minister, I have had a growing conviction that we are being asked to handle a situation that it will be quite impossible for us to carry through.' . . . I said, 'That conviction is stronger now than it has ever been,' and I went on to say, and you

can think of it what you like, 'The sooner the position is ended, the
better so far as I am concerned.'

Confirmatory evidence of these points is to be found in Beatrice
Webb's diary for August 23. After the Cabinet meetings on the
22nd, Henderson is said to have blamed MacDonald for continuing
negotiations: he would have preferred the Government to have said
what it was prepared to do and to resign if the Opposition parties
rejected the proposals, assuming that, owing to the financial situation, it was impossible to await a decision by Parliament. That
assumption, a sound one, provides the key to his desire for resignation. Sidney Webb's own opinion at that stage (on the night of the
22nd) was: 'Let the Tories come in and stand the racket.'[1]

Evidently, Henderson did not formally propose that the Cabinet
should resign. He does not appear to have pressed his opinion, or,
if he did, he failed to get support. As he said at Bristol on September 10, 'we went on talking and discussing. . . .' On the other hand,
it appears from more than one unpublished account that the
question of a Coalition Government or of a National Government
composed of members of all three parties was raised. The ex-
Ministers' Memorandum makes this assertion, but does not say
who raised the matter. It does say, however, that it was raised again
later in the proceedings by the Prime Minister, and that the Chancellor of the Exchequer expressed the view that the Cabinet would
be unanimously opposed to the formation of such a Government.
References in Beatrice Webb's diary for August 23 provide a rather
different version. It was there stated that MacDonald raised the
question of 'a Coalition Government: some of the Labour Cabinet
Ministers remaining in office'. MacDonald is alleged to have said
that the King desired this and might propose it. The suggestion
was said to have been hotly opposed by Henderson and other members. The impression left on Webb's mind 'was that J.R.M., Snowden and Jimmy *might consider it*'. Beatrice Webb's own comment
was; ' "A good riddance for the Labour Party" I said.'

It may be considered strange that this discussion about a possible Coalition or a National Government has not been publicly referred to by Labour ex-Ministers. As will be seen, they (and others)
were to seek diligently for any scrap which could possibly be presented as evidence that MacDonald had long planned such a devel-

[1] Op. cit., p. 282.

opment; and it is rather difficult to believe that they have been inhibited — in this one respect — from revealing Cabinet secrets. That applies to Snowden as much as to the rest. Possible reasons for their reticence will emerge later. But the contradictory versions of Snowden's attitude will be noted.

The subject seems to have arisen at an even earlier stage in the Cabinet's proceedings. The ex-Ministers' Memorandum refers to a discussion in the Cabinet during the course of its long sessions of August 19. Thomas is alleged to have said that if the Government could not carry out a programme on lines similar to that put forward as a basis for discussion by the Cabinet Economy Committee, they would be bound to support any Government which did. The Memorandum states that no support for his view was expressed, and then adds: 'The Prime Minister adumbrated the possibility of a National Government.' Just that!

THE ENQUIRY

Since no progress was made on the lines either of resignation or of participation in some alternative Government, the Cabinet proceeded to discuss what could be done to meet the views of the Opposition parties. Most if not all the old points of disagreement were doubtless raised again; and inevitably the main discussion was on the subject of a cut in unemployment benefit — inevitably so because only by such means could the unemployment charges substantially be reduced. The ex-Ministers' Memorandum states that the Cabinet were faced by the Prime Minister with the alternatives of a 10 per cent cut in unemployment benefit or the practical certainty of a moratorium on the following Wednesday. The differences of opinion were acute; but, in response, it seems, to a passionate appeal by Snowden,[1] the Cabinet eventually empowered the Prime Minister and the Chancellor to enquire of the Opposition parties if they would support the Government on the basis of economies amounting to approximately £76 million, including a 10 per cent cut in the standard rates of unemployment benefit.[2]

---

[1] Nicolson, op. cit., p. 459.

[2] Mowat (p. 390) gives the figure as £68½ million, 'including £12¼ million saved by a 10 per cent reduction in unemployment allowances.' These two figures were given by Samuel in his speech of September 14. They also are the figures given by Snowden on p. 941 of his autobiography, when he was discussing the particular question of the reduction of unemployment benefits. The total of £68½ million is reached, of course, by the addition of the £12¼ million to the £56¼ million of the Government's previously proposed economies. On p. 944 of his autobiography, however, when dealing at greater length with the Cabinet's

This was to be an enquiry only: on that point there is general agreement. The Cabinet as a whole remained uncommitted. Snowden wrote (p. 941) that MacDonald and he

> were instructed to meet the Opposition leaders, and to ask them, without a definite commitment, what their attitude would be. . . .

And (on p. 944):

> It was, therefore, decided that Mr MacDonald and myself should be empowered to submit tentatively to the Opposition leaders a suggestion that if we could increase the economies by £20,000,000, namely, £12,500,000 from the Unemployment Grants and £7,500,000 from other sources, they would regard that as satisfactory. We were placed in a difficult position in making this suggestion, because we had no assurance that if it were accepted by the Opposition leaders the Cabinet would agree to do it. However, we put the proposal before them. . . .

In Samuel's words (September 14), 'the contingency was put only as a possibility.'

The ex-Ministers' Memorandum states:

> A vote was taken as to whether the Prime Minister should approach the Opposition leaders to enquire whether, if the Cabinet agreed to include a 10 per cent cut, plus £7 million other economies, in their tentative proposals, this would obtain their support for the scheme as a whole. It was agreed that the Party leaders should be seen, the Cabinet not being committed to any such proposal.

This suggests that there was a dissentient minority who acquiesced. Confirmation is provided by Henderson's public statement on September 10 (to the Trades Union Congress at Bristol) that 'it was determined by a majority' to make the enquiry.

Beatrice Webb's diary (August 23) gives a different version of these events, but one which is unsupported save by Lord Parmoor. The entry reads:

> They rose at 12 o'clock under the impression that it was settled that the P.M. would resign and Baldwin would take office. However in the

decision to have the enquiry made, Snowden gave the increase as £20 million, 'namely, £12½ million from the Unemployment Grants, and £7½ million from other sources.' And on p. 948 Snowden again wrote of 'the suggestion for £20,000,000 further economies which would include a reduction of 10 per cent in Unemployment payments'. The position was that other additional economies, amounting to approximately £7½ million, were included in the figure about which enquiry was to be made. The total figure submitted in the enquiry was, therefore, approximately £76 million — the previous £56¼ million, plus £20 million.

luncheon hour J.R.M. and Snowden met the Opposition leaders again and suggested another compromise — (S.W. said that J.R.M. was not authorized to do it). . . .

This version fails to explain why the Cabinet merely adjourned until the afternoon; it is inconsistent with the passage in the same entry about Henderson's attitude towards the question of resignation; and it is contradicted on the main point by the directly authoritative accounts. Parmoor, in his *Retrospect*, quotes a passage from Snowden's autobiography in which the latter wrote (p. 948) that, when the final test came, 'the Cabinet would not agree to implement the authority they had given to Mr MacDonald and myself to submit to the Opposition leaders and the bankers the suggestion for £20,000,000 further economies which would include a reduction of 10 per cent in Unemployment payments.' Parmoor then writes: 'That any such authority was given to the Prime Minister and the Chancellor of the Exchequer, as is here described, was most vigorously denied by other members of the Cabinet, notably by Mr Arthur Henderson and Mr William Graham in the House of Commons later.' But the speeches of Henderson and Graham will be searched in vain for any such denial, nor has any public denial been made by a member of the Cabinet other than Parmoor. Henderson's statement to the Trades Union Congress at Bristol is by itself sufficient to settle the point, and to demonstrate that Parmoor's memory was sadly at fault.

The *Sunday Times* (August 23) reported that the Cabinet adjourned at 12.10 until after lunch, 'but as soon as the meeting had broken up the Prime Minister sent out messages requesting representatives of the Conservative and Liberal parties to pay another visit to No. 10 Downing Street. Within ten minutes of the summons Sir Herbert Samuel and Sir Donald Maclean, representing the Liberal Party, arrived in a taxicab. They were followed shortly afterwards by Mr Neville Chamberlain and Sir Samuel Hoare, who have been the spokesmen of the Conservative Party at all the three-party conferences during the past week. The Opposition representatives were received by the Prime Minister and Mr Snowden, and the six of them were in close conference for an hour.' The Opposition leaders left Downing Street, according to the reports in the newspapers, at 1.35 or 1.40 p.m.

In reply to the enquiry addressed to them, the Opposition leaders expressed the view that Parliament might be prepared to accept such proposals. However, they could not themselves say whether or not the proposals would be adequate to restore confidence, and suggested that this was a matter upon which the bankers should be consulted. Snowden wrote in his autobiography (p. 945):

> we received the impression that if this could be done they would regard the total of our economies as satisfactory. But they urged that this was a matter upon which the bankers should be consulted, and if they were satisfied the Opposition leaders would raise no further objection.

Samuel (in his speech of September 14) said:

> We said that in our opinion those proposals might be considered to be adequate. We did not say that they were really sufficient, but we did not say, as we had said before, that Parliament in our view would reject them. We could not express an opinion as to whether those proposals would be sufficient to restore world confidence, and whether the purpose of them would be served or not; if it was found that it would not be served, they would have to be reconsidered; but we had no reason to think, so far as we were concerned — that they would be regarded generally as inadequate. . . .

MacDonald (in his opening speech when Parliament reassembled on September 8) said:

> When it was put to the representatives of the other political parties, they said to us: 'Will this scheme secure the loan? If it does, we will support it. If it does not, we shall not.'

In his speech to the Trades Union Congress, Henderson gave his own version of the whole episode, in these terms:

> But we went on talking and discussing, and interviews were taking place between the Prime Minister, the Chancellor of the Exchequer, and the representatives of other interests outside. But it had got narrowed down to this — and this is the point I want to make — it had got narrowed down to this, shall we, instead of complying with the request for 25 or 30 more millions, shall we try them with a 10 per cent cut instead? And I remember saying: 'What? Do you want another rebuff? You have had two already.' And it was determined by a majority that they should be tried with this 10 per cent cut. The trial was made, and what was the answer that came back? 'Well, it is not very satisfactory, but if you are prepared to go to the House of Commons with it we are prepared to go to the House of Commons with it, but you will understand that our position to-day does not withdraw

from us the right in the House of Commons to move for an increase in the cut.'

The initial statement in this passage about interviews taking place was misleading. The reader should also note how extensive were Henderson's disclosures about Cabinet discussions — disclosures made, moreover, outside Parliament.

THE CABINET AGAIN

The reactions of the Opposition leaders to the enquiry made of them can hardly be described as enthusiastic, but they were certainly promising. The Cabinet met again at 2.30 p.m.

According to the ex-Ministers' Memorandum:

> . . . the Prime Minister reported that the Opposition leaders would probably agree to this. It was then suggested that these suggestions should be placed before the Bankers. Though there was a division of opinion on this, it was decided to take this step. The Cabinet was not, however, to be committed to the 10 per cent cut plus £7 million. The Bankers were to be told this and asked whether, if it were acceptable to the Government, it would satisfy New York.

MacDonald, in his September 8 speech, said:

> Again, with full consent, representatives of the Bank of England were consulted as to whether in their opinion the scheme proposed would produce the loan.

Harvey and Peacock were consulted accordingly. Little information is available about the form of this consultation. The newspapers did not report a visit by the two Bank officials to Downing Street. It is quite clear, however, that the consultation took place during the session of the Cabinet, and also that the Bankers were not seen by the Cabinet as a whole. Snowden has written (p. 946) that MacDonald and he

> put before the bankers the suggestion we had made to the Opposition leaders with the consent of the Cabinet that the total economies might be increased by £20,000,000 from the figure of £56,000,000 previously accepted.

The Bank of England's representatives, according to Snowden,

> thought that if this could be done it might satisfy New York and the credits would be granted.

According to Nicolson (p. 460) they said that they would immediately put the case to the New York bankers and obtain their opinion. Lansbury's biographer has written: 'The Bank, it turned out, had to consult the Federal Reserve Bank of America. And Mr Harrison of that Bank must make confidential inquiries in New York.' Beatrice Webb's diary for August 23 records:

> It was left to the Bank of England (Vice-Chairman) to consult the Federal Bank of U.S.A. whether they would back such a Governmental policy and their decision will be reported to-day (Sunday) when the Cabinet meets at 7 o'clock.

The form of this last statement may create a misleading impression. The approach was made, not to the Federal Reserve Bank as such, but to Harrison personally. The Bank of England, at the Prime Minister's request, asked Harrison for his opinion.

The Cabinet adjourned at 3.40 p.m., and it was arranged that they should meet again at 7 p.m. the next day (Sunday, August 23). An official statement was issued from No. 10 Downing Street, as follows:

> The Cabinet have been putting the finishing touches to a scheme which, it is believed, will meet the situation, and they will meet to hear the results to-morrow.

There is no record, nor any newspaper report, of anyone conferring with the Prime Minister at any time during the evening of August 22; and it was stated in the *Sunday Times* that, shortly after the Cabinet meeting ended, the Chancellor of the Exchequer and his wife left No. 11 Downing Street by car for their country home at Tilford. In view of the confusion about dates in certain accounts of the crisis, it is of some importance to note that the same newspaper reported that when the Opposition representatives left Downing Street about 1.40 p.m. on August 22, 'Mr Chamberlain and Sir Samuel Hoare said that their conference with the Government was concluded. Sir Donald Maclean intimated that no plans had been made for a resumed meeting.' The *Observer* reported: 'Mr Chamberlain stated, on leaving, that they had "finished for the day", and Sir Donald Maclean added that the party leaders were not returning to Downing Street unless specially requested.'

The two Liberal representatives conferred that afternoon at Lord Reading's house with their colleagues of the Liberal Advisory

Committee. Chamberlain and Hoare were also in conference that afternoon with leading members of their party. Just before half-past seven in the evening Baldwin arrived from France. According to the *Sunday Times* next day, he dined with Mr J. C. C. (now Viscount) Davidson at his house in Great College Street, Westminster. Later in the evening, it was said, Baldwin had had conversations on the political situation with Neville Chamberlain and other leading Conservatives. Chamberlain, according to his biographer,[1] gave the Leader of the Opposition a full report. We have been informed from the same source that Chamberlain, believing that it was politically urgent to get an all-party agreement and tactically desirable to split the Labour Party, went to this conference with Baldwin determined to urge him to try to work with the Labour moderates, whatever the Liberals might do. Templewood says that Baldwin had been quite content to leave Chamberlain in complete control of the negotiations, and was equally content to accept the results *en bloc*. He adds:

> The impression that he made on us when we discussed the crisis in the rooms of the Conservative Research Department in Great Queen Street was that the last thing in the world that he wished was either a return to office or the end of his holiday. 'Having destroyed one coalition,' he did not, as he continued to repeat to us, 'wish to form another.' Only if a National Government was really inevitable, was he ready to take his part in it. Chamberlain and I were inclined to be impatient when we saw him so reluctant to take the only course that seemed to us possible.[2]

[1] Op. cit., p. 193.
[2] Op. cit., p. 18.

CHAPTER IX

SUNDAY, AUGUST 23

PALACE CONSULTATIONS

The departure of the King from Ballater by special train at 6 p.m. on August 22 was reported in the Sunday newspapers. His Majesty reached Euston at 8 a.m. on the 23rd. At 10 o'clock (Morshead says 10.30), he received the Prime Minister at Buckingham Palace. After this interview, an official statement was issued in the following terms:

> On the Prime Minister's advice the King has asked Mr Baldwin and Sir Herbert Samuel to see him, because His Majesty wishes to hear from them themselves what the position of their respective parties is.

We now have Sir Harold Nicolson's account of this interview early on the morning of the 23rd. MacDonald explained the situation to the King, telling him that a reply from New York was expected before midnight:

> Mr MacDonald at the same time warned the King that it was possible that certain of his most influential colleagues in the Cabinet, and notably Mr Arthur Henderson and Mr William Graham, would not consent to these economies now tentatively put to New York. If they were to resign from the Government it would not be possible for him to carry on the administration without their assistance. The resignation of the Labour Government as a whole would then become inevitable.
> The King, on receiving this intimation, decided that the correct constitutional course was immediately to consult the leaders of the Conservative and Liberal Oppositions.

What exactly happened about consulting Baldwin and Samuel is not clear. Nicolson conveys the impression that the initiative in this respect came from the King. If so, the terms of the official announcement suggest that he asked for and obtained MacDonald's approval. Geoffrey Dawson, then the Editor of *The*

Times, recorded a telephone conversation with the King's Secretary, Clive Wigram, that morning before the interview took place. Wigram then said that the King was going to see the Prime Minister directly and 'proposed to see Baldwin and Samuel later in the day, so as to have the views of all parties at first hand'.[1] The Parliamentary Correspondent of *The Times* wrote (August 25) that the King returned to London determined to see the leaders of all parties, 'though he properly sought and received the advice of his Prime Minister before doing so.'

The only other available account of this interview is that given by Morshead, who has written that MacDonald reported to the King

> that while he and some of his colleagues favoured a ruthless policy of retrenchment, Henderson and a substantial proportion of the Cabinet were unyielding in their opposition. He accordingly felt that he would have no option but to resign, but the King urged him to remain in office and cheered him with words of encouragement and support.[2]

One thing is quite clear. MacDonald did not offer his resignation on this occasion.

By accident, the King saw Samuel before he saw Baldwin. The latter could not immediately be located. It has often been said that he had gone out for a stroll: in fact, he went to see Geoffrey Dawson, with whom he stayed talking until lunch time and whom he then accompanied to the Travellers' Club.[3] The circumstance that Baldwin could not be found when he was wanted is said to have turned the impatience of Chamberlain and Hoare to 'irritation'. In saying this, Templewood adds:

> The result was that Samuel saw the King in the morning, and Baldwin only in the afternoon, after Samuel had already opened the way to a coalition. It may well be that this timing suited Baldwin, who may have wished to come in at the end of the play. True to type, he had waited for the last moment to intervene, with the result that the scene was altogether set when he decided that the moment had come to walk on to the stage.[4]

The timing may have suited Baldwin, but the timing was not his. It was not a case of Baldwin having 'waited' and then having

---

[1] John Evelyn Wrench, *Geoffrey Dawson and Our Times*, p. 291.
[2] *D.N.B.* 1931–40, George V, p. 331.
[3] Wrench, op. cit., p. 292.
[4] Op. cit., pp. 18–19.

'decided'. Nor, when he saw the King, was it 'the last moment' for 'intervention' on his part. At that point in the course of events, it was by no means certain that the Labour Government would resign.

George V saw Samuel at 12.30 (at noon, according to Nicolson). At this interview, the acting leader of the Liberal Party, according to the account in his *Memoirs* (p. 204), advised the formation of an all-party Government, preferably under MacDonald's leadership. The passage reads as follows:

> I felt no doubt that the members of the Liberal Party in the House of Commons would support an all-party Government, formed with the single purpose of overcoming the financial crisis. A purely Conservative Administration, or a combination of Conservatives and Liberals only, would not be as effective; and a general election would offer no solution at all of the immediate urgent problem. The best prospect of securing a broad-based Government would be if there were no change of premier. I advised His Majesty to that effect.

As a description of the interview, this passage is obviously incomplete, since the resignation of the Labour Government, though possible and even likely, was not certain; and the passage has in fact proved misleading. According to Nicolson (p. 461), Samuel told the King that it would be to the general interest if the necessary economies could be imposed by a Labour Government. The best solution would be for MacDonald, either with his existing or with a reconstituted Labour Cabinet, to propose the economies required. If, however, MacDonald failed to get sufficient support from his colleagues, then the best alternative would be a National Government, composed of members of all three parties, preferably with MacDonald as Premier, and formed 'for the single purpose of overcoming the financial crisis'.[1]

[1] Samuel's own record of his advice to the King on this occasion is set out in a biography published since this book was written (John Bowle, *Viscount Samuel*, p. 271). The main passage in this record reads as follows: 'If Mr MacDonald, with this, or a reconstituted, Labour Cabinet, was able to propose economies, which were really adequate, that would be the best solution. . . . If that solution proved to be impracticable, then a National Government of members of the three parties would be the best alternative. It would be preferable that Mr MacDonald should be the Premier, unless he found that he could not carry with him a sufficient number of his colleagues. We deprecated a purely Conservative Government, as we thought it would have great difficulty in securing popular support for the necessary measures. If, however, His Majesty found that no other solution could be reached, we should of course support the Government of the day in the steps immediately necessary to save the financial situation. I said nothing as to the possibility of a Conservative-Liberal or Labour-Liberal Administration, and the King did not raise the point.'

K

Samuel advised a National Government under MacDonald only as 'the best alternative'. According to his advice, 'the best solution' was that the requisite economy measures should be carried through by the Labour Government, either in its existing or in a reconstituted form. Since 'the best solution' proved impracticable, and 'the best alternative' was resorted to, Samuel apparently did not trouble to mention the former when he came to write his memoirs.

Samuel was far from being alone in his view that the best course would be for the Labour Government to remain in office and deal with the crisis. That, of course, was MacDonald's own strongly-held conviction, and accounts for his persistence in striving for Cabinet agreement. But it was also the opinion generally held by the Conservative and Liberal leaders. Interesting confirmation is provided by Geoffrey Dawson's diary for August 23.[1] When consulted by Wigram early that morning about the King's imminent interview with MacDonald, Dawson himself urged that 'it was everything to get a plan of national economy put out in public by a Labour Government, since it was the only course that would have a permanent effect in reversing a policy of extravagance', and he 'respectfully suggested' that the King should impress upon MacDonald that 'it was his business to get the country out of the mess' and should 'dwell, with any flattery that he liked, upon the opportunity and the responsibility', adding that 'the example of Scullin, who had become almost a popular hero by facing his problem in Australia, was one that might profitably be pointed out to him'. Dawson's view was endorsed and, doubtless, acted upon by Wigram. Later that morning, Baldwin, in his conversation with Dawson, 'agreed entirely': he hoped that MacDonald would be able to carry on; and proceeded to discuss the personnel of a new Government, 'if by any misfortune he was to be called upon to form one at once.'

The important point is that Samuel and Baldwin, in their successive interviews with the King, respectively proposed and approved the formation of a National Government under MacDonald's leadership only if MacDonald found it impossible to proceed with a Labour administration—only as the next best thing.

The King's interview with Baldwin took place at 3 p.m. that day. According to Samuel, Baldwin's opinion about the situation was the same as his own. According to Nicolson, the King asked the

---

[1] Wrench, op. cit., pp. 291-2.

Conservative leader whether he would be prepared to serve in a
National Government under MacDonald. The answer was in the
affirmative. Baldwin said he was ready to do anything to assist.
Even if MacDonald insisted on resigning, he (Baldwin) would be
prepared to form a Government himself provided assurance of
Liberal support was forthcoming. In that eventuality, he would ask
the King for a dissolution when the crisis was surmounted, and to
this the King agreed.

Both Nicolson and Morshead make it plain that George V was
much impressed by Samuel's arguments in favour of a National
Government. The former has quoted from the record made at the
time by the King's Private Secretary (Wigram):

> H.M. . . . said that he (Samuel) had put the case for a National
> Government much clearer than either of the others. It was after the
> King's interview with Sir Herbert Samuel that H.M. became con-
> vinced of the necessity for the National Government.

THE CABINET SPLIT

The Cabinet met, as arranged, at 7 p.m. that Sunday, August 23.
Proceedings began (according to the ex-Ministers' Memorandum)
with a statement from the Prime Minister 'placing before the
Members the alternatives of the provisional scheme, including the
10 per cent cut, or a moratorium'. The same document continues:
'The discussion was interrupted to await the reply of New York on
the suggestion.'

From such accounts as are available, it is a little difficult to
follow what happened. From what Snowden wrote in his autobiography (p. 947), it seems that at that stage the Bank of England had
received only a personal expression of opinion from Harrison, the
President of the Federal Reserve Bank. Harrison had replied by
telephone to the Bank's enquiry, and had said that, 'while he was
not in a position to give the answer until he had consulted his financial associates, his opinion was that it would give satisfactory
assurance, and the credits would be forthcoming'. According to
Sir Henry Clay,[1] Harrison replied to the enquiry of August 22 that
'if the programme was approved by all three parties it would be
possible to raise a loan', but 'again referred the Government to
Morgans'.

The message awaited by the Cabinet was not one from Harrison

[1] *Lord Norman*, p. 390.

but from Morgans. Clay states[1] that the Prime Minister, thinking it desirable to know whether the provisional scheme would ensure the necessary credits, asked the Deputy Governor of the Bank of England, on the morning of August 23, to obtain an answer before the Cabinet meeting. The Deputy Governor is said to have explained that owing to the difference in time between London and New York, and the need to code and decode, this would be difficult; but he cabled at once to Morgans informing them of the details of the provisional economy scheme and of the proposal for loans or credits in New York and Paris, and proceeding in these terms:

> I am assured that if as the result of the adoption of the Government's scheme the loans and credits are likely to be obtainable the other political parties will promise support to the Government's programme as a minimum, they however reserving to themselves the right if they think fit of moving amendments in Parliament with a view to increasing the amount to be provided by means of economies.
>
> The Prime Minister is anxious if possible that I should be able to advise him by 7 p.m. our time as to whether there is a likelihood that the loans and credits would be forthcoming if the rest of their programme is adopted.
>
> It is understood of course that you could not at such short notice give anything in the nature of a binding commitment and could do no more than express your own personal opinions.

According to Nicolson (p. 462), the Prime Minister informed the Cabinet that no reply had yet been received to the enquiry addressed the night before to the New York bankers, but that a telegram was expected to arrive at any moment. Despite the reference to 'the night before', what happened makes it plain that the enquiry mentioned was that said by Clay to have been addressed to Morgans that morning. MacDonald, again according to Nicolson, suggested that the Cabinet should adjourn until the awaited telegram arrived. The adjournment certainly took place; and for more than an hour Ministers walked and talked in the garden of No. 10 Downing Street on that oppressively hot night. It was when the news came of the arrival of the telegram from Morgans that the Cabinet meeting was resumed.

Elements of uncertainty and confusion enter into the story because of statements made by Henderson's biographer and Snow-

[1] Op. cit., p. 391.

den. The former wrote: 'By a majority, it was agreed that New York should be asked on the telephone.' She asserted that the call was made, but gave no further information about it. And, in regard to the 'New York answer', she followed Snowden's account. Snowden wrote:

> The reply of Mr Harrison to the enquiry from the Bank of England after he had consulted the financial interests in New York was quite satisfactory. He said that if the proposals approved by the Bank of England were likely to receive a favourable response from public opinion in Great Britain that would be regarded as satisfactory, and there would be no further difficulty in raising the required credits in New York, and the French market would probably raise an equivalent amount.

But no indication is given about the mode of this further expression of Harrison's opinion. It may conceivably have been a response to the telephone call, if, indeed, any such call was made during the Cabinet's proceedings on the evening of the 23rd. In all probability, however, the telephonic communications with Harrison took place before the Cabinet meeting. The majority decision referred to by Henderson's biographer is almost certainly the decision of the Cabinet on the afternoon of the 22nd to consult the bankers about the provisional economy scheme, a step which, it is known, met with some opposition. What is quite clear is that Harrison's further reply, as set out by Snowden, was not the New York message for which the Cabinet waited in the late evening of August 23rd and the receipt of which preceded the Cabinet's crucial decision. That message was a cable from Messrs J. P. Morgan & Co. It may seem strange that Snowden made no allusion to this message; but his silence may well be accounted for by the fact that the cable from Morgans did little to clarify the position.

The waiting Ministers reassembled at 8.45 p.m. A telephone message had been received from the Bank of England that the New York telegram had arrived and that Sir Ernest Harvey was on his way to Downing Street with it. The Deputy Governor's arrival was announced by MacDonald's Private Secretary. The Prime Minister went out, took the telegram from Harvey's hand, re-entered, and read the telegram to the Cabinet.

On the 21st, before the specific enquiry had been addressed to them, Morgans had cabled their views on the situation. In their judgment, the New York market would not consider a British loan until Parliamentary action had been taken to rectify the Budgetary position. A private credit transaction they considered possible if agreement were reached by the Party leaders on a programme to be submitted to Parliament, although they added that

> it is going to take a great deal more than simply the joint declaration of three Party leaders to convince the investment and banking public here that real amendment has been undertaken and that the Government is in a position to command heavy foreign credit favours.

In their cable on the evening of the 23rd, Morgans repeated and developed these views, helpfully suggesting a possible course of action. Nicolson has summarized their reply as follows:

> In this second telegram, while expressing every desire to assist, Messrs J. P. Morgan foresaw that there was but little prospect of the American public being willing to take up a public loan, unless and until Parliament had already passed the necessary economy legislation. It would be easier to arrange some short-term Treasury transaction than to coax the public into absorbing a large loan. In their concluding paragraph Messrs J. P. Morgan & Co. enquired whether they were correct in assuming that the economy proposals now tentatively put forward by the Cabinet had the sincere approval and support of the Bank of England and the City generally, and whether the latter regarded them as sufficient to re-establish confidence.

This summary, perhaps, fails to do full justice to the nature of Morgan & Co.'s response. We are indebted to Clay for the text of the document, which reads:

> We are considering very carefully here the tentative suggestion made by the Deputy Governor as to the bare possibility of the British Government desiring to arrange some form of joint French and American credit. It is of course quite impossible to give any assurance to-day. Please tell your friends in the event that they should desire financial co-operation we shall as always do our utmost to meet their wishes. If the suggestion were to take the form of a public loan offering we are confident that until Parliament convenes and acts and until we have had an opportunity to feel out our own investment community we could render no favourable opinion whatsoever. If the suggestion however were to take the form of a short-term Treasury operation that would be less difficult and if the British Government should desire us to canvass among ourselves and our immediate friends such a suggestion we should take up the matter vigorously to-

morrow morning and be able to give you an answer by our closing to-morrow afternoon.

Kindly let us know subsequent to the results of the Cabinet Meeting which you say will be held this evening whether the Government wish us to explore promptly this possibility. The furthest we have gone to-day has been to discuss merely among ourselves the possibility of a short credit in this market of from 100 to 150 million dollars and we have as above indicated assumed that as a condition the French banking market would do an equivalent amount. When we speak of short term we have roughly in mind 90 day Treasury Bills subject to renewals for an inclusive period of one year.

In the foregoing we have as always given you the precise trend of our thought. Let us know promptly as indicated above what the Government's desires are and within 24 hours we shall be able to give you our final judgment. Are we right in assuming that the programme under consideration will have the sincere approval and support of the Bank of England and the City generally and thus go a long way towards restoring internal confidence in Great Britain. Of course our ability to do anything depends on the response of public opinion particularly in Great Britain to the Government's announcement of the programme.[1]

The concluding passages of this communication appear to have aroused considerable resentment in the Cabinet. Nicolson says that when MacDonald read them loud protests were heard by those waiting in the next room. Harvey thought that 'pandemonium had broken loose'. Such vehement protests may well seem puzzling. Morgans had been consulted about the prospects of loans and credits in the event of the Government adopting the provisional economy scheme. They had replied on that basis, knowing (and stating) that the scheme was still under consideration by the Government. They were awaiting a Cabinet decision on the economy programme, and also a notification of the course the Cabinet desired them to pursue, when they would be able to give a final judgment about the prospects. What constituted their offence, apparently, was their request for confirmation of their assumption that the provisional economy scheme was genuinely approved in British financial circles, and their emphasis upon the importance of a favourable response to the scheme from public opinion.

Those members of the Cabinet who voiced their indignation had acquiesced only with much reluctance in the submission of the

[1] Op cit., pp. 391-2.

scheme first to the Opposition leaders and then to the bankers. They objected strongly to the proposed reduction in the rates of unemployment benefit. The cable from Morgans did not present them with any alternative to acceptance of the scheme. It could hardly have been expected to do so. But its clear implication was that even Cabinet endorsement of the scheme might not suffice, and that the decisive factors would be financial and public opinion both at home and abroad. Morgans, of course, were not making any novel points: they seem rather to have taken it for granted that what they considered to be the dominant facts of the situation were generally appreciated. But whether or not these were recognized as facts, they were none the less resented by the protesting members of the Cabinet. To the latter, such a situation was intensely repugnant, since it was one which made it impracticable to determine policy solely or primarily in what were considered to be the interests of the unemployed and of the industrial Labour movement. Hence their subsequent charges of dictation on the part of the financiers, particularly the foreign financiers. There was not the slightest element of dictation in the cable from Morgans. That message, moreover, hardly advanced matters at all from the Cabinet standpoint. Sidney Webb, writing to his wife early on the following morning, described the reply which had been awaited as 'rather inconclusive'; and the ex-Ministers' Memorandum speaks of it as 'a very guarded written statement', although 'it was gathered' from it 'that New York would not be satisfied without them' (i.e. without the 10 per cent cut in unemployment benefit and the additional £7 million of economies), 'but might agree if they were included in the scheme.' The Cabinet thus found itself in the position of being unable further to postpone a definite decision on the economy programme.

After the communication had been read, MacDonald is said[1] to have made a strong personal appeal to his colleagues to accept the proposals about which the enquiry had been made, even though they comprised a 10 per cent cut in unemployment benefits. Although, he said, he was all too well aware that there would be much resentment in Labour circles, he was confident that the majority of the Party would give their support if all the facts were laid before them. Moral prestige, he argued, would be lost if the unemployed were left in a privileged position. Asking the Cabinet to agree to the

[1] This account is taken from Nicolson, p. 463.

10 per cent cut, MacDonald said that if any senior Minister felt it necessary to resign, then the Government must resign as a whole.

This statement is apparently regarded by Mowat (p. 392) as the presentation of an 'alternative' by MacDonald. 'The alternative', he writes, (i.e. the alternative to acceptance of the larger economies, including the 10 per cent cut), 'if any senior ministers wished to resign, was the resignation of the whole Cabinet.' And later (p. 394) he writes, in criticism of MacDonald, 'He then delivered an ultimatum to the members of the Cabinet, for which he and not the Opposition leaders was responsible, and offered them no alternative but resignations which he seemed only too ready to accept.' The use of the term 'ultimatum', as of the word 'alternative', is unjustifiable. MacDonald was simply pointing out the consequences of resignation by any senior dissentients. A Minister who is not prepared to acquiesce in a majority decision has no alternative but resignation. The majority, of course, has the alternative of not persisting when confronted by the threat of resignation on the part of any dissentient. If the majority adopts that alternative course, then the question of the resignation of the Cabinet as a whole may or may not arise. In this instance, MacDonald was reminding his colleagues, it certainly would arise, and the resignation of the Cabinet would be the outcome. The members of the Cabinet all had 'the alternative' of rejecting MacDonald's appeal. Mowat's remark that MacDonald 'seemed only too ready to accept' resignations is incomprehensible in this context. After days of discussion in a situation of great and increasing urgency, after having patiently tried one expedient after another, the Prime Minister was making a strong final appeal for an agreed decision, for a decision involving no resignations by any of the senior members of the Cabinet. Mowat proceeds: 'And if they had not agreed to resign, he could have brought about the same result, and was clearly ready to do so, by his own resignation.' This is even more odd. Especially so is the phrase 'agreed to resign'. The plain implication is that MacDonald's appeal was entirely bogus, and that he was determined to compel the resignation of the Ministry as a whole. For that interpretation of MacDonald's attitude, Mowat produces no evidence. Against it stands the record of the Prime Minister's prolonged (even dangerously prolonged) striving for an agreed Cabinet decision.

'During these discussions', Mowat writes (p. 392), concerning the Cabinet's responses to the Premier's plea, 'MacDonald had nothing to contribute. He sat back, absent-mindedly doodling on a blotter, waiting wearily for the end.' This is another strange comment. MacDonald had made his appeal; according to Mowat, he had confronted his colleagues with certain alternatives; indeed, according to this author's later passage, he had delivered his 'ultimatum'. From what source has Mowat secured his information about MacDonald's behaviour as Chairman while listening to the responses of his colleagues? There is a footnote reference. It reads: 'L. M. Weir, *Tragedy of Ramsay MacDonald*, p. 382.' Weir, of course, was not present. In a footnote on the next page, Mowat describes Weir's book as 'a bitter attack on MacDonald by his parliamentary private secretary, who was out of London during the crisis but seems to have obtained some inside information.' This particular piece of 'inside information' is of no importance in itself. None the less it is surprising that Mowat should have thought fit to retail it.

In regard to the discussion following MacDonald's appeal, Nicolson merely says that it was immediately evident that many important Ministers (Henderson at their head) were determined never to consent to any reduction in the rates of benefit. It has frequently been said that a vote was taken on this question, and the use of the term 'vote' is doubtless permissible. It is understood, however, that a formal vote (as distinct from the collection of opinions) is very seldom taken in Cabinet, and there is no authority for believing that such a vote was taken on this occasion. That, in all probability, is the explanation of the slight discrepancies which are to be found in the various statements which have been made about the division in the Cabinet. Such discrepancies, as will be seen, do not affect the main point.

That MacDonald had a majority of his Cabinet against him on this occasion has become one of our popular historical legends. It is an interesting example of the potency of propagandist reiteration (though much sheer carelessness enters in). The true position was stated at the time, frequently repeated in the following weeks, and never then challenged. Detailed information about the division in the Cabinet was immediately forthcoming, and has often been confirmed since; but the legend which grew up still persists. One of the latest and most glaring examples is provided by Amery, who writes: 'As they (i.e. "the recalcitrant Ministers") were in a large majority MacDonald decided that it was no longer possible for him to continue. . . .'[1] Amery appears to be entitled to the unenviable distinction of having been the first to introduce the adjective 'large'. In a still more recent 're-examination of the crisis of 1931', the author states that 'the majority of the Cabinet was not prepared to follow MacDonald in accepting the economies'.[2]

The very next day (August 24) the *Daily Herald* gave (on its front page, in heavy print) the names of 'those members of the Cabinet who resolutely declined to support a reduction in unemployment benefit'. *Eight* names were given; those of Henderson, Graham, Greenwood, Alexander, Lansbury, Johnston, Adamson and Addison. On that basis, excluding the Prime Minister himself, the division in the Cabinet was *twelve* for acceptance and *eight* against. We now know[3] that MacDonald reported to the King immediately afterwards that the voting was *eleven* for acceptance and *eight* against; but the eight names in Wigram's record of his report include that of Clynes and omit that of Johnston, and one member of the Cabinet is unaccounted for (there were in fact no absentees). Chamberlain recorded in his diary that when, with Baldwin and Samuel, he saw MacDonald on the night of the 23rd, the Prime Minister told them that *eight* ministers had refused to accept the dole cut.

The Times on August 24 understood that Henderson had been supported by *eight others*, and the eight names given by that newspaper included those of both Johnston and Clynes. On August 25, moreover, the *Daily Herald* expressed its regret for having omitted Clynes, who, it said, 'was also one of the Cabinet Ministers who felt that a reduction of the unemployment benefit would compel him to resign.' In its editorial that day, the *Herald* referred to 'the *nine* members of the Labour Cabinet who declined to agree to unemployment benefit being reduced'. It may well have been that one or more of the dissentients expressed their dissent less definitely in Cabinet than they did afterwards.

However, the number of dissentients was apparently settled at *nine*. For many years no other figure was mentioned (despite the emergence and growth of the legend already referred to). Beatrice Webb, in her diary for August 25, recorded her husband's state-

[1] *My Political Life*, Vol. III, p. 59.
[2] Graeme C. Moodie, 'The Monarch and the Selection of a Prime Minister', (*Political Studies*, Vol. V, No. I, p. 2, February 1957).
[3] Nicolson, op. cit., p. 464.

ment that *nine* members of the Cabinet had revolted.[1] It may be noted that Dalton, in his memoirs,[2] says that the voting was probably *eleven* (not including the Prime Minister himself) to *nine*. That is undoubtedly a sound conclusion.

After the formation of the National Government, Labour ex-Cabinet Ministers were naturally disinclined to dwell on the details of the split. That was particularly so with those of them who had supported MacDonald. It is interesting to note that Sidney Webb (Lord Passfield) made no allusion in his 'record' of the crisis to his own vote on the occasion in question. Similarly, when Lord Parmoor wrote his memoirs, he also was uninformative about his attitude. In view of what both peers said about the crisis, people may well have made the mistake of thinking that one or the other, or both, of them had been dissentients in the Cabinet on the night of August 23. They were not.

The biographers of Henderson and Lansbury have both stated that the dissentients numbered *ten*, without producing a tenth name. Only quite recently has an alleged tenth dissentient been named. In his history, Mowat has written (p. 392): 'Eleven ministers were ready to support the reduction in unemployment payments; ten were not.' The last name in his list of the ten is that of Lees-Smith. Mowat has a footnote in which he says that 'The authority for the inclusion of Lees-Smith among the ten is Harold Laski: Kingsley Martin, *Harold Laski* (London, 1953), p. 81'. The passage in Martin's book is a quotation from a letter written by Laski to Frankfurter on October 6, 1931. Laski wrote that seven members of the Cabinet, including Lees-Smith, threatened resignation. The date of this alleged episode is not specifically given. It is placed, however, after the 'consultation with the T.U.C.' (which was on August 20), and *before* the King returned to London from Balmoral (which was on the night of August 22–23), indeed, before he decided to return. It clearly relates, therefore, to the Cabinet meeting on the 21st, when it is known that 'a substantial minority'

[1] Op cit., p. 284. There is an editorial footnote as follows: 'According to a note in the Diary, the seven others besides Webb included Addison, Alexander, Clynes, Graham, Greenwood and Lansbury.' This hardly makes sense. Anyhow, Beatrice Webb gave two (unpublished) lists of names: the list of dissentients gives only eight names, those of Graham, Henderson, Clynes, Lansbury, Alexander, Addison, Johnston and Greenwood; the other list has twelve names, wrongly including that of Adamson, but omitting Snowden. One of the names in the majority list is that of Passfield (Sidney Webb).

[2] *Call Back Yesterday*, p. 271.

opposed any cuts in the rates of unemployment benefit, though there is no confirmatory evidence of any resignations having been threatened. Anyhow, Laski's remarks do not bear the construction Mowat places upon them. He was not dealing with the final breach on the night of August 23. And leaving aside the particular reference (in a letter which is full of inaccuracies), it is highly improbable that Lees-Smith would have confided to Laski a circumstance which he seems most successfully to have concealed from others.

No amount of effort and juggling with names has succeeded in raising the number of dissentient Ministers above ten (with a still undiscovered tenth). If MacDonald himself be included, that would still leave eleven members of the Cabinet on the other side. If, however, he be omitted, as Chairman, the existence of ten dissentients would mean that the Cabinet was evenly divided; yet those who have spoken of ten admit that the dissentients were in a minority. The correct number, plainly enough, is nine.

There is in fact no room for doubt that a majority of the Cabinet favoured acceptance. Henderson's biographer was mainly concerned to insist that the majority for acceptance was small; and 'small' was the adjective used by Snowden in his autobiography. There is also no doubt at all that the dissentients were not prepared to acquiesce in a Cabinet decision conformable to the views of that small majority. In other words, MacDonald was confronted by the threat of eight or nine resignations, including those of the Foreign Secretary, the President of the Board of Trade, and, apparently, the Home Secretary and the Secretary of State for Scotland. In such circumstances, it was obviously impossible for the Cabinet to carry on. And, of course, in regard to the issue of continuance or resignation, the precise number of the dissentients matters not at all.

In the following days and weeks there were many allusions in the press to the fact that a majority of the Labour Cabinet had supported MacDonald. The ex-Ministers' Memorandum, drawn up during the days immediately following the change of Government, states:

A minority of the Cabinet opposed the 10 per cent cut. The majority held that the Government could only adopt this proposal if there was complete or almost complete unanimity in the Cabinet. Everybody agreed that the position was such that it was impossible to continue.

Majority and minority alike, therefore, recognized the fact which

MacDonald had pointed out in making his appeal, an action described by Mowat as the delivery of an 'ultimatum'. There can hardly be any doubt about that. Certainly no disagreement was expressed. The point must be discussed, however, because it has sometimes been suggested that the Labour Cabinet could have remained in office despite the deadlock which had arisen.

This suggestion has usually been made in conjunction with (and probably as a consequence of) another suggestion, namely, that MacDonald had planned to bring the Labour Government to an end and was only too willing to take the opportunity of ending it. Snowden gave countenance to this suggestion, although, as will be seen, he did not originate it. And those who have urged it subsequently have usually brought in Snowden's words as supporting evidence. Here they are:

> When this final disagreement occurred it was evident that the Prime Minister had anticipated such a development, and had made his plans to deal with it.[1] He asked the members of the Cabinet to place their resignations in his hands (p. 950)

and (on p. 953):

> When the Labour Cabinet as a whole declined to agree to a reduction of Unemployment pay, Mr MacDonald assumed too hurriedly that this involved the resignation of his Government. He neither shewed nor expressed any grief at this regrettable development. On the contrary, he set about the formation of the National Government with an enthusiasm which shewed that the adventure was highly agreeable to him.[2]

Yet a few pages previously, Snowden had himself written that the break-up of the Labour Government was inevitable:

> A small majority of the Cabinet (and this became public property later) were in favour of these further economies, but as we could not have carried a united Cabinet in adopting them, and half the Cabinet would have resigned, the break-up of the Labour Government was inevitable. A cut in the Unemployment pay was repugnant to us all, but we had no choice in the matter (p. 948).

The apparent contradiction can only be resolved in terms of a

---

[1] Mowat quotes this sentence (p. 392), and it is probable that his subsequent assertion that MacDonald 'seemed only too ready to accept' resignations is based upon this and similar remarks made by Snowden.

[2] The assertions made in these two last sentences receive notice below.

distinction between the 'break-up' and the 'resignation' of the Labour Government. The only possible explanation is that Snowden did not believe that the first necessarily involved the second; in other words, that he thought it possible for MacDonald to carry on with a reconstituted Labour Government which had shed about half its former members. If, indeed, Snowden really thought that at the time, he must have been alone in so thinking. And, when he came to write his autobiography and penned the particular words which have been quoted, he did not discuss the practicability of a reconstituted Labour administration — for reasons which should surely be obvious enough.

It must not be supposed, of course, that those who have made use of these words of Snowden's for their own purposes shared any such view about the feasibility (still less about the desirability) of a reconstituted Labour Government. Parmoor, who quoted Snowden's last-quoted passage, went on to say that he did not agree with the conclusion that the break-up of the Cabinet was inevitable and that there was no choice in the matter of the cut in unemployment pay. But he did not suggest that resignation could have been avoided when 'the final break' actually came. His point is an entirely different one. It is, presumably, that the Labour Cabinet could have agreed to reject the proposed cut in unemployment benefit and to carry on until defeated in Parliament, or, conceivably, in view of the attitude of the Opposition parties, to have resigned as a united body forthwith. It has already been noted that Henderson would have liked the Government to resign on the previous day; and the Webbs' desire that the baby should be passed to the Conservatives was shared by many on the Labour side. Anyhow, as Henderson's biographer has written (p. 383):

> Faced with ten resignations out of a body of twenty-one, the Prime Minister's course seemed obvious. There was no surprise when he asked members to place their resignations in his hands. They did so.

THE DECISION TO RESIGN

Owing to the loose way in which even so-called authorities write, and also to the conventional jargon used by politicians themselves, what precisely was said and done in the Cabinet about resignation remains a little obscure. In itself the point is unimportant, since there is general agreement on the main issue; but it has acquired

importance because of the scope which has been given for misleading interpretations. As will be seen, the ambiguities have been
utilized by certain commentators to support the suggestion that
MacDonald acted in a high-handed manner.

In Webb's early-1932 'record', he wrote that the Labour
Cabinet

> in order not to render urgent public business impossible, empowered
> the Prime Minister to tender to the King his own resignation, which
> automatically includes the termination of office of the whole Ministry.

Parmoor, in his reminiscences, uses almost exactly the same words
(apart from the introductory clause). Snowden, as already noted,
stated that the Prime Minister 'asked the members of the Cabinet
to place their resignations in his hands. This was done . . .'; and
Henderson's biographer, in the quotation given above, employs
almost identical language; while Lansbury's biographer wrote that
'MacDonald received, in the usual form, all the Ministers'
resignations . . .'.

Nicolson's version (p. 464) is that 'The Cabinet authorized the
Prime Minister to inform His Majesty that they had placed their
resignations in his hands'. But, whatever may have been the actual
forms followed, the main point is that the members of the Cabinet
not only raised no objection to the termination of the Ministry, but
expected and even (for the most part) desired that MacDonald
should offer his resignation to the King. That, however, was not
all that happened in this connection. Indeed, it appears to have
been taken for granted that the Ministry must come to an end, and
the measures required to facilitate its termination seem to have
been dealt with incidentally. It may be of some significance that the
ex-Ministers' Memorandum makes no direct allusion to the subject of resignation in its relevant paragraph.

An entirely erroneous impression of what took place has been
created and popularized. Time and again one reads that, when
MacDonald left the Cabinet meeting to go to Buckingham Palace,
the other Ministers expected him to return with the news that his
resignation had been accepted, and, indeed, that Baldwin had been
asked to form a Government. Webb's 'record' (perhaps unintentionally, for it was highly condensed) appears to have started this
story. He wrote:

> It was taken for granted that the King would immediately send for Mr

Baldwin, the leader of the Conservative Party, and entrust him with the formation of a new Government.

Perhaps the most appropriate illustration (since it comes from a distinguished academic source and is particularly flagrant) is provided by Professor G. D. H. Cole in his *History of the Labour Party from 1914*, (p. 253):

> These were the circumstances under which Ramsay MacDonald announced to his colleagues his intention to hand in his resignation to the King and demanded from them the surrender of their portfolios (*sic*). Thus armed, he went to the King, leaving them to suppose that either a purely Tory Government, or possibly a Tory-Liberal Coalition under Baldwin, would succeed them, but he returned to announce that he himself had been entrusted with the task of forming a 'National' Government, in which Baldwin and the other Tory leaders and also the Liberals had agreed to serve under his leadership.

The ordinary reader of such accounts might well get the impression that MacDonald just went off to the Palace that Sunday night without having given any indication of what he intended to do there, apart from tendering his resignation. That, however, was not the case. And any such reader will certainly get an entirely wrong idea of what MacDonald reported to the Cabinet on his return from the Palace.

Before stating that the Cabinet authorized MacDonald to tell the King that they had placed their resignations at his disposal, Nicolson wrote (pp. 463-4):

> The Prime Minister . . . stated that he proposed immediately to inform the King of what had passed in Cabinet and to advise His Majesty to summon a conference between Mr Baldwin, Sir Herbert Samuel and himself for the following morning.

Snowden, after writing (p. 950) that MacDonald asked for the resignations to be placed in his hands, proceeded:

> This was done, and the Prime Minister immediately left the meeting to seek an audience with the King to acquaint him with the position, and to advise His Majesty to hold a conference with Mr Baldwin, Sir Herbert Samuel and himself next morning. The Cabinet agreed to this course.

From no source has any indication been given that any opposition to this procedure was expressed.

L

An important question arises. What did Snowden, and the other members of the Labour Cabinet, think would be the purpose of the proposed conference? Snowden was completely silent on the subject: the others have been almost equally reticent; indeed, no direct public allusion can be traced. Obviously, such a conference was not required for the mere object of giving the Opposition leaders information. For that purpose, another three-party meeting, summoned by the Prime Minister, and without the King, would have sufficed. The members of the Labour Cabinet certainly could not have believed or assumed that the conference was being proposed for the purpose of enabling MacDonald to advise the King to ask Baldwin to form a Government. MacDonald could have done that at the Palace forthwith, the presence of the Opposition leaders being quite unnecessary. If it be suggested that the object of the conference was thought to be the arrangement of a Conservative-Liberal coalition, the obvious answer is that Mac-Donald's own presence at such a conference was not required — unless it be contended that MacDonald's persuasive powers, as well as those of the King, would clearly have been required if such a coalition were to be formed.

Amery has actually asserted[1] that the members of the Labour Cabinet assumed that the object of the conference was 'for the purpose of handing over to a Conservative-Liberal coalition'. There is no record of any of them ever having said so; and, coming as it does from one of our leading authorities on the British Constitution, Amery's statement is most surprising. Why should a conference have been required in order to 'hand over' to a new Administration? What is meant by 'handing over' in this connection? But Amery, in his whole treatment of this episode (as of the crisis as a whole) displays much prejudice in his interpretations and is also incorrect on certain matters of fact. He omits to mention that MacDonald, before going to the Palace, sought and obtained his Cabinet's agreement to the conference proposal; and consequently implies that the Cabinet only heard of it on MacDonald's return from the Palace. His words are: 'Returning to the Cabinet he told them that he was to meet the Opposition leaders next morning, but without mentioning the object of the meeting, which they assumed to be for the purpose of handing over to a Conservative-Liberal coalition.' To this Amery has a footnote, as follows: 'His colleagues

[1] Op cit., p. 60.

afterwards thought he had deliberately deceived them. But he may well have felt bound to treat the King's wish as confidential till agreement was definitely reached.' This piles confusion upon confusion. Amery seems to have assumed that, after the interview with the King or during its course, MacDonald had agreed or decided to form a National Government in accordance with 'the King's wish', and had arranged the conference with the Opposition leaders for that purpose.

The ex-Ministers' Memorandum suggests another possibility. It states:

> It was agreed that the Prime Minister should report to the King that, with the proposed scheme, the Cabinet could not carry on and that the King be recommended to meet the three Party leaders on the following day to see whether the situation might be saved by concessions from the other leaders.

No suggestion that this was either the agreed or the assumed object of the proposed conference has ever been publicly made. The quoted paragraph is wholly unconvincing. It is dubiously consistent with the preceding statement in the Memorandum that all were agreed about the impossibility of the Government continuing; and it reads like an after-thought which might prove a useful point for face-saving purposes. That it was not in fact used is easily explicable: it was doubtless thought preferable to keep quiet altogether about the Cabinet having agreed in advance to the proposed conference.

There can scarcely be any doubt that the whole Cabinet took it for granted that the purpose of the proposed conference was to discuss the formation of a new Government. The break-up of the Labour Cabinet obviously created a major political crisis and one which might not easily be resolved. The decision to resign (to which no one, not even Snowden, raised any objection) meant that some other Government had to be formed, and formed speedily; no party had a majority of its own in the House of Commons; the crisis was urgent; and an immediate General Election was so plainly undesirable in the circumstances that it was by general consent ruled out. The possibility of some kind of all-party Government clearly existed. It had been mentioned, apparently, in the Cabinet itself on the previous day. On the morning of August 24, the *Daily Herald* referred to the subject in its main front-page article, saying: 'If a Coalition Ministry is formed it is possible, but not likely, that some members of the Labour Government might consent as individuals to serve for the "emergency" period.' There is a letter from Sidney Webb to his wife (written early on the morning of the 24th) in which he wrote:

> We meet again at 12 noon to-day, when I assume all will be settled; and we may hand in our seals this afternoon: or at latest to-morrow. I think that all that is now doubtful is the *character* of the Government that succeeds us (as *we* have all along speculated).

Though Webb made no reference, in his communications to his wife, to the conference which he knew was being held that morning, it is evident that he assumed its purpose to be discussion of the character of the new Government.

MacDonald at the Palace

The Prime Minister left the Cabinet meeting at 10.10 p.m. to go to the Palace. He was there at 10.15 and left again at 10.35. At 10.40 MacDonald was back with the Cabinet, which did not disperse until approximately 10.50 (according to the *Daily Herald's* detailed diary, the precise time was 10.47 p.m.). The times are important, in view of the many careless and highly misleading accounts which have appeared in subsequent years. Of particular importance is the fact that MacDonald returned to a waiting Cabinet. Not only has this fact frequently been ignored: it has also repeatedly been stated that the Cabinet had dispersed, either on MacDonald's departure for the Palace or before he had left the Palace. Even Nicolson seems to have fallen into what has become quite a customary error on this point (p. 464).

Snowden wrote in his autobiography (p. 950):

> Mr MacDonald left at 10.10 p.m., and the members of the Cabinet remained in the room to await his return. He came back at 10.40, and told us that His Majesty had accepted his advice to meet Mr Baldwin, Sir Herbert Samuel and himself next morning at 10 o'clock.

Henderson's biographer says that the other members of the Cabinet waited while MacDonald was away; that he returned in half an hour and informed his colleagues that the King had agreed to hold a conference with himself, Baldwin and Samuel next morning at 10 o'clock; and that 'on this the Cabinet dispersed'. The ex-Ministers' Memorandum states:

On his return from the Palace the Prime Minister informed the Cabinet that a meeting of Party leaders had been arranged for the following morning at 10 o'clock at the Palace.

It was doubtless also on his return that the Prime Minister announced that the Cabinet would meet again at 12 noon next day. The members of the Cabinet, therefore, were informed of the advice the Prime Minister intended to offer to the King, and of the acceptance of that advice. They agreed to the advice being given, and, of course, raised no objection when told that it had been given and accepted.

Nicolson, who had had verbal discussions with Sir Ernest Harvey and Sir Edward Peacock, wrote that MacDonald left the Cabinet room for the Palace in a state of extreme agitation, telling Harvey in passing, 'I am off to the Palace to throw in my hand.' The King had been dining with Peacock, and the political crisis had not been mentioned between them. After the message that the Prime Minister was on his way was received, Peacock had a short telephone conversation with Harvey, still in Downing Street, who told him that the Prime Minister on leaving had appeared distraught. All this conveys a totally different impression of MacDonald's reactions from that conveyed by Snowden's comments (quoted above, p. 142 and reproduced by Nicolson himself).

For what happened at the Prime Minister's brief interview with the King on the night of Sunday, August 24, reference must be made to Nicolson and Morshead. Nicolson quotes from Wigram's record, as follows:

> The Prime Minister looked scared and unbalanced. He told the King that all was up and that at the Cabinet 11 had voted for accepting the terms of the Bankers and 8 against. The opposition included Henderson, Graham, Adamson, Greenwood, Clynes, Alexander, Addison and Lansbury. In these circumstances the Prime Minister had no alternative than to tender the resignation of the Cabinet.
>
> The King impressed on the Prime Minister that he was the only man to lead the country through this crisis and hoped he would reconsider the situation. His Majesty told him that the Conservatives and Liberals would support him in restoring the confidence of foreigners in the financial stability of the country.
>
> The Prime Minister asked whether the King would confer with Baldwin, Samuel and himself in the morning. His Majesty willingly acceded to this request. The Prime Minister telephoned to Downing

Street to ask his Private Secretary to arrange for Baldwin and Samuel to meet him as soon as possible.

Morshead's account is in more general terms:

> At 10.15 the same evening the Prime Minister returned to the palace to tender the resignation of the Cabinet in view of its continued internal dissension. The King urged him to reconsider his own position in view of the support which the other parties were willing to lend him and the confidence which a united front would inspire among foreign creditors at a moment when the banking resources of the country were to be measured rather in hours than in days. The Prime Minister asked the King to hold a conference of the three party leaders next morning.

Amery's imaginative embellishment of Wigram's account is typical of much that has been written about MacDonald and the crisis by those who, on either side, disapproved of the formation of the National Government. MacDonald, he writes (p. 60), 'tottered into the King's room a broken man — "scared and unbalanced" was Sir Clive Wigram's description. Half an hour later he strutted out beaming with self-satisfaction. To be told by the King that he was the only man who could save England, and that the Conservatives and Liberals would support him in restoring the confidence of the world in the financial stability of the country, made an irresistible appeal to his vanity. Returning to the Cabinet he told them. . . .' Perhaps this may be regarded as an attempt on Amery's part to reconcile the testimony of Wigram and Harvey with that of Snowden.

The important point about this interview is that the King did not accept MacDonald's resignation (if, indeed, it was formally tendered), and urged him to reconsider the situation. As a consequence of his interviews that day with Samuel and Baldwin, George V was in a position to assure MacDonald of Conservative and Liberal support.

MacDonald and the Opposition Leaders

At 10.44 p.m., a couple of minutes or so before the Cabinet had dispersed, Sir Herbert Samuel arrived at No. 10 Downing Street in response to the Prime Minister's summons. At 11.10 Baldwin arrived, to be followed four minutes later by Neville Chamberlain. Sir Josiah (later Lord) Stamp and two of the Governors of the

Bank of England also arrived, remaining approximately a quarter
of an hour. It was not until about 12.15 a.m. that the Opposition
leaders left; and no official statement was issued when they did so.

Such information as is available about this meeting between
MacDonald and the Opposition leaders is derived almost entirely
from Chamberlain's diary, as quoted by his biographer.[1] It is of
considerable importance because of the light it throws upon the
time at which MacDonald decided to acquiesce in the formation of
a National Government. The passage in the biography reads as
follows:

> On the evening of the 23rd, with Baldwin and Samuel, he saw Mac-
> Donald, who said the credits could be raised, but that he could not
> keep his Cabinet.
>
> While a majority supported him, eight ministers had refused to
> accept the dole cut . . . had told the King so, recommending him to see
> the three party leaders. . . . For himself, he would help us to get these
> proposals through, though it meant his death warrant, but it would be
> of no use for him to join a government . . . would bring odium on us as
> well as himself. . . . I then intervened . . . had he considered that, tho'
> not commanding many votes in the House, he might command much
> support in the country? And would not a government including mem-
> bers of all parties hold a much stronger position? . . . Finally, I asked
> him if he had considered the effect on foreign opinion.

Both the indicated omissions and the absence of any indication
of MacDonald's response are irritating; but, years before this passage came to be published, it was known that when Chamberlain
left No. 10 Downing Street on that night of August 23 he expected
that Baldwin would be called upon to form a Government. Chamberlain had said so in a speech at Dumfries on September 11, 1931.

By a curious twist of controversy, this statement of Chamberlain's has been widely used to buttress up the theory of a Mac-
Donald pursuing his premeditated course with the deepest,
unparalleled, cunning. It has been drawn upon to support a
suggestion or charge that MacDonald concealed, even from the
Opposition leaders as well as from his Labour colleagues, a decision
he had already reached to form and lead a National Government.
Webb made the insinuation in his 'record':

> It was taken for granted that the King would immediately send for Mr
> Baldwin . . . and entrust him with the formation of a new Government.

---

[1] Op. cit., p. 193.

It is significant that Mr Neville Chamberlain, who as Mr Baldwin's principal colleague had been with him almost hourly (*sic*) in consultation with the Prime Minister, stated publicly in a speech a few days later that he had himself gone to bed that Sunday night with exactly that assumption. The Prime Minister had in mind a different development of the drama that he himself had staged.

Snowden did the same thing in his autobiography:

> I left the Cabinet meeting at 10.40 p.m. on the Sunday under the belief that the outcome of the resignation of the Labour Cabinet would be that Mr Baldwin would be asked to form a Government, and with the help of the Liberals would carry through measures of economy and additional taxation which would balance the Budget and restore national stability. Whatever, at that time, may have been in Mr Mac-Donald's mind as to a National Government with himself as Prime Minister he kept to himself, for at a meeting he had with the Opposition leaders at 11 p.m. on Sunday after his return from the Palace he gave them no hint of such a possible development. Mr Neville Chamberlain, who was present at that meeting, stated publicly a few days later that he went to bed that night expecting that next day Mr Baldwin would be called upon to form a Government.

So far there is only a hint of the suggestion referred to, but at the end of the whole passage we read:

> Taking all these things together, I think they give ground for the suspicion expressed by Mr Henderson and other Labour Ministers that Mr MacDonald had deliberately planned the scheme of a National Government.[1]

Largely, no doubt, in consequence of these references, the Chamberlain statement has been repeatedly reproduced in criticism of MacDonald. Yet it is much more reasonably accepted as evidence that at midnight, August 23–24, MacDonald had not yet come to any decision about participation in a National Government. Malcolm MacDonald made the point in a letter to Webb on January 6, 1932 to which further reference is made below. It was of course a matter of public knowledge that Chamberlain, along with Baldwin and Samuel, had seen MacDonald and discussed the situation with him very late that night: the newspapers had reported the fact. And Chamberlain's statement at Dumfries certainly established the fact that the four men had not on that occa-

[1] Op. cit., pp. 951–2 and p. 954.

sion reached any agreement about the formation of the National
Government.

The Dumfries speech has been treated as so many other speeches
have been treated. Chamberlain's words have been taken out of
their context — detached even from the rest of the sentence of
which they formed a part. *The Times* (September 12, 1931) reports
him as follows:

> Mr Henderson at the T.U.C. yesterday suggested that the National
> Government was formed in the events during the Sunday of August
> 23rd.[1] There is no truth in that statement. When Mr MacDonald in-
> timated that he was going to resign I went home thinking that Mr
> Baldwin would be sent for to form a new Government.[2]

Clearly, MacDonald had told the Opposition leaders that he intended to resign, and, when they left him that Sunday night, they
were under the impression that he would do so. Chamberlain's
remarks at Dumfries show that when he left No. 10 he did not
think he had convinced MacDonald by the arguments he had used,
as recorded in his diary. Lord Samuel's *Memoirs* confirm Mac-
Donald's indecision, for, when he wrote (p. 204) that MacDonald
'had expressed to us on the previous evening much doubt as to the
course he should pursue', he can only have had in mind this meeting late on the night of the 23rd, although the context of the passage places the meeting on the 22nd, when no such meeting took
place (see below, Appendix II, p. 380). It may be noted that it
was Neville Chamberlain who, apparently, pressed upon Mac-
Donald the suggestion of a Government drawn from all three
parties; and it is interesting that Chamberlain's biographer should
consider him to have been the 'constructive engineer' of the
National Government.

Strongly confirmatory evidence that right down until 'the last
few hours' the Prime Minister contemplated the resignation of the
whole Government and a Baldwin administration is provided in

---

[1] Henderson had said: '. . . you will remember that we resigned on the Monday though the resignation was to all intents and purposes a fairly well accomplished fact on the Sunday, and I am not quite sure that even the idea of the
formation of a National Government was not already a pretty well accomplished
fact . . .' (T.U.C. 63rd Annual Report, p. 401).

[2] It is amusing to read in Parmoor's reminiscences, after his assertion that
constitutional principle required MacDonald to advise the King to ask Baldwin
to form a Government (a strange enough doctrine) that: 'This view of the correct constitutional procedure was the expectation of Mr Neville Chamberlain,
as subsequently explained by him.'

the letter from Malcolm MacDonald to Webb already referred to. Malcolm MacDonald kept a record of his frequent conversations with his father during the last days of the crisis.[1]

The Parliamentary Correspondent of *The Times* wrote on August 25: 'The Prime Minister's friends believed on Sunday night that he would resign office, and that if his advice was sought he would urge that Mr Baldwin should be invited to form a Government with the co-operation of the Liberals, and that he and the Chancellor of the Exchequer, while unwilling to serve in the Administration, would be prepared to indicate their belief that the suggested cuts were essential if the financial situation was to be saved.' This is in line with the record in Chamberlain's diary of the talk on the Sunday night. *The Times* Correspondent, however, went on to say: 'The suggestion of the King that he should defer a final decision until yesterday morning changed the whole position, and the effort to form a National Government then began in real earnest late on Sunday evening.' In a previous sentence it had been said: 'It was the King who persuaded him at least to sleep over the situation and to return in the morning with the Conservative and Liberal Leaders.' These comments, as is now known, were in some respects inaccurate; but it is plainly true that the King's plea that MacDonald should reconsider the question of resignation, and his acceptance of MacDonald's advice to summon a conference with the three Party leaders for the following morning, gave MacDonald the opportunity of sleeping over the situation. And it is also true that Chamberlain, and the two other Opposition leaders, were provided with the opportunity late that evening of urging upon MacDonald, though without immediate success, the case for a National Government.

[1] See below, Appendix V, p. 413.

CHAPTER X

MONDAY, AUGUST 24

THE PALACE CONFERENCE

Although MacDonald did not get to bed until long after midnight, the newspapers reported, he was 'up at his usual hour, shortly after six, and went for his customary stroll in St. James's Park, accompanied by his daughter, Miss Sheila MacDonald'.

At 10 a.m. the King received the three Party leaders. They left Buckingham Palace at 11.55 a.m., when the following communique was issued to the Press:

> His Majesty the King invited the Prime Minister, Mr Stanley Baldwin and Sir Herbert Samuel to Buckingham Palace this morning, and the formation of a National Government is under consideration. A fuller announcement will be made later.

Apart from what was reported to the Cabinet by MacDonald (concerning which there were no immediate revelations), nothing more was known about this conference at the Palace at the time, although more or less imaginative hypotheses about what happened were soon forthcoming.

The memorandum in which the King's private secretary recorded what happened during the conference is now available in Nicolson's book, and must be set out in full:

> At 10 a.m. the King held a Conference at Buckingham Palace at which the Prime Minister, Baldwin and Samuel were present. At the beginning, His Majesty impressed upon them that before they left the Palace some communique must be issued, which would no longer keep the country and the world in suspense. The Prime Minister said that he had the resignation of his Cabinet in his pocket, but the King replied that he trusted there was no question of the Prime Minister's resignation: the leaders of the three Parties must get together and come to some arrangement. His Majesty hoped that the Prime Minister, with the colleagues who remained faithful to him, would help in the formation of a National Government, which the King was sure

would be supported by the Conservatives and the Liberals. The King assured the Prime Minister that, remaining at his post, his position and reputation would be much more enhanced than if he surrendered the government of the country at such a crisis. Baldwin and Samuel said that they were willing to serve under the Prime Minister, and render all help possible to carry on the Government as a National Emergency Government until an emergency bill or bills had been passed by Parliament, which would restore once more British credit and the confidence of foreigners. After that they would expect His Majesty to grant a dissolution. To this course the King agreed. During the Election the National Government would remain in being, though of course each Party would fight the Election on its own lines.

At 10.35 a.m. the King left the three Party Leaders to settle the details of the communique to be issued, and the latter said they would let His Majesty know when they were ready.

About 11.45 the King was requested to return to the Conference, and was glad to hear that they had been able to some extent to come to some arrangement. A Memorandum had been drawn up which Baldwin and Samuel could place before their respective colleagues, but the Prime Minister said that he would not read this out in Cabinet as he should keep it only for those who remained faithful to him. Probably the new National Government would consist of a small Cabinet of 12. It is quite understood that, up to now, the Cabinet had not resigned. His Majesty congratulated them on the solution of this difficult problem, and pointed out that while France and other countries existed for weeks without a Government, in this country our constitution is so generous that leaders of Parties, after fighting one another for months in the House of Commons, were ready to meet together under the roof of the Sovereign and sink their own differences for a common good and arrange as they had done this morning for a National Government to meet one of the gravest crises that the British Empire had yet been asked to face.

It should be noted that, although the formation of a National Government had been considered, and progress made 'to some extent', no final decision had been taken.

The Labour Cabinet's Last Meeting

Five minutes after leaving the Palace, the Prime Minister was with the Cabinet. The various accounts of what then took place are in some respects conflicting.

In his published 'record' of January 1932, Webb wrote:

What is known is that Mr MacDonald came at noon to the final

Labour meeting, and at once informed his astonished colleagues that, whilst they were all out of office owing to his resignation, he had actually 'kissed hands' as Prime Minister of a National Government, which would confine itself to what was required to meet the actual financial crisis and would then promptly proceed to a General Election, at which the leaders of the three political parties, without anything in the nature of a coalition or a 'coupon', would severally appeal to their respective followers.

This was in several respects inaccurate. MacDonald could hardly have said that his colleagues were all out of office owing to his resignation. He had not then resigned, and they were not then out of office. MacDonald had not then 'kissed hands' as Prime Minister of a National Government: he was still Prime Minister of the Labour Government. Only a provisional agreement to form a National Government had been reached at that stage.

Beatrice Webb's diary for August 25 contains a similar error. She wrote that at the Cabinet meeting MacDonald 'announced that he had accepted a commission to form a National Government'.[1] It is highly unlikely that MacDonald made his statement in that form, but, if he did, he was not entitled to do so: he had not at that stage been offered any such commission. Webb's letter to his wife, written in the afternoon or evening of that day (August 24), put the matter more accurately: 'J.R.M.' (he wrote) 'announced at noon that he had been asked, and had agreed, to head a non-party Emergency Government of about a dozen Ministers, personally selected from all parties, for duration of the crisis only, perhaps only five or six weeks.' The Parliamentary Correspondent of the *Daily Express* was probably correct when he wrote on August 27 that MacDonald told the Cabinet that the King had 'practically asked' him to form a National Government, and that he had 'agreed to try and do so'.

The ex-Ministers' Memorandum stated:

On Monday at noon the Cabinet met and the Prime Minister at once reported that he had agreed to be the head of a Government including members of the Conservative and Liberal parties. It was to be a co-operation of persons and not a coalition of parties. Its business would be confined to dealing with the emergency, though the London Passenger Transport Bill might be passed and perhaps some measures of a non-controversial kind. Its emergency programme would be within the general lines of the tentative proposals which had been discussed,

---

[1] Op. cit., p. 284.

including some such adjustment of the Sinking Fund as the financial
authorities might agree to, the financial authorities being the Treasury.

The reference in Snowden's autobiography (p. 951) is as follows:

> . . . Mr MacDonald reported that it had been decided to form a
> Government of individuals whose task would be confined to dealing
> with the financial emergency. Mr Baldwin and Sir Herbert Samuel
> were prepared to join such a Government, with Mr MacDonald as
> Prime Minister.
>
> The resignations of the Labour Ministers had already been given
> to Mr MacDonald, and it was agreed that he should place them in the
> hands of the King that afternoon.

In commentary after commentary it has been said that, when
MacDonald announced that a National Government was to be
formed under his leadership, his Cabinet colleagues were stunned
— rendered almost speechless with amazement. Henderson's biographer, for example, says that MacDonald was heard 'with stupefaction', and that even Snowden was 'completely unprepared'.
There was no suggestion, she wrote, in MacDonald's tone or
manner of regret in the break-up of the Labour Government:

> No hint was thrown out that he cared to know the views of any of his
> colleagues, or recognized that they might feel they ought to have been
> consulted, or at least prepared. He did not appeal for support from
> his old associates in this new venture. On the contrary, he gave them
> the sense that he was glad to be rid of them. The meeting, which was
> largely silent, was over in a few minutes. Henderson came out, too
> shattered to speak.[1]

We have been told, with at least equal frequency, and by
Henderson's biographer herself, not only that MacDonald had for
a long time premeditated forming a National Government, but also
that this was widely known. One of the few important pieces of
information about the crisis given by Dalton in his memoirs[2] is that
he saw Henderson at the Foreign Office on the morning of August
24 *before* the Cabinet meeting at noon, and was then told by
Henderson that MacDonald was 'determined on the formation of a
"National" Government, containing Tories and Liberals, with himself as Prime Minister'. If that was so, Henderson's stunned surprise at MacDonald's announcement shortly afterwards is difficult
to understand. MacDonald's critics can hardly have it both ways.

[1] Op. cit., p. 385.
[2] Op. cit., p. 271.

Nicolson has given a rather different second-hand account of this Cabinet meeting, as follows (p. 467):

> He (MacDonald) entered the Cabinet room with a confident, or as one of his colleagues described it, a 'jaunty' air, and at once informed the assembled Ministers that it had been decided to form a 'Cabinet of Individuals' to deal with the emergency. He himself was to be one of these 'individuals'; he invited any who so desired, to join him in this patriotic act of self-sacrifice. There was a hush when he made this astounding announcement. Mr Arthur Henderson flung himself back in his chair and emitted a low whistle. Mr Herbert Morrison, at that date a very junior Minister, broke the silence with the words: 'Well, Prime Minister, it is very easy to get in to such a combination: you will find it very difficult to get out of it. And I for one am not coming with you.' One by one around the table each of the Ministers signified his unwillingness to join. Mr Ramsay MacDonald found himself deserted, except by Mr Thomas, Lord Sankey and a most unwilling Philip Snowden. The Cabinet dispersed at 12.25.

This directly contradicts the statement made by Henderson's biographer that MacDonald made no appeal for support. Nicolson's statement that each Minister in turn signified his unwillingness to join the new Government is inconsistent with his next remark about the exceptions. It is also difficult to reconcile with other (and in some instances probably more authoritative) accounts which speak of the silence of Ministers. The assertion that Mac-Donald invited any Ministers who so desired to join him is not confirmed by other accounts; but, whether MacDonald did so or not, his announcement certainly implied that invitations would be forthcoming.

In dealing with the 1931 crisis, Nicolson explained that he had been much assisted by verbal discussions with certain named persons. The only member of the Labour Cabinet thus mentioned is Mr Herbert Morrison. Morrison voted in support of MacDonald on the night of August 23. It was widely assumed in Labour circles in after years that his sympathies had been with MacDonald; and, whatever may have been unjustified in that assumption, there is little doubt that Morrison's political prospects were adversely affected by it. It may be noted that the Parliamentary Correspondent of *The Times* wrote on August 25, 1931: 'Among the other members of the old Cabinet Mr Herbert Morrison is believed to be a loyal supporter of Mr MacDonald'; while the *Daily Herald* on the same day said: 'Mr Herbert Morrison may also be included in the Ministry, and this is regarded as an indication that the new Government will put the London Traffic Bill on the Statute book.' On August 26, however, the *Herald* reported that several members of the late Government had denied rumours that they were to join the new Ministry, and added: 'Mr Herbert Morrison is one of these: he has never been asked to take office in the new Government nor has he ever been considered in that connection.' Nicolson's account of the breaking of the silence by Morrison at the Cabinet meeting on the 24th, and of his refusal then to join the new Government, is no doubt based upon information supplied by Morrison himself. No such incident has been mentioned by other ex-Ministers; and, whatever may have been said at the Cabinet meeting, and despite the denial reported by the *Herald* on August 26, it did not apparently prevent MacDonald from giving Morrison a direct personal invitation to join the National Government afterwards. Mrs Mary Agnes Hamilton has recorded in her reminiscences: 'After the meeting (of the Parliamentary Labour Party on August 28), I lunched with Herbert Morrison; to him, as to nobody else, a direct personal appeal had been made; he had had a severe struggle in his mind between loyalty to Mac and loyalty to the party.' And, although Morrison rejected the Prime Minister's appeal, he was, Mrs Hamilton wrote, 'troubled and unhappy.' He had been, as she says, 'a great MacDonaldite.'

Beatrice Webb's diary for August 25 records that MacDonald's colleagues listened to his announcement

> with the usual English composure — Henderson intimating that discussion would be out of place, after which the meeting proceeded to wind up the formal business about documents, etc.; passed unanimously a vote of thanks to the P.M. proposed by Sankey, and without further leave-taking left the Cabinet room.

An interesting, and perhaps the most reliable, version of the meeting is contained in the letter written by Sidney Webb to his wife immediately after the Cabinet dispersed, before he went to lunch:

> He (MacDonald) announced this very well, with great feeling, saying he knew the cost, but could not refuse the King's request; that he would doubtless be denounced and ostracized, but could do no other. We uttered polite things, but accepted silently the accomplished fact.

Neither in this letter nor elsewhere did Webb mention the alleged refusal to join the new Government of each Minister in turn (or of each of them save Thomas, Sankey and Snowden). And, in regard to this final Cabinet meeting, as in regard to other incidents, almost everything said about MacDonald's behaviour is contradicted by someone else.

Snowden has told us in his autobiography (p. 954) that:

When the members of the Labour Cabinet were leaving after the Prime Minister's announcement that he had agreed to form a National Government, he asked me and Mr Thomas and Lord Sankey to remain behind. We then had a frank conversation about the new situation which had so unexpectedly arisen. He asked us if we were prepared to join him in the Government which was to be formed. In view of my position as Chancellor of the Exchequer, and the exceptional responsibility I had for helping to get the country out of its difficulties, I felt that there was no other course open to me than to assist the new Government, provided I could get certain assurances as to its character and its purpose. The definite assurances which were given to me were:

(1) That the new Administration would not exist for a longer period than to dispose of the emergency, and that when that was achieved the political parties would resume their respective positions.

(2) That the Administration would not be a Coalition Government in the general sense of the term, but a National Government for one purpose only.

(3) That as soon as the financial crisis had been settled there should be a General Election, and at that Election there would be no merging of political parties and no 'Coupon' or other party arrangements.

(4) That the Administration which was being formed would not propose any party legislation of a controversial character, but would confine itself to the one purpose for which it was being formed.

Although Snowden rather conveys the impression that these assurances were given in order to resolve his doubts, they were actually based upon the provisional agreement reached by the three leaders.

Nicolson has pointed out (p. 467) that:

A Memorandum written by Sir Herbert Samuel while the Conference was still sitting emphasizes some of the points in the above record (i.e. Wigram's record quoted above). It was clearly understood that the National Government now agreed to be formed would not be a Coalition in the ordinary sense, 'but a co-operation of individuals': it was agreed that, when the emergency had been dealt with, the respective Parties would return to their ordinary positions: the ensuing election would not be fought by the National Government as a Coalition, but by each of the three Parties, acting independently. On such conditions a National Government would be formed under Mr Ramsay Mac-Donald to impose economies to the amount of £70 million, which would include a cut of 10 per cent in unemployment benefit and increased contributions to the Unemployment Insurance Fund of about fourteen million pounds.

It appears, indeed, both from Webb's 'record' and from the ex-Ministers' Memorandum, as quoted above, that these points were all mentioned by MacDonald in his announcement to the Labour Cabinet. It had been intended, it is true, that the Prime Minister would submit the provisional agreement only to those members of the Cabinet who were prepared to support him; and, in form, doubtless, MacDonald acted accordingly; but he communicated the substance of the agreement to the full Cabinet.

Since the proposed new Cabinet was to be a small one — of about a dozen members — who, in Webb's words, were to be 'personally selected from all parties', MacDonald could not, in making his announcement, invite all or any of his colleagues to join it (although he may none the less have invited them 'to join him' in the general sense). In such a Cabinet, obviously, only four or five places at most could be assigned to Labour members; and it would have been futile to invite Henderson or any of his associates to join. What MacDonald did, when the Cabinet dispersed, was to detain the three leading Ministers who had supported him in the previous days (Snowden, Thomas and Sankey) and invite them to participate in the new Cabinet. What MacDonald would have done if Snowden, Thomas and Sankey, or any of them, had refused to enter the proposed Government, it is of course impossible to say; but it is extremely unlikely that he would have gone forward. Thomas, when he left Downing Street, informed the Press representatives that he would be a member of the new Government, and *The Times* next morning said that the fact that Lord Sankey also remained at No. 10 for a considerable time after his colleagues had left was construed as a hopeful sign that the Prime Minister would be able to rely on the continuation of his important work in the Indian Round-Table Conference.

While MacDonald went to the Cabinet meeting from the Palace, Baldwin and Samuel doubtless proceeded to submit the provisional agreement to their respective colleagues.[1] What did the ex-Ministers not detained by MacDonald do when they dispersed? Beatrice Webb's diary (August 25) records that after the Cabinet meeting, 'Sidney joined up with Henderson and Lansbury and some six others, and went off to lunch at the Office of Works[2] to discuss the situation.' In Sidney's letter to her on the previous afternoon, he had immediately written, 'I am going to lunch with a scratch dozen or so of my colleagues to talk it over,' and had afterwards added:

> At the lunch (8 present) we agreed to make no statement to-day and none to-morrow unless we were attacked, and then only to say we reserved ourselves for the meeting of Parliament and the Parliamentary Labour Party. (Half a dozen others who were not present are expected to agree.) But bitter attacks and controversy were expected. It is believed that J.R.M. will take with him Thomas, perhaps Snowden, perhaps Sankey, and if asked also Amulree — Henderson thinks Lloyd George will be there nominally for the sake of his name, along with Herbert Samuel and perhaps Reading for the Liberals.

MACDONALD AND THE JUNIOR MINISTERS

Webb's letter to his wife concluded with the words:

J.R.M. had a meeting of the Under-Secretaries to-day and made it

---

[1] *The Times* (August 25) reported that the body of Conservative ex-Ministers who had been in daily touch throughout the crisis of the previous week had consisted of Neville Chamberlain, Sir Samuel Hoare, Lord Hailsham, Sir Philip Cunliffe-Lister, Sir Bolton Eyres-Monsell, Sir Kingsley Wood, and, since his arrival on the Saturday night, Baldwin; while Sir Geoffrey Fry and Geoffrey Lloyd had been in constant attendance as personal secretaries at 24, Old Queen Street, which had been the headquarters of the party. It was also stated that Sir Herbert Samuel and Sir Donald Maclean had held a number of their meetings at Lord Reading's house in Curzon Street, while Lloyd George had been kept in close touch with events at his house in Addison Road. A meeting of the 'Liberal Shadow Cabinet' was said to have been held at the same time as the Cabinet meeting (12 noon). Samuel, of course, had a special problem arising from the serious illness of Lloyd George, for whom he was acting as deputy. According to his *Memoirs* (p. 205), Samuel was able to keep in touch with Lloyd George throughout, although interviews, with one exception, were not permitted; and Lloyd George fully concurred in every step that was taken.

[2] This was Lansbury's office, and it had already become a meeting place for the dissentients in the Cabinet. Lansbury's biographer has written (p. 269) of the Labour Cabinet's discussions that: 'Only gradually did a division of opinion become clear, and it was marked, to outside observers, by the increasing number of the Cabinet Ministers who came back with the First Commissioner of Works after each meeting to talk with him in his big room in Storey's Gate overlooking St James's Park. After the first meeting there were only three: before the last there were ten out of twenty-one. The names are not recorded: one of his earliest allies, to his surprise, was Clynes; next was Graham; but the great shift in opinion occurred, as ever, when Henderson changed his mind.'

clear that he wanted some of them. Shiels reports a very bitter feeling among them, even Pethick Lawrence (who had not been consulted by Snowden).

The meeting thus referred to, which took place at No. 10 Downing Street at 2.30 p.m. that afternoon (August 24), was a meeting of all Ministers not in the Cabinet and all Junior Ministers. Mowat (p. 396) has described it as 'a farewell meeting'. It was certainly not intended to be such when it was summoned. Its timing proves that conclusively. The original purpose of the gathering, according to MacDonald, was to inform the Ministers concerned of a cut in their salaries. On August 21, the Labour Cabinet not only provisionally accepted the greater part of the proposed economies (the £56½ million), but also gave immediate instructions in regard to certain cuts in salaries.

Dalton, in his diary,[1] wrote that MacDonald was not speaking the truth when he told this meeting of its original purpose. He based this assertion on the fact that the summonses had been issued only on the previous evening, 'when the "National" Government was already decided on.' In his entry for the previous day, Dalton had recorded how the village policeman had brought the message to him in the Wiltshire Downs (he was not on the telephone) in the dusk of that evening, Sunday, August 23. That, of course, was before the waiting Cabinet at No. 10 had received the reply from New York. The National Government had not then been decided on in any sense of the phrase.

MacDonald's remarks on this occasion did not pass altogether unnoticed in the Press at the time. The Parliamentary Correspondent of *The Times* wrote on August 26:

It is said that when the Prime Minister met the junior Ministers in the late Government on Monday afternoon he intimated that he would not expect any of the younger members, merely out of loyalty to himself, to follow him in the course he had taken. It was obvious that such action might prejudice their future career in the Labour Party, and he would not ask for such sacrifices. The absence from the new Administration of some of those who supported the Prime Minister in last week-end's struggle may thus be due to the fact that in their own interests the Prime Minister deliberately refused to invite them to serve.

[1] Quoted, op. cit., p. 272.

There was an allusion in the *Daily Herald* also, on the same day, when Hannen Swaffer wrote:

> One thing that emerges from all the drama of a fateful week is that Ramsay, with that large-mindedness with which his comrades always credit him, did not ask any of the younger men in his Cabinet, merely because of loyalty to him, to join his new Administration. He was going possibly into the political wilderness himself. There was no reason why they should follow him.

Doubtless, MacDonald was alluding to what he said on this particular occasion (and possibly to other actions of a similar kind) when, in a speech at Easington on October 12, 1931, during the Election campaign, he said: 'I quite understand why my colleagues did not join the National Government. I have not a word to say against them, for, as a matter of fact, I advised some of the younger men not to do it.'

Nicolson has written (pp. 467–8) that:

> MacDonald addressed the junior Ministers 'very earnestly and impressively'.[1] He assured them that he had no wish that they should accompany him into the wilderness; they were young men, with their lives before them; they must consider their future careers; it would in the end be more profitable for them to dissociate themselves from himself and the National Government and to join what would now become the Labour Opposition in the House.

Nicolson added:

> Most of the junior Ministers followed, but without much subsequent gratitude, this unselfish advice.

Mowat has referred to this incident of the crisis in these somewhat churlish terms (p. 396): 'On the other hand, he (MacDonald) showed some sympathy with the feelings of his former colleagues when he held a farewell meeting with the junior ministers. . . .' That the incident may have had a much deeper and important significance has not occurred to him. Although it took place within a couple of hours or so of the provisional agreement to form a National Government, which makes it all the more striking, commentators have usually chosen to ignore it. Attlee, however, one of the Ministers present, alluded to it in his autobiography. The passage deserves quotation:

---

[1] The reference here is to Weir, op. cit., p. 387.

MacDonald informed us that the Labour Government was at an end and that he, with Philip Snowden, J. H. Thomas and Lord Sankey, were going into a Coalition Government of which he was to be the head. He said that this was only a temporary measure. He did not wish any of us to join and said that there would certainly not be a 'coupon' General Election. He would soon be back with us. These remarks were received with scepticism by those who knew him best. Having already distributed the offices in the new Government, he would have been embarrassed if any Labour Ministers had wished to join, though this did not prevent him in the future from denouncing them for deserting him. Probably he had counted on more members following his lead than the handful who did so.[1]

Writing in 1954, Attlee forgot that the offices in the new Government had certainly not been distributed at 2.30 p.m. on August 24. Dalton has published his own longer version of the incident. Writing in 1931, he said that MacDonald none the less expressed the hope that some of the junior Ministers would follow him:

> ... He has not called us here in order to try to form any case, or to ask us to join him. Most of us are young men, with our political careers before us. He realizes that he is committing political suicide. He is not going to ask any of us to do the same, or to put our heads into the noose into which he will put his. But ... perhaps some of us *would* be willing to travel the same road with him. The best plan will be for him to write to us individually and enquire.[2]

MacDonald certainly asked one of these Ministers to remain in office. Shinwell has recorded[3] that he refused a request made by MacDonald over the telephone almost immediately 'when I went home after he formed his National Government' (presumably when Shinwell went home after the meeting of the junior Ministers). That Shinwell had been invited and had declined was reported in the *Daily Herald* on August 26. Like Morrison, he had been a strong MacDonaldite.

THE NATIONAL GOVERNMENT

At 3 p.m. that afternoon (August 24) Baldwin and Samuel were again in Downing Street. At 4.10 p.m. MacDonald saw the King at Buckingham Palace, and, according to the subsequent official

---

[1] *As It Happened*, pp. 73–4.
[2] Op. cit., pp. 272–3.
[3] *Conflict without Malice*, p. 110.

announcement, tendered the resignation of the Ministry. This time
the resignation was accepted, and MacDonald in turn accepted the
commission to form a National Government. The full terms of the
announcement were:

> The Prime Minister this afternoon tendered to his Majesty the resig-
> nation of the Ministry, which was accepted by his Majesty, who en-
> trusted Mr Ramsay MacDonald with the task of forming a National
> Government on a comprehensive basis for the purpose of meeting the
> present financial emergency. Mr Ramsay MacDonald accepted the
> commission, and is now in conference with Mr Stanley Baldwin and
> Sir Herbert Samuel, who are co-operating with him in the constitution
> of such an Administration.

Nicolson quotes Sir Clive Wigram's record, as follows:

> The Prime Minister arrived looking worn and weary and was received
> by the King. The Prime Minister tendered his resignation as Prime
> Minister of the Labour Government which the King accepted. The
> King then invited him to form a National Administration. Mr Ramsay
> MacDonald accepted the offer, and kissed hands on his appointment
> as the new Prime Minister.

The conference between the three leaders was resumed. At 9.15
p.m. an official statement was issued in the following terms:

> The Prime Minister, since kissing hands on appointment by his
> Majesty this afternoon, has been in consultation with Mr Baldwin,
> Sir Herbert Samuel, and Mr Snowden as to the names to be sub-
> mitted to the King for inclusion as Ministers in the new Government.
> Considerable progress has been made.
>
> The specific object for which the new Government is being formed
> is to deal with the national emergency that now exists. It will not be a
> Coalition Government in the usual sense of the term, but a Govern-
> ment of Co-operation for this one purpose.
>
> When that purpose is achieved the political parties will resume their
> respective positions.
>
> In order to correct without delay the excess of national expenditure
> over revenue it is anticipated that Parliament will be summoned to
> meet on September 8, when proposals will be submitted to the House
> of Commons for a very large reduction of expenditure and for the pro-
> vision on an equitable basis of the further funds required to balance
> the Budget. As the commerce and well-being, not only of the British
> nation, but of a large part of the civilized world, has been built up
> and rests upon a well-founded confidence in sterling, the new Govern-

ment will take whatever steps may be deemed by them to be necessary to justify the maintenance of that confidence unimpaired.

Although Snowden made no reference to the fact in his autobiography, it should be noted that (with MacDonald, Baldwin and Samuel) he participated in the discussions about the personnel of the new Cabinet.

On the same night of August 24, Baldwin issued a statement, in the course of which he said:

> ... The crisis with which we are faced demands prompt and immediate measures, and a dissolution of Parliament at this stage, followed by a General Election, would be disastrous. This fact dominates the situation at the moment.
>
> The only means by which the national emergency can be met is close co-operation between all parties. For this purpose we Conservatives have consented for a limited period of time to enter a National Government, which is to be formed for the express purpose of carrying out such measures as are required to balance the Budget and restore confidence in our national credit, and there is no question of any permanent Coalition.
>
> The National Government has been allotted a definite task, and on its completion it is understood that Parliament should be dissolved as soon as circumstances permit, and that each of the parties should be left free to place its policy before the electors for their approval. By this means no party will be called upon to sacrifice any of the principles in which it believes. But the gravity of the crisis is such that it is the bounden duty of every one who studies the welfare of our country to put aside party differences for the time being and to co-operate in the national interests. In that task we Conservatives will play our part boldly and courageously.

Ex-Ministers and T.U.C.

Other important developments occurred on August 24. The agreement reached by the group of ex-Ministers at lunch-time, as reported by Webb to his wife immediately afterwards, was not destined to be carried out. The ex-Ministers concerned did not succeed in reserving themselves for the meeting of Parliament and the Parliamentary Labour Party. No attack made upon them was the cause of this failure.

Citrine was to tell the Trades Union Congress at Bristol on September 7 that, on hearing that a National Government, or what purported to be such, was being formed,

We had consultations at once with officers of the Labour Party, and we put forward the view most strongly that an immediate conference should take place of the two national bodies, together with the Consultative Committee of the Parliamentary Party, as we believed, from the Trades Union Congress side, it was imperative that the Movement should know at the first opportunity where we stood in relation to the new Government. As to our own attitude we had no doubt, but we thought it advisable that we should have a meeting to explore the position fully. That meeting took place. . . .

The announcement that a Joint Meeting of the three bodies (i.e. the General Council of the Trades Union Congress, the National Executive of the Labour Party, and the Consultative Committee of the Parliamentary Labour Party) would be held on August 26 was made on the 24th by Citrine himself. He went on to say:

It is obvious that nobody can commit the Trades Union Congress and the Labour movement to participation in, or support of, a National Government without their consent. That consent has not been asked for, and has not been given. Until the properly constituted bodies — namely, the Labour Party executive and the Trades Union Congress General Council — have considered the matter and reached a decision it must be understood that our support of the Government ceased with the resignation of the Cabinet. I think the opinion of the trade unions at any rate will be that in resigning office rather than carry out the policy of drastic economies at the expense of the unemployed, which the other parties have endeavoured to impose, the Ministers who resigned have acted as Labour Ministers would be expected to act by the Labour movement.

The Labour Correspondent of *The Times*, reporting this announcement next morning (August 25), pointed out that, while any decision reached at the Joint Meeting would require ratification, there was little doubt that it would be ratified; and that, since the trade union vote was the ruling factor in the Labour Party Conference, Citrine had indicated in advance what the decision was likely to be. Citrine (he went on) was speaking for the trade union movement and was not prejudging the action of the executive of the Labour Party:

Nevertheless he did not speak until after he had had an opportunity of learning the opinions of at least some members of the party executive. He was, in fact, in consultation with Mr Henderson immediately before, and one outcome of the exchange of views was the resolution to obtain an authoritative decision from the executive bodies of the three main branches of the Labour movement.

From Dalton's diary it appears that what he calls 'a council of war' was held at Transport House in Henderson's room on the afternoon of the 24th. Dalton went there straight from the meeting of the junior Ministers. Among those present were Lansbury, Ernest Bevin, Citrine, Stanley Hirst (the Chairman of the Party executive), and J. S. Middleton (the Assistant Secretary of the Party).

Two points in Citrine's statement of the 24th have particular interest. The first is the importance he attached to a decision by the General Council and the National Executive, and his apparent indifference to the Parliamentary Party. The second is the ambiguity of his references to the resignation of Ministers. The Ministry as a whole had resigned. Citrine was not speaking of that. He was certainly not thinking of MacDonald himself and any other Ministers who might join or support the new Government. He was thinking of the others. Only some of these had threatened resignation; and, doubtless, Citrine's approval was confined to them; but, being awkwardly placed, he used the ambiguous expression 'the Ministers who resigned'.

Next morning it was reported in the press that J. H. Thomas, on his own initiative, had attended a meeting of the executive of his union (the National Union of Railwaymen) in London on the 24th. His position was that of an official who had been seconded for political duty during his period of office in the Labour Government. Thomas is said to have made a long statement of his reasons for acting with MacDonald. The executive refrained from expressing any opinion upon his action, but, it was said, while it would do nothing until informed that Thomas had joined the new Government, its intentions were not concealed. Thomas's 'leave of absence' from union duties was held to have terminated when the Labour Government resigned, and the executive would not hesitate to recall him, so that Thomas would then have to choose between Ministerial or trade union office, though his choice was certain. The 'unofficial opinion' of the executive was said to be one of regret that Thomas had acted in opposition to the General Council of the T.U.C. Thomas himself made a statement after the meeting of the N.U.R. executive, in which he said:

No one deplores more than I do the break-up of the Labour Government. No member of that Government could be, or is, happy in contemplating any economies in the social services; but the grave financial position makes it imperative, in my judgment, that the first and only consideration should be that the financial stability of the country must be placed beyond all doubt. I am satisfied that fundamentally the country is sound, but it is the duty of all, regardless of personal consequences, to contribute their bit to pull her through the present crisis. That is the only motive I have, and that is the spirit in which I undertake a task which I know will lead to misunderstanding and probably abuse; but it is my duty as I see it, and I will not flinch from it.

The reactions of Beatrice Webb to the news of the 24th have considerable interest. Her diary entry for 6.30 p.m. that day reads:

Just heard over wireless what I wished to hear, that the Cabinet as a whole has resigned, J.R.M. accepting office as P.M. in order to form a National Emergency Government including Tories and Liberals: it being also stated that Snowden, Thomas and alas! Sankey will take office under him. I regret Sankey: but I am glad the other three will disappear from the Labour world — they were rotten stuff: each one of them for different reasons.[1]

In the diary entry for August 25, after her husband's return from London, Beatrice Webb was much interested in the problem of the future relations of MacDonald, Snowden and Thomas with the Labour Party. She expressed the view that, owing to the Party's constitution, the need for being a member of an affiliated organization, MacDonald and Snowden would probably find themselves

[1] Op. cit., p. 283. A later passage in the same entry indicates that, just as Webb himself was willing in the Cabinet to accept the cut in unemployment benefit, so his wife's reactions to the change of Government were not due to any opposition to that cut. She wrote: 'The first result of J.R.M.'s defection may be the consolidation of the Labour movement, political and industrial, under Henderson's leadership — with a sterner outlook, a more disciplined behaviour and a more scientific programme. The danger in front of the Labour movement is its deep-seated belief that any addition, under any condition, to the income of wage-earners is a good thing in itself. That was why it was so fatal to start state subsidized insurance, it was bound to end by becoming unconditional outdoor relief — and that "addition" to the livelihood of the poor was certain to increase the area of unemployment. It is a most demoralizing form of voluntary idleness. Under capitalism the wage-earner's life is often so hard, and the wage-earner is so irresponsible, that idleness, with a regular pittance, is comparatively attractive to large bodies of men — they won't accept and won't keep work they don't particularly like and are not accustomed to — and when they do accept it they are not over keen to bestir themselves. And yet the typical Trade Unionists, though when administering their own out-of-work benefit, they insist an all sorts of conditions, resent these conditions being attached to the state scheme. That is the danger of the Labour Government and always will be, as far as I can see.'

excluded from membership. No reason for this view was given: presumably she thought it probable that MacDonald and Snowden (and Thomas also) would be expelled from their respective constituency parties. But Thomas, she thought, so long as he was not expelled from the N.U.R., 'which is not likely,' would remain technically a member, though he would never again be elected to a responsible position in his own organization. The problem was one which was to continue to worry Beatrice Webb for some time.

All the announcements made on August 24 made it clear that the new Government was intended to be, not a coalition of parties, but a Ministry of individuals drawn from all parties. They also made it clear that the new Government was to be formed for one specific purpose, that of dealing with the emergency; and was expected, therefore, to be of short duration. Obviously, a party might support the new Government: the Conservatives and Liberals were expected to do so. Similarly, a party might oppose it. Whether or not the Labour Party would do so remained to be seen. It was expected that it would formally constitute the Opposition in Parliament, and that Henderson would be its leader. The Labour Correspondent of *The Times*, for example, wrote on August 25:

> Mr Henderson has led the opposition in the Cabinet to the proposals which the Prime Minister approved. He will become at once, upon relinquishing office, the natural leader of the Labour Party in Parliament if, as is expected, the party resolves to go into Opposition.

But the character of the Party's opposition to the new Government was an uncertain factor in the situation, though one which was bound to be of the utmost importance. It is one of the surprising features of Mowat's history that he appears to be unaware of the significance of the attitude actually adopted by the Labour Party, and completely ignores its effects upon the development of the crisis.

Bitter hostility from certain elements in the Party was inevitable. The attitude of the General Council of the Trades Union Congress was known. But, in view of the circumstances in which the Labour Cabinet broke up, the formulation of any agreed policy would clearly raise awkward problems. And it was not anticipated that Henderson and his ex-Ministerial and other Parliamentary colleagues would take up a position of unqualified and uncompromising hostility to the new Government. It was extremely difficult to see how they *could* do so. In this connection, so vital to an understanding of the crisis, the views expressed by the *Manchester Guardian* on August 25 may well be recalled. That newspaper deplored having to make the assumption that the Labour Party would become actively hostile or, at any rate, non-co-operative. It recognized that Henderson would have to display great gifts of leadership. His responsibility was stressed. 'It was mainly owing to his stand that the minority in the Cabinet against cuts in the dole was so strong and that Mr MacDonald found it impossible to carry on.' But it was 'one thing to lead a revolt like that of the nine Ministers; it is another to develop that revolt into a challenge to a National Government . . .'.

> The omens are unfavourable, but it is impossible to doubt that, although formal support may be withheld, Mr Henderson and his colleagues will be able to give generous aid. After all, Mr Henderson is as much impressed with the reality of the emergency as the other members of the Cabinet Committee of Five. He and his colleagues agreed to almost the whole of the proposals in the economy scheme. Indeed, if report be correct, they went some way towards supporting the drastic revisions of the insurance scheme itself; the final difference came on the matter of degree as much as of principle.
>
> It is thus impossible for the Labour leaders to cut themselves aloof from the economy scheme, however strong the pressure from their rank and file and however great the temptation to make electioneering capital. The Labour party will be severely tried, but it may yet have the wisdom to sympathize with, if it cannot welcome, Mr MacDonald's bold constitutional experiment.

Of special interest also is the editorial in the *Daily Herald* on that same morning of August 25. The formation of a National Government was attacked in severe terms; and particular emphasis was given to the charge that the Federal Reserve Bank of New York had been allowed 'to dictate, as the condition for a further credit to the Bank of England, the policy to be pursued in relation to unemployment benefit'. This was described as 'acceptance of the dictatorship . . . of international finance', and 'surrender to the City'. The article declared that the national organizations of Labour would reject, by overwhelming majorities, any scheme which involved new privations for the unemployed. But the references to MacDonald and 'those members of the previous Ministry who join him' were entirely free from personal animosity. These men were said, accurately, to be entering the new Government 'as individuals, not as accredited representatives of the Labour Movement', while the Labour Party was entering a new phase, 'without leaders who have rendered it services which will make their names live with lustre in history.' The editorial proceeded:

> Fully aware of the consequences, Mr MacDonald and his immediate Labour colleagues who propose to act with him are walking a path which leads to the political wilderness. Profoundly wrong as their attitude is, we know that the Labour Movement as a whole is big enough and generous enough to salute their sincerity. The plans they are to sponsor must be intensely repugnant to them. But, regardless of their personal interests, not heeding the pain of a break with the associations of a lifetime, they are following what they, mistakenly, deem to be the line of duty. The *Daily Herald* will decline to countenance any personal attacks upon them, but it will answer their case with reason and argument.

Even so, Dalton has recorded in his diary that the Trade Union leaders had sent for 'X of the *Herald*' (presumably the Editor) during the 'council of war' at Transport House on the afternoon of August 24, and had made him alter the whole emphasis of the editorial he had proposed to publish, making it more adverse to MacDonald and the new Government than it otherwise would have been. In the following days, to judge from the same source, Ernest Bevin kept the *Herald* well under his control.

Dalton's same entry for August 24 tells us that Henderson considered the situation only as 'an interlude in the life of the Party' and said, 'we mustn't drive J.R.M. and the others out.' Dalton himself was far from sharing the spirit of his 'Uncle Arthur'. The diarist 'nephew' reveals his own reactions in an entry for August 27:

> With J.R.M., P.S. and J.H.T. I never had any relations at all, and was always conscious of suspicion and dislike, which I heartily reciprocated. It is a cleaner air I breathe to-day, and the prospects of a real Labour Government, full of youngish men, under Uncle's Premiership, are bright, though still speculative, within one or two years. And I can hardly fail to be in the *next* Cabinet.

In another entry Dalton refers to his 'first feeling of sheer joy, when the Lost Leaders decamped...'.

Apart from its editorial, however (though alluded to in it), the *Daily Herald* carried on August 25 a 'startling disclosure' by its

Political Correspondent about an 'attempt by U.S. banks to dictate the internal policy of Great Britain'. Behind the report that the Federal Reserve Bank of New York was prepared to extend further large credits to the Bank of England lay, it was said, 'an amazing fact':

> The late Government was informed by the Federal Reserve Bank that such credits would only be granted provided that specific and considerable economies were at once made in the administration or in the actual benefits paid under the Unemployment Insurance scheme. This virtual ultimatum from New York bankers played a vital part in dividing the late Cabinet on the issue of a 10 per cent reduction in unemployment benefit. Insistence by the Bank of England on the need for credits — even on these terms — heightened the existing clash within the late Cabinet. It has been made absolutely clear that the credit will not be forthcoming unless and until measures which the U.S. bankers consider satisfactory are put into operation by the new Cabinet.

This allegation was given extensive publicity in the United States, and, according to the *Economist* (August 29), aroused resentment there. The New York Correspondent of *The Times* (August 26) stated 'on the best authority' that there was no truth in the *Herald's* assertion.

The Federal Reserve Bank, as we have seen, had, like the Bank of France, granted considerable credits to the Bank of England. In regard to the loans or credits sought by the Labour Government, the Federal Reserve Bank was not itself involved. Harrison, its Chairman, had only been asked for advice on the prospects of raising a loan on the New York market. The same request had been made to the Government's agents, Morgans. The opinion of both Harrison and Morgans was that there was no likelihood of raising a loan until the British budgetary position was definitely put in order. They were of opinion, however, that it might be possible to arrange a short-term credit on the basis of the economy scheme tentatively submitted to them. There was no ultimatum from the New York bankers. They were not, in fact, enthusiastic about providing credits, and were afterwards to be subjected to criticism at home for granting them. But they were responsibly anxious to assist the British Government, which needed the credits urgently; and they gave their expert opinion on the prospects, just as the Bank of England had done. That opinion was shared by the

French and other Continental experts. There was no demand from
them that unemployment insurance benefits should be reduced; no
demand that any specific measures should be taken; although they
doubtless held the widely prevalent view that the British budgetary
situation could not be rectified without economies in unemployment insurance expenditure. However, the impracticability of raising the required loans or credits except on the basis of an economy
programme comprising reductions in unemployment benefit could
be plausibly attributed to an attempt on the part of the 'U.S. banks'
or 'the international financiers' to dictate British domestic policy.
Such an interpretation of what had happened was likely to evoke a
strong reaction from the British public, and more particularly from
the Labour movement: it could be used to exploit both national
sentiment and the prevalent mistrust of the mysterious operations
of the financial world. Much was to be heard about what came at
once to be called 'a bankers' ramp'.

CHAPTER XI

FIRST REACTIONS

THE NEW CABINET

On August 25, the Prime Minister had another day of conferences with the leaders of the three political parties. At 5.20 p.m. he drove to the Palace and submitted to the King his list of the proposed members of the new Cabinet. MacDonald remained with the King for about half an hour. On his return to Downing Street, he said: 'The barometer is setting fair. We have very nearly finished our preliminaries.' At 7 p.m. the names of the new Cabinet Ministers were officially announced, together with the names of eight other senior Ministers.

The Cabinet consisted of ten members, four drawn from the Labour Party, four from the Conservatives and two from the Liberals. The Labour members, in addition to the Prime Minister, were Snowden, Lord Sankey, and Thomas, all of whom retained their previous offices. Baldwin became Lord President of the Council; Sir Samuel Hoare received the important appointment of Secretary of State for India; Neville Chamberlain and Sir Philip Cunliffe-Lister being the other two Conservatives. Sir Herbert Samuel and Lord Reading were the two Liberal members of the Cabinet, the first as Home Secretary, the second as Foreign Secretary.

Little information is available about the process of Cabinet-making. Samuel has told us in his *Memoirs* (p. 205) that in the conferences with MacDonald and Baldwin to allocate the offices in the Government, he found both ready to treat the Liberal Party with all fairness, taking into account the large Liberal vote at the last General Election and not only the small Liberal numbers in the House. Samuel, however, had trouble with Lloyd George about the Liberal appointments. 'Not being willing to let bygones be bygones,' Lloyd George 'raised strong objection to one or two of my suggestions for junior posts'; and Samuel, being only Lloyd

George's deputy in the leadership of the Party,'could not insist', though 'those exclusions gave rise to difficulties afterwards'. The Liberal element in this first National Government was drawn exclusively from those who continued to accept Lloyd George's leadership. Simon and his friends were kept out. Lloyd George himself was far too ill to take office.

The eight other appointments announced on August 25 included Lord Amulree, who retained the post he had held in the previous Labour Cabinet as Secretary of State for Air; four Conservatives (Sir Austen Chamberlain, Sir John Gilmour, Sir Henry Betterton, and Lord Londonderry); and three Liberals (Sir Archibald Sinclair, Sir Donald Maclean, and Lord Lothian). The office of Secretary of State for War was not filled at the same time as the other major appointments. *The Times* said on August 26 that MacDonald was very anxious to retain the services of Tom Shaw in that capacity. Shaw had been one of the majority supporting MacDonald when the final break came in the Labour Cabinet. Shaw, however, evidently declined to serve, for, on the 26th, the appointment of the Liberal Marquess of Crewe to this post was announced. Two days later, the *Daily Herald* reported that Shaw would not seek re-election to the House. The office of Lord Privy Seal was also left vacant for the time being. It is possible that MacDonald was anxious to find a Labour occupant of this post also. It was reported in the press on the 26th that a meeting of all the Whips in the late Government had been held on the previous day, and that they had unanimously agreed to refuse to take office in the new Administration.

On the evening of the 25th, the Prime Minister broadcast an address to the nation in which he explained the nature of the financial crisis and the need for swift and effective action to restore confidence.[1] He opened with a personal reference, as follows:

---

[1] In view of subsequent controversy, it is perhaps desirable to quote from this part of MacDonald's address. He said: 'It is essential that the confidence of the world in our credit should be restored; otherwise we shall not be able to maintain the value of the pound sterling, and the results of that should be very carefully considered. First of all, if there was any collapse in the pound we should be defaulting in our obligations to the rest of the world, and our credit would be gone. This would be fatal, since this country, above all others, depends on the maintenance of its credit, having to buy as we do so large a part of our food and raw materials from abroad. Then the pound sterling is the greatest medium of world trade, and the basis of the money of many other countries. Thus the commerce and well-being, not only of the British nation but of a large part of the civilized world, have been built up and rest upon the confidence in the pound sterling, and if that confidence be destroyed it means a dislocation of world trade from which everyone, and most of all the working people of this country,

I speak to-night under unusual and, to me, rather sorrowful circumstances. I have given my life to the building up of a political party. I was present at its birth; I was its nurse when it emerged from its infancy and it attained to adult years. At this moment I have changed none of my beliefs and none of my ideals. I see that it is said that I have no Labour credentials for what I am doing. That is true. I do not claim to have them, though I am certain that in the interests of the working classes I ought to have them. Be that as it may, I have credentials of even higher authority. My credentials are those of national duty as I conceive it, and I obey them irrespective of consequences.

MacDonald's only reference to the Labour Cabinet's discussions was in these words:

There was no disagreement in the Labour Cabinet that economies of a fairly drastic kind would have to be made.

He disclosed for the first time officially what was already well-known, namely, that there was a proposal to cut unemployment benefit by 10 per cent without touching children's allowances; and dealt with the point at some length. MacDonald also referred to the suggestion which had already been made that the crisis was due to 'a bankers' "ramp", or a conspiracy, or something of the kind, against a Labour Government', and emphatically declared the charge untrue:

We were never presented with any political ultimatum. We never found in the attitude or the conversations of those with whom we were negotiating any political bias one way or the other. They told us, when we put up proposals to them, whether in their opinion those proposals would meet the circumstances required to give confidence, so that a

will suffer. Further, if the value of the pound were to fall suddenly and catastrophically, not by plan, as some people suggest, but without plan, by the force of economic circumstances without control — should that happen, prices would rise much faster than wages and incomes could be adjusted, even if adjustments were possible, and conditions similar to those in Germany, when some millions of marks were given in exchange for the pound sterling, would arise by the widening of a vicious circle. The people who would suffer most are the people not with large, but with the smallest incomes. . . . Things are happening which if allowed to go on will speedily produce a crisis. In those circumstances it is no use discussing the theories of banking, Macmillan reports, who is to blame, and so on. This threatened cloud has to be dispelled, and dispelled immediately. . . . When the danger has been removed we can have an assize and a trial and a verdict; but my colleagues and myself are determined that the assize shall not be a coroner's inquest. Everyone from whom we have borrowed, or who has placed deposits in our keeping, must be assured that the Budget will be balanced, and that assurance is to be given at once, not only as a declaration of intention but as a programme with essential details,' loan might be floated. When they were doubtful they were perfectly willing that tests should be imposed.

Finally, the Prime Minister spoke of the new Government:

> It is not a Coalition Government. I would take no part in that. It is not a Government which compels any party to it to change its principles or subordinate its distinctive individuality. I would take no part in that either. It is a Government, as has been described, of individuals. It has been formed to do this work. If the work takes a little time, the life of the Government will be short. When that life is finished, the work of the House of Commons and the general political situation will return to where they were last week, and those who have taken risks will receive either our punishment or our reward. The election which will follow will not be fought by the Government. There will be no coupons, and, I hope, no illegitimate prejudices. . . .

On Wednesday morning, August 26, the formalities incidental to the change of Government were carried through at Buckingham Palace.[1] That evening the King left Euston Station in order to resume his holiday at Balmoral. Meanwhile, a conference of all the appointed Ministers was held, and then the Cabinet itself held its first meeting.

THE NEW OPPOSITION

In its editorial that morning the *Daily Herald* denounced the new Government as 'a bankers' Government'. 'People of all parties', it was said, 'will feel a sense of humiliation that it is possible for international finance to break Governments,' adding, 'One of the conditions laid down by the banks is that part of the price for saving the Pound is to be paid by the very poorest people in the country.' The editorial asserted that already a demand was being made for the continued existence of the new Cabinet 'beyond the time by which its specific work has been brought to an end,' and that the course of events would run inevitably with, and not against, this demand. Matters outside the scope of economy plans, it

---

[1] Lord Templewood has written (op. cit., p. 22): 'MacDonald, having worked himself up into taking his critical decision, at once relapsed into a mood of doubt and depression. When he appeared at the Privy Council for the swearing in of the new Cabinet, he looked so mournful in a black tie and frock coat, that the King laughingly said to him: "You look as if you were attending your own funeral. Put on a white tie and try to think it is your wedding." ' This story may be contrasted with Snowden's oft-repeated 'Duchesses' story, see below, p. 418.

argued, would arise for discussion and decision, and it would be difficult for the Cabinet to end its own life. The editorial also fore-shadowed one of the alternative proposals which were to be put forward by the chief organizations of the Labour movement: the mobilization of British capital invested abroad.

Both *The Times* and the *Manchester Guardian* that same morning gave what purported to be authoritative information about the case ex-Ministers were likely to make for themselves. Both newspapers proved to be well-informed. The *Guardian* indicated the lines upon which ex-Ministers would attempt to disavow all responsibility for the economy scheme; a feat which on the previous day it had de-clared impossible. In regard to the economy proposals outlined to the Labour executive bodies on August 20, and those which were pre-sented to the Opposition leaders on the 21st,

> they would say, I think, that they were led step by step inside the Cabinet to accept, as part of a general scheme to meet a serious emer-gency, proposals to which they were really opposed. They accepted them reluctantly in the interests of the unity of the Cabinet and in the light of the reading of the situation given to them. They cannot, they would argue, be held to the details, because in some cases at least they did not express a final view on them because they wished to see the scheme as a whole, and in particular to see the final balance as between economy and taxation and other revenue-producing expedients.

In reference to the Joint Meeting of the three Labour Commit-tees due to be held that day (26th), the Labour Correspondent of *The Times* said that, although a break with MacDonald, Snowden and Thomas was inevitable, it was to be made without reproaches and without recrimination:

> That note is, I am informed, to be very clearly sounded to-day. The differences are deep, but they are not to be embittered by personal attacks. There is not to be a heresy hunt and neither by word nor by deed is there to be a suggestion of expulsion from the party. Some things will be settled by the facts of the case. Mr MacDonald will no longer lead the party and he will lose the *ex officio* place he has had on the National Executive. Mr Thomas's position is different, because he is an elected member of the executive. It is expected in some quarters that he will resign. So far, however, as the dissident Ministers can control events, nothing will be done in the way of proscription which would make impossible the reunion of the leaders when the time comes for 'political parties to resume their respective positions'.

The qualification, 'so far as the dissident Ministers can control events,' was to prove important.

Comment in the *Manchester Guardian* on the ex-Ministers' attitude was not dissimilar. Their general feeling was said to be one of sympathy with MacDonald's personal position and with his aims:

> The present mood among all sections of the movement is one of sadness that the break between the Prime Minister and his old colleagues should appear to be so complete. Although the experiment of the National Government is for so short a period no one seems to contemplate that the Ministers who take part in it will be likely to seek to return to their old place in the Party.
>
> It is taken for granted that the Party must pass into Opposition, and that with all the goodwill and sympathy in the world it cannot take any other than a hostile attitude towards some of the most critical of the items in the economy scheme.
>
> The prospect pleases no one (except the warriors of the I.L.P.). ... Even if the Prime Minister were to attend to-morrow's meeting, as he is entitled to do, he would not affect the situation or swing over the Labour movement to support him. Mr MacDonald is more likely to attend the meeting of the Parliamentary Labour Party which has been called for Friday. By then, however, an anti-Government policy will have been determined.

The Times Correspondent, it is of interest and importance to note, said that although the number of Labour M.P.s prepared to follow MacDonald would be in doubt until Friday, the conjecture of 20 was more likely to be accurate than one of 50. The *Guardian's* Labour Correspondent, on the previous day, said that the Parliamentary force which would follow MacDonald was estimated by some at no more than 20 or 30; and the editorial spoke of 'only a handful of supporters', just as the *Daily Express* wrote (also on the 25th) that the Prime Minister could command 'only a fraction of his Party in Parliament now'.

The Labour Joint Meeting (August 26)

The joint meeting of the T.U.C. General Council, the National Executive of the Labour Party, and the Consultative Committee of the Parliamentary Labour Party, took place on the afternoon of Wednesday, August 26. The official report of this conference gave only the terms of the resolution adopted, which was as follows:

> That this joint meeting of the Trades Union Congress General Council, the National Executive Committee of the Labour Party, and the

Consultative Committee of the Parliamentary Labour Party, having considered the position created by the formation of the new Government, is unanimously of opinion that it should be vigorously opposed in Parliament and by the Movement throughout the country; they express their approval of the action taken by the Ministers of the late Government in declining to render their support to the new administration; and recommend the Parliamentary Labour Party to constitute itself the official Parliamentary Opposition.

The Report submitted to the Trades Union Congress on September 9, 1931, added:

It was also agreed that a joint manifesto should be issued to the Movement without delay, and this was published the following day.

The Report presented to the Labour Party Annual Conference early in the following October said that statements were made by Henderson, Clynes, Lansbury and Morrison; and that the resolution was adopted 'after general discussion and separate consideration of the position by the three Committees'.

Next day (August 27) the Labour Correspondent of *The Times* said that the conference had begun at 2 p.m. and continued, with half an hour break, until after 7 p.m. The decision to oppose the new Government was not only unanimous but emphatic. Agreement upon alternative measures, however, was not so easy. The Correspondent recalled that the General Council had on the previous Friday repudiated the scheme of economy which had the approval of the Labour Cabinet as a whole, and that — as had been disclosed by J. H. Thomas[1] — the final and more drastic scheme had the approval of a majority of the Cabinet, 'so that apparently several Ministers who have since resigned were prepared, a few days ago, to go as far as the Ministers who remain in office.' It was not surprising, therefore (the Correspondent continued), that a certain liveliness marked the proceedings when the conference came to consider the differences between the General Council and former Ministers. The latter, he said, 'were severely taken to task for having ventured to approve proposals without first ascertaining the views of the General Council upon them.' A good deal of feeling was shown, it was said, by representatives of the General

---

[1] See below, pp. 184–5. This disclosure had already been made by all the chief newspapers (including the *Daily Herald*, the *Manchester Guardian*, and *The Times* itself). Thomas was mentioned, presumably, because he was the first member of the Cabinet to make a public statement on the point.

Council. The note of discord was allowed to die down, but the underlying policy differences remained to be settled. The conference was to reassemble that afternoon, but a joint sub-committee would make a preliminary attempt to arrive at agreement in the morning.[1]

On the afternoon of August 26, the *Evening Standard* — and subsequently other evening newspapers — published a letter addressed by the Prime Minister to all unofficial Labour M.P.s. According to an announcement issued from Downing Street afterwards, the letter was marked 'Personal' (a fact not mentioned in the *Evening Standard*) and was never meant for publication. In it MacDonald asked Labour M.P.s 'to think over the situation without prejudice or passion before reaching their decision' as to which way they would take; explained the general situation as he saw it,[2] emphatically repudiating the 'Bankers' ramp' contention; and appealed to them to suspend judgment until Parliament met. The letter ended:

All this has caused us great pain. When it is over, the party will be left untrammelled as to its policy and programme, and we beg that during these trying days both sides will express their views so that the very hard issues involved may be dispassionately considered.

J. H. Thomas addressed a message to members of the N.U.R. (published in the *Railway Review* and reproduced in *The Times* on August 27) explaining his attitude. In the course of this statement he said:

Eventually a majority of the Labour Cabinet was obtained for a definite programme of economy and taxation. It is regrettable, however, that a minority of the Labour Cabinet announced that they intended to

[1] The *Daily Express* report (August 27) said: '. . . At times the discussions were somewhat acrimonious. Trade Union leaders accused ex-Ministers of having supported proposals opposed to T.U.C. policy, and personal attacks were made on some of them. The charge was put forward that certain members of the late Government had agreed to all the economies except the 10 per cent cut in unemployment benefit. The answer given to the T.U.C. was that efforts had been made to reach a compromise with the object of keeping the Labour Government in office.'

[2] One passage in this connection ought perhaps to be singled out for quotation. MacDonald wrote: 'The crisis was approaching with rapid strides. Latterly it had become a question of hours, and shelter had to be found immediately. The Government strove hard to agree about this, so that its work in other fields might be continued. It failed, and we had to face the consequences. To go on as though this approaching calamity could be avoided, in our opinion, was not possible if the Party was to escape responsibility for it.'

resign, and this made it impossible for the Labour Government to continue in office.

Thomas used similar words in a letter to the Executive Committee of the Labour Party in his constituency of Derby:

> Unfortunately, although a majority decided that there was no alternative, a minority felt quite conscientiously that they had no other course than to resign. It was therefore felt that the Cabinet as a whole should resign. That course was decided upon, but it did not avert the crisis. They were faced with a situation which it was a question, not of weeks or days, but of hours, to save.

The Committee considered his letter on the night of the 26th and decided to place the whole matter before a special meeting of the delegates to the Derby General Council of the Party, to which Thomas was invited.

THE LABOUR JOINT MANIFESTO, AUGUST 27

The outstanding event of Thursday, August 27, was the publication of a Joint Manifesto by the three Committees of the Labour Movement. This Manifesto repudiated all responsibility for 'the new Coalition Government', and called for firm resistance to it. Full expression was given to the 'Bankers' ramp' theory of the crisis,[1] and all the proposed economies were condemned. The Manifesto constituted an acceptance of the policy of the General Council of the T.U.C., a repudiation of the policy of the Labour Cabinet, and an implied criticism of all the ex-Ministers. It endorsed the chief alternative proposals which had been put forward in the previous week by the General Council, viz.: taxation of fixed interest-bearing securities, and suspension of the Sinking Fund; and added 'measures to reduce the burden of War debts'; but it gave priority over all these to 'mobilizing the country's foreign investments'.

The Labour Correspondent of *The Times* (August 28) said justly that, though three sets of hands were set to the document, 'the

---

[1] 'Forces in finance and politics made demands which no Labour Government could accept' — 'a situation caused by a policy pursued by private banking interests in the control of which the public has no part' — 'financial interests have decided that this country is setting a bad example to other countries in taxing the rich to provide for the necessities of the poor' — 'a financial crisis . . . aggravated beyond measure by deliberately alarmist statements in sections of the Press, and by the fact that a protracted campaign has created the impression abroad that Great Britain is on the verge of bankruptcy.'

dominant voice is that of the General Council slightly subdued out of deference to the feelings of the Parliamentary leaders who have, since they left the Cabinet, accepted the essentials of the General Council's policy.' He went on to point out that 'a majority of the Cabinet did, in fact, accept the full scheme which the manifesto assails, and the Cabinet as a whole (although not unanimously) had accepted the earlier scheme which the General Council rejected and for which it sought to substitute other proposals'; and that (while the manifesto declared that the new Government's policy had aroused the entire Labour movement to determined opposition) all the items in that policy recited by the manifesto, with the one exception of the cut in unemployment benefits, had the approval of the Labour Cabinet, 'and a cut in benefits (it may be repeated) had the approval of a majority of the Cabinet.'

The Joint Meeting also passed a resolution, 'in view of the impending General Election,' calling upon all sections of the Labour Movement immediately to strengthen their organizations and to provide the finance requisite to ensure a majority Labour Government.

This Joint Manifesto of August 27 virtually shattered the hopes which had been entertained that the ex-Ministers would be able to exert an effectively moderating influence upon the Labour opposition to the new Government and its policy. It was widely, indeed generally, regarded as a capitulation by them to the T.U.C. General Council. It certainly committed them to a course of action which involved them in great difficulties. Snowden wrote in his autobiography (pp. 956–7) that this manifesto removed any doubt he might have felt as to the wisdom of his action in joining the National Government. He described it as 'a shameful travesty of the facts which had led to the resignation of the Labour Government, and a gross misrepresentation of the purpose for which the National Government had been formed.'[1] It was 'the first indication of the line the Labour leaders were going to take in repudiating responsibility for economies to which the Labour Cabinet as a whole had agreed', and it 'did much to change my views about the

---

[1] The passage in the manifesto to which Snowden objected in this connection read as follows: 'Fundamentally, it is an attempt to reverse the social policy which, in this country, has within limits provided for the unemployed, the aged and the sick, the disabled, the orphaned, and the widowed. Unemployment benefit is attacked on the ground that it strengthens resistance to wage reductions. These are the motives which impel the new Coalition Government in its policy of drastic cuts in social expenditure.'

political honesty of my late Labour colleagues, and to make me doubt whether any future coming together would be possible.'

LIBERAL AND CONSERVATIVE PARTY MEETINGS

The full Cabinet did not meet on August 27, but the Committees which had been appointed were at work in an effort to complete their tasks for the next Cabinet meeting, fixed for the following Monday afternoon (August 30). The Prime Minister left London for Lossiemouth on the night of the 27th (not on the 26th as stated by Nicolson). *The Times* reported that MacDonald's colleagues 'urged him strongly to take a few days' rest in view of the heavy strain which has been placed on him during the last fortnight and of the arduous duties which he will be called upon to perform when Parliament reassembles'.

Friday, August 28, was marked by meetings of all three political parties. In the cases of the Liberal and Conservative meetings, full reports of the speeches made were issued to the press.

The Liberals (M.P.s, Peers, and candidates) met at 11 a.m. that day. Once again they were temporarily reunited: indeed, the gathering was quite a remarkable demonstration of unity. Although Sir John Simon was absent in Scotland, a message was read from him in which he congratulated all Liberal friends who had been invited to join the National Government, and promised his support of 'any administration which pursues retrenchment and handles the Indian problem with determination as well as with sympathy'. Lord Grey of Fallodon, however, did attend (for the first time since the War) and did so, in his own words, 'in order to demonstrate as emphatically as I can my entire agreement' with the action taken by the Liberals who had joined the new Government. The gathering was addressed by Lord Reading, Samuel, Maclean, Lord Grey and the Marquess of Crewe; and the first-named informed the assembled Liberals that their incapacitated leader, Lloyd George, was 'in complete accord with what is being done'. With virtual unanimity (there seems to have been one lone dissentient), the meeting agreed to support the new Government.

Samuel's speech on this occasion was naturally the most informative, and has already been alluded to more than once. In the course of his narrative, he described the suggestion that there had been 'a bankers' manoeuvre, an international scheme to overthrow the Labour Government', as 'stuff and nonsense'. Other points he made of particular interest and importance were (1) that at the three-party conference on August 20 there was complete agreement 'that no disservice to the country would be greater than to have an immediate general election', and (2) that the new Government was a temporary combination, but, in his view, it could not abandon the task which it had undertaken until it had seen it well on the way to completion. Both Samuel and Maclean paid warm tributes to MacDonald and Snowden. Both also emphasized that the Conservative leaders had completely refrained from raising any controversial political issues. After this gathering, the Liberal Parliamentary Party held a further meeting.

The Conservative meeting (also of Peers, M.P.s and candidates) was held at 11.30, and lasted three-quarters of an hour. Baldwin addressed the gathering, and gave his explanation of the decision to join the new Government and of the conditions upon which the Government was formed. In a reference to his interview with the King on the afternoon of August 23, he said: 'In the circumstances of that meeting and at that time there was nothing for anyone in my position to do but promise full co-operation to tide over the crisis, whatever it might involve.' Baldwin emphasized that there were two problems, first, that of balancing the Budget, and second, that of dealing with the balance of trade, which 'can only be dealt with by tariffs'. The new Government, he said, was formed for the purpose of passing legislation necessary to effect economy and to balance the Budget. 'The Government exists for no other purpose except such purposes as may fall to the lot of any Government while it is in office.' Baldwin added:

> Now I know as well as anybody here the difficulties and dangers of any form of combination, especially when there is a big matter of principle dividing us. In this matter of balancing the Budget we are all agreed in the Government, and we are all agreed in this call. After that our agreement ends and we part company.
>
> We then get to point 2 . . . the tariff, which we know is absolutely essential to complete the work which is being begun by the rectification of the Budgetary finance. When this Parliament dissolves, when the economies are carried and the Budget is balanced, you will then have a straight fight on tariffs and against the Socialist party.

A resolution supporting the Conservative leader 'in his decision to take part in the formation of a National Government to deal with the present financial emergency' was proposed by Lord Hail-

sham, seconded by Brigadier-General Sir Henry Page-Croft, supported by Colonel John Gretton, and passed unanimously.

The Parliamentary Labour Party, August 28

At 2 p.m. that day the Parliamentary Labour Party assembled.
The meeting was also attended by the National Executive of the
Labour Party and by the General Council of the Trades Union
Congress. The presence of the General Council was described in
Dalton's diary as 'an innovation, suggested by Uncle, to mark
unity'. According to the report in *The Times*, the members of the
Council took no part in the proceedings, which lasted nearly three
hours. A statement was made by Henderson to the press after-
wards, but no detailed report of the speeches was issued.

MacDonald, who had left for Lossiemouth the previous evening,
was not of course present: nor did Snowden attend. Both, according to *The Times*, sent apologies for absence, which were read.
Henderson, according to the *Manchester Guardian*, stated that
letters were read from both of them, and that the letters were
merely apologies for absence. The *Daily Herald* reported that
letters were read from MacDonald and Snowden intimating that
they were not going to attend the meeting:

> The Prime Minister's letter explained that he had only received
> notice of the meeting after making arrangements to leave London for
> Lossiemouth, and, therefore, much to his sorrow, he was unable to
> attend.
>   Mr Snowden's letter indicated that what there was to say on the
> policy of the new Government had been stated by the Premier in his
> letter to Labour M.P.'s. As the Party had determined its own policy,
> he saw no useful purpose in attending the meeting.

On the day after the meeting, the Press Association issued the
following:

> When the Prime Minister's attention was drawn to suggestions that
> he had ignored the meeting of the Parliamentary Labour Party, he
> said: 'There is no question of ignoring it at all. I am grieved beyond
> words that it was impossible for me to be present, but the letter of
> invitation did not, in fact, reach me until yesterday, and I had made
> arrangements to leave for Lossiemouth.'

J. H. Thomas neither attended nor wrote. Lord Sankey, however,
was present, and so was Malcolm MacDonald.

In Snowden's autobiography (p. 953) the following passage appears:

A meeting of the Parliamentary Labour Party was held on 28th August. Mr MacDonald did not attend it, nor did he send any message or appeal. This was naturally taken as an indication that he had finally separated himself from the Party and did not want its support. I do not know if Mr MacDonald had an invitation to attend this meeting. I was not aware of it until after it had been held. Labour members have since complained that Mr MacDonald and myself did not attend this meeting. Even had I known of it my presence would have been useless, for the day before the Trade Union Council and the Committee of the Parliamentary Labour Party had issued a public manifesto which made any change in their attitude to the National Government impossible.

This statement of Snowden's is in several respects remarkable. It implies, not only that he sent no letter of apology for absence, but also that he received no invitation. It is also strange that he should have been unaware that the meeting was to be held, in view of the announcements which had appeared in the press, one of which at least had even given the time and place. Equally odd is Snowden's expression of ignorance about whether or not MacDonald had an invitation, in view of the statement issued on MacDonald's behalf by the Press Association on the day after the meeting. Dalton, in his memoirs, suggests that Snowden's memory was clearly at fault. That may well have been the case, the lapse of memory extending even to the letter of apology which there is no doubt he wrote and equally no doubt was read to the meeting. But no such excuse can extend to the distinction he attempted to draw between himself and MacDonald. The passage can only be understood in its context, as part of a criticism of MacDonald for not consulting the Labour Party (or any member thereof) before agreeing to the formation of a National Government; and, as such, it is typical of much in Snowden's book and illuminating about his methods of controversy. Let it be assumed that Snowden forgot that MacDonald sent a letter, just as he forgot that he had sent one himself. The assertion that the absence of any message or appeal from MacDonald was naturally taken to mean that he had finally separated himself from the Party and did not want its support could with similar justification be applied to Snowden himself; and yet, from his own account, Snowden had certainly not separated himself from the Party.

Furthermore, there is plenty of evidence (including Henderson's own statement after the meeting in question) to show that the leaders of the Labour Party drew no such conclusion about Mac-Donald, whatever their hopes (or fears) may have been. There is the additional point that if, as was indeed the case, the Party's attitude towards the new Government had been determined, and publicly announced, prior to the meeting, then it would have been as useless for MacDonald to attend as Snowden declared it to be in his own case. If the *Daily Herald's* report was accurate, Snowden had not only said *in his letter* that it was useless for him to attend, but had also drawn attention to MacDonald's letter to Labour M.P.s as an adequate statement of the case for the new Government.

Henderson gave the meeting a narrative of the events of the previous fortnight. According to the *Manchester Guardian*, his review was 'studiously colourless and fair'. He was followed by Lord Sankey, who explained his reasons for joining the National Government. Dalton has recorded that Sankey's justification was partly based 'on the importance and imminence of the Second India Round-Table Conference'. According to the same source, Sankey said: 'They were none of them leaving the Labour Party. Nothing would ever drive *him* out.' It was afterwards reported (and Dalton also records) that Sankey began by saying that he believed Mac-Donald had saved the country, and that Henderson had saved the soul of the Labour Party. Accounts agree that Sankey was listened to respectfully and sympathetically. Among the speakers who followed, according to Dalton, were Lord Arnold, Dalton himself, Ben Tillett, and James Sexton. Malcolm MacDonald also spoke: according to the *Manchester Guardian*, he made a courageous defence of his father and the other Labour members of the National Government, but a reference he made to the Cabinet Economy Committee 'brought a sharp contradiction' from Henderson. This evidently related to the point, already dealt with, concerning the form of the proposals submitted by the Committee to the full Cabinet. Dalton's diary records: 'Malcolm MacDonald announces that he will go with his father, and attacks Uncle for going back on understandings and on "the report of the Committee of Five". This brings Uncle to his feet to deny the accusation and, in particular, to repeat that the Committee of Five made no report.' Henderson's point, presumably, was that the Committee had presented no formal report and made no specific recommendations.

All this discussion took place on a resolution approving that adopted by the joint meeting on August 26 and the manifesto issued on August 27. The resolution was passed with six or seven dissentients, one of whom, according to the press, was Malcolm MacDonald, the others all being members of the I.L.P. group. The Parliamentary Labour Party thus committed itself to vigorous opposition, and also, in a general sense at any rate, to the policy of the Joint Manifesto.

The meeting then proceeded to elect officers for the forthcoming session of Parliament. The Deputy Leader of the Party in its previous period of opposition had been J. R. Clynes. It was Clynes, however, who nominated Henderson as Chairman, and therefore as Leader, of the Party. There was no other nomination, and the proposition was carried with five or six dissentients, all members of the I.L.P. group. Henderson stated afterwards (and evidently told the meeting) that he had felt very strongly that Clynes should have advanced to the leadership, particularly in view of his own position as Secretary and Treasurer of the Party, but that 'forces had been too strong' for him. Dalton's diary for August 24 (evidently not written up on that day), recording the 'council of war' at Transport House that afternoon, said that Henderson was very unwilling to become Leader, 'but in the next few days he gradually yields to pressure from all sides.'

On Henderson's proposition, Clynes and Graham were unanimously elected Joint Deputy Leaders. The Party Whips were then reappointed *en bloc*; and arrangements were agreed upon for the election of a Parliamentary Executive Committee to replace, according to the usual party practice, the Consultative Committee which had functioned when the party was in office. It was also agreed that a further meeting of the Parliamentary Party should be held, probably on the day before Parliament met; and, according to Henderson's subsequent statement, it would then consider the recommendations of the Executive with regard to questions of policy. It may be noted, therefore, that the determination of actual Parliamentary policy was to remain in the hands of the Parliamentary Party. Henderson said in his press statement that the 'two outside committees' of the Labour Movement (the National Executive and the General Council of the T.U.C.) 'having had their position adopted by the Parliamentary Party', all three were now working for common action and in agreement. He added:

Exception has already been taken to the General Council figuring in these proceedings, but those who take that exception seem to forget how the Labour Party was created and how it is organized, and so I have no apology to make on that score. In fact, I have no hesitation in saying that so far as I am concerned I prefer more rather than less consultation between these bodies. . . .

Accounts of this meeting agree that none of the speeches were recriminatory, and that there was no bitterness in the references to MacDonald and Snowden. In reply to questions put to him when he made his subsequent statement to the press, Henderson said:

With regard to the National Executive, nobody has attempted to exclude the members of the Executive from this meeting, and Mr MacDonald as a member of the National Executive was invited but he did not come. No attempt has been made to exclude any person. They are still continuing to be members of the party, and no such attempt has yet been made. Mr MacDonald could have come just as Lord Sankey came, and so could Mr Thomas and Mr Snowden. Letters were read from both Mr MacDonald and Mr Snowden. They were merely apologies for absence. We have not heard from the others.

Some significance may have attached to Henderson's remark that no attempt to exclude MacDonald and his associates from the party had 'yet' been made. Reporting the joint meeting of August 26, the *Daily Express* said that no official consideration was given to the future position of MacDonald, Snowden and Thomas, adding: 'The general feeling was that it would be wiser to avoid any discussion of expulsions from the Socialist Party on the ground that efforts to maintain unity would be seriously prejudiced.'

The result of these party meetings on August 28 was, therefore, that the Liberal and Conservative Parties, as anticipated, had unanimously agreed to support the new Government, while the Labour Party had almost unanimously decided vigorously to oppose it, and to do so on a basis which diverged widely from the policy which the previous Cabinet had accepted in general terms but had failed to agree in implementing. Although there was still a loophole of which the Parliamentary Labour Party might take advantage if it wished, and felt strong enough, to pursue a course of discriminating opposition to the new Government, the hope that it might do so had dwindled almost to vanishing point.

o

CHAPTER XII

THE PRE-PARLIAMENT INTERLUDE

On the Eve of Parliament

The period of ten days which ensued before the meeting of Parliament was marked by (1) continuous Cabinet preparations, (2) the development of the Opposition campaign, (3) speculation about the Government's majority in the House of Commons, (4) indications of Labour support for the Government and Labour Party action against Labour supporters of the Government, and (5) signs of pressure for an early General Election in Conservative circles. There were two main governing circumstances. One was an easing of the financial situation: the other was uncertainty about popular reactions to economy cuts and increased taxation. The two factors were closely linked; for a tendency might well develop, stimulated by Opposition propaganda, to deny the gravity and even the reality of the financial crisis and to question the necessity for cuts and increased tax burdens.

The formation of the new Government had led to an immediate improvement in British credit abroad; the position of sterling strengthened; and on August 28 the Treasury announced that credits had been successfully negotiated for the Government in New York and Paris to a total of about £80 million. The Cabinet met, as arranged, on the afternoon of August 31, the meeting lasting about $3\frac{1}{2}$ hours. On September 1, it met again for just over three hours. On the 2nd, there were two meetings each of two hours' duration; and that day Parliament was summoned for September 8. On the afternoon of the 3rd there was another two-hour meeting, and the Cabinet then adjourned until the following Monday evening, when it met again for a final session before Parliament assembled. The Prime Minister issued a message to the nation in the following terms:

To-morrow Parliament will meet. The Government will ask from it, and is certain to obtain, a vote expressing its confidence. I appeal to the nation also to give us its confidence and to banish from its mind all notions that the crisis which confronted us was not a real and a dangerous one, or that we could have met it with any measure less vigorous than those we shall ask Parliament to sanction. We had to face it and all its potential consequences. We had to act with decision and speed: and the great thing we have already secured is that, instead of the House of Commons meeting to deal with a condition of financial collapse, it is meeting to deal with proposals to avert that grim possibility and to bring the country back to an even keel.

The completion of the Administration itself was carried through during these days. On September 3 most of the remaining Ministerial appointments were announced, and five further appointments were notified on the following day. The distribution of the Cabinet and other Ministerial offices between the parties was as follows: 31 Conservatives, 13 Liberals, 9 Labour and 1 non-party member of the previous Government. Four further Liberal appointments (mainly of Whips) were to be announced on September 14.[1]

OPPOSITION ATTITUDES

Meanwhile, there was intense political activity on the side of the Labour Opposition. Members of Parliament naturally spoke in their own constituencies. In this early phase, ex-Ministers and others were far from pursuing the same line. That also was not surprising. Those ex-Ministers who had supported the Prime Minister at the time of the final breach were obviously in an extremely difficult predicament. For the most part they confined themselves to expressions of disagreement with the formation of the National Government. In some instances, the chief ground advanced was doubt whether the proposals of the new Administration would conform to the general line upon which the Labour Government had been working.[2]

---

[1] The full list of Ministerial appointments is given in Appendix VI below.

[2] Lees-Smith, for example, said in a speech at Keighley (his constituency) on September 2: 'The Budget must most certainly be balanced, but I have grave doubts as to whether the new Government will balance it in the right way. The proposals which the late Government were considering were that it should be balanced partly by economies and partly by a very substantial sum from direct taxation. I doubt whether the new Government will adhere to the proposals for new taxation, and, in that case, the treaty between rich and poor which the late Cabinet were considering will be broken.' There proved to be no foundation for Lees-Smith's anxiety. Wedgwood Benn, at Aberdeen on August 29, said that he found it impossible to support the National Government: 'he had to consider what would be the probable course of its policy and administration, and experience showed that in such circumstances it was always the forces of reaction which triumphed.'

Their references to the Prime Minister and those associated with him were often strikingly complimentary, and they invariably disclaimed any intention to indulge in recrimination.[1] But that was also true of others, like Greenwood and Clynes, who had been on the other side when the break came.[2] That there were many leading figures in the Labour movement who took from the start a very different attitude towards MacDonald and his colleagues is plain enough from the Webb and Dalton diaries, but for the time being they refrained, for the most part, from expressing their emotions publicly. The official organ of the I.L.P., however, was more straightforward, and described as 'pernicious nonsense' the advice not to indulge in recrimination towards the Labour Members of the new Government.

Other ex-Ministers, during these same days, moved in varying degrees towards the position of the Joint Manifesto, which of course set the tone for Labour propaganda throughout the country. As a rule, they did not deny the reality and gravity of the financial crisis.[3] It would have been difficult for them to do so, anyhow, in

[1] Wedgwood Benn, for example, said (Aberdeen, August 29) that he desired to pay tribute to the great careers of the Prime Minister and Snowden, 'whatever difference of opinion there might be, no one would be found to doubt their sincerity and courage.' Lees-Smith (Keighley, September 2) said he hoped that during the coming controversy no word of bitterness would be addressed to MacDonald or Snowden: 'he profoundly disagreed with their decision to enter the National Government, but it was a sincere decision, and he recognized the fact that no two living men had done more than they had to create the Labour Party.' Herbert Morrison, in a speech at South Hackney (September 7) said, 'he had always had a high regard for the Prime Minister and for Mr Snowden, and he hoped none would forget in five minutes their great life's work for Labour and Socialism — work which would endure and be remembered when many lesser lights were forgotten. He could respect their courage and believe in their sincerity. But what they were doing was wrong. . . .'
[2] Addressing his constituents at Colne on September 6, Greenwood told them he felt very unhappy: 'I have parted company with men who were in the Labour movement when I was a child. Nothing will ever tempt me to say a word against the men who built up that movement. . . . Two weeks ago the break came between old comrades, and they separated because they took different views of the immediate situation. I am not going to widen the breach between old comrades. . . . I do not come to say a single unkind word about the Prime Minister, the Chancellor of the Exchequer, or the Secretary for the Dominions, or the two or three who have followed them.' Clynes, speaking at Manchester on August 27, said: 'I hope that our differences will be discussed without bitterness or abuse, and I am fully persuaded of the sincerity and honesty of the Prime Minister.' That this attitude was far from being confined to ex-Ministers may be illustrated by Harold J. Laski's article in the *Daily Herald* on August 29, in the course of which he wrote: 'No one, I think, doubts that Mr MacDonald, and those who have gone over with him to reaction have acted from the highest motives; their sincerity is not in question. What is at stake is their sagacity. . . .' Laski was to be one of MacDonald's bitterest critics.
[3] Pethick-Lawrence, Financial Secretary to the Treasury in the Labour Government, said in a letter which he circulated to the members of the Par-

the circumstances in which they were placed. But William Graham got near doing so, in an article for the *Daily Express* on August 31, when he referred to 'a financial crisis, in the reality of which only a fraction of the Labour movement believes'. Increasing emphasis was placed by ex-Ministers on the proposal to mobilize British capital invested abroad; a proposal which, so far as is known, was never mentioned during the Labour Cabinet's discussions, not even by the General Council of the T.U.C. And the twin themes of 'dictation by the bankers' and a 'bankers' ramp', which were being widely developed in the country, were given countenance in one form or another. Johnston, interviewed in *Forward*, said that 'the money-lenders and their political parties . . . demanded a cut of the unemployed benefit. They want humanity crucified on a cross of gold. We declined absolutely and resigned.' Pethick-Lawrence, in his letter to the Labour M.P.s, contended that it was wrong 'to lower the dignity and credit of the country as a whole by shaping our internal policy to accord with the behests of foreign financiers'. Addison (at Swindon, August 26) said: 'The pistol that had been put to our heads all the time was not held in the hands of the T.U.C., but in the hands of the controllers of the money market and, according to the reports made to us, the demands were very emphatic,' and (at Chesham, September 5) said that the demand to meet the financial crisis by reducing the amount paid to the unemployed was put forward by the Bank of England ('he was not satisfied on the evidence before them that that specific demand in that form was put by the foreign lenders'). Dalton, at Bishop Auckland, asserted (September 1) that 'the first Labour Government was destroyed by a Red Letter and the second by a Bankers' Order'. He had coined this remark in his speech at the meeting of the Parliamentary Labour Party on August 28, recorded it in his diary, and was evidently pleased with it.

liamentary Labour Party before its meeting on August 28: 'The financial situation was undoubtedly exceedingly grave, and the continued and increasing foreign withdrawal of deposits from our banking system was on a scale to threaten even the existence of the gold standard in this country. No Government could view such a position without the utmost alarm. It is true that the actual working of the gold system to-day is causing great havoc all over the world. But the consequences of going off it are incalculable and might involve a large number of our people in great individual sacrifices. Ministers were right, therefore, in my opinion, in putting up against such a course a most strenuous resistance.' Greenwood, in his Colne speech, said: 'The crisis was real, not an invention. It was a normal development of capitalist organization. During the last few weeks we have been, given society as it is, trembling on the very verge of national ruin.'

It is also of interest and some importance that the first public speech which seems to have been made by an ex-Minister (that of Addison at Swindon on August 26) gave what purported to be an account of the proceedings in the Labour Cabinet.[1] It was this disclosure, no doubt, which the *Manchester Guardian* had in mind when speaking (in its editorial on August 27) of 'the recrimination that is already taking place about what happened in the Cabinet'.

THE 'MANCHESTER GUARDIAN' AND THE OPPOSITION

The decision of the directing executives of the Labour movement to go into active opposition, and the near unanimity with which it had been accepted by the Parliamentary Labour Party, gave rise to speculation about both the new Government's majority in the House of Commons and the likely outcome of the eventual General Election. That the Government would have a majority adequate for its immediate purposes was never in doubt, but, as *The Times* commented on August 31, the majority would be none too large. On the face of things, MacDonald and his fellow Labourites in the new Cabinet seemed at first to be almost without support from the Labour Party in the country. 'It is pretty certain,' wrote the *Manchester Guardian* on August 27, 'that only the merest handful of Labour members — if, indeed, any at all — will support the Government.' The paper's Labour Correspondent reported the general opinion that 'exceedingly few' Labour members, 'perhaps none at all, outside the Ministry,' would side with MacDonald. The *New Statesman and Nation* (August 29) said that 'the whole Labour movement has almost as one man repudiated the new

---

[1] As reported in the *Manchester Guardian* on August 27, Addison said: 'A detailed scheme of economies or reliefs to the Exchequer, including the most dreadful curtailments to the extent of £56 million, had been accepted, subject to the overriding condition that sacrifices would be called for by those who were able to bear them, including those who were profiting by the fall in prices in the value of fixed dividends. . . . Subsequently we were told the sum thus provided was not enough, and further proposals were made which were entirely workable and which would have saved the Exchequer an additional large sum fully adequate to meet what was demanded. The total was not wrong. The total was enough with what was otherwise proposed — more than enough — to balance the Budget, but we were told that the way we were doing it was wrong. More must be provided in the way of further cutting down the amounts paid to the unemployed, in addition to the very heavy sacrifices which the other proposals meant in connection with unemployment insurance and the workers generally. I am not at liberty to tell you the prodigious demands that were made, but finally we were told that it would be acceptable to the Conservatives and the Liberals, provided it was acceptable to the bankers, that a further 10 per cent deduction must be made from unemployment pay.'

National Government and its policy'. Beatrice Webb (in her diary for September 2) wrote of 'the swift, cold and practically unanimous repudiation of MacDonald, Snowden and Thomas by the entire Labour world'. 'The Labour Party', she concluded, 'emerges stronger — far stronger and more united than they were three weeks ago.'[1]

On August 25, as we have seen, the *Manchester Guardian* had considered it impossible for the Labour ex-Ministers to oppose the entire economy scheme, and had hoped that the Labour Party would extend a measure of co-operation to the new Government. Its assumption was quickly proved unsound: its hopes completely shattered. The decision of the joint meeting of the Labour executives on August 26 was described as 'momentous'. The *Guardian's* editorial analysis of the position of the Labour Opposition (on the 27th) is important both in itself and because of this newspaper's later attitude. Though inclined to despair, the *Guardian* still pleaded for Opposition restraint and even for a measure of Opposition co-operation. It was alarmed at the prospect of a General Election provoked, as it feared might be the case, by Labour exploitation of unpopular economy measures.[2] Next day (August 28)

[1] Op. cit., pp. 285–6.
[2] The more important passages in this editorial were as follows: 'One could have understood a reluctance on the part of the Labour Party to give formal support to the new Government if it had been accompanied by a suspension of judgment on the measures that are to be presented. That would have been a normal reaction to the situation. After all, the whole of the Cabinet supported the economy scheme, with the exception of the reduction of insurance benefit, and on that single point the forces were almost equally divided. The party might well have said that as ex-Ministers were committed to the economy scheme and recognized its necessity the decent thing would be to judge of the proposals on their merits when they were produced. Whether the ex-Ministers would have preferred this course one can only conjecture. If they did, they have been overborne by the weight of mass feeling in the party, which has brushed aside all the finer shades of tactics. It is another revelation of the commonplace that Labour is only happy when in opposition. . . . It is a rather astonishing sidelight on the irresponsibility which animates the party. The Labour decision implies that the party condemns the idea of a coalition for a specific end which the existing Government found itself unable from its internal weakness to accomplish. On a minor matter of politics or on a highly controversial one there might be room for argument. But when the issue at stake is the financial stability of the country one despairs that a great party can show itself so blind and reckless. It is now being said that the issue was not the saving of British credit but a sinister manoeuvre by British and foreign bankers to destroy a Labour Government and reduce the British standard of living. If that were true it would mean that two of the members of the Cabinet Committee of Five were entirely deluded from the beginning, and that the whole Cabinet argued for hours on successive days in ignorance of essential facts. A defence on such grounds has a weak sound, and is made no better by the suggestion that Mr MacDonald and Mr Snowden were active dupes who misled their colleagues. The fact is, of course, that

it reported the joint Labour Manifesto under the headlines, 'Labour Declares War. Root-and-Branch attack on the Economy Plans. Working Up to the Election.' The Manifesto compelled the *Manchester Guardian* to recognize that the policy of the T.U.C. had been adopted, and that the ex-Cabinet Ministers, by implication, disowned all responsibility for the economy proposals they might have agreed to in Cabinet. Editorially, it expressed its impatience. It pointed out that 'the idea of party co-operation, and finally of national government, arose in the first instance from the knowledge that a financially sound policy would be liable to unscrupulous electoral attack', and said that it was 'only too evident' that the Labour movement was about to lend itself to an attack of precisely that nature. The greatest consequential disadvantage, in the paper's view, was that the Government would have an incentive to prolong its own life. A dissolution of Parliament would involve the risk that the Government's work would be largely or wholly undone. And the *Guardian* considered it very undesirable that a Coalition Government should continue after the crisis which gave it birth had passed.

Dealing with the three-party meetings on the 28th, the *Manchester Guardian* said next day that

Ministry and Opposition are, therefore, based on purely party lines,

Ministers were under no illusion, that they were impressed with the gravity of the financial position, immediate and prospective, and were firmly agreed that the Budget must be balanced. . . . An enormous responsibility will rest upon Mr Henderson and his Front Bench. The natural instinct of the Labour rank-and-file, once again in opposition, all restraints removed, will be to attack the economy proposals all along the line, to treat all cuts in wages and salaries, all reform of the insurance system, all interferences with social services, as equally offensive. It will be so easy to propound an alternative scheme of stiff taxation on the rich and (with an eye on an early election) to build up a reputation as defenders of the rights of the weak and iron hammers of the oppressors of the poor. . . . A Labour Opposition could be so guided as to shed no scrap of its attachment to Labour principle and yet to recognize that the Government it is attacking is performing, from a sense of duty, a highly distasteful task. The front for criticism of the ordinary sort will be wide, but the Labour Party can surely show itself big enough and tolerant enough to realize that this is a purely temporary and passing phase in our politics from which all parties will be glad to free themselves. The cohesion and loyalty of the Labour Party have been amply demonstrated; it can lose nothing in the estimation of the electorate by restrained Parliamentary conduct and by a large measure of courageous co-operation with the Government in putting through its principal financial measures. There will be room for reasoned argument on details and for the presentation of alternative proposals. The worst thing that could happen to British politics would be that the next few months should be turned of set design into an electioneering campaign leading up to the miserable climax of an appeal to the country on the crudest and most inflammatory grounds. From that only the Labour Party can save us.'

and the Government is not really a national but a coalition Government, formed by the almost exact fusion of two parties against one.

Much concern about this situation was expressed:

> It is an alignment which plays into the hands of the Labour Party, and it does not appear likely that that Party will be over scrupulous about the use it will make of its opportunity.

The *Manchester Guardian* was anxious, therefore, that the new Government should get through its work as expeditiously as possible. 'It bids fair, under assiduous Labour Party misrepresentation, to be the most unpopular Government of modern times.' The man in the street, the editorial explained,

> will have no real gratitude to a Government which has rescued him from dangers which he only dimly apprehends and which the Labour Party is prepared to tell him were mostly imaginary. Under such circumstances the odium attached to the Government will be an ever-increasing one, and the longer it puts off an appeal to the country the greater will be the chances of a clear Labour majority after the next election.

That prospect the paper viewed with great apprehension because

> the instinctive reaction of the Labour Party to the crisis has been to assert the absolute sanctity of wages and unemployment benefit, to say that whatever and whoever else suffered the working classes shall not suffer at all. The issue has been officially represented by the Labour movement as being not between solvency and bankruptcy but as being simply between rich and poor. That is a dangerous doctrine.

The *Manchester Guardian* had quickly moved from fear of a General Election provoked by root-and-branch Labour opposition to advocacy of an Election at the earliest possible moment because of the likelihood that the Labour campaign would become increasingly effective. The *Economist*, it may be noted, fully shared the *Guardian's* apprehensions about the efficacy of Labour propaganda, but, from the outset, set its face against an early General Election. The prospect of such an Election, it declared on August 29, was 'disastrous'. The following week (September 5) it maintained that the Labour Opposition's attitude made it all the more desirable that the National Government should remain in office and should not run the risk of an Election. The *Economist* was particularly anxious that party differences within the Government

— it was doubtless thinking primarily of the tariff issue — should be kept in abeyance. 'Until calm weather is restored, the helm of State should remain in firm, responsible hands.'

The fears expressed by these two Liberal journals had not been shared by Samuel in his speech to the Liberal Party meeting on August 28. Expressing great disappointment at the attitude of the official organization of the Labour Party, he said:

> Taking up a partisan and class attitude, they would fall into a great error of judgment, the same mistake which the T.U.C. Council made when they plunged the country into the general strike. The nation would not have it, and when he spoke of the nation he included the whole body of the working classes. The typical British working man knew quite well when it was necessary to adopt a national rather than a class attitude. This was one of those occasions when those who thought they would succeed by an appeal to more ignoble methods would find that they were greatly mistaken.

However, the apprehensions of the *Manchester Guardian* concerning the outcome of a delayed General Election were rather strikingly reinforced from the other side on August 31, when William Graham, in his *Daily Express* article, declared, on the 'confident assumption' that the new Government would have to continue until the Budget of 1932:

> What is described as the record of the Labour Government will be speedily forgotten; and to the present crisis there will probably be little reference long before Xmas. Partner in another Coalition, nothing can now save Liberalism as an independent force. . . . Conservatives will be denied the opportunity of proceeding with the major items in their programme; electorally they will suffer most because of the terribly disagreeable things, affecting millions of the electorate, that the National Government must do. Nor will that tendency be materially influenced by the attitude of Labour in virtually united Opposition. In an electorate approaching thirty millions there are now great, but essentially simple, mass movements; the trained students of politics and economics and the long view are in a hopeless minority. . . . The next election will be fought, not by a Labour Government on an admittedly difficult defensive, but by a Labour movement united and eager. . . . At one stroke, without an election, and with time to prepare for an election on unusually favourable ground, they (the Labour leaders and members) have been relieved of their anxieties. Yesterday they dreaded a contest: to-day they are almost within sight of their clear majority in the British House of Commons.

In the House on September 8, 1931, W. J. Brown (then sitting as an Independent Labour member, and a spokesman of the extreme Left) said of Graham's statement that he did not think he had ever read a more disgraceful public pronouncement. It was certainly candid. In the same debate, Churchill expressed the view that it was not merely candid but even brazen. Graham was counting on the short memories of the electors; but there were many others in the Labour Party who were confident of electoral victory no matter how soon the Election might come, and this feeling was to be a factor of major importance in the following weeks.

LABOUR SUPPORTERS OF THE GOVERNMENT

When writing of 'purely party lines' and 'the almost exact fusion of two parties against one', the *Manchester Guardian* implied that the Prime Minister and his Labour colleagues in the new Government were a negligible element in the situation. And, unlike Samuel, it drew no distinction between the Labour Party as an organization and the general body of Labour voters and sympathizers. Under the impetus provided by the General Council of the T.U.C., the Labour Party machine had acted with great promptitude and no little skill. Within the Labour movement, it had no organized challenge to meet; and its decision to go into vigorous opposition, reinforced by the disciplinary powers and other forms of pressure at its disposal, gave it what seemed overwhelmingly decisive influence. Graham, in his *Express* article, had gone so far as to describe the new Government as 'a coalition in which there is now no Labour element'. Appearances, however, were deceptive. Indeed, the action taken by MacDonald and Snowden, the two men who had been the outstanding leaders of the Party, was bound to have very considerable effect upon its members. Opinion in the Labour movement was in fact genuinely and deeply divided; and that division was inevitably found in the ranks of the Parliamentary Party itself. Very large numbers of Labour men and women found themselves confronted by a conflict of loyalties. On the one hand, there was loyalty to and confidence in the former leaders of the Party, approval of or sympathy with the action they had taken, and concern for what was believed to be the national interest: on the other side, deep-rooted loyalty to the Party, and, in many instances, involvement in its organization. The fact that the phase of National Government was expected to be brief, and the consequential hope that the breach would soon be repaired, was, more often than not, the determinant of the choice made. The most congenial course was to stay put.

At first, Labour support of the new Administration seemed to be confined to the Labour members of the new Cabinet and those other members of the previous Government who subsequently accepted appointments in the new one. Lord Amulree's retention of his office as Secretary of State for Air has already been noted. On August 29, Sir William Jowitt, in a letter to his constituency Labour Party, announced that he had been invited and had agreed to continue as Attorney-General. Malcolm MacDonald had at an early stage declared his intention to support the National Government, and his name appeared in the second list of appointments. On September 1, it was announced that Mr Craigie Aitchison, Lord Advocate for Scotland in the Labour Government, had decided to back the new administration, and he was appointed to the same office in it. Next day, the second Labour back-bencher, Sir Ernest Bennett, announced his support. *The Times* that day (September 2) stated that the Prime Minister had received letters from several prospective Labour candidates telling him that they refused to follow the official decision of the party. It said that many of those members who had gone into opposition had done so because they did not want to cut themselves off from the official Labour Party, but that there had been much searching of heart and hope that the existing differences would soon be forgotten.[1] *The*

---

[1] On September 1, the *Daily Herald* published a letter from Sir Ben Turner, M.P., to the Prime Minister, in the course of which he wrote: 'It must be a deep wrench to you, as it is to many of us, to be unable to act in co-operation as in the past, but I think that time will be the best factor in bringing us all together again. . . . I am sure no one can utter a word of blame or condemnation for either you or Snowden having taken the line you have with the knowledge that you must possess, and the feelings that you have expressed regarding the danger to the nation. Of course I am unable to depart from the position of the Labour Party, but I hope that the Party as well as both you and Snowden will retain personal acquaintances and friendships.' The *Manchester Guardian* (on August 31) published a report of a speech made by Joshua Ritson, Labour M.P. for Durham, in which he said: 'I am not going to stand here and condemn Mr MacDonald. Mr MacDonald undoubtedly feels that he is right. You remember he was right during the war, and whatever we may say now no man suffered more than he did for what he felt was right then. We feel that he has been rushed into believing that the finances of the country were in such a state that he would have to take very drastic measures. That being his view, he has acted upon it, knowing what it would cost, and when a man is prepared to lose all that he has in the sense of fellowship, friendship and the leadership, I am not going to stand here and coldly condemn. But the Labour Party will have to go on. We have an able leader in Mr Henderson.'

Times estimated that about ten or a dozen Labour members of Parliament would support the Government, in which case its majority would be between fifty and sixty. These included another ex-Minister, G. M. Gillett, whose name was also to appear in the second list of appointments to the new Administration. On September 3, according to *The Times*, the Government were pleased at the support they were continuing to receive from members of the Labour Party. That day it was announced that two more back-benchers, Holford Knight and J. A. Lovat-Fraser, had declared their support. With the adhesion of D. S. T. Rosbotham, the Labour member for Ormskirk, it was known by September 7 that at least 11 Labour M.P.s would vote with the National Government; and it was believed that half a dozen or more would abstain from voting. *The Times* that day reckoned that the Government could probably count on a total of 336 as against 276 for the Opposition, although there would be absentees, of course, on both sides. These figures did not include the Speaker, the Chairman of Ways and Means, and the Deputy Chairman, who do not take part in divisions. The Speaker was a Conservative; the other two were Labour members.

During these days before Parliament assembled, action had begun to be taken in the constituencies against Labour members and supporters of the Government. The Prime Minister wrote to the Secretary of the Seaham Divisional Labour Party after the formation of the new Government, explaining the grounds of his action, saying that he was aware of the pressure that would be brought to bear upon his friends in Seaham and placing himself unreservedly in their hands. The Executive Committee of the Seaham Party met on August 29 and unanimously passed a resolution recommending the full delegate meeting (summoned for September 12) to oppose the National Government and to ask MacDonald to resign his seat. The Prime Minister, who resided at Hampstead, was a member of the Labour Party there. On August 31 the newspapers announced that the General Council of the Hampstead Labour Party had 'expelled' him. In reply to the Seaham Party Executive's resolution, MacDonald wrote that he would not, under any circumstances, carry out his intention to put himself in the local Party's hands, 'whilst it involves the desertion of a duty, which I consider to be imperative, to protect the great mass of wage-earners in this country from a serious disaster.' It was reported on September 7 that the Blackhall Miners' Lodge (in the Seaham division) had passed a resolution condemning the decision of the Divisional Executive to recommend that MacDonald should be asked to resign. So matters rested when Parliament assembled.

J. H. Thomas, after he had joined the new Government, was called upon to resign from it by the executive committee of the N.U.R. He wrote in reply refusing to do so, and tendered his resignation as Political Secretary of the Union. The executive met on August 31 (with Thomas present) and accepted his resignation, but ruled that he was not entitled to his pension. *The Times*, in reporting this next day, also reported that the Derby (No. 2) branch of the N.U.R. had adopted a resolution assuring Thomas of their 'full confidence'. On September 5 Thomas attended a meeting of the general council of the Derby Labour Party, which was also addressed by his Labour colleague in the representation of the two-member Derby constituency, W. R. Raynes, who had decided to oppose the National Government. By 103 votes to 48 a resolution was carried declaring that membership of the National Government was incompatible with membership of the Labour Party, and withdrawing the party's endorsement of Thomas as prospective candidate for the constituency. After the meeting Thomas stated that he would contest Derby whenever an election came 'as an independent Labour man'. The existence of substantial minorities in both these cases (which soon became clearer in the case of Seaham) is indicative of the differences of opinion in Labour ranks.

As already noted, Snowden had decided not to seek re-election, and had informed his chief Cabinet colleagues of that decision before the crisis came. Late on the night of August 22, in view of the likelihood of the Labour Cabinet's resignation, Snowden wrote a letter conveying his decision to the Chairman of the Colne Valley Divisional Labour Party, and this was published in the press on the 29th. The executive of that party met on that day, and while expressing appreciation of Snowden's valuable services, deprecated his action in joining the National Government, and approved the official decisions of the Labour Party. In certain other cases of supporters of the National Government, resolutions were passed by the local Labour parties (usually unanimously) either calling upon the M.P. concerned to resign his seat or terminating the candidature of the M.P. or candidate. On September 2, for example, the East Fulham Labour Party unanimously decided to terminate the candidature of H. B. Usher, MacDonald's personal secretary, who had notified the party on August 28 of his intention to give full support to the Prime Minister and had placed himself unreservedly in the Party's hands.

Among well-known members of the Labour Party who signified their support of the new Government in these early days was Clifford Allen (afterwards Lord Allen of Hurtwood), the former Chairman of the I.L.P.[1] An excellent illustration of the state of mind of many members who were far from satisfied with the official line of the Party is to be found in the article entitled 'Some Questions for the Labour Opposition Chiefs' which appeared in *Forward* on September 5, and was written by Joseph F. Duncan, Secretary of the Scottish Farm Servants' Union. The article ended with the words, 'in such a general salvation it is only right we should search for a scapegoat to offer as a sacrifice.'[2]

CONSERVATIVE AND LIBERAL OPINION

If the superficial near-unity of the Labour Party concealed wide divergencies of view, the apparent unanimity of the Conservatives was also, though much less, deceptive. No open hostility on that side to the National Government was expressed; but desire for a speedy termination of the experiment scarcely hid the feeling in some quarters that it could and should have been avoided. Amery's letter to *The Times* on August 28 provides an illustration: in the course of this communication he said that a number of his colleagues, including the leader of the party,

> inspired by the most patriotic motives, and for reasons which seemed convincing to them, have now agreed to join a so-called National Cabinet, on the basis of postponing a remedy for the real crisis, in order to patch up the Budget situation.
>
> We are told this is to be for a few weeks only, and that then the members of the new Government will 'bow to partners' and rejoin their respective parties for the battle on the main issue. Experience shows how difficult it is for a Cabinet to deal with one issue only. New issues arise which must be dealt with, and which each tend to justify the prolongation of a Government's existence and to consolidate it.

Amery has told us in his memoirs that he was unconvinced that Baldwin could not have insisted on including a tariff or formed his

[1] See Allen's letter to the *Manchester Guardian*, September 5, 1931.
[2] See Note at the end of this Chapter.

own Government; and in his diary he actually wrote: 'even Neville (Chamberlain) loses his head, and sells the pass in the first fortnight of serious crisis.'[1]

There was a significant passage in Lord Hailsham's speech at the party meeting on August 28, when he said:

> I have heard — not here but outside — a suggestion that it would have been better for us to stand aside and to claim, as we could have claimed, to form a Government of our own. I am not going to discuss whether that would have been electorally wise or electorally foolish. It was not a possible alternative, for this reason — that whether we attempted to pass the economies first and dissolve afterwards or to dissolve first and pass the economies afterwards the process must have taken several weeks, and, as our Leader has told us, it was a matter not of weeks but of days and ultimately of hours within which the situation was to be retrieved.

Later in his address, Hailsham said that there was going to be an election soon, how soon Baldwin could not tell them, but he (Hailsham) hoped it would be within a couple of months or so.

The situation in regard to an election was summed up by the Parliamentary Correspondent of the *Manchester Guardian* on August 31 in these terms:

> It is among Liberals especially that there is least expectation, or, for that matter, desire, of an early general election. Sir Donald Maclean gave a strong hint yesterday that the task might take longer than some people expected, and that if more time were needed it would have to be given.[2] One must suppose that he expressed also the judgment of his Liberal colleagues in the Cabinet. In the Cabinet it is the Conservative and Labour Ministers who have most stressed the shortness of the partnership and the nearness of the dissolution. One finds the same thing in the rank and file. It is Conservatives especially who talk of an early general election.

TRADES UNION CONGRESS

The reassembly of Parliament almost coincided with the opening of the Trades Union Congress at Bristol. The latter started on

---

[1] Op. cit., p. 61.

[2] The text of this passage in Maclean's speech (August 29), as reported, was as follows: 'Nobody can tell how long this Government will be in office, but it was well to remember that the objective was the thorough re-establishment of British credit. If that took longer than was at present anticipated by some people the nation would insist on the necessary time being given to it. When that is accomplished then let the nation have the choice, without let or hindrance, to decide which party shall be its future leaders.'

Monday, September 7. On the same day the second session of the Indian Round-Table Conference formally began. At Bristol, the chief events that day were Arthur Hayday's presidential address and Citrine's long statement on the financial crisis.

The main points of Citrine's review have already been dealt with; the President's speech deserves more than passing notice. Hayday not only expressed unqualified opposition to the new Government and its policy: he also gave unqualified endorsement to the 'Bankers' ramp' theory:

> Political and financial influences of a sinister character working behind the scenes have taken advantage of the difficulties arising from the policy pursued by private banking interests, which are not subject to any public control, to dictate to the British Government and people a fundamental change in national policy. Secret forces have broken the Labour Government. These same forces have created a new Government without the authority of Parliament or the people by methods equivalent to dictatorship. The policy of the new Government has likewise been dictated. . . .
>
> At the bidding of irresponsible and uncontrolled financial interests whose very existence is hardly known to the public the social policy of this country which has set an example to the rest of the world is to be violently reversed. These recent events have revealed the existence of an imperious international financial combination possessing the power to bring to its knees even a country like ours, wealthy, solvent, and productive; and to threaten it with financial ruin unless it agreed to change its policy and curtail its social expenditure. Political parties, with the exception of our own, have come under the dominance of finance along with the Government of the day. The Labour Government was destroyed by it. It has brought about a financiers' revolution more ruthless and complete than a military dictatorship could accomplish. . . .
>
> It is a matter of the gravest significance that behind the scenes, where the destruction of the Labour Government was planned, the one inescapable demand which the Labour Cabinet was required to meet was the reduction of unemployment benefits. No other proposal, no alternative plan, that the Labour Cabinet could have formulated would have been accepted as an alternative to this demand.

Note

Extracts from Joseph F. Duncan's article in
Forward (September 5, 1931)

While we are all getting ready to loose the excommunications

P

perhaps someone who knows what it is all about might give us some facts to go upon. So far we have got an ample supply of rhetoric, but a tantalizingly meagre output of facts upon which those of us who have to find our way from newspaper reports find it very difficult to come to any understanding. The first point on which I would like to have some enlightenment is how far the members of the Labour Government are satisfied that there was a financial emergency which required to be tackled immediately. I was under the impression from the reports of the overtime being worked by the Labour Cabinet that the members were engaged in the task of finding some way of pegging sterling and of balancing the Budget. Tom Johnston seemed to be under the same impression, and he was a member of the Cabinet. If I understand him aright, the Cabinet went together along the road to drastic economies, which would have entailed burdens on the workers, but the members parted company when it came to the question of reducing unemployment benefit. . . . I think we are entitled to some plain and unequivocal statement from the members of the late Cabinet as to the nature and extent of the financial crisis they attempted to surmount. If it is to be passed over in the offhand way that Graham handles it, as if it were entirely a matter of a game in party politics, what some of us will want to know is why the late Cabinet called the Tory and Liberal leaders into consultation. That appeared to those of us who had only the barest of newspaper reports to guide us, an attempt to form a temporary coalition to ensure credits from America, and to enable an emergency budget to be passed as speedily as possible. Unless there was a very grave crisis which had to be overcome without delay, there was no justification for the Labour Cabinet attempting to arrange its policy with the Tories and Liberals before it was submitted to the Labour Party as a whole. . . .

I suppose I may as well put my head on the block right away and say that I do not recognize anything sacred about the amount of unemployment benefit which is paid at any particular time. . . . I want to know where the cuts were to fall, and what the nature of the 'contributions' the workers were to be called upon to pay, as Tom Johnston puts it, before I can say how heinous was the reduction of unemployment benefit in comparison. . . .

What I would like to know is who delivered the ultimatum which roused the Labour Cabinet and induced those who were prepared to agree to a cut in unemployment benefit to resign with their fellows rather than be dictated to. That is the crucial point on which definite information is essential. If those who refused to bow to such dictation can assure us that the financiers were not merely stating the conditions on which they would lend, but were also dictating the means the Government of this country should take to balance its budget then the sooner the facts are made known to the public the better. The propaganda value of such material in the long run would compensate largely for the muddle we are in now. But we must have something more than vague statements about Bankers' ramps and other fudge of that kind. Finally, I should like to know whether any attempts were made to find out the possibilities of alternative ways of meeting the crisis (that is, assuming there was one!) by adopting the proposals vaguely outlined in that wordy Manifesto issued by the National Executives. Pethick-Lawrence gives definition to the only suggestion which appears to apply to the immediate crisis, the proposal to mobilize foreign securities. That, of course, could only have been adopted if the Tories and Liberals agreed. Were they asked, and if so, what did they reply?

CHAPTER XIII

THE NATIONAL GOVERNMENT AND THE HOUSE OF COMMONS

SEPTEMBER 8, 1931

The proceedings in the House of Commons on September 8 began with an episode which not only aroused immediate protests and much subsequent adverse comment but also indicated that the full power of the Labour party machine both outside and inside Parliament was to be exerted upon Labour M.P.s. The Speaker announced that he had received letters from Sir Robert Young and Mr (afterwards Sir) Herbert Dunnico resigning their offices as Chairman and Deputy-Chairman respectively of Ways and Means. He read the letters in turn. The essential part of Sir Robert Young's communication was as follows:

On 26th August, as a result of the changed political situation, I wrote a letter to my constituency and said:

'The Chairman of Ways and Means is appointed for the duration of Parliament. It is, however, a Party nomination but subject to the approval of the House of Commons. I was appointed by unanimous consent. Nevertheless should the Prime Minister on the one side, or the Labour Party on the other side, think I should resign I shall certainly do so.'

I sent a copy of the letter to the Prime Minister, the Leader of the Opposition, and to the executive of the Amalgamated Engineering Union. The Prime Minister did not ask me to resign. My trade union executive, however, expressed the opinion that I should tender my resignation and with that opinion, I understand, many Members of the party to which I belong, agree. That being so I feel, and I am sure the House will sympathize with my feeling, that were I to remain Chairman my position would be uncomfortable, invidious, and untenable. I therefore humbly tender my resignation to the House.

Dunnico wrote as follows:

Two years ago, with the approval of all parts of the House, I was elected Deputy-Chairman of Ways and Means.

I am now informed that the Opposition party has withdrawn that approval.

The duties of the Chair are difficult, exacting, and arduous even when they are exercised with the consent and support of all parties. In the absence of that general support the duties of the office could not be performed satisfactorily.

I must, therefore, humbly ask you to tender to the House my resignation of the office to which I was appointed....

The Prime Minister thereupon moved the appointment of Sir Dennis Herbert (later Lord Hemingford) to be Chairman of Ways and Means, and this was subsequently agreed to, but not before two points of order had been raised concerning Sir Robert Young's letter, Mr (later Lord) Hore-Belisha asked if any steps would be taken to secure that hon. Members accepting office in the service of the House should in future be responsible to the House and not to outside bodies; and Sir Basil Peto enquired whether it would be in order for him to move that the House do not accept Sir Robert's resignation, in view of the reason alleged for it, namely, that a certain body unconnected with the House had intervened. The Speaker, however, answered in the negative.

The debate which followed took place on what was in reality, though not in form, a motion of confidence in the new Government. The procedure adopted was as unprecedented as the circumstances in which the House met. The difficulties arose from the need to secure a vote of confidence from the House, and to make urgency procedural arrangements, before proceeding to submit a Supplementary Budget to a Committee of Ways and Means. What happened was that the Prime Minister first presented a message from the King under the Royal Sign Manual, which was read by the Speaker, as follows:

The present condition of the National finances, in the opinion of His Majesty's Ministers, calls for the imposition of additional taxation, and for the effecting of economies in public expenditure. His Majesty recommends the matter to the consideration of his faithful Commons, and trusts they will make provision accordingly.

Some argument followed, in the course of which MacDonald explained that the Government desired to know at the end of the day whether or not they had the confidence of the House, and the Speaker said that he proposed to treat the Motion for setting up the

Committee of Ways and Means as a Reply to the Royal Message, allowing a full and wide discussion. The Prime Minister then moved that the House should resolve itself on the following Thursday into a Committee to consider the Ways and Means for raising the supply to be granted to His Majesty.

MacDonald opened with an explanation of the financial crisis and a statement of the case for the formation of the National Government. In the course of his remarks he said that his view was, and remained unmoved, that the previous Government, in co-operation with other parties, should have faced the crisis. He also dealt at some length with the talk about a bankers' plot, and emphasized the purely advisory function of the bankers:

> I want to impress upon the House the fact that these transactions as regards the State were precisely of the same nature and conducted in precisely the same way as any loan transactions conducted in private life between companies or between individuals and banking companies. I wish to state, specifically and emphatically, and this has been reported to my colleagues before, that never in the whole process of the negotiations carried on by the Chancellor of the Exchequer and myself, with the approval of the Government, and reported to it immediately after each interview, did the banks interfere with political proposals. They simply confined themselves to giving us expert advice as to the effect of the proposals on the possible yield of the loan.

The central theme of the Prime Minister's speech was the need for immediate action in the circumstances which had arisen on August 23:

> Hon. Members who are representing Labour but not more adequately than I am and than I shall be doing, have to remember what would have happened if nothing had been done to avert what was maturing over our heads. Sterling, as I say, would have gone off the gold standard without management or control. It would have tumbled.

It is of considerable importance to note that in his speech Mac-Donald made no disclosures about the discussions in the Labour Cabinet. He made one or two passing allusions to the Cabinet Economy Committee without raising controversial points; and he also referred (as already noted) to the communication of the various schemes, by instructions, to the representatives of the other two parties.

Henderson, who followed, began with references to his long

collaboration with MacDonald. He said that the personal aspect of the case appealed to him very strongly:

> By the change that has taken place we have lost three if not four of those who have been in the very forefront of the battle, and who, especially in two cases, have been associated in the building up of the movement.

He then turned to the National Government, and maintained that 'neither by its composition nor the manner of its formation' was it entitled so to call itself: 'We have the largest party on this side of the House, notwithstanding the baker's dozen of defections which have taken place. . . .'

The Opposition leader then plunged into an account of the proceedings in the Cabinet Economy Committee, and was soon challenged by Ernest Brown for doing so. Continuing to deal with what he had said either in the Committee or in the Cabinet itself, Henderson criticized MacDonald for not having called together or met his party. He incidentally admitted, as already noted, that the whole Cabinet were agreed about seeking the co-operation of other parties. The next part of the speech was a contention that the crisis was largely due to the effects of propaganda, national and international, but especially Conservative, about Socialist extravagance; and Henderson proceeded to quote the *Daily Mail* for August 1929 in proof of a further contention that the unsatisfactory Budgetary position was largely due to the previous Conservative administration. This was followed by an attack on the Liberals for having urged further expenditure upon the Labour Government; and a criticism of Baldwin for a speech at Worcester on August 3 in which the Conservative leader had said that, although the Conservatives were prepared to support the Government in restoring financial equilibrium, the responsibility was the Government's. Henderson then came back to the discussions in the Cabinet Economy Committee and the Cabinet, stressing the point that he had from the early stages reserved his decision until he could see 'the complete picture', and also emphasizing the provisional acceptance of the £56 million of economies. Although twice at this period of his speech he said he had to be careful because of Ernest Brown, Henderson none the less went on to make his assertion about the report to the Cabinet that the economies had to be increased by from £25 million to £30 million, which led to

the interventions by MacDonald and Samuel already dealt with
(p. 115). His next point was that in the Cabinet on the Saturday
morning (August 22) he had, in effect, expressed the view that
resignation was desirable, and Henderson proceeded to give an explanation of his reasons. He first dealt at length with the Labour
Party's attitude towards provision for the unemployed, in order to
establish that the question of reduction in the benefits was a major
issue for the Party. His further remarks in this connection related
to the joint meeting on August 20 and to Snowden's alleged statement about cuts in unemployment benefit (see above, pp. 90–1
and p. 96). In passing, Henderson apparently accepted completely
what MacDonald had said about the bankers, and said:

> I am not laying down any complaint about the bankers. I would not
> dream of doing so. I think the banker is just like anyone else. If he has
> to find money for me, he ought to be in a position to lay down his
> conditions.

Next morning *The Times* said that Conservative and Liberal
opinion was that the Prime Minister had taken care not to widen
the breach between his former colleagues and himself, but that
even some members of the Opposition regretted that Henderson
had laid so much emphasis on the party position rather than on the
crisis itself. Henderson's speech was described as 'mainly an
account of what had happened at meetings of the late Cabinet and
its sub-committees, and was clearly thought by many to be in
questionable taste'. The Parliamentary Correspondent of the *Manchester Guardian* said that MacDonald 'was more successful in
illuminating the nature and possibilities of the crisis than anyone
else; and after all that is the gravamen of the whole business.'

> Even from the Government side he was the only person who forced
> attention all the time to the meaning of a catastrophic collapse of
> the pound. It was a point which Mr Henderson chose completely to
> ignore. . . . Nearly all his efforts were directed to justifying his and
> his colleagues' rupture with the Prime Minister, and this is not of
> palpitating interest to anybody now.

The *Economist* (September 12) wrote that MacDonald's speech
was 'as accurate in detail as it was forceful in its simple lucidity. In
very trying circumstances the Prime Minister was at his best. . . .'
Churchill, who followed Henderson in the debate, said that during
the latter's speech he had 'felt at times quite shy . . . as if I were

listening to a family quarrel'. Sir Godfrey Collins, later, said that Henderson had appeared to him to be speaking 'with the mind of a party manager'; and Colonel Josiah Wedgwood, from the Labour benches, said that Henderson 'recommends accuracy in the reporting of Cabinet wrangles, which is really no cure for the condition in which the country finds itself'.

Churchill showed that he had not been at all enthusiastic about the formation of the National Government:

> Some may think that it would have been better to have given the most complete assurances of support to the Socialist Administration in respect of all the economies and financial measures that they were willing to take. . . . I am not at all sure that . . . they might not have got through their own difficulties themselves, without bringing this extraordinary political disturbance upon the country. However, the deed is done. It was done from high motives, disinterested motives, and we have got to make the best of it.

But, Churchill contended, Henderson's action had anyhow to a considerable extent blighted the hopes with which the Government had been formed. 'Now that the largest party in the House is in irreconcilable opposition, it is true that the term "National Government" can no longer be properly used', and 'of course confidence will not return and judgment is suspended'. He had been told that adverse monetary currents were still flowing. Both he and Amery raised the question of a General Election in their speeches on this occasion. Churchill said that the Labour Opposition's challenge had to be taken up. Referring to Graham's statement, he said that the benefits the Labour Party would reap from delay were obvious.

> With every day that passes the short, shifting memories of our electorate will fade. . . . In six months' time it will not be the Socialist Government that will be in the dock, but the Government of the day.

Churchill dwelt on the effects of uncertainty about the election:

> The position of the Government must be precarious if their tasks and labours are prolonged. From every point of view the business of this country will be prejudiced until we reach some finality.

Churchill asked for an assurance that there would be no substantial or new departure in Indian policy; and insisted that there could be no industrial revival without a tariff. But his main point was that:

> there will be no restoration of confidence at home or abroad until the

Socialist party has been again decisively defeated at the poll. . . . We need a Government instrument commanding the support of the majority of people of this country.

Amery argued that the pound was not being saved by the formation of the Government: it had had a respite — 'that is something' — but it was still under suspended sentence of execution. His solution was a tariff. That solution could not be carried out by the Government nor by the existing House of Commons. It could only be applied in a House of Commons with a clear and decisive mandate from the country behind it, and by a Government which was of one mind on this great issue. Amery, therefore, urged a General Election at the earliest possible opportunity.

The Times next morning said that there was regret that Churchill had raised the question of a General Election so soon, and that it was felt that his remarks would do little to help the Government. The *Economist* (September 12) was perturbed both because Amery and Churchill insisted on the need for tariffs and because of their call for an early election. It considered all talk of a dissolution to be 'ill-conceived and dangerous'. How, it asked, would the Bank of England maintain the exchange during a four weeks' electoral campaign during which the future policy of the country would be thrown once again into the melting pot? It was particularly anxious to prevent the revival of the tariff controversy, over which the component parts of the Government 'must split'. 'The one thing that matters', it declared, 'is to steer the ship into port.'

Left-Wing spokesmen were also much in evidence during this debate, and were at least as critical of the official Opposition as of the Government. Maxton foretold 'a real, genuine, economic collapse', 'a breakdown of your economic system', in 'a very few weeks'. W. J. Brown held that there was not a halfpennyworth of difference between the two Front Benches:

This (Labour) Front Bench was prepared to agree that cuts should be made in the wages of civil servants, in the pay of teachers, in the pay of the Army, the Navy and the police. They were prepared to agree that there should be economies even in Unemployment Insurance provided they stopped short of a cut in the standard rate of benefit. What is the difference between the two sides? The difference is that one will go ten-tenths of the way, and the other will go nine-tenths of the way.

Brown declared that any propaganda about the unreality of the crisis was a lie. The crisis was real and desperate, and no real statement of policy had come from the Opposition Front Bench. He proclaimed that the only solution was the overthrow of the capitalist system. Sir Oswald Mosley's speech was of a different order. It was a plea for a constructive industrial policy, the reconditioning of our industries by the use of our capital resources, the expansion of the home market by scientific protection, and continued borrowing to deal with unemployment and provision for the unemployed. Mosley, who made several references to the arguments advanced by J. M. Keynes, advocated deficit budgeting; and bitterly attacked banking policy, Snowden's orthodoxy, and the Labour Party's acceptance of it in the past as well as their talk of a bankers' ramp:

> To talk of a bankers' ramp in order to get rid of the Labour Government, in face of the figures of industry, and the obvious argument that the bankers are not going to ruin themselves in order to unseat a few hon. Members, really reaches the height of dialectical absurdity. Anyhow, we shall have the test of this matter in the next few weeks. If it was a bankers' ramp to get rid of the Labour Government, the bankers' ramp has come off. You are out and the bankers have won. If it is just a bankers' ramp, now things will get better. If it was all a frame-up, unemployment will now be lessened.

Replying to Labour interruptions, Mosley added:

> They have not yet found out what has lifted them from that side of the House to this, and in their dazed and bewildered condition, even when their seconds are trying to bring them round and tell them what has happened, they are ungrateful.

Wedgwood, from the Labour benches, made a characteristic contribution to the debate. He could not make up his mind. He rather favoured devaluation of the pound. He had no confidence in any solution that had been put forward that day, and not much in his own. He did not know how he was going to vote. Chuter Ede, the only other back-bench Labour speaker, did know: with the overwhelming mass of the Labour party, he said, he was prepared 'to take up the challenge that has been thrown down by the financial interests of this country'.

Baldwin's intervention in the Debate was, in the main, a justification of his decision to participate in the formation of the National Government, in terms similar to those which he had used in addressing his own party meeting:

... it was a matter of hours to make a supreme effort to maintain the credit of the country, and no man to whom the appeal might be made to carry on the Government in those circumstances had any right to refuse, however difficult or disagreeable, or however impossible, the task might seem . . . there was no alternative, and I had to say that I and my colleagues would readily give such help as they could give to the Prime Minister for the accomplishment of this task . . . because it is essential to show the world not only that we are prepared to make the sacrifices which will be necessary to achieve the balancing of the Budget, but that it is actually done as a fact.

But Baldwin went on to emphasize the responsibility resting upon the Opposition, in regard to the way in which they presented their case:

If foreigners feel that there is a large section of the community in Great Britain at this time which does not realize the gravity of the issue or is reluctant to face the difficulties, that mere fact itself will tend to render nugatory a great deal of what we may do, and will prolong, possibly to a dangerous period, the length of time in which we hope to recover financial stability and the credit of our country in the eyes of the world.

Alexander wound up the debate for the Opposition. The first part of his speech was again devoted to the discussions which had taken place in the Labour Cabinet, and what he said has already been dealt with (p. 97 and pp. 115–16 above). The rest of his speech was a discursive treatment of reparations and war debts, the question of balancing the Unemployment Insurance Fund, protection, long-term German loans, 'wicked propaganda', and, finally, mobilization of overseas assets.

The Government reply was entrusted to Samuel. Like Baldwin, he refused to be drawn into the tariff controversy, and dealt first with the facts of the financial situation and the reality of the crisis. In reply to Churchill, he pointed out that both the Conservative and Liberal leaders had given assurances of support to the Labour Government:

Our advice constantly was, that in order to preserve the unity of the nation, the late Government should continue in office provided they were willing to take measures that were adequate to the situation. . . . We all of us offered our support to the then Government if they would continue in power, and, further than that, we pledged ourselves to vote in Parliament for whatever measures of economy might be essential and to share any unpopularity in constituencies affected thereby.

Samuel then dealt at length with the attitude of the Liberal and Conservative representatives in the negotiations preceding the resignation of the Labour Government on the subject of cuts in unemployment benefit; and ended with an appeal to the Opposition leaders to give the Government whatever support they could in order to meet the crisis, pointing out that the loan which had been obtained had, of course, only temporarily redeemed the situation.

In the division which followed, the Government received its vote of confidence by 309 to 249. Analysis showed that, including the tellers, the Government supporters were:

243 Conservatives

53 Liberals

12 Labour

3 Independents

14 Conservatives were paired: three were absent unpaired. Five Liberals were also absent unpaired. The number of Labour members supporting the Government was one larger than had been anticipated, Major A. G. Church voting with the Government.

The Opposition vote, including the tellers, was made up of 242 Labour and 9 Independents. The figure for Independents includes Sir Oswald Mosley and the three other members of the New Party; and the two Irish Nationalists, Devlin and Cahir Healy. The remaining three were former Labour members then sitting as Independents (Oliver Baldwin, W. J. Brown and E. J. Strachey). There were 14 Labour pairs. Of the 12 Labour members absent unpaired, 7 were apparently accounted for. The remaining five definitely abstained: they were Sir Norman Angell, R. D. Denman, Miss Picton Turbervill, G. R. Strauss and Colonel Wedgwood.[1]

---

[1] In *After All* (pp. 257–9), Sir Norman Angell has a few interesting notes written at the time. They show that on the next day (September 9) the abstentionists were threatened with the withdrawal of the Labour Whip; and also that they attended a gathering in the Prime Minister's room at which MacDonald gave a detailed account of the crisis to his supporters. Sir Norman's comments on Dalton's behaviour during the whole crisis episode are also of interest. More important is his statement that MacDonald pressed him very much to join those who were coming over to the National side: '. . . I refused finally to take the plunge. And I have felt since that it was no credit to me that I did refuse. The motives of refusal were, I am afraid, mainly that I shrank from facing the censure of old friends in the Labour ranks — censure for "ratting", for "betrayal of the cause", for failing to stand by old comrades. This ought not to have weighed with me at all. But it did. Other motives were sounder.'

There was one feature of the debate which foreshadowed coming events. The London Correspondent of the *Manchester Guardian* reported:

> Every now and again a belligerent note was struck out of the Opposition which surprised many people by its fierceness. Perhaps this mood will pass as the House adjusts itself to the new situation and the sense of dispossession weakens among the Labour members. But it is not a pleasant phase to observe at the moment. It led to frankly ungenerous treatment of the Prime Minister by many of his former followers. Jeers and mockery and even mimicry of his graver accents all seemed fair methods of controversy to many of his old followers, and, of course, he hardly ever mentioned the word 'Bank' but the Opposition benches boiled over with wrath. They have got the bank complex very badly, and the plot theory is obviously going to be worked to death by the Labour back-benchers.

THE EMERGENCY BUDGET

On September 9 the Government secured the passage of its business motions. The first, restricting private Members' time for the remainder of the session, was carried after some debate by 308 votes to 215. The second and third, providing for the termination of proceedings on the Budget resolutions at specified times on September 10 and September 19 respectively, were agreed to without a division. The House then disposed of the Committee, Report and Third Reading stages of the non-controversial Public Works Loans Bill introduced by the previous Government.

Next day (10th) Snowden presented his Emergency Budget. The estimated deficit on March 31, 1932, was £74,679,000; and for the following year the Chancellor estimated a deficit of £170,000,000. The economy proposals, to be submitted on the following day, would amount to £70 million and would save about £22 million in the rest of the current financial year. Provision for the Sinking Fund, it was proposed, should be reduced from £52 million to £32,500,000, which would suffice to meet contractual obligations; with consequential reductions of the deficits (for the current year of £13,700,000 and for the following year of £20 million). Snowden's proposals to meet the net deficits of £39 million and £80 million respectively involved increased taxation, 70 per cent of which was direct and 30 per cent indirect. The standard rate of income tax would be raised from 4s. 6d. to 5s. in the £. All the personal allowances would be reduced, except that for earned income, which would be slightly raised. The Chancellor proposed to increase all surtax payments by 10 per cent. His suggested increases in indirect taxation involved higher duties on beer, tobacco, petrol and entertainments. He estimated surpluses of £1½ million for both the current and following years. Snowden also announced that the Finance Bill would include clauses designed to facilitate the conversion of the 5 per cent War Loan to a lower rate of interest at the first suitable opportunity. The Chancellor concluded an unusually brief Budget speech with a peroration which brought a remarkable demonstration of applause from the Government benches.

The Times reported next day:

> The temper of the Opposition was very different. The back-benchers filled the air with snarling, irrelevant and ignorant interruptions unworthy of any serious Parliamentary occasion, and particularly discreditable on this occasion as betraying in presumably national representatives either indifference to or incapacity to understand a national emergency. Their attitude was the more incomprehensible because Mr Snowden's speech today was confined — in view of the Economy Bill to-morrow — merely to explaining his proposals for fresh taxation and revealed that the blow was to fall mainly on the direct taxpayer — a feature which might have been supposed to appeal to them.

According to other reports, however, the jeers and petulant cries left Snowden unaffected, and his domination was such that those concerned were soon reduced to compulsory silence. Snowden wrote in his autobiography (p. 972):

> It was evident that at that time the relations between myself and all my late Cabinet colleagues had not become embittered, for at the close of my speech two of them handed across the table notes expressing warm congratulations upon it.

It is important to note that in this speech Snowden made no reference at all to the discussions in the Labour Cabinet. In his passing reference to the economies which were to be submitted next day, however, he said:

> It may almost be sufficient if I say that nine-tenths of the items under

which economies are proposed were adopted and approved by the late Government.[1]

Graham, who followed for the Opposition, after repudiating the suggestion (not made by Snowden) that ex-Ministers ever failed to recognize the need to balance the Budget, complained that Snowden had given no indication of the nature and scope of the proposed economies. Having been corrected by Snowden about what the latter had said on the subject, as quoted above, Graham proceeded at some length to discuss what had happened in the Labour Cabinet. His main points were, (1) that the figure of £56 million was never finally accepted, and was always subject 'to the presentation of a complete picture', and particularly to some statement of policy about reduction of debt charges and the Sinking Fund; (2) that it was specifically put to the Cabinet that unless a 10 per cent cut in unemployment benefit was included in the programme it would not restore confidence; (3) that the views of other political leaders conveyed to the Cabinet also emphasized that they reserved the right to move increases to the amount involved if the suggestion was not accepted in that form; and (4) that it was 'because of an outside insistence upon that specific point, which we refused to accept, that the late Government broke'. Graham's brief concluding remarks on the Budget proposals were naturally of a preliminary nature.

The speeches which followed on September 10 present few points of special interest, although it should perhaps be noted that Pethick-Lawrence, who wound up, said in the course of his final remarks:

> I do not speak in terms of exaggeration. I choose my words with the utmost care. I am not speaking the language of hyperbole. I am speaking with deliberate intention and a careful use of words and I say that this Government has been formed for the express purpose of placing the neck of this country underneath the foot of foreign finance.

Henderson was in Bristol that day addressing the Trades Union Congress. Once again, and this time at still greater length, he reviewed the proceedings and discussions of the Labour Cabinet. He repeated the points made in his House of Commons speech two days before. His additional comments on the tariff issue, and on the

---

[1] Dr Thomas Jones recorded in his diary for September 14 (*A Diary with Letters*, p. 11):' P.J.G. (P.J., later Sir James, Grigg) full of admiration for Snowden — "something really great about him." He had put through the Tories and Liberals the identical Budget which he had proposed to the Labour Cabinet.'

possibility of forming a National Government in July, have also been noted above (p. 77 and footnote p. 56).

CABINET SECRETS

The subsequent proceedings of Parliament, from Friday, September 11, until its prorogation on October 7, cannot be reviewed in any great detail; but the general course of those proceedings and their main features must have attention. Most subsequent comment has concentrated upon the prolonged wrangle which developed between the Labour ex-Ministers and Ministers about the negotiations which had preceded the resignation of the previous Government. Much severe criticism, invariably directed in after years exclusively against MacDonald, Snowden and Thomas, has been made of the 'revelations' about Cabinet discussions and 'disclosures of Cabinet secrets'.

It was doubtless inevitable that there should be disclosures, and some consequential recrimination. Ex-Ministers were in an unenviable position: they were constantly being attacked from one side for having 'run away', and, on the other, they encountered not only the implied rebukes of the Trade Union leaders but also the contemptuous criticism of the I.L.P., of Mosley and the New Party, and of Left Independents like John Strachey and W. J. Brown — not to mention the puzzled queries from more moderate elements in the Labour Party. They had to explain themselves, and they had neither been nor were all of one mind. Their explanations could hardly be made without reference to the course of the complex discussions on the Labour Government's economy and taxation proposals; and such explanations began at once, long before Parliament assembled. In such circumstances, the Labour Ministers in the National Government could hardly refrain for long from replying to the actual or implied criticisms of their conduct and from dealing with the ex-Ministers' versions of what had happened. The new Government's proposals were subjected to attack before they were submitted to Parliament, and before any details of them were known. When the proposals were submitted, Ministers not unnaturally advanced, as a major argument in defence, the similarity (and for the most part the identity) of their proposals with those which the whole Labour Cabinet had provisionally accepted. A process of gradual revelation in debate was scarcely avoidable. Moreover, the tentative proposals of the Labour

Q

Government had already been disclosed to others. As *The Times* pointed out on September 12, every one knew that they had been submitted at various stages, by direction of the Cabinet, to the leaders of the Opposition parties, so that they had long ceased to be secrets confined to the Cabinet alone. Disclosures had also been made to the joint meeting of the T.U.C. General Council and the National Executive of the Labour Party; and the information had been passed on by Citrine to the general public in his speech to the Congress on September 7, the day before Parliament met.

The real nature of the controversy must be understood. It was not in any important sense a dispute about the content of the proposals agreed, or provisionally accepted, or considered, by the Labour Cabinet. It arose because the ex-Ministers in Opposition contended that they had not been committed to any of the proposals and were, therefore, entitled to oppose any or all of them; and in fact proceeded to oppose all of them. On this basis, and on this basis alone, could those ex-Ministers who had threatened resignation and those who had supported MacDonald unite, and all join the T.U.C. General Council and the Party organization outside Parliament, in 'vigorous opposition'. The Graham Memorandum contains an illuminating passage, as follows:

> Finally, it must again be pointed out that the Economy Committee of the Labour Government all accepted the repeated declaration of the Foreign Secretary that neither he nor anybody else was bound until the complete picture, including both economies and new revenue, was supplied. As is well known, that complete picture was never forthcoming: and of itself that would be sufficient ground for all members of the late Cabinet taking the view that they were not even morally committed to any of the proposals. On that basis there should be little difficulty in reconciling the opinion of those who, in presence of what they believed to be a financial crisis, were prepared to go beyond what other colleagues would endorse.

It has been seen how the process of disclosure was begun by Addison in his Swindon speech on August 26, and, in Parliament itself, by Henderson and Alexander on the first day (September 8), and how Graham in the House and Henderson at Bristol carried it further on September 10. MacDonald, however, had kept carefully within the correct limits on the 8th, and Snowden, not even alluding to the Labour Cabinet's discussions, had done the same on the 10th.

It was the Second Reading of the National Economy Bill (on Friday, September 11, and Monday, September 14) which provoked the most striking Parliamentary 'wrangles'. Even so, further disclosures of what had taken place in the Labour Cabinet were very limited, although previous disclosures then received considerable fresh publicity. On two occasions requests were made for the production of supposed Cabinet documents said to have been referred to; but the Speaker pointed out that there were no such documents. On the 11th a Labour back-bencher (McShane) raised the rule that specific papers referred to should be produced to the House, the Speaker replying that he understood there was no paper to be produced. The same reply was given on the 14th, when another Labour member (MacLean) asked for Papers, so that Members might judge whether statements made about Cabinet discussions and figures alleged to have been agreed upon at Cabinet meetings were correct.

The Debate on September 11 was opened by MacDonald, who explained the nature of the Bill and the Government's economy proposals. The Bill empowered the Government to give statutory effect to the proposed changes by Orders-in-Council, the powers to be granted for one month. The aggregate of the economies was £70 million. In his speech, MacDonald mentioned that the lowest of the tentative economy schemes put forward by the previous Government had amounted to £56 million, and he asked whether the difference of £14 million was a difference of principle or not. It was largely accounted for by the proposed cuts in the standard rate of unemployment benefit: for men from 17s. weekly to 15s. 3d.; for women from 15s. to 13s. 6d.; and for adult dependants from 9s. to 8s.

Two relevant 'wrangles' occurred during MacDonald's speech. In neither instance did he go beyond what was already known to persons outside the Labour Cabinet. The first arose from his statement that while the Government's taxation scheme would produce £80 million, the former Government had begun its discussion on the basis of £88 million, which would have included taxes on tea and sugar. In reply to interventions from Lansbury, the Prime Minister made it clear that this referred to the Cabinet Economy Committee; that the figure had been communicated to people outside the Cabinet by the instructions of the Cabinet; and that the Cabinet were told that only gross figures could be mentioned regarding taxation for ordinary Budget reasons. The second was the outcome of a statement by MacDonald that the Government were pursuing a policy that was not only laid down as a possibility by the former Government but one which that Government had actually begun to apply. In this connection, he mentioned two things: first, the five point cut on the Civil Service; and secondly, that instructions were given to Ministers to approach the various people affected by proposed cuts and to open negotiations with them, as in the case of the initial instructions given to the Minister of Education to begin negotiations on a 20 per cent cut. Mac-Donald prefaced these remarks by saying that it was no Cabinet secret, being in the records of the Departments. When the Speaker had dealt with the question about production of papers, Mac-Donald said that the conversations he had mentioned were reported outside and known to have been opened up, and beyond that he would not go. Lees-Smith, the former Minister of Education concerned, said that he was not instructed by the Cabinet to open conversations on a 20 per cent basis but on a 15 per cent basis, though, in fact, conversations had not been opened by the time the Cabinet resigned. MacDonald, who had said that it was at first on a 20 per cent and then on a 15 per cent basis, said that he was perfectly willing to leave the matter as Lees-Smith had stated it. He had, in fact, skilfully secured an important admission.

MacDonald stressed one general point about the Labour Cabinet's economy proposals:

> We were told that all these schemes were tentative, everybody knows that; it is no secret. It has been in the newspapers again and again, and it has been in the newspapers quite authoritatively communicated by both sides that there were various schemes. There were at least three schemes. Do let the House remember that these schemes were tentatively put together by the body of men who held supreme political authority in this country and that these tentative schemes, by the instructions of those in authority, were handed to the Chancellor of the Exchequer and myself to communicate to the representatives of the other two parties and to the representatives of the Bank of England. I have previously explained why this was necessary. Can anyone imagine the extraordinary nature of the position; the governing body of the country, especially in the circumstances with which we were faced, producing schemes and asking the Chancellor of the Exchequer and myself to go and communicate them to the representatives of the other two parties and then when they have asked us to do that to hold themselves in a position to say, 'We are not responsible.'

The two ex-Ministers who spoke subsequently that day, Clynes and Johnston, did not go any further into the Labour Cabinet's proceedings, but both of them repudiated any responsibility for the economy proposals. Clynes, who followed MacDonald, repudiated 'those repeated implications in the Prime Minister's speech that those of us on this side had accepted, sanctioned and approved the various items to which he referred', and endorsed Graham's remarks of the previous day, summarizing the attitude of the ex-Ministers to the proposed economies in these words, 'that the various items were in the nature of an economy or proposed Budget agenda to be finally decided in the light of a complete picture. That complete picture was never presented.' Johnston, in his speech towards the close of the debate, not only gave full expression to the 'dictation of international finance' theory, speaking of 'alien influences' and describing the new Government as 'a Wall Street Government', but also disclaimed all responsibility 'for this cruel and unnecessary attack upon British standards of civilization'.

In winding up the debate on the 11th, J. H. Thomas dealt with the subject in a devastatingly effective manner. He revealed no Cabinet secrets, confining himself to what was already known, and, indeed, being content to base his case on Henderson's own account of what had happened:

> Why did we sit then, in the midst of this crisis, day after day, if, at the end, we never intended what we were dealing with? You will not get over the fact that if the Leader of the Opposition himself said that as evidence of our anxiety to balance the Budget we provisionally agreed to this, then either we agreed that the Budget ought to be balanced, or the £56 million meant nothing.

During the prolonged 'wrangle' which ensued, Lansbury asked a question about permission to give an account of what happened in the Cabinet, and MacDonald replied:

> It is perfectly clear that nothing that has been said up to now has been kept in the Cabinet, because on the Cabinet instructions those figures were communicated to the leaders of the two parties.

When the debate was resumed on September 14, Greenwood at once renewed the controversy: he made no further disclosures, but repeated what had now become the ex-Ministers' stock argument — that they were in no way bound by the proposals they had provisionally accepted. Greenwood was followed by Samuel, who, in the course of his speech, gave, with the full assent of the Prime Minister, a long and detailed account of the course of events as known by or reported to the Conservative and Liberal representatives; an account confirmed afterwards by Neville Chamberlain. The important points in this statement have already been noted (see pp. 85, 87, 105–6, 121 and 123 above).

There were a number of interruptions during Samuel's speech, which itself of course disclosed no Cabinet secrets. Some of the interruptions were questions about the discussions in the Cabinet, and Snowden made several brief statements in reply. It may be noted that he prefaced one of them with the remark that 'all this disclosure of what took place in the Cabinet' had not originated with the Labour Ministers in the National Government. That was true; and Snowden was to repeat the point during the Election campaign. Snowden's references on this occasion to the joint meeting on August 20 have already been given (p. 91 above). On the general issue, Snowden mentioned Henderson's statement about the provisional acceptance of the £56 million of economies, and said, 'Therefore, if right hon. Gentlemen sitting there challenge the figure of any particular item, then they must deal with some of the other items.'

The controversy cropped up from time to time later in the same week. Snowden made a passing allusion to it next day (September 15), simply saying that he was not going to enter into the contentions which had occupied so much time as to the extent to which the late Government were committed to a large measure of economy, since the admission about the £56 million was sufficient. On September 17, there was a long 'wrangle' at question time arising out of the cuts in naval pay. MacDonald had said that every Department had been requested to make its observations about proposals regarding cuts, and that the Admiralty, so far as he could charge his memory, had replied in certain terms. A long argument followed about the rule, which the Speaker reaffirmed, 'that if quotations are made from a document the demand can be made for its production in this House.' It was contended by Opposition members that MacDonald had quoted from a document; to which he answered that he had not done so, having only charged his memory, and having only intervened at all because of a question from Alexander (the former First Lord of the Admiralty) about the Admiralty's reply. He pointed out, in regard to the rule, that the question was not whether there was a document but whether the document was textually quoted. Lansbury, not for the first time, pressed for permission to publish documents and to make a statement explaining his resignation. He seems to have confused the resignation of a Ministry as a whole with the position of an individual Minister who resigns, and his plea met with no response. MacDonald then said that ex-Ministers must not put questions indicating knowledge of the situation but conveying an inaccurate impression, because, if they did so, 'they compelled Ministers to reply.'

LABOUR MINISTERS AND THE OPPOSITION

The relations between the Opposition and the Labour members of the National Government were becoming increasingly strained. *The Times* reported on September 12 that MacDonald had suffered almost constant interruption, 'much of which was either fatuous or flippant.' A Liberal member spoke during the debate on the 11th of 'the personal venom' displayed. It had begun to affect the Opposition Front Bench. Graham's reference in his *Express* article to there being 'now no Labour element' in the Government has already been noted. On September 11, saying that he was speaking for Labour in the new Government, MacDonald had added: 'they can take the label from my back but they cannot take the label from my mind.' Clynes, who followed, denied that in anything MacDonald had said he had spoken for Labour; then referred to Thomas as 'the right hon. Member for Derby for the moment'; and later spoke of the Labour Ministers as 'they whose pockets are filled with demands from their constituencies for their resignation'. Thomas later protested at these references, and Clynes readily expressed his willingness to withdraw anything that had offended him. Snowden wrote in his autobiography (p. 978):

> A section of the Labour members subjected the Labour Ministers to daily insults; the most offensive insinuations, innuendoes and expressions were constantly flung across the floor. But I am glad to say that these actions were not approved by the more sensible members of the Opposition. I received a number of letters from members of the Labour Party expressing their disapproval of this conduct of the minority of their colleagues.

Such disapproval, however, was seldom publicly expressed; and in the House of Commons it was not directly voiced at all.

Two speeches in the debate on the Budget proposals on September 15 provide further evidence of the reluctance with which some Labour members were adhering to the Opposition. Sir Norman Angell,[1] in saying that he was continuing to associate himself with the Opposition, emphasized that he was doing so 'only after giving full weight and consideration to the fact that the pound *was* in danger, and that the flight from the pound would have been a catastrophe which, once it had happened, we could not have stemmed.' The veteran Trade Union leader, Sir James Sexton, made a highly emotional speech about his severance from MacDonald and Snowden, 'the political gods whom I once worshipped,' men he had 'gloried in': 'It is with a sore heart that I find myself in this position, particularly in view of the fact that I personally — and they say that confession is good for the soul — was in favour of the formation of a National Government.'

The Labour supporters of the Government received a recruit from the House of Commons on September 10, when R. D. Denman, who had abstained on the vote of confidence, announced his decision to join MacDonald. On the 16th it was announced that Markham, the Labour M.P. for Chatham (now Sir Frank Markham), had accepted the post of Parliamentary Private Secretary to the Prime Minister. It was reported on the 10th that three Labour peers, Lords Rochester, Marks, and Dickinson, were Government supporters. They were soon to be joined by Earl De La Warr and Lord Gorell. The Opposition peers were thus reduced from 19 to 12, Lords Sankey and Amulree being Ministers.

In MacDonald's constituency of Seaham, several miners' lodges had protested against the decision of the executive of the Divisional Labour Party to recommend that MacDonald be asked to resign his seat. On September 12, a delegate meeting of the Divisional Party confirmed the executive's resolution, but it did so only by the narrowest possible majority, by 40 votes against 39. The large minority, it appeared, was partly due to resentment that MacDonald had not been given an opportunity of addressing the Party. Sidney Webb had written to his wife on September 7 that Dr Marion Phillips, then Chief Woman Officer of the Labour Party, who had been in Seaham, 'said the women were weeping at losing

[1] Angell, together with Strauss, Wedgwood, and Miss Picton Turbervill, had voted with the Opposition on the 14th (Second Reading of the National Economy Bill). They were four of the five Labour members who had abstained from voting on the 8th.

J.R.M. and that many of the miners felt the same; she thought there would be a widespread feeling for him.'

There is no doubt that many (probably the great majority) of the Opposition members were at first confident that the General Election, when it came, would sweep out MacDonald and his Labour associates. Much evidence of that is to be found in the Parliamentary debates. Indeed, hopes were such that some thought popular resentment at economy cuts and increased tax burdens would produce a Labour victory. The bulk of the Opposition displayed an aggressive mood from the start of the proceedings in Parliament. And no theme was more persistently exploited than the suggestion that the cuts, and particularly that in unemployment benefit, would be, and were designed to be, the prelude to a general attack on wages. At the same time there were ominous signs that a reaction against parliamentary methods might develop, or be developed. Certain statements made foreshadowed the influential criticism of, and reaction against, parliamentary democracy in the following years. Clynes said of the National Economy Bill (September 11) that:

> This disturbing and this revolutionary Measure may well be taken as fully justifying the drastic manoeuvres which a Socialist majority in a future Parliament will have to take to give effect to its will.

Brockway, on the same day, used similar language; and declared also that the Opposition would not be confined to Parliament, but would try to organize industrial action. Johnston, also on September 11, expressed agreement with Brockway, and said that he doubted for the first time in his life whether gradual evolutionary progress was possible. On the 18th, Aneurin Bevan declared:

> If this Committee imagines for a moment that we are going to confine ourselves to sterile Parliamentary opposition at a time when they are making use of the most ruthless class policy that this House has ever carried out, if they think that we are going to repeat the docility of 1921–1929, they really must think that all the guts have gone out of Englishmen.

He concluded with these words:

> As far as we are concerned, there is one thing about which we are pleased in the present crisis, and that is that the change over of this party from there to here has clearly exposed the class issue. We shall

carry it through to a final conclusion, be the circumstances what they may.

On September 15, Dalton made the challenge to a General Election from the Opposition Front Bench. Snowden took it up, saying that he admired the way in which his old associates had been cheering to keep their spirits up, 'knowing — knowing — that only a few weeks, possibly, remain before the place that knows them now will know them no more.' Snowden was probably right in suggesting that Dalton was indulging in bravado. In the latter's diary for September 11 he wrote that his belief that Labour would have a majority at the next Election had subsided a little; though he still thought it possible that Labour's strength would be 'very nearly' maintained. However, the course of events in the next few days, which seemed greatly to strengthen the position of the Opposition, made its attitude increasingly challenging.

THE INVERGORDON 'MUTINY'

It was during the debate on September 15 that the news reached the House of Commons of the unrest or 'mutiny' in part of the Atlantic Fleet in harbour at Invergordon.

The pay and other allowances of naval ratings had been reduced in 1925 in accordance with the recommendations of an official committee, but the reductions were applied only to new entrants, on the ground that it was unfair and inexpedient to disturb the implied contract with those who had enlisted on the higher scales of pay. The pre-1925 entrants, therefore, had remained on the higher scales. The National Government (following its Labour predecessor) proposed no general reduction in the scales of pay in the Navy. No alteration was proposed in the 1925 rates. What was proposed, in regard to the ratings, was that those who had continued to enjoy the higher rates should now accept the 1925 rates. It was an assimilation of the pay of men who entered before 1925 to that of the men who had entered subsequently.

According to the statements made in the House of Commons on September 17 by the Prime Minister and the former First Lord (Alexander), the Admiralty, when asked by the Labour Government for their observations on the proposed cuts, said, while expressing some doubt, that they thought the men would loyally accept them, provided there were cuts all round in the public services and in unemployment pay.

A decision to apply the proposed cuts appears to have been taken without further investigation, and the orders were issued by the Admiralty without any preliminary explanation to the men concerned. Part of the Atlantic Fleet was already at sea in preparation for routine exercises. The trouble arose on the battleships still in harbour at Invergordon. The first news about pay reductions appears to have reached the naval ratings from the wireless and from the newspapers on Sunday, September 13. Apart from any questions concerning the accuracy of the reports, and apart also from the question of Communist influences at work, the cuts naturally gave rise to grievances, and involved hardships, in some cases considerable, arising mainly from commitments entered into on reasonable expectations.

On the evenings of the 13th and 14th successive batches of ratings on shore leave discussed the matter and arrangements were made for concerted action. A letter was drawn up imploring the Admiralty to amend the proposed cuts, saying that reasonable cuts would be accepted, but announcing the men's decision unitedly to refuse to sail until definite assurances of revision had been given.[1] On the 15th, the men on all the ships at Invergordon (the petty officers and chief petty officers mostly excepted) refused to muster. No violence of any kind occurred; nor was any disrespect shown to officers. It was a kind of passive resistance. Faced with this situation, the Admiral in charge acted promptly and sensibly. He cancelled the sailing orders, and recalled the ships already at sea (hence the reports of 'the recall of the Atlantic Fleet'); and the Admiralty ordered all the ships to return to their home ports for investigations to be made into the complaints.

In the House of Commons on September 16 Sir Austen Chamberlain (the First Lord) made the following statement:

The Board of Admiralty have had under their earnest consideration the representations received from the Officer Commanding the Atlantic Fleet as to the hardships involved in certain classes of cases by

---

[1] The text was as follows: 'We, the loyal subjects of His Majesty the King, do hereby present to my Lords Commissioners of the Admiralty our representative to implore them to amend the drastic cuts in pay which have been afflicted on the lowest paid men of the lower deck. It is evident to all concerned that this cut is the forerunner of tragedy, misery and immorality amongst the families of the lower deck, and, unless a guaranteed written agreement is received from the Admiralty and confirmed by Parliament stating that our pay will be revised, we are resolved to remain as one unit refusing to sail under the new rates of pay. The men are quite agreeable to accept a cut which they consider reasonable.'

the reductions ordered by His Majesty's Government in naval rates of pay. Their Lordships have directed the ships of the Atlantic Fleet to proceed to their home ports forthwith. Personal investigation will then be made by the Commanders-in-Chief and representatives of the Admiralty into those classes of cases in which it is alleged that the reductions press exceptionally on those concerned. His Majesty's Government have authorized the Board of Admiralty to make proposals for alleviating the hardship in these classes as soon as the facts have been ascertained by the contemplated investigation.

Captain W. G. Hall asked leave to move the adjournment of the House in order to discuss the matter, but the Speaker ruled that it did not come under the provisions of the relevant Standing Order, because it could just as well be debated on the next day. And next day, after many questions and answers (to some of which reference has already been made), Captain Hall again asked leave to move the adjournment. The Speaker raised no objection, and Captain Hall secured the requisite support. A brief debate took place later that day (September 17) in accordance with the provisions of the Standing Order. There were only two speeches (those of Captain Hall and Sir Austen Chamberlain), followed by a short comment from Alexander. The discussion was conducted in an admirably restrained manner by the two Opposition speakers and in a most conciliatory spirit by Sir Austen.

The Prime Minister had already announced on the 16th that various cases had been brought to the attention of the Government in which particular classes of persons affected by the proposed cuts were said to be unfairly affected; and said that the Government believed that the difficulties could be adjusted. On the 21st he announced the Government's decision that the simplest way of removing just grievances was to limit reductions as regarded teachers, police, and the three Defence Services, to not more than 10 per cent, the higher ranks of commissioned officers in the Defence Services excepted. This general decision made the review of the naval reductions, already begun at the home ports, of secondary importance. The naval ratings who had joined after 1925 remained unaffected by the cuts.

OFF THE GOLD STANDARD

Inevitably, the news of Invergordon had an adverse effect upon the financial situation. Assessments of its influence vary, but it was certainly all the greater because of the use of the term 'mutiny' and the scare headlines in the newspapers, particularly in the foreign press. Mowat has suggested (p. 404) that Invergordon served as 'a scapegoat'; but he himself had said (p. 403): 'whether really a mutiny or not mattered little; any news that the British navy, of all things, was faltering was enough to make the nervous foreigner decide that Britain was really near its last gasp.' In fact, the reactions to Invergordon were never assigned by Government spokesmen a more than contributory significance. The financial position had been worsening from other causes; and the deterioration became increasingly rapid on September 16 and the following days. To the general public, none the less, it came as an unexpected shock when, on the night of Sunday, September 20, it was officially announced that the Gold Standard was to be suspended. Beatrice Webb recorded (diary, September 23) that 'when, on the Sunday afternoon, two ex-Cabinet Ministers and two ex-Under-Secretaries were discussing the probable character of the P.M.'s summons to Henderson to return to London, not one of them had the remotest inkling that the decision was "to go off the Gold Standard".'[1]

The withdrawals of funds from London, greatly reduced after the formation of the National Government, had never stopped. On September 16 they accelerated sharply, £5 million being withdrawn that day. On the 17th, the figure was £10 million; on the 18th, nearly £18 million; and on the 19th, a Saturday half-day, over £10 million. The credits of £80 million were almost exhausted. During the two months or so from the middle of July, funds amounting to more than £200 million had been withdrawn. On Saturday (the 19th) the Bank of England addressed a letter to the Prime Minister and the Chancellor of the Exchequer advising the suspension of their obligation under the Gold Standard Act of 1925 to sell gold at a fixed price. Consultations followed, and, after a meeting of the Cabinet on Sunday afternoon (September 20), the Bank's advice was accepted.[2]

[1] Op. cit., pp. 289–90.

[2] The terms of the Bank's letter were as follows: 'I am directed to state that the credits for dollars 125,000,000 and francs 3,100,000,000, arranged by the Bank of England in New York and Paris respectively, are exhausted, and that the credit for dollars 200,000,000 arranged in New York by His Majesty's Government, together with credits for a total of francs 5 milliard negotiated in Paris, are practically exhausted also. The heavy demands for exchange on New York and Paris still continue. In addition, the Bank are being subjected to a

The official statement issued that night from No. 10 Downing Street announced that the Government would introduce immediately a Bill to suspend for the time being the operation of Subsection (2) of Section (1) of the Gold Standard Act of 1925, and would ask Parliament to pass it through all its stages on Monday, September 21. It was also stated that the Bank of England had been authorized to proceed accordingly in anticipation of the action of Parliament; and that the Stock Exchange would not be opened on the Monday. The announcement concluded:

His Majesty's Government have no reason to believe that the present difficulties are due to any substantial extent to the export of capital by British nationals. Undoubtedly the bulk of the withdrawals have been for foreign account. They desire, however, to repeat emphatically the warning given by the Chancellor of the Exchequer that any British citizen who increases the strain on the exchanges by purchasing foreign securities himself or assisting others to do so is deliberately adding to the country's difficulties. The banks have undertaken to co-operate in restricting purchases by British citizens of foreign exchange, except those required for the actual needs of trade or for meeting existing contracts, and, should further measures prove to be advisable, his Majesty's Government will not hesitate to take them.

His Majesty's Government have arrived at their decision with the greatest reluctance. But during the last few days the international financial markets have become demoralized, and have been liquidating their sterling assets regardless of their intrinsic worth. In the circumstances there was no alternative but to protect the financial position of this country by the only means at our disposal.

His Majesty's Government are securing a balanced Budget, and the internal position of the country is sound. This position must be main-

drain of gold for Holland. Under these circumstances the Bank consider that, having regard to the above commitments and to contingencies that may arise, it would be impossible for them to meet the demands for gold with which they would be faced on withdrawal of support from the New York and Paris exchanges. The Bank therefore feel it their duty to represent that in their opinion, it is expedient in the national interest that they should be relieved of their obligation to sell gold under the provisions of Section (1) Sub-section (2) of the Gold Standard Act, 1925.'

The reply to the Bank was: 'His Majesty's Government have given the most serious consideration to your letter of the 19th instant in which you informed them of the grave difficulties with which you are faced in meeting the obligation placed on the Bank of England by the Gold Standard Act of 1925 to sell gold in the form of bars to any person making a demand in accordance with the Act and of the dangers which you apprehend if that obligation is maintained. His Majesty's Government are of opinion that the Bank of England should place such restrictions on the supply of gold as the Bank may deem requisite in the national interest. They will be prepared to propose to Parliament forthwith a Bill giving indemnity for any such action taken by the Bank.'

tained. It is one thing to go off the Gold standard with an unbalanced Budget and uncontrolled inflation; it is quite another thing to take this measure, not because of internal financial difficulties, but because of excessive withdrawals of borrowed capital. The ultimate resources of this country are enormous, and there is no doubt that the present exchange difficulties will prove only temporary.

On Monday, September 21, the Gold Standard (Amendment) Bill was passed through all its stages in both Houses and received the Royal Assent. The bank rate was raised to 6 per cent.

In his opening speech in the House, Snowden elaborated the points made in the official statement issued the previous night. Dealing with the causes of the accelerated drain, he said:

> Unfortunately, however, we could not present a united front. Speeches were made and articles were written by prominent people advocating inflation and repudiation, which had a most damaging effect. There was political uncertainty, and the news of the unrest that occurred in the Navy was recorded in scare headlines in every foreign newspaper. At the same time, in the general atmosphere of nervousness, difficulties developed in foreign countries, and people began to scramble to liquidate their positions. This was as much due to nervousness about their own position as to a loss of faith in sterling.

In a broadcast address the same evening, the Chancellor repeated these points, but attributed 'the chief cause of the drain on sterling' to the nervousness of foreign banks about their own position and what they might be called upon to meet. When he came to write his autobiography, Snowden put the point about lack of unity more plainly, writing: 'The opposition of the Labour Party to the Budget proposals had given the impression abroad that the country was not united.'

Mowat (p. 403) attributes the continuance of the drain partly to 'uneasiness caused by Conservative efforts to work up an early general election'. Later he has a considerable passage (pp. 406–7) on Conservative pressure for an election prior to the suspension of the Gold Standard. He has nothing whatever to say about the effects of the Labour Party's opposition, and, indeed, very little at all about the Opposition's attitude throughout this period. Any uncertainty created by Conservative pressure for an election would have been of little importance had it not been for the nature of the Opposition campaign and fears of its success at the polls.

It is of some interest to note that the *Economist* (September 26), while ignoring the Opposition campaign, referred to 'the reckless and ill-considered propaganda launched by a section of the Conservative Party in favour of a General Election' and to the reports of insubordination in the Navy as factors which had contributed to the loss of foreign confidence. But, in the *Economist's* view, such factors were not mainly responsible:

> While the formation of a National Government and the rectification of the British Budget did much to reassure opinion abroad as to our determination to maintain British credit on a firm basis, these domestic developments had done and could do nothing in themselves to alleviate the international crisis whose repercussions last week began to extend to financial centres such as those of Holland, Switzerland and Scandinavia. The consequent scramble to increase banking liquidity, in face of a violent slump in security values, resulted in the repatriation of balances held in London, causing a strain on sterling which could not, in any case, have been indefinitely supported.

In his speech on the 21st, Snowden said that he saw no reason why sterling should depreciate to any substantial extent or for any length of time 'provided, and this is vital, that the finances of our country are administered with proper care'. The country could face the position with calmness, because the Budget was balanced, and the danger of uncontrolled inflation removed. These points were expanded in his subsequent broadcast address.

The decision to suspend the operation of the Gold Standard Act provided the Labour Opposition with some very plausible arguments. The National Government, it was contended, had been formed to maintain the Gold Standard, and had failed to do so. In particular, the economy measures had failed to achieve their object, were no longer necessary, and should be withdrawn. Moreover, since no serious depreciation in the value of the pound sterling was anticipated, the fears previously expressed had clearly been greatly exaggerated. Such arguments were to be extensively employed in the subsequent Election campaign. The reply given to them was that had it not been for the formation of the National Government and the measures it had taken and was taking, a disastrous inflation would have occurred; and that since the Gold Standard was now suspended the need for economy and a soundly balanced Budget was all the greater.

Henderson, who followed Snowden on September 21, argued that the Government's programme had failed, and that, as proof of the genuineness of the expressed desire for unity, the programme should be withdrawn. The Parliamentary Correspondent of the *Manchester Guardian* reported that 'this blunt proposal galvanized the Opposition into furious cheering'. But Henderson's general tone was conciliatory, and, after asking questions about the kind of control envisaged for exchange operations and to prevent the exploitation of prices, he concluded:

> If the answers are at all satisfactory, though I have not had an opportunity . . . of consulting the whole of my colleagues, the advice we will give is that we will not oppose the Bill, and by that means we will make our contribution to that unity that has been referred to.

In the event the Opposition Front Bench did not oppose the Bill, but they were unable to carry with them large numbers of their back-benchers. No less than 112 Labour members voted against the Second Reading. The attitude of the more extreme elements was strikingly aggressive, and is well exemplified in the following passage from Aneurin Bevan's speech on September 21:

> The first thing that emerges from this Debate and from the speech of the Chancellor of the Exchequer is that in this matter the Opposition is more powerful as an Opposition than it was as the Government. The Chancellor of the Exchequer has now admitted that this is not a National Government at all. The world does not believe in it; it does not take it on trust; it thinks that it is unrepresentative of the British electorate. It is considered that at all costs an election must be postponed, because the Government would be kicked out. At any cost this unrepresentative Government must be kept in power, in order to keep together the miserable shreds of capitalist credit in Great Britain. And the Opposition on this side of the House, although it is an Opposition, still has the ability to blow such a blast through those shreds that the world could see the bare bones beneath.

THE CLOSING STAGES

Before passing to the subject of pressure for an election, some references must be made to Parliamentary proceedings after the suspension of the Gold Standard and before the dissolution.

Much subsequent controversy arose from an incident at question time on September 21, the day on which the Gold Standard (Amendment) Act was passed. When the Prime Minister, as al-

R

ready noted, announced the Government's decision to limit the proposed cuts, he was asked whether he would also consider granting a concession to the unemployed. He answered:

> The handling of the unemployment cuts was necessitated by special conditions of borrowing, and they must remain.

This reply was often to be used as evidence that conditions had been attached to the credits granted to the Government, and in support of the charge of 'dictation' by the foreign bankers. It was repeatedly quoted, not only in the period immediately following, but also in after years. But MacDonald's reply to a further supplementary question almost immediately afterwards on the 21st was always ignored. Asked whether he would now admit that the grants to the unemployed were cut down at the dictates of foreign bankers, he replied:

> I say most emphatically that that is not true.

On the 22nd, Snowden was asked whether, in the recent credits, any conditions, political or economic, were imposed. His answer was 'No, Sir'. A Member at once enquired, without eliciting a reply, how that answer could be squared with the statement made by the Prime Minister the day before about conditions of borrowing. On the 24th, when asked if the Prime Minister's statement was incorrect, Baldwin replied that he could not answer for the contents of anyone's mind except his own, and reminded the questioner of Snowden's 'comprehensive' answer. Next day, in debate, Johnston quoted the Prime Minister's first answer on the 21st, and the replies of Snowden and Baldwin, saying that either the Prime Minister or Snowden was wrong. In all this, MacDonald's emphatic denial on the specific point was passed over. Had it not been, the suggestion of inconsistency could not have been made. MacDonald's successive replies on the 21st did not then give rise to any such suggestion.

Mowat (p. 384) has written: 'MacDonald himself, however, repeated the charge (i.e. that conditions had been attached to the credits), partly as a means of excusing his actions. In Parliament on September 21 he claimed that reductions in unemployment payments could not be reversed because of "special conditions of borrowing", though later parliamentary questions brought firm denials of this, including one from Snowden himself.' Mowat went on to suggest that the explanation of 'these conflicting statements' lies in the meaning of words like 'advice' and 'dictation'; and says that obviously foreign bankers did not dictate to the British Government, but gave advice about the conditions under which loans would be obtainable which conditions included a balanced budget and savings at the expense of the unemployed. Mowat is undoubtedly right about 'dictation' and 'advice', but dubiously so about 'conflicting statements', and he is misleading about Mac-Donald having 'repeated the charge'. In fact, MacDonald emphatically denied the charge.

The relations of the Labour Ministers with the Labour Opposition did not improve during the closing days of the 1929–31 Parliament. It is true that the opposition to the Government's emergency legislation was, on the whole, neither vigorous nor effective. That was particularly so in regard to the Budget Resolutions and the Finance Bill; in which respects, indeed, according to Snowden, the Opposition 'miserably collapsed'. But the attitude and arguments of the Opposition remained unchanged, except for the new arguments provided by the suspension of the Gold Standard and for the fleeting hopes that aroused. 'Wrangling' about what had happened in the Labour Cabinet was not prominent. Henderson himself, and Graham also, were only conspicuous by their absence from the Opposition Front Bench. There was a passing allusion by Thomas on September 22 to the acceptance of the £56 million of economies, but it was made only in reply to a direct appeal by Alexander in connection with the cuts in naval pay. It led Shaw, however, to make his only intervention in these debates. His remarks were very brief. He said 'quite deliberately' that 'neither in honour nor in fair play' was he 'bound in any way to any proposal that was submitted to the Cabinet', although he 'went a tremendous way personally — out of loyalty and affection — a fantastic way.' Shaw, as noted, had voted with the majority in support of MacDonald at the time of the final break in the Labour Cabinet.

The familiar agreed line of the ex-Ministers was expressed in perhaps its most unqualified form in a speech by Clynes at Bradford on September 20, when he is reported to have said:

> He and others in the Cabinet discussions had made it plain that they were committed to nothing, either to any items singly or to all of them collectively, until they had a complete picture before them of what it

all meant, at which time they would decide their course of action. That complete picture was never presented to the Labour Cabinet and no opportunity of that kind was given to them to reach a final decision.

Morrison, in one of the few brief speeches he made on the National Economy Bill, was more skilful than most of his colleagues. He evaded the issue of his own responsibility for the economy proposals by refusing to reveal Cabinet secrets, and audaciously expressed amazement, surprise and pain at what he called the irresponsible way in which Government supporters, and 'particularly right hon. Gentlemen', treated the secret proceedings of the Cabinet. He justified his opposition simply on the basis that it was the duty of the Opposition to oppose. 'This Bill is the Government's business, and it is for us to attack it and to tear it to pieces if we like, and we are going to do what we like in this respect.'

Throughout the proceedings on the Finance Bill, Snowden avoided all reference to the subject, just as he ignored the many gibes and insinuations directed against him, until his final speech in the Third Reading debate on October 2, his last speech in the House of Commons. He was fully entitled to write in his autobiography (p. 979):

> I ignored the offensiveness of a section of the Labour Party until the Third Reading of the Finance Bill, when the official spokesman of the Labour Party, who had been a minor Minister in the Labour Government, made a speech which gave me the opportunity to say frankly what I thought about their attitude and their action in running away from their duty to deal with the financial situation.

The Labour spokesman on that occasion was Attlee, who had opened the debate with a speech which was nothing more than an elaborately prepared personal attack upon the Chancellor of the Exchequer. The latter's devastating reply was, he afterwards wrote, really the measure of his deep disappointment with the action taken by the Labour Party, his sense of outrage at 'their hypocritical conduct in disowning proposals to which the majority of them agreed as members of the late Government'.[1] Even so, his references to these proposals were brief and general: he made

---

[1] Attlee himself had denounced Snowden's establishment of the Economy Committee presided over by Sir George May, although he had voted in favour of it at the time.

no disclosures of Cabinet secrets. When dealing, however, with a speech made by Henderson in the country, he did refer to Cabinet discussions on the tariff question. In doing so, he based himself on statements made by the *Daily Herald*, as already noted (p. 78 above). His references to the previous February have also been quoted previously (p. 48 above). But the speech marked Snowden's complete estrangement from his late colleagues and his Party. It was doubtless made in the knowledge that he had been expelled from the Party (the notification of this to him was dated the previous day, and the *Herald* had reported the fact on September 30). And Snowden himself quotes in his autobiography a press report which said that, while the Labour Party had been stunned into silence before the conclusion of the speech, the mood on the Government benches changed 'to one of strained astonishment at the unlimited capacity of Snowden's invective'. It was, indeed, a foretaste of what was to come from Snowden during the election campaign.

CHAPTER XIV

APPEAL TO THE PEOPLE

ELECTION SPECULATION

The position of the National Government was undoubtedly weakened by the suspension of the Gold Standard; and in these circumstances Conservative pressure for a General Election increased. It was urged that the Government needed a clear popular mandate; and also that the problem of the adverse trade balance must now be dealt with.

The question of a General Election had overshadowed the political scene from the moment the Labour Cabinet broke up. After Parliament reassembled it soon began to come to the forefront; and, after a hardly perceptible interlude following upon the suspension of the Gold Standard, it became dominant.

Two closely connected issues were involved: when was Parliament to be dissolved, and on what basis would the ensuing Election be contested? When the National Government was formed, assurances which were apparently clear had been given on both points. That Government was regarded as a purely temporary expedient. Its life was expected to be short. When its task was completed, Parliament would be dissolved, and the three parties would contest the General Election independently. The task itself, however, proved not to have been so clearly defined as had been thought at the time. Then, as noted above, the official pronouncements declared the one specific purpose of the Government to be that of dealing with 'the present financial emergency', with 'the national emergency that now exists', of putting 'British credit in a position of security'. In Baldwin's first statement, on August 24 (see p. 168 above) the words used were: 'carrying out such measures as are required to balance the Budget and restore confidence in our national credit.' In his speech to the Conservative party meeting on August 28, however, Baldwin had said (see p. 188 above) that the only purpose of the new Government was that of 'passing legislation necessary to effect economy and to balance the Budget', and had gone on to say that there would then be an Election at which the Conservatives would have a straight fight on tariffs and against the Socialist party.

In the circumstances of the time there was no inconsistency in these statements. It was assumed that with the passing of the necessary legislation the national emergency would be over, and that the party struggle over longer-term policy could then be resumed. There was no question, as Baldwin had said, of a permanent coalition. The election, as MacDonald had declared, would not be fought by the Government. And the reasons for that seemed obvious enough. They were stated, from the Conservative side, by Lord Hailsham on September 3, when he said:

> The National Government was formed for one purpose and one purpose only, to balance the Budget. It is absolutely essential to finish that task quickly, to do nothing else, and to have an immediate dissolution and an appeal to the country on the Conservative Party's reconstructive programme. The country could not be saved by economies alone. We must have a constructive programme; and so long as the National Government lasts the Conservative Party cannot proceed with their constructive programme of tariffs and Imperial development, for no one would be so foolish as to believe that the Liberals would agree to such a programme.

It is true that in some quarters the idea that the National Government should be brought to an end as soon as possible was not at all congenial. There were hints, as noted above, that the Government's task might take longer than was anticipated. In Liberal circles there was a scarcely concealed desire that the Government should continue in office after the immediate emergency was surmounted in order to deal with the wider aspects of the crisis. From the outset the *Economist* considered the achievement of budgetary equilibrium only 'the first, and easiest stage on the painful road to recovery'; and rejected the view that the Government was simply a stop-gap administration formed to deal with one isolated issue. Liberals agreed with Conservatives that 'the country could not be saved by economies alone'. They agreed, too, that the National Government could not carry out a tariff policy. On that issue, as the *Economist* said on August 29, the Government would split 'from top to bottom'. And, precisely in

order to avoid the raising of the tariff issue, the *Economist*, even at
that early stage, was anxious that the new Government should have
a long tenure of office and that a dissolution should be indefinitely
postponed.

The Conservative desire for an early General Election was both
natural and unconcealed from the start. It was strengthened by the
attitude of the Labour Opposition and fear that the new Government would become unpopular. This anxiety, as we have seen, was
expressed by Churchill when the House of Commons met on
September 8. But Churchill was neither in the Government nor
very favourably disposed towards it. The same is true of Amery
who also raised the question of an Election on the same day. Such
early talk about an Election was, as *The Times* said, 'very properly
condemned as distracting.' Neville Chamberlain recorded in his
diary on September 3 that important Conservatives outside the
Cabinet had proposed to him that he and his Conservative colleagues within the Cabinet should urge the abandonment of the unpopular economies and an appeal to the country on the full tariff,
incidentally getting rid of Snowden and Samuel. Chamberlain gave
cogent reasons for rejecting the proposal, but was clearly disgusted
by it: 'I made no comment on the cynical nature of the proposal
that four of the Cabinet should engage in this discreditable intrigue against our colleagues.'[1] It may well have been that the
'important Conservatives outside the Cabinet' were, or included,
Amery and Churchill.

After Snowden's Budget speech, and the progress made with the
emergency legislation, talk of a General Election naturally developed, and, said *The Times*, was 'better justified'. That newspaper,
however, under Geoffrey Dawson's direction, soon advanced the
idea that any appeal to the electorate should be made by the
National Government itself and not by the parties separately. An
editorial on September 16 granted that 'even a premature appeal
to the country would hardly be more mischievous than protracted
uncertainty', and also that 'outside forces' might soon grow too
strong for the maintenance of the existing harmony in the Cabinet
'without convincing proof that it is what the country desires'. But,
the question was asked,

Is there any real reason why the appeal to the country, whenever it
may come, should not be made — on a broad programme of recon-

[1] Feiling, op. cit., p. 194.

struction which will include a tariff — by the National Government as such?

The notion that after the events of the last month, and in face of an emergency which still persists, it can merely dissolve in the chaos of the old three-party system is altogether too light-hearted to bear examination.

The combination of men who are serving under Mr MacDonald are not — it has been said again and again by all of them — a Coalition in any ordinary sense. There has been no sign so far of the weakness and inaction which come from the compromise of principles in the desire to hold together. . . . Surely this task of national recovery would be better carried through to the end by the men whose bond of union is that they had the courage to begin it?

The Times conceded that there might be withdrawals because of disagreement, and also that, in effect, the suggested appeal to the country would be for the support of the Conservative platform. This editorial was written by Dawson himself. Dawson's diary shows that he had previously put his view to Baldwin, and later to MacDonald, and had found both 'receptive'.[1]

This new approach to the Election problem evoked a favourable response in many quarters. Sir Evelyn Wrench has expressed the view that 'few leaders in *The Times* can ever have had more immediate results'. Certainly its development by *The Times*, and the paper's unwaveringly persistent advocacy of a 'national' as against a party appeal, exercised great and growing influence in the subsequent days, an influence which may well have been decisive, particularly in regard to Conservative opinion.

On the Liberal side, the pressure for an election aroused considerable anxiety. The Liberal Parliamentary Party meeting on September 17 found itself obliged to devote its attention to the matter. Writing that night, the London Correspondent of the *Manchester Guardian* said that, with one dissentient, the opinion was that the Liberal Party could accept no responsibility for a General Election until there was full assurance of the crisis being really over. He referred to 'the obvious feeling' in the House of Commons that the country's financial position could not be regarded as finally secure. There was, however, a widespread belief that a movement had been set on foot by some responsible people to bring about the formation of a Conservative-Liberal Coalition

[1] Wrench, op. cit., pp. 292–3.

Government committed to full Protection; and the Correspondent said that the Conservatives were deluding themselves about the number of Liberals who would be likely to support them.

Editorially, on the 18th, the *Manchester Guardian* recognized the strength of the Conservative case for an early election — it could hardly have done otherwise, in view of its editorial on August 29 — but said that the case rested entirely on one assumption —

> that the stability of the pound can be maintained during the month or so that must elapse between the decision to dissolve and the holding of the elections.

Only the Government could judge about that.

> If the Government should decide that elections are to be held it could only be because the Government was perfectly satisfied that the immediate crisis — so far as the stability of the pound is concerned — was over.
>
> To hold elections to the jeopardy of the pound would imply a scandalous irresponsibility on the part of the Government and a neglect of its primary obligations, indeed of the sole purpose for which it came into being. For it is evident that the holding of elections would put an additional strain upon the pound and the stability of the exchanges.

This was written, apparently, on the assumption that the parties would contest the election independently; and the *Manchester Guardian* declared that the proposal was 'simply a device for giving the Tories a long spell of power'.

The Parliamentary Correspondent of *The Times* wrote on the 18th that political opinion was steadily hardening in favour of an early General Election on a national appeal by the National Government. There was, he said, a certain amount of opposition in the City to an early General Election on the ground that foreign opinion would be nervous about the result. But it was generally agreed, he argued, that on a national appeal there could be little doubt about the result, the Opposition being prepared for the loss of some 30 to 50 seats; although the same could not be said with certainty of an appeal on strictly party lines.

Samuel has stated in his *Memoirs* (p. 209) that he wrote to the Prime Minister on September 18, on behalf of his colleagues and himself, protesting against a General Election being precipitated, 'in breach of the undertakings that had been given.' Writing that night (published on the 19th), the London Correspondent of the *Manchester Guardian* said that the Conservative wire-pullers were moving heaven and earth to rally Liberals to the idea of an early election and a new 'National' Government, a Conservative-Liberal coalition, committed to protection. MacDonald, he said, was the arbitral figure. The Conservatives were confident they could win with him, but doubtful in their hearts if they could do without him. They were calculating, also, that if they could detach half the Liberals they would have wrecked the Liberal Party for good. Liberal Ministers held that an election would hold serious risks for the pound sterling:

> Certainly they are of the opinion that this Government, which was called into being for that purpose, has not yet placed the pound beyond all possibility of danger.

The Conservatives, on the other hand, appeared to think that the danger to the pound sterling would be to have no election and to leave Great Britain before the world possessed of a Government impotent to deal with the adverse trade balance which is undermining our credit abroad quite as much as the unbalanced Budget did.

Editorially, the *Manchester Guardian* came out that day (the 19th) with a plea for the formation of a 'real National Government'. Its central argument has considerable significance. It was that the differences between Ministers and ex-Ministers had been shown to be differences 'not of principle but of more or less':

> The recent debates which have given so painful an exhibition of recrimination between Ministers and ex-Ministers have at least had one useful result. They have shown that the Opposition leaders while they were in office were not only able to follow Mr MacDonald a large part of the way since taken by the Government, but that they have considerable difficulty in showing, even now, in precisely what particulars and on what principles they would differ from the Government if they were themselves in power.

Since Henderson and his colleagues were no more anxious to see the collapse of the pound than was the Government, such differences ought not to be allowed to stand in the way of a truly National Government. The *Manchester Guardian* suggested that MacDonald should openly invite Henderson to state the terms on which he would be willing to co-operate: it did not, however, express any confidence about the response to such an invitation.

Naturally enough, the *Economist* was not attracted by the project of an election fought by the National Government; but it was not unduly alarmed, because it saw no prospect of such a plan taking practical shape. The Conservatives would insist on a high protective tariff, and the Liberal Party as a whole would refuse to co-operate on that basis. But, even if an agreed programme were arrived at, 'the result of the election would still be in doubt.' In these circumstances, the *Economist* maintained that a dissolution would mean the inevitable collapse of sterling, and 'to court that eventuality would be an act of irresponsibility beyond pardon'.

TOWARDS THE DISSOLUTION

The dramatic decision of September 20 to suspend the Gold Standard produced a new situation. For a day or two the election controversy appeared to be suspended along with the Gold Standard. On the 20th itself, MacDonald wrote to Samuel as follows:

> Although I have acknowledged by word of mouth receipt of yours of the 18th with a resolution on the discussed Election, passed by the Liberal Advisory Committee, you would no doubt like to have it in writing. There was a great deal to say from a purely political point of view for an Election now, but the objections to it both from the financial and the long-range political view were so overwhelming that I could not have agreed to it. I was prepared to carry on, going right through the programme that was necessary to maintain sterling, but the sudden collapse at the week-end created a new situation which I hope we are going to unite in facing. Obviously there is not even a theoretical justification for an Election now.[1]

MacDonald doubtless assumed that in the new and unexpected phase of the crisis upon which the country had entered that day, a General Election in the immediate future was impracticable. At the same time he plainly realized that his Government might not maintain its unity in face of the new situation. He expressed the hope that it would do so. It was a hope which soon seemed likely to be disappointed; and one reason for that was that events quickly demonstrated the unsoundness of MacDonald's assumption.

It could be argued, and was to be argued, that since the crisis with which the National Government had been formed to deal had

[1] Samuel, *Memoirs*, p. 209.

not been surmounted, and since the national emergency, so far
from being almost over, had entered upon a graver phase, the time
had not yet come for a dissolution of Parliament and its expected
corollary, the termination of the Government itself. The *Economist*, for example, wrote powerfully on these lines on September
26. Its plea was: 'Let the present navigators stay at the helm and
carry on.'

But the same set of facts could be drawn upon in support of the
other side. The chief argument which had been employed in the
preceding days against a General Election had fallen to the
ground: it was no longer possible to contend that an election would
imperil the maintenance of the Gold Standard. And, it was argued,
the real danger to the pound lay not in a dissolution of Parliament
but in postponement. The new phase of the crisis could be, and
was, itself attributed largely to the political uncertainty and to the
inadequacy of the measures so far being taken by the Government.
It could be dealt with effectively (so the argument ran) only by a
Government capable of taking the further steps required, resting
on a clear expression of approval from the electorate, and assured
of a majority for several years. To the contention that an immediate
Election (by which was meant an election as soon as the Government's emergency legislation was passed) would be a breach of
the many assurances given at the time of the National Government's formation, the answer given was that with the failure to
surmount the crisis on the basis of the Government's original programme, those assurances were inapplicable, an entirely new and
unanticipated position having arisen.

If an election were to be held as soon as the then current Parliamentary business was disposed of, was it to be conducted by each
party independently or by the National Government or by some
new combination? Although some elements in the Conservative
Party had pressed, and continued to press, for an Election at
which that party would fight independently on an unqualified
tariff programme, the desirability of appealing to the electorate on
as wide a basis as possible was recognized by the Conservative
Ministers and the bulk of their adherents. Before the suspension
of the Gold Standard, as we have seen, *The Times* had urged a
national appeal by the National Government itself on the basis of a
modified emergency-tariff policy. In doing so, it expressed an influential and growing body of opinion by no means confined to the

Conservative ranks. After the operation of the Gold Standard had been suspended, the case for such an appeal, in the event of an Election, was greatly strengthened. The question was how far agreement on an appeal of that kind could be reached within the National Government and among its supporters.

On September 17, the Parliamentary Correspondent of *The Times* had pointed out the unlikelihood of the Government trying to put a tariff policy into force without an election, since, with a nominal majority of between 50 and 60, it could not risk the defection of even only a dozen Liberals. And, according to this Correspondent, Opposition members were freely admitting that they would be defeated if an Election were held before the end of November. He added significantly that:

> One of the great assets of the present National Government is the faith which large masses of electors who voted for Labour candidates at the last election have in Mr MacDonald, Mr Snowden, and Mr Thomas.

Labour members who had visited their constituencies in the previous week-end had reported that this was true even of some of the unemployed.

As things happened, election speculation was scarcely interrupted by the shock of the suspension of the Gold Standard. Within a day or two it was again the dominant theme in the newspapers. And there were important developments on the very day of the passing of the amending Act (September 21). A meeting of the '1922 Committee' (the organization of the Conservative backbenchers) declared unanimously for the immediate imposition of an emergency tariff, and for an early Election on the basis of a national appeal by the National Government. This, of course, meant continued acceptance of MacDonald's leadership. Snowden wrote in his autobiography (p. 989) that a resolution to this effect was sent to Baldwin on the 22nd, and, without giving further dates, proceeded:

> Under this pressure from their party, the Conservative members of the Cabinet raised this issue. Mr Baldwin came into my room at the House and gave me a frank statement of the position in which he was placed by this decision of his Party. He, himself, was very anxious to stand by the conditions upon which the National Government had been formed, but Party pressure was too strong for him.

The other important move on September 21 was on the side of the Liberals. In the debate on the Budget resolutions on the 15th, Sir John Simon had delivered a closely reasoned speech in which he had contended that the system of free imports would have to be abandoned and an emergency tariff imposed. The speech had had much influence. On the 22nd, the Parliamentary Correspondent of *The Times* reported that steps were being taken to ensure that the Prime Minister knew of the strong feeling among Liberal members in support of what amounted to a tariff policy; and said that the Liberal leaders would be surprised to learn how many of the rank-and-file members were determined to support the Prime Minister in whatever measures he and the majority of his Cabinet colleagues might think necessary to maintain the financial stability of the country and to restore the balance of trade. A memorial to that effect, for presentation to MacDonald, had been signed on the night of the 21st by 22 Liberal M.P.s, and more signatories were expected. It was afterwards reported that this memorial had been promoted by Hore-Belisha and Ernest Brown.

On the afternoon of September 22, MacDonald left London for a few days' rest at Sandwich. It was stated next day that he was feeling the effects of fatigue and overstrain. He returned on the morning of Friday, September 25.

The Times renewed on the 23rd its plea for as wide an area of political co-operation as possible. Two things, it said, were clear: first, that the National Government had saved the country from uncontrollable inflation, and, secondly, that its work could only be permanently effective if there continued to be a National Government with a national appeal. The *Manchester Guardian* that same day denounced the Tory party, which, it said, cared only about tariffs, and was proposing to delude simple electors by calling itself the 'national' party. A thin covering of Labour and Liberal names would be provided; but the *Manchester Guardian* found it very difficult indeed to believe that MacDonald could lend his name to such a trick, or would be willing to play the part of decoy duck; and considered it quite incredible that the bulk of the Liberal party or the official Liberal policy could in any way endorse the full Tory tariff programme. Only a small number of Liberals would be willing to support Simon, and 'whether large or small, there is no longer any point in calling them Liberals'. The editorial concluded by saying that if the Tories insisted on a General Election, it was the duty of all Liberals to fight them to the full extent of their power.

That day (September 23) the Liberal Parliamentary Party held a well-attended meeting, 50 out of the 58 M.P.s being present, and Sir Herbert Samuel presided, absenting himself from the Cabinet meeting which was going on at the same time. The Liberal gathering lasted two hours. The tariff issue was not discussed; and no resolution was submitted against an election; but Samuel was asked to convey to the Prime Minister how strongly opposed to a dissolution the meeting was. The chief subject of discussion was the Hore-Belisha memorial to the Prime Minister. It was claimed that 29 Liberal Members, including Runciman, had signed it; though no member of the Government had been asked to do so. The London correspondent of the *Manchester Guardian*, writing that night, said that the bulk of the 29 intended the manifesto to be a pledge of support for a tariff if the Prime Minister plumped for a tariff. The words used in the memorial were 'any measures which you think it essential to take in the interests of the finance and trade of the country'. The result of the discussion was entirely negative. The differences of view in the Liberal Parliamentary Party remained unresolved.

Rumours of internal dissensions in the Conservative Party were described by *The Times* on September 24 as without foundation. The four Conservative members of the Cabinet, it said, were

> entirely agreed that the temporary suspension of the gold standard has not made the necessity for an emergency tariff any the less urgent, and that only by an appeal to the country as soon as the business now before Parliament has been disposed of can that tariff be satisfactorily put into operation.

The belief was expressed that there was a substantial majority in the Cabinet in favour of tariffs.

The Conservative business committee (or executive) met on the 24th. According to Neville Chamberlain's diary, far-reaching decisions were taken unanimously.[1]

> All were in favour of the national appeal by a national government under MacDonald, provided the programme embodied the full tariff. All agreed that the election should be at the earliest moment. All agreed that, if we went to election with R.M. as P.M., we must accept

[1] Feiling, op. cit., p. 195. See below, p. 258, however, for Amery's version.

him as P.M. when we come back. . . . Truly, the Conservative Party is a wonderful embodiment of good sense, patriotism, and honesty. What would have been the astonishment of the Socialist executive, if it could have overheard the Conservative executive agreeing to allow the man, who has all his life actively opposed them, now to have the credit of carrying out their own policy just when the whole country has come round to it.

These decisions were not reported in the press at the time. *The Times* said next morning (September 25) that there was no reason to change the view that there would be an early appeal to the country by the National Government; the only matters still in doubt being the time and the exact nature of the appeal. Editorially, it stated the case for an election:

The present Government has the power to postpone a General Election. What it cannot postpone is rumour and clamour about it and the consequent uncertainty which is a daily source of anxiety to the world. The risk of the defeat of a national appeal must be taken some time, and the force of such an appeal will certainly gain nothing by delay. Provided only that the appeal is truly national, the sooner it is launched and the quicker it is answered, the less will be the risk of failure and the greater the power for good which success will bring.

The *Manchester Guardian* (through its London Correspondent) said on the 25th that the Conservatives were in a position to force an election, but that no decision to do so had been taken, because they were waiting for MacDonald to decide whether he would go to the country as head of 'a so-called National Government'. The Correspondent added that MacDonald had never been a free-trader of the stricter kind, and his problem was 'to settle the larger question whether he can allow himself to be the head of a virtual Conservative Government'.

After referring to the meeting of the Conservative business committee and Neville Chamberlain's diary, Mowat has written (p. 407):

It was clear now, if it was not in August, that MacDonald was a prisoner of the Conservative majority in his own government, and could regain his freedom only by resigning.

Putting aside the fact that there was no Conservative majority in the National Government, and the other fact that MacDonald, by resigning, could bring that Government to an end, it is both amus-

s

ing and instructive to contrast Mowat's view of the situation with that presented by Amery. The latter writes in his memoirs that:

> ... once stuck to the MacDonald Tar Baby the Conservative leaders found disentanglement increasingly difficult and unattractive. Coalition became an end in itself, and MacDonald, as the embodiment of the 'national' idea, soon discovered that he was indispensable, and so master of the situation. . . .
>
> Baldwin and Neville insisted on an election, and MacDonald was in no position to refuse. Nor was he unprepared to go with them on policy. But policy, in his view, was a minor matter compared with keeping the Coalition intact and himself at the head of it. The Conservatives were prepared to continue the Coalition, but only on terms which would force Samuel and other intransigent free-traders to resign. On the 23rd Baldwin still thought that after the election the King would send for him as the leader of the largest party. On the 24th he told us at the Business Committee (of which I was still a member) that, after meditating till 3 a.m., he was inclined to think that MacDonald might be allowed to stay on for a while. Neville bluntly said that, if MacDonald wanted to stay, nothing could stop him. Hailsham urged Baldwin to tell MacDonald that we were willing to go on serving under him. All the rest, except myself, were of the same opinion, and no one urged Baldwin to push his claim, or even took the view that the Party would insist on having him. But (quoting his diary): 'we were all agreed as to the great importance of pitching our tariff demands high enough to make sure of getting rid of Samuel, and, if possible, Reading.'[1]

Allowing for Amery's dislike of both Baldwin and MacDonald, this provides substantial confirmation of Neville Chamberlain's account. It also suggests that the Conservative leaders did not all at that time fully grasp the strength of MacDonald's position, which the events of the next few days were to disclose.

MacDonald returned to Downing Street on the morning of Friday, September 25. In the afternoon there was a brief Cabinet meeting at the House of Commons. Its business was understood to be largely of a routine nature, mainly concerned with India. Soon afterwards the Prime Minister left for Chequers and spent the week-end there. Samuel meantime (on the 24th) had circulated to the Cabinet a memorandum stating the Liberal case against an early election.

The *Manchester Guardian's* London Correspondent (writing on

[1] Op. cit., p. 67.

the night of the 25th) took the view that whether or not MacDonald decided to remain Prime Minister there would be an election. There were, he wrote, only a few cool heads among the Conservatives (or Tories, as he habitually called them) who feared the risks of going to the country without MacDonald as leader:

> These more judicious Tories acknowledge (1) that the only justification for an election now is that the country should be offered something as nearly approaching a National Government as is possible after the self-exclusion of Labour, and (2) that the absence of Mr MacDonald would seriously diminish the chances of success. But when did the cool heads among the Tories prevail in a crisis?

On the 26th *The Times* declared editorially that 'the only way to counteract the evil wrought by the ever-present threat of a General Election is to have a General Election'. It considered that events were moving rapidly towards it. The call to the Prime Minister was clear: he was 'marked out to be the protagonist of a national appeal'. Not the slightest doubt existed that the whole of the Conservative Party and at least a large section of the Liberal Party would accept his leadership; and he might be perfectly certain that his new supporters did not intend to use him for their own party purposes but to follow him in a national purpose.

> Indeed the economic and political situation has changed so completely during the last few weeks that party prejudices and jealousies based on the old situation are altogether obsolete.

The Parliamentary Correspondent that day described as 'utterly false' the suggestion that trouble was brewing because some backbench Conservatives 'were said to regard Mr MacDonald's position at the head of the National Government as destined to last only till his electoral value was exhausted'. If there ever had been any irresponsible talk of that kind, he proceeded, it was entirely foreign to the views of the party leaders and of the great majority of the Conservative rank-and-file:

> Mr MacDonald's leadership throughout the crisis has made a profound impression on the country. There can be no question of his being 'taken for a ride' and then 'bumped off', and any suggestion of the sort would be deservedly unpopular. It may be added that Mr Baldwin, so far from having impaired his position by his loyal support of the Prime Minister, has greatly improved it during the last three weeks. Nothing is more remarkable than the new hold which he has

established on the House of Commons in circumstances which are peculiarly difficult, but which happen to suit his particular gifts. The two men are clearly working together in the closest harmony and to the great advantage of the nation.

As to the Liberals, their line of action in the event of an election could not be in much doubt, according to the *Manchester Guardian's* Correspondent. The proposal holding the field, he said, was that the Government should issue a manifesto signed on behalf of the three parties in favour of a policy of national reconstruction and what would be described as an emergency tariff. That, he declared, would be equivalent to the dismissal of Sir Herbert Samuel, Sir Donald Maclean and every other Liberal Minister; although their places could be filled by Sir John Simon and other emergency-tariff Liberals. For the time being, however, Liberal efforts were directed to the prevention of an early General Election. Maclean, in a speech at Wadebridge on September 26, described the agitation for an election as 'irresponsible', and an election itself as 'autumn insanity'. Snowden at this stage appears to have shared the opposition of the Liberal leaders to an election. So also, but with much greater passion, did Lloyd George, who was visited during the week-end by both Reading and Samuel.

On Monday morning (September 28) *The Times* made a special appeal to Liberals, setting out what it considered to be 'overwhelming reasons' for a General Election:

Within a fortnight the present Government will have passed the legislation which it was formed to pass and for which alone it has a secure majority. Owing to circumstances quite outside the control of the present Government, that legislation, though it has saved the nation from the disasters of a collapse of the currency, has not gained for the nation that considerable breathing space which in happier times it would have secured. Sterling is not worthless, but it is unstable; and even if no calamitous developments are likely for some little time to come, so long as this country has an unstable currency, no one can guarantee the course of events from one day to another. . . . A General Election is the only way to end a dangerous and damaging uncertainty and to equip a British Government with full powers to meet whatever dangers may arise.

The paper's Parliamentary Correspondent that day said, significantly, that 'the national appeal should be for a free hand'.

MacDonald's Attitude

The Prime Minister returned from Chequers on the morning of the 28th; the Liberal Advisory Committee met that morning; and the Cabinet discussed the situation in the afternoon. Important Labour meetings were also held that day in preparation for the Annual Conference of the Party, due to be held at Scarborough on October 5.

No decisions were taken by the Cabinet. Next morning (29th) the Parliamentary Correspondent of *The Times* summed up the position in these terms:

> while the Conservative members of the Cabinet believe in an early election, the Liberal members are opposed to it, and the Labour representatives, with the exception of Mr J. H. Thomas, have not committed themselves.

Thomas's remarks, upon which this comment was based, hardly bore the construction placed upon them:

> Mr Thomas in a statement yesterday morning repeated his declaration at Derby on Sunday night that an appeal to the country could not be long delayed. He added: 'I do not know whether or when a General Election will take place, but I do not think an appeal to the country can be long delayed, and I believe Mr MacDonald will go to the country as the leader. I intend to stand at Derby under his leadership.'

The Prime Minister was said to be 'again looking tired and worn', and complained of severe headaches. He was persuaded to leave the House at an early hour of the evening in order to obtain a much-needed rest.

None the less, the position had been clarified in one vital respect. MacDonald's own attitude had been publicly explained. In a statement circulated by the news agencies, his friends declared that

> it could be safely assumed that if there was an immediate General Election Mr MacDonald would not lend himself to the plans of any one party. The more he considered the situation the more he was convinced that what was required above everything else was national unity. It was with the object of attaining that unity that the National Government was formed, and it was with the carrying out of a national programme that it had been at work. If all the parties would not come in and form part of that national unity, they anticipated that the Prime Minister would find himself in a position in which he would

be compelled to tell the country that he found it impossible to secure national unity, and would therefore have to stand out of the Government. On the other hand, he might have to appeal for a big united central block which would concentrate upon immediate national needs, and would ask the nation to give it power to deal with those needs as they arose. What the Prime Minister really wanted was a 'doctor's mandate' to deal with the position in which the country now finds itself.

MacDonald had not committed himself to an immediate General Election. He was still adhering to the original conception of the National Government; and his relations with the Labour Party were involved. Sir Clive Wigram wrote to the King that day (September 28) as follows:

He (the Prime Minister) does not like the idea of smashing up the Labour Party at the head of a Conservative association. He does not know how to run with the hare and hunt with the hounds. He has hopes of sitting tight now and attracting a following of the Labour Party. This may take a long time.

In quoting this, Nicolson himself comments:

Mr MacDonald himself was divided in mind. On the one hand, he felt that an Election was in fact essential and believed that it would prove to the world that in making his difficult decision he had correctly interpreted the wishes of the nation as a whole. On the other hand, it was repugnant for him to fight the friends with whom he had been associated all his life. . . . Mr MacDonald must have known that the mass of the Labour members regarded him as a traitor to the cause: nor, in any case, would the Conservatives have permitted him to sit tight.

In regard to the last point, MacDonald could none the less confront the Conservatives with his resignation and the consequential break-up of the National Government. As to the attitude of the Labour Party, there were some slight grounds for MacDonald's hopes, quite apart from the indications of Labour support for him in the country. Dealing with a rumour that some Opposition members were contemplating support of the Government, the *Manchester Guardian's* London Correspondent, on the 25th, had accounted for it by reference to the fact that Henderson certainly and Graham to some extent had not shared the bitter mood displayed by the bulk of the Opposition, whose displeasure at the attitude of their two leaders had been manifested. The *Manchester Guardian's* own appeal for a truly National Government, and its insistence upon the narrowness of the differences between the Labour Ministers and the ex-Ministers, have already been noted; and even on September 29 its editorial showed that it was still, unhopefully, hankering for such a development.

The effect of the disclosure of MacDonald's attitude and conditions on the 28th was quickly apparent and far-reaching. To some it seemed that the expected early Election might not take place after all. The statement made on the Prime Minister's behalf certainly ruled out the prospect of a national appeal on a full tariff programme, and thus nullified the hopes of Conservatives like Amery. It kept open the possibility of retaining Samuel and the other Liberal Ministers, together with Snowden; and thus threatened the hopes of the main body of Conservatives, if not of all the Conservative Ministers. The Liberals, as will be seen, were greatly relieved and momentarily delighted. *The Times*, which had always pleaded for the widest possible national appeal, had no difficulty in falling into line with the Prime Minister. Its Parliamentary Correspondent wrote on the 29th:

> One notable feature of the political developments during the past few days has been the complete conversion of Conservative members to the view that, whenever the appeal is made to the electorate, it should be made by Mr MacDonald. Even some of those who were pressing last week that Mr Baldwin should conduct the campaign agreed yesterday that the Prime Minister was the one person who at this juncture should lead the fight for a strong National Government in a new Parliament. For this reason there was a general inclination to regret the insistence which some back-bench Conservative members have placed on the need for a tariff. It is now clear that Mr MacDonald will not agree to conduct a campaign on a programme which is in any way limited. If he does come forward it will be for the purpose of asking for a free hand to meet every situation as it arises with the most suitable weapons. If the Conservatives insist on a Protection and Free Trade contest they will be faced with the prospect of an election on the old party lines, and nobody at Westminster is prepared to gamble on the result of such an election at this juncture.

It is important to understand that political opinion at this time was much influenced by the instability of government resulting from the three-party 'system' and by the fact that under such a system the results of general elections were highly speculative.

The editorial in *The Times* on the 29th took up the idea of a 'doctor's mandate'. The phrase, it said, was 'excellently apt':

Mr MacDonald's view . . . is clearly on the highest level of public spirit and political realism. It will not surprise anyone who looks back to the Prime Minister's own part in the formation of the National Government. . . . It puts the case as rational men and women of every class and party would wish it to be put. . . . Yesterday's reminder that Mr MacDonald's historic decision to form the National Government was itself made at heavy personal and political cost was not unreasonable or untimely.

The Times attacked alike 'the rampancy of protection' and 'the extremism of free trade':

The attitude attributed to Mr MacDonald is a rebuke to extreme partisans, and no camp has a monopoly of them. Among the complaints of 'Tory clamour' and 'Tory plots' it is possible to detect hardbitten party spirit masquerading in the guise of public virtue quite as easily as in simpler-minded bursts of constructive enthusiasm on the other side.

The editorial, however, insisted that an early appeal to the electorate was necessary.

The *Manchester Guardian's* editorial that day (September 29) appears to have been written before the disclosure of the Prime Minister's attitude. It was an attack upon the 'Tory trick':

The Conservatives have pressed for an election precisely because they are not satisfied with the kind of policy that would be carried out by a Government representing the mass of the supporters of all three parties. They want a Government that will carry out a Conservative policy, and that, at the same time, will be called 'National'.
. . . If the Government found it necessary to reconstruct itself before the election it would consist, to all intents and purposes, of the Conservative party, a few repudiated leaders of the Labour party, and a certain number of Liberals, most of whom, like Sir John Simon, had for some time been out of sympathy with the policy of their own party.

The Tories, it was said, wanted MacDonald as a kind of figurehead; and the article concluded:

All that the present Government has achieved might have been done more usefully and intelligently with the full approval of the Opposi-

tion. The Conservatives have preferred to work for their bogus
'National' Government and an immediate election. We trust that Mr
MacDonald will not help them to achieve either.

But the Monday night letter from the paper's London Correspondent (published on the 29th) told a different story. The election, it seemed, was far from being a foregone conclusion:

It is known now beyond a doubt that the Prime Minister refuses to
lend himself to a raging, tearing Tory campaign for a tariff. The Tory
pressure has been extreme. I am told on excellent authority that Mr
MacDonald went away last week largely to escape it. And now he has
had the pluck to tell them that their conception of a National Government and a national policy is not his.

The Tories, he declared, had been thrown into dismay: all their
plans were upset.

No official report of the meeting of the Liberal Advisory Committee on the 28th was issued; but the opposition to an early election was understood to be unanimous, and there was also general
refusal to agree to a purely protective tariff. It was decided, however, that the Liberals would be prepared, on the lines of Samuel's
memorandum to the Cabinet, to consider without prejudice any
proposals put forward as a remedy for the immediate difficulties
arising from the adverse trade balance. The *Manchester Guardian's*
Correspondent had interpreted MacDonald's conditions to mean
that the Liberals must remain in the Government; and he concluded from the decision of the meeting that the Liberals desired
to strengthen MacDonald's hands as far as they could consistently
with their convictions.

THE EXPULSIONS

No statement was issued about the important decision taken that
same day (September 28) by the National Executive Committee of
the Labour Party. It was a decision first reported on September 30
in the *Daily Herald,* and officially made public on October 1; and
the letters communicating it to the persons concerned were not
written until October 1. It was then announced (as reported in the
Herald the previous day) that the National Executive had decided
that 'automatically and immediately' all members and supporters
of the National Government cease to be members of the Labour

Party.[1] There was of course nothing 'automatic' about this 'decision'. According to his biographer, Henderson voted against it, though he did so alone.

It is one curious feature of the commentaries on the 1931 crisis that they give very little attention to this expulsion of MacDonald and his associates from the Labour Party. Mowat, for example, makes only the most casual mention of it. In many cases, undoubtedly, silence on the subject may be attributed to the difficulty of reconciling the expulsion with the customary assertion that MacDonald 'left' his Party. In his *British Political Parties*, R. T. McKenzie discusses at very great length the 'emergence and exodus' of the Leaders of the Labour Party (and of MacDonald in particular) without a single reference to the expulsion. The significance of the date at which the decision was taken has also passed almost unnoticed. It was taken not only before the Election was decided upon but also at a time when the Liberals and Snowden were still opposing an Election, and when MacDonald was still uncommitted. It was taken on the day when MacDonald had renewed his appeal for national unity, and announced his determination to proceed only on a non-party basis. It may be contended that the threat of an Election was the occasion of the decision, although it would be equally plausible to hold that the occasion was the imminence of the Labour Party Conference. The ground of the expulsion, however, was association with the existing Government, which had been in being for over a month. And, although the expulsion decision was not publicly reported until September 30 (in the *Herald*), it was certainly known to MacDonald and his asso-

---

[1] Snowden subsequently published in his autobiography (p. 987) the text of the National Agent's letter to him, dated October 1, as follows: 'The National Executive Committee, at its meeting on Monday, 28th September, gave anxious consideration to the political situation and the developments which point to a grouping of the opponents of the Labour Party and an attack upon it at an impending Election. It was strongly felt that no distinction could be made in the attitude of the National Executive Committee to the actions and negotiations leading to the threatened anti-Labour combination from that shown in the establishment of the New Party by Sir Oswald Mosley earlier in the present year. Consequently it decided that Members of Parliament and others who are associated or in future associate themselves with the present Government thereby cease to be members of the Labour Party. It is my duty to convey this information to you and to express the regret of the Executive Committee that the decisions of representative Committees of the movement which have already been approved by the Trade Union Congress at Bristol and which will undoubtedly be approved at the Annual Conference of the Party at Scarborough have not been accepted by certain of its representatives, amongst whom are numbered some who have been largely responsible for the creation of its policy and practice.'

ciates on September 29, and probably very soon after it was taken. Dalton recorded in his diary for September 29 that MacDonald was

> said to be very angry, and more inclined than before to an election, because he has heard (quite correctly) that our N.E. yesterday decided, without waiting for Scarborough, that those Ministers, M.P.s and candidates who had associated themselves with the National Government could no longer be regarded as members of the Labour Party.[1]

In view of MacDonald's attitude towards an Election, as reported by Wigram to the King on the 28th, there can scarcely be any doubt that the news of his expulsion from the Labour Party was a contributory factor in his subsequent decisions.

THE LIBERAL PARTY

The King returned to London from Balmoral, according to plan, early on the morning of September 29. MacDonald, who had a long talk with Baldwin that morning, was received at Buckingham Palace at 1.55 p.m. and did not leave until 3 p.m. The only information about this interview is derived from Nicolson (p. 492). According to him, MacDonald explained that a deadlock had arisen, adding that it might become necessary for him to ask the King to summon another Palace conference. The King's answer was that he would be glad to do so, but that such a conference would have to 'come out with a settled policy':

> The country (he said) had to be saved and there should be a combination of all decent-minded politicians towards this end: Party differences should be sunk.

The Cabinet then met; and after its adjournment there was a meeting of the Liberal members of the Ministry. No decisions of a conclusive nature were reached at either gathering. The Parliamentary Correspondent of *The Times* reported next day (September 30) that the prospect of a General Election had been brought definitely nearer, 'on the only basis on which a General Election is tolerable — that is, an appeal by Mr MacDonald, as head of a National Government, for a popular mandate to go ahead with the work of reconstruction, and to use any and every means, including a tariff, which may be found to be necessary.' The Prime Minister's position was said to be 'by no means an easy one': he

[1] Op. cit., p. 285.

was obviously 'finding great obstacles, even in the present Cabinet, both to an immediate election and to the programme which it will require'. It seems clear, from this and other comments, that MacDonald had now decided in favour of an early election if a satisfactory basis could be secured. For that, as the same Correspondent said, a programme was necessary 'which would receive the support of the Conservative Party, a substantial section if not the whole of the Liberal Party, and of those Labour members who placed their country before their party in the recent crisis.' Accordingly, the whole object of the conversations going on was to discover whether a national programme on those lines could be framed. MacDonald was said to be

> naturally anxious to avoid any reconstruction which might give the country the idea that the official Liberal Party was opposed to him even though it would be possible to replace the present Liberal members of the Cabinet by other Liberals who are equally distinguished.

The Liberal members of the Ministry, at their meeting on the evening of September 29, considered a formula proposed as the basis of a joint election manifesto. The formula (according to *The Times* on October 1), though drawn in the widest possible terms, included an undertaking by all supporters of the National Government to give it powers to deal with the situation as it develops by every possible means 'not excluding tariffs'.[1] The only decision taken as a result of this Liberal meeting was that Samuel should visit Lloyd George at Churt next day (30th). The Parliamentary Correspondent of *The Times* said (on October 1) it was understood that Lord Reading intimated at this meeting that he would not necessarily regard a decision to hold an immediate election as a reason for resigning from the Cabinet; but that for the most part the Ministers present did not commit themselves. He added:

---

[1] *The Times* described the formula as 'prepared by the Prime Minister'. Snowden, in his autobiography (p. 990) writes of it as 'proposed by the Conservative members of the Cabinet'. Chamberlain's biographer (though giving no dates) makes Chamberlain the author of the formula. Amery (p. 68) does likewise, and says that Chamberlain thought it would serve to dispose of Samuel. Amery quotes his diary for September 29, as follows: 'Drove home with Neville who was reasonably encouraging. His view is that MacDonald is the key, and that it is essential to get him, and no less essential to keep out Samuel.' His entry for the following day, September 30, reads: 'Business Committee where we learnt that MacDonald had completely agreed to a formula skilfully drafted by Neville which we were assured contained all we wanted. . . . The general feeling was that it was strong enough anyhow to keep out Samuel and most of the Liberal Ministers though it would probably be accepted by Reading.'

It was indicated that the Prime Minister was very anxious to retain the services of Sir Herbert Samuel as a member of the National Cabinet; but it was generally understood that if Sir Herbert Samuel felt it impossible to remain the Prime Minister would still proceed with his plans and invite the co-operation of those other Liberals who have indicated their willingness to give him a free hand and who are probably not fewer than 25 in number.

The Parliamentary Labour Party also met on the 29th in the morning. According to *The Times* the Labour members were in a much more optimistic mood when they met, being under the impression that an election had been postponed; but as the day progressed they became more depressed. At the meeting Henderson contradicted rumours that overtures were taking place for a 'more representative National Government', and, according to an official announcement afterwards,

> Mr Henderson declared that there was no truth in these rumours, that so far as he was concerned not a single word on such a subject had passed between him and any member of the Government or anyone acting on their behalf, and further that he would never dream of entering into conversations of such a character or of committing himself in the slightest without first consulting the party.

On the morning of September 30, *The Times* editorial displayed a slight impatience in reiterating its arguments in favour of an immediate General Election. Some fresh impetus to cohesion and decision was required:

> The alignment of parties in the House of Commons under the late Government contained all the elements of a deadlock, and, if they once again become active, they will not be merely dangerous but fatal.
>
> Fortunately for the country a new solvent exists in the shape of the Prime Minister, who, being now adrift from all parties, has an opportunity, rarely accorded to a statesman, in a situation which clearly demands unprecedented remedies. Mr MacDonald has rightly allowed it to be known that he will not identify himself with any party's policy and that he will not merely pass from the leadership of one party to the leadership of another. But that does not mean that he need simply wait for a united front before he takes the lead. On the contrary, if he will only take the lead, there is little doubt that a united and very wide front will form itself behind him. His retirement from politics merely on the ground that unity among his present colleagues was unattainable would be a national disaster. Nobody else can weld

together the forces making for national stability. If he disappeared from the scene, the old party wrangles would inevitably be resumed — a consummation wholly contrary to the national desires and the national interests, and quite unrepresentative of a situation in which inexorable events have eliminated dogmatism from the views of all reasonable persons, whether Socialists, Liberals, or Conservatives. But if he sets up his standard as a national leader, the response is already assured.

There was, however, another factor in the situation: the physically incapacitated Leader of the Liberal Party. The Cabinet met at noon on September 30, and before Samuel left for Churt to see him, Lloyd George had made his views known in vigorous terms. *The Times* (October 1) wrote of a flood of matter issued by the news agencies, 'which threatened fire and slaughter against any Liberal who might co-operate in an immediate national appeal.' A statement issued by the Press Association said that Lloyd George remained unalterably opposed to an early General Election, and added:

> The view taken by those concerned principally with the Liberal Party machine in the constituencies is that if Sir Herbert Samuel decides to support the National Government in an immediate appeal to the country it will mean a complete break between him, together with those members of the Parliamentary Liberal Party who support him, and Mr Lloyd George, plus the Liberal party candidates in the country.

Samuel and Maclean went down to Churt late that afternoon and spent about an hour with the invalid, who had obviously a special personal reason for being violently opposed to an early Election. No statement was issued after their visit.

The political situation remained apparently unchanged during October 1. In fact, if not in form, however, the Liberal Ministers (and Snowden) had moved to the position that they could not prevent an immediate election, and were prepared to remain in the Government if agreement could be reached on a common platform. On the morning of the 1st, the National Liberal Federation issued a reply to the statement published on the previous day which had given expression to Lloyd George's views. It read:

> A statement published to-day makes certain allegations regarding the attitude of 'those principally concerned with the Liberal Party

machine in the country', 'the Liberal Party machine', and 'the Liberal
Party candidates in the country'.

It must be stated that no decision on the issues referred to has yet
been reached by the National Liberal Federation (which is 'principally
concerned with the party machine in the country') or by the Liberal
candidates, who have their own organization.

Until this is done no statements regarding the action of these bodies
have any foundation.

After an audience of the King in his capacity as Foreign Minister, Lord Reading in turn made a visit to Churt towards mid-day.
Lloyd George was opposed to an early election in any circumstances. It was said (by 'alleged "friends" from whom', said *The
Times*, 'he may well pray to be saved') that he was prepared to consider tariffs if the election were postponed, but to come out as a
free-trader if it were held immediately. A meeting of Liberal Ministers was held at 5.30 p.m. on October 1, and lasted nearly an hour.
Samuel and Maclean reported Lloyd George's opposition to an
election, and also their reply to him

> that the impression in political circles was that the Prime Minister had
> definitely decided to appeal to the country, and that Liberal Ministers
> generally felt that his decision would not be a sufficient reason for
> withdrawal from the National Government if a suitable basis for a
> manifesto to the electorate could be found.

The Cabinet met at 6.30 p.m. At 7.30 it adjourned until 10 p.m.,
and then continued until 11.30. In the interval a meeting of the
Liberal Advisory Committee or 'Shadow Cabinet' had been held.
It was understood (said *The Times* next day) that a revised wording
of the formula was under consideration. In the new form the Prime
Minister's supporters would pledge themselves to support any
policy which might be found necessary to restrict imports, including prohibition, tariffs, or any other methods. The Liberal Shadow
Cabinet, it was stated, accepted the view that an immediate appeal
to the country need not necessarily be followed by the resignation
of the Liberal Ministers, but no agreement was reached on the
wording of the formula. In these circumstances, it was not perhaps
surprising that no definite decision was arrived at during the final
session of the Cabinet that night, but *The Times* reported that
sufficient progress had been made to justify the hope that a final
decision would be taken when the Cabinet met again at 2.30 p.m.
that day (October 2).

Amery (p. 69) quotes his diary on the night of October 1. There were frequent divisions in the House of Commons, and he got details at intervals:

> At ten-thirty our people came out in the depths of gloom, Philip telling me that Samuel had swallowed the formula 'hook, float and sinker' and that there was no way of getting rid of him. Later they came out more cheerful, reporting that Samuel's colleagues had gone back on him, that Samuel himself has asked for a modification of the formula, and had been refused; finally things ended at midnight with Samuel being given till two-thirty next day to say 'yes' or 'no' to the formula as it stands.

It is plain enough that in this long-drawn-out phase of the crisis most, if not all, of the Conservative leaders would have preferred not to reach agreement with Samuel and his closest associates.

A curious announcement was issued that night, apparently on official authority, by the Press Association, asserting that the five Liberal Ministers (Samuel, Reading, Sinclair, Maclean and Lothian) had decided to remain in the Government, 'despite the advice tendered them by Mr Lloyd George', and 'in view of the possibility of an immediate General Election'. As *The Times* remarked, certain sections of the Liberal machine had already caused general surprise by the propaganda issued during the crisis; and this statement was at any rate premature, since no decision had been taken by the Liberal Ministers. Amery's assertion that it was issued by Samuel is almost certainly incorrect. However, the London Correspondent of the *Manchester Guardian*, while admitting that the statement was premature, was of the opinion that it could not be said to be altogether untrue in spirit, since the Liberal Ministers were still negotiating about the basis of a joint appeal to the country. That meant, he insisted, that by that very act they were repudiating Lloyd George's leadership.

Editorially, the *Manchester Guardian* was up in arms on the morning of October 2, under the heading, 'The Snatch Election.' The probable formula, it was said, was that the electorate would be asked to give the Government a blank cheque. It was a masterpiece of tactics. The Liberal Party would be split, and not merely by Simon and his followers. Liberals, it was maintained, could not decently co-operate with the Conservatives in a long-term policy; and it could only be hoped that those who were now willing to put co-operation with the Conservatives on a more or less permanent footing and were undoubtedly good Liberals (the *Manchester Guardian* excluded the Simonites from this category) would in due course retrace their footsteps:

> In the meantime those Liberals who maintain the consistency of their dislike to Conservative policy in general and to tariffs in particular, even in times of national emergency, will have to struggle on as best they can, pending the return of Mr Lloyd George to active political life.

THE CRITICAL PHASE, OCTOBER 2–5

MacDonald was away from London for the whole of October 2. In the early morning he left for Durham to keep an engagement to address the delegate meeting of the Seaham Divisional Labour Party that evening. By the same train travelled many delegates to the Labour Party Conference at Scarborough. *The Times* (October 3) said that MacDonald left with the firm impression that the Cabinet would reach a definite decision in his absence when it met in the afternoon. That, however, did not happen.

October 2 was an extremely busy and trying day for Samuel. Early in the morning he had an audience of the King. Information about this interview is limited to Nicolson's quotation from the King's own diary, as follows:

> Received Sir Herbert Samuel at 10.30. He was quite impossible, most obstinate, & said he would not look at tariffs & that there was a deadlock as regards Conservatives and Liberals in the Govt.
>
> God knows what can be done! . . . Am much worried by the political situation & can't see a way out.

Nicolson comments that the King's anxiety was not caused by any personal feelings about Free Trade or Protection: what worried him was the prospect that, if the Liberals left, MacDonald also would resign and that the whole apparatus of National Government would then come crashing down.[1]

There were then communications by telephone with Lloyd George at Churt, followed by a meeting of the Liberal Ministers. That led to a hurriedly summoned meeting of the Parliamentary Liberal party, to which Lords Reading and Lothian were specially invited, and which was attended by 42 M.P.s (including Ministers). Both Reading and Samuel explained the position from their

[1] Op. cit., pp. 492–3.

respective standpoints. According to *The Times* (October 3), Reading conveyed the impression that if the Prime Minister decided on an immediate election, he would be prepared to stand by him. Samuel, however, was less clear: he told the Liberal Members that an immediate election was now unavoidable, and it was gathered that he would be prepared to consider any methods of restoring the trade balance, including the prohibition of imports and a tariff system, if the Government decided that such steps were necessary, though he would not sign anything which might imply his adhesion to a general system of protection in the future. The general view of the meeting, according to the London Correspondent of the *Manchester Guardian*, was that while Liberals could not commit themselves beforehand to tariffs they would not exclude tariffs if it could be shown on investigation that the trade position demanded them.

The position in regard to the proposed formula is rather obscure. *The Times* said that it had been rewritten on a number of occasions during the discussions, but that the Liberals were saying on the previous night (October 2) that the questions in dispute had been narrowed down to the fine point of whether the formula should be of a positive or negative kind—

> that is to say, whether the Government should ask for a mandate to use any remedy, not excluding tariffs, or whether tariffs should be definitely included as one remedy which will be applied.

No resolution about the formula was submitted to the Liberal meeting; and a demand that one should be submitted was defeated by a narrow majority (19–17). It was then agreed that Lord Reading and Samuel should be given a free hand to inform the Cabinet that the wording of the formula was not acceptable and that an effort should be made to obtain further amendment.

The Cabinet met at 2.30 p.m. At 3.45 there was half an hour's adjournment so that Samuel could consult his Liberal colleagues again. This further consultation proved unfruitful, for the Cabinet, after another half-hour of discussion ended without having taken any definite decision. Writing that night, the *Manchester Guardian's* Correspondent could not conceal his pleasure at the turn events had taken. Something like a Free Trade reaction, he said, had occurred: there was growing recognition that a formula could not be found to satisfy both convinced Free-Traders and 'convinced and feverish whole-hogger Protectionists'; indeed, it was even doubtful whether there would be any further search for a formula. However, he thought the Liberal Ministers were now likely to propose that the Government should ask simply for a free hand and would then trust to MacDonald to see that the free hand was not abused in the interests of the Protectionists. The Tories might not agree, in which case MacDonald would have to decide whether or not to go to the country with such Liberal support as he could get, and he had not concealed his wish to carry the whole Liberal Party with him.

On the morning of October 3 *The Times* published a letter from Lord Grey of Fallodon, in which he insisted that the primary and paramount issue was that of economy and sound finance, and that the Government must have power to deal with emergencies:

> It would therefore be unreasonable for free-traders, in supporting a National Government, to qualify their support by stipulating that tariffs should be excluded from the powers given to the Government for dealing with really emergency situations.

Grey expressed concern about the attitude of an important section of the Conservative Party, and the danger, 'very great' and 'very serious', of any attempt to exploit the national emergency as a means of carrying a full party programme. His letter concluded with the words:

> if tariffs are to be made the issue, the election will degenerate into a party fight, and the national cause will be in jeopardy.

The Times reported that while the Cabinet meeting was in progress on October 2, Grey visited the House of Commons, and conferred with Maclean, Isaac Foot, and Leif Jones, three of the keenest free-traders among the Liberals. The paper's Correspondent wrote of a general assumption that, whatever Samuel might do, Reading, Sinclair and Pybus among the Liberal Ministers would agree to continue under MacDonald's leadership, adding:

> Until Sir Herbert Samuel makes up his mind the question of inviting the co-operation of Sir John Simon and his supporters does not arise, though Mr MacDonald is in the strong position of knowing that, however the situation develops, he can rely upon the support of a substantial section of the Liberal Members of the House of Commons.

On the night of October 2, Runciman, addressing his constituents in Penzance, said that he was prepared, in the matter of tariffs, to support any steps found necessary to restore the trade balance.

MacDonald returned to London from Seaham early on the morning of Saturday, October 3. On his journey north he had had enthusiastic cheers from large crowds at each stopping-place. The Seaham meeting had been arranged at his request. The Executive Committee of the local Divisional Labour Party had agreed to it reluctantly, but the extreme narrowness of the vote by which its resolution (condemning the National Government and calling upon MacDonald to resign his seat) had been carried at the previous delegate meeting had been due to the strong feeling that MacDonald should have been given the opportunity of speaking to the delegates before any resolution was passed. Even so, there was no question of rescinding the resolution. The meeting was simply for the purpose of enabling MacDonald to explain his position; and, at the last moment, the Executive Committee decided that it should be private. There were numerous questions following MacDonald's speech, but no discussion took place and no resolution was submitted. MacDonald stated afterwards that he was thoroughly satisfied: he had had a most heartening reception and a good hearing: it had been a wonderful evening, 'very, very satisfactory.' He came back to London, however, to face a position of apparent deadlock.

The Prime Minister was informed by Thomas of what had happened at the Cabinet meeting on the previous afternoon. At 9.15 a.m. he was received in audience by the King, and remained at the Palace for nearly an hour. Information about the interview is again derived solely from Nicolson, who has written that MacDonald told the King that 'he was beginning to feel that he had failed and had better clear out'. The King, however, urged him to 'brace himself up to realize that he was the only person to tackle the present chaotic state of affairs'; that it was his positive duty to find a solution; and that

> even if Mr MacDonald were to tender his resignation, he, the King, would refuse to accept it.[1]

The Prime Minister afterwards left London for Sir Philip Sassoon's home at Trent Park, going on to Chequers in the afternoon, and remaining there until Sunday night (October 4), when he returned to Downing Street.

The executives of the various Liberal Party organizations met on

[1] Op. cit., p. 493.

the Saturday afternoon (October 3). They were addressed by
Samuel and Sinclair, and a long discussion followed, at the close
of which, it was afterwards stated, confidence was expressed in
Samuel. After the latter had withdrawn, the meeting discussed and
adopted the following resolution:

> The Executives of the National Liberal Federation, the Women's
> National Liberal Federation, and the National League of Young
> Liberals unitedly endorse the action of the leaders of the party in
> offering all the resistance in their power to the precipitation of an un-
> necessary and dangerous General Election in the midst of the national
> crisis.
>
> They recognize that our leaders have gone very far in the attempt
> to maintain national unity at this time. At this moment the proposal of
> a general tariff would have the most unhappy effects upon the minds
> of the electorate, since it would inevitably cause a further addition to
> the cost of living at a time when the electors are already subject to cuts
> in wages and allowances and the heavy new taxes imposed by the
> Budget as well as by the probable rise in prices due to the departure
> from the Gold Standard.
>
> The most vital and urgent need at this time is to settle the currency
> problem by rapid negotiations with other nations. In these circum-
> stances it ought to have been possible to concentrate upon that vital
> issue and to put aside questions of party controversy. The permanent
> fiscal policy of the country ought only to be settled by the deliberate
> judgment of the electorate in normal times. We adhere as firmly as
> ever to the view that free trade is ultimately the only basis upon which
> national and international prosperity can be restored, and we deplore
> that a favourable moment for bringing about a reduction of world tariffs
> should be imperilled by insistence upon a tariff policy in this country.

This was not interpreted by *The Times* (on October 5) as an
absolute declaration in favour of free trade which would tie
Samuel's hands in any further discussions. And it was followed on
the 3rd by an announcement from Sir John Simon, in these terms:

> I cannot help feeling that the game of formula hunting has gone on
> long enough. The reality of the national crisis is not in dispute, and
> in such circumstances the best course is for the country to put its
> confidence in the Prime Minister, which I feel sure it is quite ready
> to do. That is the course that I mean to follow. I have the best of
> reasons for knowing that this is also the view of many other Liberal
> members of Parliament, and we are forming an organization at once
> for the purpose of carrying it into effect.

The Liberal Party headquarters issued the following answer:

> Sir John Simon's threat to form a new organization is regarded by
> Liberal headquarters with complete equanimity. Sir John Simon has
> not addressed a Liberal meeting outside his own constituency for
> nearly two years. He has long ceased to attend the Liberal Shadow
> Cabinet meetings, and in June last definitely withdrew from the
> Liberal Party. Liberals throughout the country for some time have
> regarded Sir John as a Conservative endeavouring to keep one foot in
> the Liberal camp for purposes best known to himself. His contem-
> plated action will not receive a fraction of support from any section of
> the party. Its real purpose will be limited to the obtaining of funds to
> enable those members of the Parliamentary Party who have been most
> closely identified with Sir John Simon's subversive tactics to fight
> their present constituencies at the General Election.

On Sunday, October 4, Samuel made another visit to Churt. He
has recorded in his memoirs (p. 211) his note at the time:

> . . . I had a very long conversation with Lloyd George. In the course of
> it he expressed himself very strongly against any lasting alliance be-
> tween the Liberal Party and the Conservatives. He said that he him-
> self would not contemplate it, and he added, with some emotion, 'If I
> am to die, I would rather die fighting on the Left.'

Samuel also spent half an hour with MacDonald, after the latter's
return that night to Downing Street.

That week-end was a period of suspense. No Cabinet meeting
was held either on the Saturday or the Sunday. All turned on Mac-
Donald's decision. As the Parliamentary Correspondent of *The
Times* wrote on the Monday morning (October 5), the members of
the Cabinet were at any rate united on one point — that Mac-
Donald should be allowed to have his week-end in peace. By that
morning, as he wrote on the following day, 'a point had clearly been
reached at which the Prime Minister, who has intentionally taken
his time in eliciting and considering the views of the other party
leaders associated with the National Government, must make his
own decision on its future.'

Early on Monday, October 5, MacDonald visited Lloyd George
at Churt. The journey was fruitless. Mowat writes (p. 408): 'his
blandishments were unavailing.' The Prime Minister returned, as
The Times Correspondent put it, 'with the knowledge at least
that Mr Lloyd George was as violently opposed as ever to an im-

mediate General Election.' According to Samuel, Lloyd George 'phoned him after MacDonald had left and tried to extract a promise from him to stand firm. According to *The Times*:

Mr Lloyd George's position was understood to be that if an election were not postponed he would at once raise the tariff issue and challenge the Prime Minister to declare his policy on this one item alone. Everything else would be subordinated to the old party controversy between Free Trade and Protection. Mr Lloyd George would present himself to the country as a convinced Free-Trader — a position which, as his friends have been cynically remarking in the House of Commons, he has in reality adopted during the last few months for the first time in his life. If, however, he were successful in postponing a General Election, then it is understood that he would be prepared, illogical as it may sound, to consider the necessity of introducing tariffs to meet the present emergency.

When the House of Commons assembled that afternoon, Henderson and many ex-Ministers and other Labour Members were away at Scarborough, attending the Labour Party Conference. No Cabinet meeting was held until very late in the evening, though some of the leading Ministers met in the afternoon. MacDonald himself was busy with a series of interviews. A meeting of Liberal Ministers took place at 9 p.m. The Cabinet met eventually at 9.30.

At 9.30 p.m. also, a meeting convened by Hore-Belisha was held of those Liberal M.P.s who were prepared to support a national appeal, whatever action might be taken by the official Liberal Party machine. Attended by over twenty members, the meeting made preliminary arrangements to set up an organization; and Sir John Simon was authorized to convey the feelings of the meeting to the Prime Minister. This information, according to *The Times* next day, was in MacDonald's possession while the Cabinet was sitting. *The Times* also stated that misleading assertions had been made in the official statement issued by the Liberal Party headquarters on October 3. The facts were, it said, that Simon had spoken at a demonstration in Devon in February, and that he had resigned, not from the Liberal Party, but from the Parliamentary Party, because it was supporting the policy of the late Government which led up to the financial crisis, a decision unanimously endorsed by the Liberal Association in Spen Valley, Simon's constituency.

The Cabinet meeting ended at 11.30 p.m., and it then became known that unanimous agreement had been reached and that a statement would be made in the House of Commons as soon as possible. The Liberal Ministers met afterwards and all decided to continue in office.

THE DISSOLUTION

The agreement reached by the Cabinet was a development which had been quite unexpected earlier in the evening. The editorial in *The Times* next morning (October 6) had plainly been written before the news arrived. Headed 'A Time for Decision', it urged that the policy by which the Prime Minister stood should now be pressed firmly 'against fanatics on both sides':

> The Prime Minister is ready to make himself the rallying-point of every shade of opinion which agrees that, until the peril of a financial collapse is finally repelled, Liberals, Conservatives, and Socialists should concentrate upon the highest common policy. He is not asking Conservatives to vote Liberal nor Liberals to vote Conservative, nor has he turned Liberal or Conservative himself. On the contrary he has quite firmly and quite rightly insisted that he will not become the agent of party policy. If he sponsors a national appeal he is under an obligation to the country to see that the answer to it is not abused. For his own sake, equally, he is right to make it clear beforehand that it is no part of his plan to go to the country as head of a National Government and to return from it as the prisoner of a party. The policy which he would ask the country to support presupposes that a National Government would carry it out. In demanding a free hand to shape economic reform as the facts require he is asking for a discretion which could not be entrusted save to an Administration as comprehensive as he desires to make it.

This editorial came down heavily upon both the Liberal press and Amery:

> The makers of difficulty have not, of course, been wholly or chiefly the protectionists nor are they worse afflicted by party spirit than their opponents. From the moment when an appeal to the country became inevitable, the whole Liberal press abandoned itself to an incredible campaign of violence in the effort to prove that the Liberal Party should not be called upon either to sacrifice its theories or to expose them to the peril of the polls. Day in and day out the world has heard of 'Tory trickery', and of how Mr MacDonald had either succumbed to it or baffled it. But it has been clear that the more Liberals wrote and spoke about Tory wickedness the more they were thinking about Liberal salvation. . . . And their oracle at Churt seems to have out-

topped them all with the suggestion that Liberals might condone a tariff if they were let off an election and oppose it if they were not.

As for Amery, who had written a letter to *The Times* in reply to Lord Grey, and whose view was that Conservative candidates should be 'pledged to the full policy of protection', his argument and claims were described as 'utterly lacking in perspective'. His letter was 'the same letter which he would have written in 1923, when an ill-timed tariff policy created the first Labour Government', and 'for other reasons it is equally ill-timed at the moment':

It would be easier to accept Mr Amery's view as representative if it were not the same view which he has advocated with force and consistency throughout his whole political life.

Amery had written that the tariff was the indispensable first step in balancing the national trade account; his letter went on:

Why should those of us who hold that conviction be branded as narrow-minded and factious partisans because we are not prepared to accept some disingenuous formula for the sake of securing as nominal allies those who do not mean what we mean, and who would seek every opportunity in Parliament or in a Government to delay, to emasculate, and, if possible, wreck the measures we believe to be vital? We are told that national unity demands it. Why is the mutual cancelling out of two policies in futile inaction or half-action a more 'national' course than insistence on definite action in accordance with what is now the view of the great majority of the nation outside the party caucuses?

On what basis and how had the Cabinet reached its unanimous decision towards midnight on October 5? According to Samuel's account in his memoirs (p. 211), he found himself in the end without a single supporter on the specific question of a joint Government manifesto, but definitely refused to give way:

Finally, the others did so. At the very last moment, suddenly and unexpectedly, the Conservative insistence on this point relaxed, and we came to an agreement. Each party was to draw up its own manifesto in its own terms; the Prime Minister would issue, over his signature alone, a general pronouncement in a form to which we could all assent.

Samuel has given the text of a letter he wrote to Lloyd George on the following day (October 6), as follows:

A very strong effort was made in the Cabinet last night to avoid the general election. Both Reading and I pressed it, and it received support from an unexpected quarter. The Conservatives, however, were adamant, and it was clear that the Cabinet would certainly break up if the postponement of an election was made a *sine qua non*. The deadlock continued over tariffs, but was at last resolved when the suggestion was made that each of the Parties should make its own statement, and that instead of a joint declaration signed by representatives of the three sections there should be only an individual manifesto signed by the Prime Minister, its terms to be approved by Baldwin and myself. This preserves the individuality of the Liberal Party and frees us from any concession in the form of words to be used with regard to tariffs. Not one of our Ministers would have been prepared to resign on the issue of the election only, nor would the Parliamentary Party or the National Liberal Federation have supported us in any such action. We can now draft our manifesto in our own way, and I will send it to you as soon as there is anything ready, in the very earnest hope that you will endorse it.

Ramsay Muir, who brings this with him, will tell you further about the situation.

It is not certain who made the suggestion which broke the deadlock. Mowat (p. 408) attributes it to Neville Chamberlain, but there is no supporting evidence. Amery (p. 69) says that it was Snowden's suggestion: Snowden, however, made no allusion in his autobiography to its authorship. According to the account given by Lothian to Thomas Jones, the agreement arose out of a statement made by Snowden, to which both Samuel and Baldwin in that order assented.

On Tuesday, October 6, at 9.15 a.m., the King received the Prime Minister. Nicolson has quoted from the Royal diary:

P.M. came at 9.15 to-day to say that at last the Government have found a formula on which they can make an appeal to the Country. He has worked hard and shown great patience. Lloyd George, as usual, has been impossible. The Prime Minister asked for a dissolution which will take place to-morrow and the General Election on October 27. I am very pleased and congratulated him. Had an interesting talk with General Smuts. He is a very sound man.[1]

In the House of Commons that afternoon, at question time, MacDonald announced that he had asked for a Dissolution and that the

[1] Op. cit., p. 493.

King had consented. Next day, after the King's speech had been read in both Houses, Parliament was prorogued by Royal Commission; and in the evening the Dissolution Proclamation was published in the *London Gazette*, nominations being fixed for October 16, polling for October 27, and the meeting of the new Parliament for November 3.

CHAPTER XV

THE ELECTION CAMPAIGN

THE MANIFESTOS AND THE ISSUES

After the publication of the dissolution proclamation on the evening of October 6, the Prime Minister issued an Appeal to the Nation. The important passages in his Manifesto were:

The present National Government was formed in haste to meet a swiftly approaching crisis. It stopped borrowing, imposed economy, and balanced the Budget. World conditions and internal financial weakness, however, made it impossible for the Government to achieve its immediate object. Sterling came off gold, and the country must now go through a period of recovery and readjustment during which steps of the utmost importance, nationally and internationally, must be taken to secure stability and avoid a recurrence of recent troubles....

As it is impossible to foresee in the changing conditions of to-day what may arise, no one can set out a programme of detail on which specific pledges can be given. The Government must therefore be free to consider every proposal likely to help, such as tariffs, expansion of exports and contraction of imports, commercial treaties and mutual economic arrangements with the Dominions....

The Government is to be comprehensively national, and not sectional, in the obligations which it is to keep before it....

While our present conditions last these things cannot be done by political parties fighting partisan battles on platforms and in Parliament. But they must not involve a loss of political identity, because the immediate tasks are temporary and, when finished, will be followed by normal political activities. They do mean, however, a willing co-operation between all political parties acting together through their representatives, and shouldering joint responsibility for discussion, examination, and action. National unity through the co-operation of parties — all the parties, by preference, if that were possible — is as essential now as it was in August.

In August the combination had to be improvised hurriedly both as regards the Government and its supporting parties and groups in

Parliament. Now, with these prospects before us and so many world indications of uncertainty still threatening, it is essential that the nation's support of Government policy is placed beyond the shadow of a doubt. Parliament has to be endowed with fresh life and mandates. So an election is unavoidable. The working of Parliamentary institutions, of democratic responsibility, and of constitutional practice, demands it. An election, of the result of which there must be no uncertainty, is also necessary to demonstrate to the whole world the determination of the British people to stand by each other in times of national difficulty, and to support any measure required for placing themselves and their credit in an unassailable position.

The Times, on the morning of October 7, was naturally enthusiastic: the leadership of the Prime Minister was, it said, no mere political convenience, and he would lead into action the 'vast body of moderate opinion which is neither afraid of nor exclusively wedded to any particular experiment'. On the 8th it referred to the Prime Minister's use of the word 'temporary' and to his phrase about the subsequent resumption of 'normal political activities', and commented:

But 'temporary' is a relative term. Who can doubt to-day that the task must be longer, more urgent, and more difficult than it was in the days before — through no fault of the National Government — sterling fell from the gold standard? Who can doubt that the task could never be carried out at all save by a National Government of which every member and supporter had unreservedly recognized that the dogmatisms of former party politics are now completely obsolete? The appeal which Mr MacDonald has addressed to the nation is addressed also to his own colleagues. He asks them in effect to unite not only in name but also in fact. His appeal is not an essay in political philosophy but a call to action; and its character should encourage all his colleagues to see that the force behind a national appeal is neither dissipated in the constituencies nor destroyed in the next Parliament. . . . In one quarter and in one quarter only is the appeal likely to fall upon deaf ears. . . . Unhappily there is one party so wedded to its prejudices, and with so low an opinion of the spirit and intelligence of our people, that its co-operation cannot be expected. So far as can be gathered from the depressing deliberations at Scarborough, the Socialist Party has declared against any and every measure to meet the immediate emergency, except what Mr Snowden has called 'the usual clap-trap about going to the supertax-payer'. They are against economy. They are against tariffs. They are against bankers. Most of their leaders have only achieved consistency by the simple process of asking their party to forget the past — a past which includes their 'provisional' agreement to very large economies, their tentative suggestion of a revenue tariff, and Mr William Graham's outline of an emergency Budget practically indistinguishable from that brought in by Mr Snowden. They now seek to obtain the forgiveness of their followers by a rehash of the old doctrine that everything should be publicly owned or controlled — a doctrine in which there is not a single fragment relevant to the present emergency. The Prime Minister cannot hope that those who deserted him — and deserted their duty — will now repent. But he can reasonably hope that their hostility will not be shared by humbler folk, and he can appeal over their heads to those for whom they arrogantly claim to speak.

The reactions of the extreme Protectionists may be judged from Amery's comments in his memoirs:

> MacDonald, in fact, got his way. The battle would be fought with him as the embodiment of the national conception, entitled to remain leader when it was won. In a typically woolly manifesto he appealed to the nation to pull together, and promised that any proposal likely to help, including tariffs, would be considered. Baldwin and Samuel each likewise appealed for unity under the national label, and then proceeded to enunciate opposite policies.[1]

In the Liberal camp it quickly became clear that, quite apart from Simon and his associates, there was distress, confusion and disunity. The Liberal press was anything but enthusiastic, the *Manchester Guardian* bitter in its resentment. *The Times* was soon proved wrong in suggesting that rejection of MacDonald's appeal would be confined to the official Labour Party. The reaction of the invalid at Churt was rapid and vigorous. Frank Owen says: 'Lloyd George was beside himself with rage. He had been betrayed! From then onwards, his resentment of Samuel was never assuaged.'[2] Even on October 7 *The Times* wrote of 'Lloyd George's outburst', for, on the previous day, a statement had been issued in the following terms:

> It is understood from those in close touch with Mr Lloyd George that he considers the decision of Liberal Ministers no longer to oppose an immediate General Election and to commit themselves to the consideration of a tariff policy as a gross betrayal alike of the interest of the country and of the party to which they profess allegiance.

[1] Op. cit., p. 69.
[2] Frank Owen, *Tempestuous Journey*, p. 720.

Their continued adherence to the National Government, it is argued, may result in fastening the shackles of Protection on the country for a generation, and will wreck the Liberal Party.

Even at this late hour it is hoped by those who stand by Mr Lloyd George's attitude that all Liberals who still believe in free trade should unite determinedly in its defence. Such a demonstration, if too late to save the situation to-day, would provide in the Liberal and free trade candidates who survive the General Election a nucleus of a new progressive party.

Liberal dismay and disunity were such that a hurriedly summoned meeting of the Parliamentary Liberal Party on the afternoon of October 6 was unable to reach any decisions. That day also 24 Liberal M.P.s met and constituted the organization of Liberal Nationals. Sir John Simon was appointed Chairman; an executive was elected, with Hore-Belisha as Chairman; Walter Hacking (Secretary of the Manchester Liberal Federation) was appointed chief organizer; and offices were opened. Thomas Jones records a lunch on that day at which, among others, Isaac Foot was present — gloating over the discomfiture of Sir John Simon and his Liberal supporters. 'They were waiting last night, while the Cabinet sat, to be called in — but Samuel stayed on.'[1]

It is much to be regretted that no study of the General Election of 1931 was made at the time on the lines of the extremely useful studies of the 1945 and subsequent General Elections sponsored by Nuffield College. No comparable study can be made now; nor, anyhow, would this be an appropriate place for any attempt of the kind. But the main features of the campaign and its outcome must be recorded.

The campaign was opened by the Prime Minister with a broadcast speech on the night of Wednesday, October 7. This was essentially an expanded version of the Appeal he had issued on the previous evening. MacDonald explained why an Election was necessary; outlined the tasks confronting the Government; and asked both for approval of its formation and actions and for power and freedom to deal with the immediate difficulties of the situation:

When formed last August the Government contemplated a brief life, finishing by a re-establishment of security and an immediate return to normal political conditions. The new situation makes that impossible for some time to come, and the Government has been compelled to

[1] Op. cit., pp. 15–16.

ask the country for a mandate and support which can be weakened by no faction and by no opposition either organized or disorganized.

The first task of the Government was to stabilize the pound sterling. The second was to deal with the adverse balance of trade. On this subject MacDonald said:

> We shall try to increase our exports, which is the best way, and to reduce our imports. A reduction in imports may mean some form of prohibition of certain luxuries and other unnecessary things, or it may mean a tariff, which would act as an impediment to their coming into the country. The Government must be free to consider when that expedient is to be used and how it is to be used.

MacDonald appealed for the subordination of ordinary party issues to national interests. He hoped that 'every party would join up', but, if that was not to be, then he looked to 'the vast majority of the electors of all classes and parties'. There was nothing in his speech which could be described as recrimination or invective. Only once, right at the outset, did he make any reference to the Labour Government, when he said:

> When the late Government shirked the unpleasant duty of carrying out what it admitted to be its duty, a National Government was formed to finish the deserted work. The result was promising at first, but world conditions and events in the House of Commons and outside weakened the confidence which the new Government had begun to establish, and when certain naval incidents — exaggerated and misrepresented — were known all over the world, the task for which the Government had been formed could not succeed. Perhaps it was never possible, but the country would have been disgraced had no one tried, and tried with all their might, to save the situation.

And later MacDonald made what might be interpreted as an indirect allusion to the Opposition propaganda, saying:

> Let me strike the note on which the election should be fought. This is no bankers' ramp, no mere anxiety of the City. The City may have been guilty of sins both of omission and commission. When we have reached the state of stability these things can be dealt with. Reforms can be made. There can be changes in the relation between banking and industry, between currency and commerce. For the moment we must bend our energies to the immediate difficulties which beset us. We must see to it that when the manufacturer produces goods he knows what value he is to get for them. When the workman brings

home wages we must see to it that his wife knows how much bread and cheese, tea and sugar, she can buy with her shillings. In a comprehensive sentence, that is our case and our care.

This time MacDonald did not emphasize the 'temporary' nature of the Government. His phrase 'impossible for some time to come' will have been noted. And in another passage he said:

We cannot work in the midst of speculation as to whether we are to live or not to live. We were improvised to do something definite. We have to undertake a new task, the length and complexity of which no man can foresee. Whatever the man in the street may say or think, the parliamentary position was impossible. Are we to be allowed to govern, or are we not? This must be settled once and for all by an election.

Baldwin's election manifesto was issued on October 8. It was a brief document. His points were (1) that it was necessary to extend the period of co-operation inaugurated by the formation of the National Government; (2) that the national trade account had not been balanced yet, and the disaster of a fluctuating and falling currency had to be prevented; and (3) that it was imperative for the Government to 'have a national mandate giving it freedom to use whatever means may be found necessary after careful examination to effect the end in view', adding that 'the country must show in no uncertain manner that it will have nothing to do with a party whose programme could only convert a situation grave already into one of chaos and catastrophe'. Baldwin then gave special attention to the problem of the adverse balance of trade:

I am prepared to examine any method which can effect what is required. I recognize that the situation is altered by the devaluation of the pound, but in my view the effect of that devaluation can be no valid substitute for a tariff, carefully designed and adjusted to meet the present situation. I shall therefore continue to press upon the electors that in my view the tariff is the quickest and most effective weapon not only to reduce excessive imports, but to enable us to induce other countries to lower their tariff walls.

In regard to what he called the desperate position of agriculture, Baldwin said:

we shall require such a free hand as will allow us to use prohibitions, quotas, or duties as may seem most effective in the circumstances.

u

And he hoped that the Canadian Government would renew its invitation to the proposed Ottawa Conference on imperial economic unity.

Ramsay Muir's visit to Churt proved unsuccessful. 'We did our best', Samuel has written, 'to secure Lloyd George's participation.' Lloyd George refused to sign the Liberal Manifesto. And, on October 8, Major Gwilym Lloyd George resigned his post as Parliamentary Secretary to the Board of Trade, and his brother-in-law, Major Goronwy Owen, resigned his office as Comptroller of the Household. The official Liberal Manifesto was issued on the 9th. After indicating that the Liberal Party had been opposed to a General Election, it declared that in view of the Prime Minister's decision to appeal to the country the Liberal Ministers had felt it their duty to co-operate with him in maintaining a strong and stable Government composed of men of all parties. The situation was no less critical than when the National Government was formed; the vital need was to avoid any inflation of the pound:

> At home it is imperative both to keep the Budget balanced and to secure a favourable balance of trade, by whatever methods, whether related to currency, to the expansion of exports or the restriction of imports, which might be found necessary and effective for that purpose.

The Manifesto then stated:

> We are strongly of opinion that no issues of controversy between the parties supporting the Government should have been introduced at this election. Having regard, however, to pronouncements that have been made, we feel bound to declare our view that whatever emergency measures might be found to be necessary to deal with the immediate situation, freedom of trade is the only permanent basis for our economic prosperity and for the welfare of the Empire and the world.

Emphasizing the need to maintain sound finance, and declaring that the Labour Party's programme of expenditure would defeat the aims of balancing the Budget and preventing inflation, the Manifesto referred to the case for electoral reform, the forthcoming Disarmament Conference, and the problem of India, and concluded with an appeal to the electorate 'to use its power to ensure that Liberal ideas shall have a powerful expression and an effective influence both in the Government and in the coming Parliament'.

Lloyd George issued a separate pronouncement in the form of a letter to his constituents in the Caernarvon Boroughs. He denounced the election itself as 'the most wanton and unpatriotic into which this country has ever been plunged'. For it, he blamed the 'Tory Party managers'. After criticizing the return to the Gold Standard in 1925, and the foreign loans policy of City financial houses, he maintained that no new mandate was required to deal with the currency question, and that tariffs were no help. The Tory attitude, he said, had resulted in an accentuation of the differences 'even inside what is known as the National Government', and the election would intensify class differences:

> The Tory leaders have deliberately provoked dissension, because they saw a distinct party advantage in fighting an election now. This tricky attempt to utilize the national emergency to smash the political influence of organized labour may achieve a temporary triumph, but in the long run it will do nothing but provoke exasperation and accumulate mischief. I sincerely trust that the nation will mark resentment at this unworthy and reckless manoeuvre by withholding its support from candidates who are seeking to profit from the intrigue.

Lloyd George ended by declining 'to assist a mere Tory ramp to exploit a national emergency for Tory ends'.

The Labour Party's Manifesto was issued on October 9. It was a long document, beginning with the assertion that the capitalist system had broken down even in those countries where its authority was thought to be most secure. The Labour Government, it declared, 'was sacrificed to the clamour of bankers and financiers'. The National Government, having failed completely in its original object, 'now seeks from the electorate a mandate for the impossible task of rebuilding capitalism':

> this ill-assorted association of life-long antagonists seeks a blank cheque from the people for purposes it is unable to define. Acutely divided within itself, headed by men who are now acting in direct contradiction to their own previous convictions, certain, in the near future, to split into fragments, it makes the shameless pretence of being the instrument of national unity. The Labour Party is confident that the country will not be deceived by claims so arrogant and so dishonest.

What was described as 'a coherent and definite programme' followed. Socialism was said to provide the only solution for the evils resulting from unregulated competition and the domination of vested interests. The Manifesto accordingly pressed for the extension of publicly-owned industries and services, and for 'coordinated planning'. In a minority position, it was said, the Labour Government had suffered from intolerable restrictions. Asking for power to press forward rapidly with its programme,

> it will tolerate no opposition from the House of Lords to the considered mandate of the people: and it will seek such emergency powers as are necessary to the full attainment of its objectives.

The banking and credit system, the Manifesto proceeded, must be brought directly under national ownership and control. An international conference to arrive at a concerted monetary policy was advocated, and the reopening of negotiations with a view to the cancellation of Inter-Allied War debts and reparations. Tariffs were opposed. Labour's alternative was the reorganization of the most important basic industries as public services owned and controlled in the national interest, with import boards endowed with adequate powers of regulation and purchase. There followed certain familiar items of Labour policy. And the Manifesto concluded with an unqualified condemnation of the reduction in the rates of unemployment benefit, the increase in contributions, 'the introduction of Poor Law tests and machinery into the administration of unemployment insurance,' and the Economy Act as a whole. A pledge was given 'to reverse immediately the harsh policy of the present Government'.

Thus the stage was set. It presented a situation of considerable complexity. On the one side was the loose alliance of parties and groups supporting the National Government, each fighting independently, but agreed in much, and conforming, in greater or less degree and with more or less reluctance, to a common platform. On the other side was, first, the official Labour Party and its associated organizations; and, secondly, Lloyd George and his supporters, with influential backing in the Liberal press. There were also Mosley's New Party; the Communist Party; and a contingent of independent candidates.

Inevitably, minor clashes occurred between the component elements in the 'National' alliance; and the major conflict over the tariff issue between the main body of the Conservatives and the official or Samuelite Liberals was only partially kept in the background. To the ardent protagonists on both sides of the tariff controversy, it was the supreme issue of the Election. They sought to make it so in the minds of the electors. Their failure was not due simply, or even primarily, to the fact that advocacy of the rival creeds was restricted by the acceptance of a common platform. That platform left much scope for such advocacy, and the restraint it should have imposed was exercised much more by the leaders than by the rank-and-file. Moreover, it was on this issue that the Government candidates were most obviously vulnerable. Their known differences of view on the subject, extensively expressed during the campaign, could be and were vigorously exploited by the Government's opponents. But the truth was, not only that the climate of opinion on the fiscal controversy had been changing, but that the bulk of the electorate were not easily convinced that it was the chief issue of the Election. Indeed, they seemingly endorsed the view, plainly implied in the very decisions of the political leaders to form and to continue the National Government (and to oppose it), that the tariff issue was a subordinate one.

The struggle which overshadowed all else was that between the official Labour Party and the National Government. The explanation is not that the various supporters of the Government succeeded in concealing their differences by attacking the Labour Party. There was nothing artificial about their condemnation of the attitude that Party had taken up towards the crisis. Its vigorous and increasingly virulent opposition to the National Government was the major cause of the election and its central issue. The General Election of 1931 was as much a verdict on the formation of the National Government as on whether or not it should continue to function. And, as the campaign proceeded, it resolved itself more and more into a contest between the Labour Ministers and the Labour Party. The renewed and embittered controversy about the discussions in the Labour Cabinet was not the cause but an incidental consequence of this. MacDonald (to use Amery's phrase) was 'the embodiment of the National conception', the key figure in the Government: without him the Government would not have been formed in the August, nor could it have survived in October. He and his associates had thwarted the attempt to make protection the basis of the appeal to the country, and so saved the Government. They also constituted the chief obstacle to the attempt on the Labour side to make Socialism the great Election issue. They stood in the way of a clear-cut campaign for and against 'the Tories', irritating the ardent Protectionists like Amery, infuriating the fanatical Free-Traders whose chief mouthpiece was the *Manchester Guardian*, and keeping the official Labour Party on the defensive. In these circumstances, that Party largely concentrated its attempts to counter-attack upon its former leaders, and particularly upon MacDonald. The contest in the Seaham constituency, and to a lesser extent that at Derby, consequently became of outstanding public interest. For the same reason, repeated opportunities were offered to Snowden, who took full advantage of them, and whose independent and effective role in the campaign was its other most conspicuous feature.

Arrangements in the Constituencies

From the standpoint of the 'National' alliance, it was obviously undesirable that, as a general rule, there should be more than one candidate supporting the Government in any single-member constituency. It was indeed requisite that the Government vote should not be split in any constituency where such a split would risk the loss of the seat. On the whole, the necessary, and even the merely desirable arrangements were made with surprisingly little difficulty, despite the fact that they were left substantially in the hands of the localities themselves. The central party and group organizations, and the leaders, provided guidance and exhortation only: no authoritative decisions were applied from the centre.

Mowat has written: 'It was the coupon election all over again, though, let it be granted, without the coupons.' The qualification nullifies the assertion; and all that Mowat apparently has in mind is the fact that the great majority of the candidates supporting the National Government were Conservatives, just as the majority of Coalition candidates in 1918 were Conservatives. The parallel ends there: and it is difficult to see how the situation could have been otherwise. 'As in 1918,' writes Mowat, 'the lion's share of the National candidates was taken by the Conservatives.' But the simple facts were (1) that 78 per cent of the Government's supporters seeking re-election were Conservatives, and (2) that the candidates already adopted in seats which had been held by the Labour Party were for the most part Conservatives, and so far from the Conservatives increasing the number of their candidatures in such constituencies a substantial process of withdrawal took place.

The only alternative to what was done would seem to have been a 'share-out'; an allocation of the National candidatures between the various parties and groups in accordance with some agreed principle of division cutting across or going beyond the actually accepted principle that Government supporters seeking re-election for their old constituencies should not be opposed.

At the time of the dissolution, the Government representation was as follows:

Conservatives	-	-	-	263
Liberals	-	-	-	-	58
National Labour	-	-	-	15
Independents	-	-	-	4

Naturally enough, Government supporters seeking re-election had a strong claim, and expected, not to be opposed by a rival supporter of the Government. With few exceptions, they were not so opposed. The great majority of them, of course, were Conservatives. In fact, 24 seats which had been Conservative were contested by Liberal candidates despite Labour opposition. In 18 of these constituencies the Liberal candidate had been second in 1929. Churchill and Lord Eustace Percy were among those so opposed. In 21 other constituencies previously held by Conservatives but not on this occasion contested by the Labour Party, the Conservative candidates also had to meet Liberal opposition. In no fewer than 19 of these 21 seats, it should be noted, Labour had fought in 1929. The other exceptions are of interest, and in some instances of considerable importance. Some of the constituencies represented by Liberal and Labour supporters of the Government in the previous Parliament were seats which the Conservatives had expected to win when the Election came; and the local Conservative associations and adopted candidates were naturally reluctant to withdraw. In most cases, however, they did so.

There were four instances in which the Conservatives decided to contest constituencies which had been held by Labour supporters of the Government. One of these was Preston, at which the retiring Labour member on the Government side (it was a double-membered constituency), Sir William Jowitt, the Attorney-General, did not seek re-election. He contested instead (unsuccessfully) the two-membered Combined English Universities seat, where two Conservatives were among his opponents. Another was the case of S. F. Markham at Chatham. Here there was a special complication. In the initial stages of the campaign Markham had taken charge of the National Labour organization which was formed, and had not at first intimated his intention to seek re-election. The case gave rise to some difficulty (see below, pp. 302–3), but, under protest, Markham eventually withdrew. The third instance was that of Central Wandsworth, where Major A. G. Church decided not to seek re-election. He was eventually nominated for the University of London seat against the former Independent member, Sir Ernest Graham Little, and was unsuccessful. In the remaining case, that of Everton (Liverpool), the former Labour member, Derwent Hall Caine, did not withdraw, and was supported in his campaign by the National Labour Committee against both Labour and Conservative opponents. This was one of two instances in which a National Labour candidate fought both Labour and Conservative candidates, and the result was therefore of particular interest (see below, p. 332).

Similarly, little trouble arose about the former Liberal M.P.s who were Liberal Nationals. Only two of them were opposed by Conservatives, although one of these was a junior Minister, A. E. Glassey, in East Dorsetshire. The local situation in Dorsetshire was not favourable to Conservative-Liberal co-operation; and in two of the other three constituencies in the county there were straight fights between Conservatives and Liberals, the Labour Party not presenting candidates on this occasion. In the East Dorset case, as in the other, that of Ashford in Kent, the local Conservatives could contend, with justification, that there was no danger of a split resulting in a Labour victory. In Heywood and Radcliffe, the retiring Liberal National member, Colonel England, eventually withdrew. In the Western Isles, the Liberal National had a straight fight against his Conservative opponent.

With the Samuelite Liberals the position was nothing like so happy, because of the tariff controversy, and particularly because of a letter sent at the very outset of the campaign to Liberal candidates and associations by Ramsay Muir, Chairman of the National Liberal Federation. This letter is discussed below (pp. 298–301). Three Liberal Ministers had to meet Conservative as well as Labour opponents: Sir Herbert Samuel at Darwen, Sir Donald Maclean in North Cornwall, and Milner Gray in Mid-Bedfordshire. The position of these Ministers gave rise to a good deal of controversy. Another Minister, E. D. Simon (afterwards Lord

Simon of Wythenshawe) also had Conservative opposition in Penryn and Falmouth, but this was a rather different case, Simon having deserted his former constituency of Withington in an attempt to succeed Sir Tudor Walters, the retiring Liberal member for Penryn. Apart from Ministers, eight other Samuelite constituencies were contested by Conservatives, one of these being Withington, when no Labour candidate appeared.

Problems for the 'National' alliance were also presented by those constituencies held at the dissolution by Opposition Labour members. In many of these the local Conservative associations and candidates had anticipated victory at the next Election, and they could hardly be expected to withdraw. Indeed, the Conservatives had adopted candidates in the great majority of instances. On the other hand, it was desirable, from the standpoint of the 'National' alliance, that the non-Conservative elements in the Government should secure substantial support in the new Parliament. This was a more difficult problem in the case of the Labour supporters of the Government than in that of the Liberals, whether Liberal Nationals or Samuelites. The National Labour elements in the localities were entirely unorganized, save perhaps to some very slight degree in the seats formerly held by National Labour representatives; and the proposed National Labour candidatures had to be hurriedly improvised. It could hardly be expected that Conservative candidates already chosen would withdraw in their favour. Broadly speaking, the only opportunities left for such candidates were in a few strong Labour seats, where the Conservatives and Liberals had either not adopted candidates or were not keenly anxious to fight, and where in any event the prospects seemed far from good. In the outcome, only eight such candidates were nominated, and two of these (at Gateshead and Newcastle Central) in fact supported another Government candidate, although they were too late formally to withdraw. This was also the position of the National Labour candidate at Colne Valley, Snowden's old seat, who withdrew in fact though he could not do so in form, on Snowden's advice, and supported the Liberal candidate against his Labour and Conservative opponents. Even so, the National Labour candidates in South-Eastern Essex and Peckham contested seats in which there were Conservative candidates.

In the case of the Liberal Nationals, local arrangements were made with very little difficulty. Apart from the 19 constituencies, previously held by Liberal Nationals, in which the Conservatives withdrew and in which, with two exceptions, they had achieved second place in 1929, there were 11 others where the Conservatives refrained from adopting candidates in order to give Liberal Nationals straight fights against Labour. In half of these the Conservatives would have had good prospects of success.

The chief trouble, in regard to former Labour seats as in regard to seats formerly held by Government supporters, arose as between the Conservatives and the official Liberals or Samuelites. In this connection it should be realized that, at this period, the Liberal Party rather than the Labour Party provided the main opposition to the Conservatives in many parts of the country. In 1929, Labour was in the third place in no less than 149 constituencies, and in 39 others presented no candidate at all. The trouble would have been much less than it proved to be had it not been for the publication on October 10 of the Ramsay Muir letter already mentioned. In this letter, addressed to Liberal associations and candidates, the Chairman of the Liberal Federation said:

> We need not look for any arrangement with the Conservatives. They will do their best to destroy us, except possibly in the constituencies where we alone have any chance of defeating Labour. There will be no pact and no coupons.

> We shall do well to concentrate upon those seats which we have a fair chance of winning, especially those where there is no chance of a Labour victory. We must not abstain from fighting Protectionist sitting members merely because they support the Government, except in cases where the effect of our putting up a candidate would be a Labour success.

> We ought to try (besides holding our own seats) to fight every Labour member (not being a supporter of the Government) where we come second on the poll, and every Protectionist candidate whom we can hope to unseat without letting Labour in.

Muir said that the Party had practically no funds at its disposal, and the need for financial help was 'extremely urgent'. He described the election as a 'wild gamble with the nation's fortunes', and said that its sole cause was the desire of the Conservative Party to turn a national emergency to party advantage. In a long reference to the tariff issue, he wrote:

> Liberals must support the National Government as Free-Traders or not at all. In the national interest we have no right to palter with Free Trade.

We have supported the National Government and we shall support its successor in all measures necessary to meet the national emergency. We are ready for any impartial and scientific inquiry into fiscal policy. But we must be satisfied that its conclusions are sound before we vote for them. Will the Conservatives pledge themselves to drop their agitation for tariffs, if an impartial and scientific inquiry shows that they are wrong?

Muir went on to suggest questions which might be addressed to candidates of other parties who wanted to secure the Liberal vote, for example:

Will you oppose the imposition of food taxes or other burdens on the people in view of the heavy burdens already imposed?

If an inquiry is held by the Government and the conclusion is adverse to tariffs will you cease to advocate them?

In conclusion, Muir said that the Liberals could not hope to do very well in the election: 'the dice are loaded against us.'

Baldwin took up the matter in the opening speech of his campaign at Birmingham on the evening of October 9, before the press publication of Muir's letter. On that day the decision of the Darwen Conservatives to oppose Samuel had been announced. Baldwin said:

I regret to see that Sir Herbert Samuel, leader of a large section of the Liberal Party, is being opposed in Darwen. I know perfectly well what local feeling is at these times ... but I do not think that to oppose a leader of the party that forms part of the National Government is quite what I should call playing the game, but it is only fair to remember that it is much easier to play the game if two people do it instead of one. And I have been perturbed by some news which has reached me from London this evening, just before I came to this meeting, that there has been issued instructions to Liberal candidates and Liberal chairmen, which I am informed may appear in the Press to-morrow. And if the purport and tone of that is as has been described to me, I am perfectly certain that Sir Herbert Samuel knows nothing about it and will be the first to repudiate it; because if this be the fact, and if such instructions have been issued to Liberal candidates, then I feel that the co-operation which I desire and for which I would strive would become not only very difficult but almost impossible.

Muir's own reply to this on October 10 was not helpful. He said:

the plain fact is that Protectionist candidates are opposing Liberal Free-Traders, and it is natural that Liberal Free-Traders should oppose Protectionists. The assumption that the basis of co-operation between Liberals and Conservatives must be that Liberals must in every case give way to Conservatives is an entirely illegitimate one. On such a basis no co-operation is possible.

Samuel made no reference to the matter until October 12, when he said, in a speech at Darwen, that he gathered Muir's letter

was written under the impression that many Conservative candidates might insist on a full protectionist programme for immediate application. He hoped that that would not prove to be the case.

He went on to urge the necessity 'to use language of restraint', and from that standpoint criticized a speech made in Darwen in support of his Conservative opponent by Sir Henry Page Croft.

It was not until October 19 (three days after nomination day) that Samuel, in response to a further reference by Baldwin to the Muir letter, gave a fuller explanation of it. Speaking at Finsbury Park Empire on the 17th, Baldwin said:

When great sacrifices are demanded, difficulties are bound to arise. I think they arise sometimes unnecessarily. At Birmingham I appealed to Sir Herbert Samuel to repudiate a document which had been issued to the Liberal candidates and chairmen, because that document, in my mind, was entirely opposed to the spirit of the manifesto of the Prime Minister. I said that I was afraid that the publication of such a document, if allowed to go uncontradicted, would make co-operation in many places difficult, if not impossible. I am very sorry myself that my fears have proved only too right in a few constituencies, and the fact of the publication of that document has undoubtedly caused a great deal of trouble in many constituencies in the country. . . .

Samuel's remarks on the 19th were as follows:

I knew nothing of the letter in question until after it had been circulated. It was written before the dissolution of Parliament and was based on the supposition that the election might not be fought on a broad and simple national issue, as it was afterwards stated by the Prime Minister, but that a main issue might be whether the new Parliament should be pledged to establish a general system of protection. As the election has proceeded it has become more and more plain from the speeches of the head of the Government and many others that that is not so.

The appeal on behalf of the Government is to be genuinely national with the programmes of all parties subordinated to the common cause. Some constituencies, unfortunately, offer exceptions to this rule. But wherever the rule is observed, the conditions which Mr Ramsay Muir was anxious to guard against do not apply, and so the conclusions which he drew do not apply either.

Samuel added:

Broadly speaking, considering the great difficulties in the way which many people thought could by no possibility be overcome, it is remarkable how the parties supporting the Government have shown a spirit of co-operation. That spirit must, of course, be mutual. I have done my best to promote it. I am sure that Mr Baldwin has done and will do the same.

The trouble would also have been less had it not been for the activities of the more extreme Protectionists, supported as these were by the Beaverbrook and Rothermere newspapers. In an editorial on October 13, *The Times* considered that neither side was wholly blameless in the case of the opposition to Sir Herbert Samuel, but that in the case of Sir Donald Maclean it was 'as misguided as it is disruptive'. The article went on:

It is unhappily all too clear that in this and in other similar cases those forces which did their unsuccessful best to dictate to the Conservative leaders eighteen months ago are now following the same short-sighted course. It cannot therefore be made too clear that this stirring up of local associations to change a national into a party battle is directly opposed to the views of Mr Baldwin. . . . All these partisan candidatures, whether of fanatical Free-Traders or of fanatical Protectionists, can only confuse the electorate by representing that the fiscal issue is the only issue at this election; and all are equally to be condemned.

Despite all the complications, however, the efforts made to avoid splitting the National Government vote were strikingly successful. The outstanding failure was the maintenance of the opposition to Samuel, Maclean, and two or three other Liberal Ministers. The Conservatives were called upon to make the bulk of the sacrifices, and their response, on the whole, was remarkably satisfactory. Indeed, their behaviour compared favourably with that of the Samuelite Liberals. It must be remembered that no one anticipated the magnitude of the National victory which was actually achieved: it was that which produced a much greater discrepancy than had been envisaged between the number of Conservative seats and the number of those won by non-Conservative supporters of the Government. The Conservative central organization, when criticized, pointed out that their candidates had been withdrawn, or they had refrained from nominating candidates, in fifty constituencies in most of which they had had a well-founded hope of winning. In fact, this happened in some 57 constituencies (in 13 in favour of National Labour candidates, and in 44 in favour of Liberals of one variety or another). The total number of Conservative withdrawals and abstentions was greater still. On a more optimistic estimate of the prospects, the Conservative organization could have made an even stronger defence.

The criticism had been voiced by the Prime Minister himself in a speech at Dawdon on October 13. After repudiating a charge that Tory funds were being provided for National Labour candidates, MacDonald said:

> As a matter of fact we are finding that we shall probably have to fight some Conservative candidates who were thrust into Labour seats against our candidates. Darwen is not the only case, and so far as I am concerned I am not going to tolerate parties saying they are supporting the National Government and putting in party candidates and using the National Government to increase their party's strength in the House irrespective of the National Government. This is an independent co-operation. The leaders know each other and trust each other to play a perfectly honourable game in the national interests. The whole trouble is coming from local organizations which refuse to respond to the advice of the leading men.

As will be noted, this was not a criticism of the central Conservative organization. It led, however, to a letter from Lord Stonehaven, the Chairman of the organization, to Lord De La Warr, the Chairman of the National Labour Committee, in which the statement referred to above was made. Lord Stonehaven added:

> Not a single case can be produced to substantiate the allegation that Conservative candidates have been thrust into Labour seats against National Labour candidates. On the contrary the Conservative Party has done its best to try to make room for National Labour candidates sent down at the last moment to constituencies where Conservatives have long been in the field.

De La Warr replied to Stonehaven on the same day (October 14) expressing appreciation of the latter's efforts and those of Baldwin, but regretting that the attitude of the leaders was not entirely shared by some of their followers in the country. De La Warr pointed out that the first list of National Labour candidates numbered 35; that this number had been reduced to 25 in order to avoid splitting the National vote; and that 10 of these were still being opposed. He mentioned in particular the cases of two former M.P.s who were being opposed, those of Hall Caine at Everton and Markham at Chatham.

It must be conceded, however, that the National Labour candidatures in seats not formerly held by MacDonald's supporters presented special difficulties for the Conservatives. Even in the cases of the Samuelite Liberals, a clear field was left them by the Conservatives in more than twenty constituencies, eight of them previously Liberal seats. The outcome was that, whereas in 1929 there had been only 102 straight fights (83 in which Labour was concerned), in 1931 there were 409 (Labour being concerned in 375 of them). Moreover, of the three- and four-cornered contests, only 52 involved the three main parties, Conservative, Liberal and Labour.

There were 67 Unopposed Returns, as follows:

Conservatives - - -	49
Liberal Nationals - - -	7
Liberals - - - -	5
Labour - - - -	6

The nominations for the contested seats were:

Conservatives - - -	519
Liberal Nationals - - -	39
Liberals - - -	121
National Labour - - -	21
Labour - - -	513
Communists - - -	25
New Party - - - -	23
Others - - - - -	29

LIBERAL DISUNITY

During as before the Election campaign, the Liberals were in a state of great confusion. On October 7 the Executive of the National Liberal Federation passed a vote of confidence in Samuel. It was also decided to issue an urgent appeal for funds. That was taken by *The Times* next day to mean that money would not be forthcoming from Lloyd George's Fund. On the 8th came the resignations of the two Ministers who were members of Lloyd George's family. More important, the chief permanent official of the Liberal Party, Colonel Tweed, resigned all his appointments in connexion with the official party organization. The Liberal Nationals that day announced the adhesion of Runciman to their group.

On the 9th the *Manchester Guardian* bitterly declared that the Liberal Party was divided into three, 'though for the sanity of the electors it is to be hoped that representatives of all three groups will not appear in any one constituency.' This paper held that if the Government were returned to power it would be a Tory Government, 'and those who expect to co-operate with it on any other basis will sooner or later have a painful awakening.' The editorial concluded roundly:

> this sham unity, this temporary and embarrassing alliance of tigers and sheep is worth less than nothing. Taking as it does increasingly every day the form of an alliance against Labour, it is perhaps the greatest threat to national unity that we have.

The *Manchester Guardian* had travelled far since August 29, when it was urging the earliest possible appeal to the country in order to forestall the disaster of a Labour success. No doubt that even then it wished to see the alliance of Protectionist tigers and Free-Trade sheep brought to a speedy end. But the prospect of a tariff being imposed by means of this alliance was more than it could stand. The alliance became an intolerable menace, not because it was anti-Labour, but because it might be pro-tariff. For the *Manchester Guardian* the tariff was now the primary issue, and the Tories were blamed for having made it so:

> It is as clear as anything in politics can be that for the Conservative Party the 'National' Government means tariffs first and foremost. The tariff is for them the test question.
>
> One would have thought that this simplified matters for the Liberal party. Co-operation with the Tories would not be easy anyhow, but co-operation for the purpose of foisting a permanent tariff system on the country is a betrayal of everything that Liberalism has fought for in the past.

The division of the Liberal Party into three parts was perhaps an over-simplification. There was the Liberal Council, whose Executive Committee, however, on October 8, endorsed Lord Grey's attitude and brought itself into line with the Samuel position. There was also the Liberal Free Trade Campaign Committee, under the chairmanship of F. W. Hirst, and with distinguished academic support, which issued a manifesto on the 8th reaffirming unqualified faith in free trade. Samuel's position was indeed one of very great difficulty; and it was certainly not eased by Ramsay Muir. In the circumstances, he balanced with considerable skill; but went out of his way to make an attack upon Sir John Simon personally, though not upon the Liberal Nationals as a body.

The publication of the Liberal manifesto, of Lloyd George's personal manifesto, and of the Ramsay Muir letter, did not improve matters. The *Manchester Guardian* (October 10) had no use for Ramsay Muir, since his letter suggested that 'where advocacy of Free Trade might result in handing the seat over to Labour Free Trade should take a back seat':

> Mr Muir's letter, in fact, puts sincere Liberal Free-traders in an extraordinarily difficult position. Liberals who still believe in Free Trade and have not been overcome by the sudden anti-Labour mania exhibited at Liberal headquarters, will be compelled to vote for a Labour candidate in preference to the Liberal in cases where the Liberal is relying on Conservative support. For, in general, such Liberals, even if they do get in, cannot be trusted to vote for Free Trade or any other Liberal principle in the new House of Commons. And that, in turn, is very unfair to those Liberal candidates who really do mean to stick to Free Trade, who do not care two straws about a 'National' Government which compromises their Liberalism, and who can still regard a Labour Member of Parliament with the equanimity which was, until recently, usual among Liberals.

The *Manchester Guardian* declared that the 'National' Government and Liberalism were incompatible, and that there could be no Liberal Party worth the name until it broke with the 'National' Government. It dismissed the Liberal manifesto on the ground that no adequate explanation was given in it why the Liberals needed to work with the Conservatives. MacDonald and Snowden were held chiefly responsible for 'bad Budgeting'. Henderson and his colleagues were said to have 'suddenly had a pistol put to their heads'. The Government's economies were 'crude and unjust'. Lloyd George's manifesto, on the other hand, received the *Man-*

x

chester Guardian's unqualified approval. The effrontery with which the *Manchester Guardian* reversed its attitude towards the August crisis and the formation of the National Government is as striking as its invective, which became increasingly less restrained as the campaign proceeded. Its references in the passage quoted to 'the sudden anti-Labour mania' and to 'equanimity' are particularly instructive in the light of its editorials during the last week of the previous August.

Colonel Tweed also attacked the Ramsay Muir letter. He declared that he associated himself completely with Lloyd George's attitude of opposition to the Government; and he particularly objected to the passage in the Muir letter which suggested that the Liberals should concentrate on those seats where they had been second at the last Election, for in 253 seats, according to Tweed's reckoning, the Liberals had been third. Muir's reply was significant. He said:

> A year ago, when I was in charge of the organization committee, I received a definite promise of a certain sum towards running the next election. In virtue of that promise, commitments were made with a number of candidates. That sum was suddenly withdrawn, and without warning, and the result was to place the headquarters of the party in a great difficulty. An immediate attempt had then to be made to raise fresh funds but in face of this situation it was held to be necessary to concentrate attention upon those seats which we were most likely to win and therefore undesirable to advise all the constituencies to try to put up a fight.

The Muir letter, even if drawn up before the dissolution, was plainly the consequence of an intimation that Samuel and his associates, if they persisted in their attitude, would have no financial assistance from Lloyd George. On October 12, a statement was issued on behalf of the latter, that the fund associated with his name would be placed at the disposal of Liberal candidates who were unequivocal Free Traders. That, presumably, left the matter as it found it.

Labour did not fight the 1931 Election without allies. No formal alliance, of course, was entered into with Lloyd George, although Henderson visited Churt on October 10. But the Labour Party, Lloyd George, and the chief Liberal newspapers, had a common enemy in the National Government. Labour's decision not to contest a considerable number of constituencies where the Liberals provided the chief opposition to the Conservatives was doubtless influenced by this consideration. Almost from the outset of the campaign, as noted above, the *Manchester Guardian* moved strongly towards the Labour side. On October 10 it had suggested that the Liberal free-trade vote should be given to Labour in preference to Liberals fighting with Conservative support. Less than a week later, reinforced by Lloyd George's election broadcast, it made its advice more specific.

In his broadcast, Lloyd George said:

> There is no real probability, in my judgment, of the return at this election of an independent Socialist majority. . . . The danger is therefore all in the direction of Protection. I earnestly hope therefore that Liberals will in every case cast their votes for free-trade candidates at this election. So many Liberal candidates have been withdrawn, very unwisely, as I think, and so many are quite indistinguishable from Tory protectionists, that the choice left to the electors is too often between a food taxing Tory and a free-trade Labour candidate. Between the two I should have no hesitation in the circumstances which govern this election. I am neither a Tory nor a Socialist, but a Liberal. But I weigh probabilities. Protection is the impending peril. I should use my vote to avert that calamity.

The *Manchester Guardian* adopted this argument. The greatest danger, it declared, was that the Conservative Party would come back in such numbers that it would be able to flout the Liberal and Labour supporters of the Government, who would be cast aside or absorbed. It endorsed Lloyd George's view that it was impossible for the Labour Party to obtain a clear majority of its own; and argued that the right course was, in Lloyd George's words, 'to reduce the Protectionist membership of the next House of Commons to such proportions as will ensure that the whole question of our trade balance and of national reconstruction shall be given unbiased consideration.' 'A clear Conservative majority', said the *Manchester Guardian* on October 16, means 'Protectionism, full and complete.'

> The free-trade test, though not the only one, is the one that can be applied with greatest safety. The more Free-Traders there are in the House, whether Liberal or Labour, the less likely is the Government — whatever its nominal party composition — to introduce a policy that will be harmful to the best interests of British industry and to the general recovery of international trade.

On the 17th, the *Manchester Guardian*'s advice to Liberal voters went beyond Lloyd George's broadcast words. It was expressed in these terms:

> A Liberal candidate who has virtually signed away his Liberalism by promising (explicitly or by implication) a 'free hand' to Mr Mac-Donald and tariffs to the Tories ought not to be supported any more than a professing Tory. In such a case a Liberal would have no option but to vote Labour. But it would be absurd for a Liberal to vote for a Labour man in preference to a Liberal if the latter besides being a Liberal was the more sincere Free-Trader and stood a better chance of defeating the Tory.

The same advice was given, perhaps in more definite form, on October 21. In the majority of cases (those which would really decide the election), the Liberal voter had to make up his mind 'between voting Labour and voting (in effect or without disguise) Tory':

> It ought now to be plain to all that the Tories aim at a majority large enough to put their full programme into force, and that such genuinely progressive elements in the Government as may survive the election will certainly disappear soon after. The only possible way of preventing this is for Liberals to vote Labour.

Henderson quoted this advice, and made it one of his chief points in his broadcast on October 23.

Speaking at Liverpool on October 21, Baldwin reproved the *Manchester Guardian*. Its article, he said, was ungenerous, petty in its terms, and very unlike that great paper, which hitherto had been the greatest organ of Liberal opinion in the country:

> Frankly I do not understand it. It makes the position of Liberals, both in the Cabinet and the Government, very difficult. It arouses distrust among many in my own party, a distrust that is only too easily aroused at a time when it is essential for the nation — Conservatives, Liberals and Socialists who are liberal minded — to work together for the common cause. It is like a nasty-tempered member of a football team, when he sees the other side will beat his own, and says of them: 'I will just kick these fellows on the shin, for I don't like their faces.' That spirit does not tend to help the game.

The *Manchester Guardian* replied on the 23rd that it had never heard of such an incident on the football field. Baldwin's assump-

tion 'that everybody with any pretension to public spirit must be
on his side' was, it declared, preposterously wrong:

> We are most definitely and emphatically not on Mr Baldwin's side.
> We wish to see his side beaten. We regard the 'National' Government
> as one of the gravest dangers before the country at the present moment.

The Government, said the *Manchester Guardian,* was not national:
it was anti-Labour: and it was not a unity within itself. Men like
Samuel and Baldwin were proclaiming themselves as believers respectively in Free Trade and Protection but willing to examine the
position after the election:

> Why after the election? Why cannot they make up their minds now,
> so that the electorate would have something to go on? The answer is
> obvious; they cannot. Then why pretend?

Lloyd George purported to regard Protection versus Free Trade
as the central issue: the *Manchester Guardian* and its Liberal supporters undoubtedly considered it to be the issue which mattered
most. So also, of course, did many Conservatives. The *Manchester
Guardian* would not admit that it was putting party before nation.
When would anyone make such an admission? it queried: 'Nobody
supports a political party because he believes that it will be bad for
his country.' That was Amery's attitude, too. To him the talk of
putting nation above party was humbug:

> I disliked the whole humbug about a National Government above
> Party, and feared that a clear national verdict for the causes for which
> I had worked so long would be weakened and frittered away in order
> to hold together a Coalition which had no other object than to per-
> petuate its own unnecessary existence. . . . I had no doubt that we
> could have secured an ample majority for a purely Conservative
> Government on a straight issue.[1]

On this subject of nation and party much nonsense is often
talked and no doubt was talked during the 1931 Election. None the
less, it will be generally conceded that a course of action recognized
to be in the national interest may be detrimental to a party's immediate prospects; and that the subordination of party interest to
the wider national interest is sometimes necessary and frequently
desirable. That is granted in time of war or at other periods of
grave national emergency. In 1931, this issue turned on the ques-

[1] Op. cit., p. 70.

tion whether or not the situation was in fact one requiring such a subordination of party interests. Opinions differed, as they were bound to do, but the affirmative answer was widely and genuinely believed to be true.[1] And those who gave it considered that the activities of the extremist Free Traders and Protectionists were in danger of obscuring the real issue of the election. *The Times* emphasized this danger throughout. On October 20 it wrote:

> Unhappily there are signs that some Conservatives and some Liberals are falling into the trap laid for them by the Socialist Party, and even more obviously by Mr Lloyd George, and are doing their best to see that this election is fought on the old party lines of Tariffs versus Free Trade and in the old party spirit. Lord Grey, in his speech at South Shields on Saturday, rightly deplored attempts to distract the country by giving prominence to minor issues, and doubted whether some Conservatives could 'spell, write, or speak any word except "Tariff" '; but he would have crowned his admirable advice if he had extended it to those Liberals who can certainly see nothing except free trade. The free-trade Bourbons are no whit better than the tariff Jacobins.

The *Economist*, consistently deploring the appeal to the electorate, viewing the attitude of the official Labour Party with alarm, and staunchly opposed to the 'economic insanity' of high or permanent tariffs, found it increasingly difficult 'to detect upon what issue the majority of the electorate thinks they are voting'. Its strong free-trade convictions did not prevent it from recognizing that the tariff issue was one of 'comparative unimportance'. It admitted that if the Conservatives secured a clear majority of their own there might be a danger of the 'tariff monomaniacs' trying to force their policy upon their own leaders. But the *Economist* was not at all sure that the election would produce such a result, although by October 24 it had come to the view that a majority for the Government was almost certain. Such a majority, it declared, would be

> rightly interpreted as the justification of Mr MacDonald's action, and the condemnation of that of Mr Henderson and his colleagues, and as a vague expression of the desire for a strong Government to tackle big problems.

That, undoubtedly, summed up the position accurately enough. The *Economist* held that, in the nature of things, the results could

---

[1] Some discussion of the matter is to be found in the author's *The Essentials of Parliamentary Democracy*, (1935), pp. 159–63.

give no proof whatever of any majority demand that any particular line of policy should be followed; and that, whatever the National majority, 'there will be no conceivable mandate for Protection.'

ELECTIONEERING

'The stridency of the campaign was another unpleasant reminder of 1918 — and of 1924.' So Mowat has written. The blame for this he attributes very nearly exclusively to the supporters of the National Government. He writes much about their abuse of their Labour opponents. But 'the most powerful weapon against the Labour Party was fear', and 'everything was done to create panic'. It was no wonder, he says, that the *Manchester Guardian* called it 'the most fraudulent election campaign of modern times'. The *Manchester Guardian* did so on October 28, the day after the poll. Perhaps, in another sense, it was no wonder, for the *Manchester Guardian* was almost beside itself with rage at the results. In a letter, dated November 1, Miss Violet Markham wrote to Dr Thomas Jones:

> And I have been thoroughly incensed this week with the *Manchester Guardian* which is indeed laying hands on the Ark of the Covenant. The leading article on Wednesday talking of the 'monstrous fraud' of the Election was I thought deplorable.[1]

It is a commonplace of British politics that the Conservatives (with or without allies) never win an Election, according to their opponents, unless they employ unfair methods. Doubtless the defeated, irrespective of party, always attempt to explain away their failure on some such grounds; but the 'parties of progress' (perhaps just because they believe themselves to be such) are rather more prone to this sort of thing than the Conservatives. Certainly, the General Election of 1931, like all General Elections, presented some unpleasant features; and, as always happens, there was mutual recrimination about the methods employed. Mowat's treatment of the matter would be less open to criticism had it been less hopelessly one-sided. He has relied too much on the *Manchester Guardian*, which bitterly opposed the National Government throughout the campaign, and the *Economist*, which, from start to finish, deplored the fact that there was an Election at all.

It is simply not true that the atmosphere was one of panic; or

[1] Op. cit., p. 21.

that the electors were driven by fear. Writing on October 29, the *Manchester Guardian* itself said:

> There is agreement that it was panic, but the panic had not manifested itself beforehand in any open way. There has been no turbulent terror, none of the exasperation of temper in which panic often makes itself manifest. *It has been a remarkably quiet election.*[1]

A panic which had not manifested itself in any open way 'beforehand' was, indeed, a strange sort of panic. The 'agreement that it was panic' existed only among the partisans of the defeated, and was very far from comprising all of them. Since the panic manifested itself only in the voting, all that the *Manchester Guardian* was really saying was that the vote for the National Government was amazingly large; but to the *Manchester Guardian* the only feasible explanation of an overwhelming verdict for its opponents, at that or any other Election, is panic or some other regrettable emotion. Mowat himself says that 'the dominant mood, as in 1918, was one of sullenness, of meetings of grim, silent audiences'. Indeed, as has happened on other occasions, the British electors largely kept their own counsel, and gave all the politicians a shock. What can safely be said is that an impartial observer from Mars would not have concluded that the Labour Party and its allies were less to blame than their opponents for the 'stridency' of the campaign. The verdict of such an observer might well have been given in the opposite sense.

The 1931 General Election was the first in which broadcasting played a full part. Mrs Hamilton has written[2] of the persistence of the view that the B.B.C. made an unequal allocation of time as between Government and Opposition. She attributed this to the effect of Snowden's broadcast, since his 'vitriol counted for more than one', but she asserted that 'numerically the allocation was perfectly even'. That was not so as between Government and Opposition. Apart from the Prime Minister's initial broadcast on October 7, ten broadcast addresses were given, in the following order: Baldwin, Clynes, Lloyd George, Simon, Snowden, Graham, Samuel, Baldwin, Henderson and MacDonald. There were thus six speeches on the Government side and four on the Opposition side. The Conservatives, however, had only two, both given, it

---

[1] Author's italics.
[2] *Remembering My Good Friends*, p. 113.

will be noted, by Baldwin. The three sections of the Liberals each had one. No fewer than five were allocated to the rival Labourites, three to Opposition Labour and two to National Labour. Although Mrs Hamilton's statement was incorrect, it is difficult to see how a fairer distribution of the broadcasting time could have been made, unless, indeed, the more extreme Conservative Protectionists had been given an opportunity.

No doubt the choice of speakers on the Government side was skilful; but the prominence given in the broadcasting to the Labour speakers on both sides exemplifies the main feature of the campaign as a whole. *The Times* wrote on October 21:

> The debt which the nation owes to Mr MacDonald, Mr Snowden, and Mr Thomas becomes clearer every day. It is no disparagement of the admirable part which has been played by leaders of the other political parties to say that the election campaign is turning upon the fact that these three members of the late Socialist Cabinet did their duty when their colleagues ran away.

The conflict between the Labour Ministers and their former colleagues was the heart of the whole matter. The charge that the ex-Ministers had run away from the crisis was, undoubtedly, the chief feature of the campaign on the Government side. From the beginning, too, the Labour Party machine directed its strongest efforts against MacDonald and his associates, and particularly against MacDonald himself. The driving force behind these efforts was provided by the General Council of the Trades Union Congress, under the leadership of Ernest Bevin and Citrine.[1]

Apart from the continued repudiation by ex-Ministers of any responsibility for any of the economy measures considered and 'tentatively' proposed by the Labour Cabinet, the Labour Party's propaganda suggested that the National Government had been planned by MacDonald in advance, and asserted that MacDonald

---

[1] Ernest Bevin had for long been bitterly opposed to MacDonald — and to Snowden — but he was more antagonistic personally to MacDonald than he was to Snowden, or than Snowden himself was to MacDonald. After the first Labour Government, as R. T. McKenzie has reminded us, Bevin pulled every string to oust MacDonald from the Labour Party leadership, co-operating even with Snowden for that purpose. At that time, Bevin had not emerged from his original anti-parliamentary phase, and, indeed, was never to become a Parliamentarian in anything but a formal sense. Events were then still moving up towards the General Strike. Bevin, like the whole of the Labour and Socialist 'Left', intensely disliked the minority Government experiment. At the 1925 Labour Party Conference he moved a resolution against any repetition of Labour Minority Government, and was soundly trounced and defeated by MacDonald.

and his Labour associates had deserted to 'the enemy', that they were entirely dependent on Tory support, and that they were 'prisoners' of the Tory Party. Citrine set the tone immediately after MacDonald's broadcast on the day of the dissolution. He said that MacDonald had 'surrendered to his masters in the Tory Party who had dictated a General Election':

> Mr MacDonald would be kicked downstairs just as soon as the Tories deemed it expedient, and what better fate could he expect who had intrigued for months past behind the backs of his colleagues to form a National Government?

On October 14, the General Council of the T.U.C. issued its Election Manifesto. For its opening words the General Council owed an unacknowledged debt to Dalton:

> Fellow workers, the first Labour Government was destroyed by a 'Red Letter'. The second Labour Government has been destroyed by a Bankers' Order. . . . It has been deliberately broken because it refused to reduce the workers' standard of life.

What, it was asked, was the history of the 'National' Government?

> It was formed by the Prime Minister behind the backs of his Labour colleagues. It was a secret alliance with those forces of reaction against which the trade union movement has fought throughout its existence. . . .
> This Government is an unstable alliance between the Conservative Party and divided remnants from the Liberal Party, together with a few Labour deserters who have abandoned the principles by which they stood not two months ago. In this strange combination the Conservative Party is master, the Prime Minister its docile servant.

On the previous day (October 13) Henderson made his adoption speech at Burnley. Its main passage must be quoted because it constitutes Henderson's nearest approach, in a public pronouncement, to endorsement of the 'plot theory'. Speaking of the Government, he said:

> There was only one point in their programme on which they really did agree, and that was the necessity for inflicting a crushing defeat upon the Labour Party.
> The astonishing thing about this discreditable manoeuvre was that the combination responsible for it had at its head the former leader of those political forces it was now proposed to destroy. What the

Labour movement or the Parliamentary Labour Party had done to deserve to be whipped by National Government scorpions was not easy to understand, as it must be remembered that Mr MacDonald, before forming his new combination, suffered no reverse at the hands of the Parliamentary Party. In fact he was the leader of Labour at the beginning of August, and when next he met his old colleagues in September he had become the head of a new administration without explanation of any sort or kind.[1]

Though it was difficult to understand the real inwardness of this move, it must be obvious that Mr MacDonald, by consenting to this election, was permitting himself to be used by his life-long opponents to smite his life-long political friends, who had denied him no opportunity in political life, but, on the contrary, had given him unstinted confidence and honour.

The suddenness of the change-over was all the more remarkable in view of the fact that the possibility of a National Government had been in Mr MacDonald's mind for months, and had even been the subject of conversation without its having once been brought before any official meeting of the Labour Party. Moreover, it must be stated that when the definite move was made to bring a National Government into being, the reasons advanced were that it was necessary because of the paramount importance of promoting national unity and re-establishing confidence abroad. How was the first of these two desirable objects to be achieved or maintained by an openly avowed attempt at bringing about a crushing defeat of the Labour Party?

It will be noted that Henderson did not commit himself to any assertion that the National Government had been planned months in advance; but the ambiguity of his comments led to them being interpreted as an endorsement of what so many of his associates were saying on the subject. MacDonald himself so interpreted them, and replied next day (October 14) in a speech at Blackhall Colliery in his Seaham constituency, in the following terms:

I find it is going about a good deal that the National Government was devised months ago. I am very sorry Mr Henderson stated that yesterday, because he must know it is not true. The simple truth is this: every one of you who followed the events of the last ten days of the Labour Government knows that if I can be blamed for anything it is for carrying on negotiations too long. Why did I carry them on ten days when, at the end of the second or third, I began to doubt if it was

---

[1] Henderson was evidently speaking of the Labour M.P.s and the reassembly of Parliament in September. As a description of the formation of the National Government, this passage is a masterpiece of omission and evasion.

possible to get Cabinet unity? I carried them on because I wanted to keep the Labour Government in office. I knew that in front of us were Indian problems, disarmament problems, matters relating to our relations with America, a new coal agreement, and the Geneva International Conference on coal. I wanted the Labour Government to face the facts. A minority of the Government compelled the rest of us to give up our places, and I declined to run away and allow it to be said that a Labour Government in time of crisis had not the courage to face unpopularity.

In his opening election speech at Easington two days before (October 12) MacDonald had said:

I strove until almost the last sand in the glass had gone through to keep the Labour Government in office. That was my policy. My policy was not to go out but to remain in. I failed. Then the National Government had to be hurriedly constructed, because there was no time to lose.

The official Labour organ, the *Daily Herald*, under Bevin's close supervision, completely abandoned the attitude of 'no recrimination' announced on the formation of the National Government. During the election campaign it sank low, even by the standards of the less reputable national newspapers. A special interest attaches to one incident which may be selected from the mass of illustrative material available.[1] On October 13, the *Herald* came out, under a banner headline 'Premier's Secret Tory Bargain', with the story that MacDonald had entered into a secret pact with the Conservatives by which 'the whole resources of the Tory Party machine', including funds, were to be placed at the service of the National Labour candidates. The story was accompanied by a photograph of Baldwin and MacDonald, obviously whispering together, with the caption, 'Are they whispering to each other about pacts in the constituencies?' The *Herald* said:

The finishing touches were put to the Tory–MacDonald pact yesterday at a joint conference of the two publicity staffs which, under Sir Patrick Gower and Sir Robert Donald, are to work in the closest co-operation.

[1] Two other incidents perhaps deserve mention. The first is the *Herald's* front page story on October 17: 'Girls' Secret Air Dash to Seaham: R.A.F. Pilot Mystery.' The second is its featured statement on October 22 that the National Government, if returned to power, would as one of its first acts put an end to the Indian Round-Table Conference.

Every National Labour candidate who is returned will be, in fact, neither 'National' nor 'Labour' but just plumb Tory.

That is the chief effect of the secret bargain.

The Pact also has a financial side.

The MacDonald Labour candidate will be, in everything but the bare title, Tory candidate.

In return for this promise of support, and for the withdrawal of Tory candidates, pledges, the exact terms of which are being kept secret, are being extorted from all these candidates. . . .

Mr MacDonald has a secret fund. Money paid him by wealthy people who remain discreetly hidden. But this fund will not be enough to pay all the expenses. To fill the gap the funds of the Tory organizations in the constituencies will be available. And these will be supplemented, if necessary, by a grant from the central Tory campaign fund.

The Tories are paying the MacDonald piper. And 'National Labour' has had to agree that they shall call the tune.

Alongside this was a report by Hannen Swaffer that MacDonald had arrived in his constituency at Seaham without a single cheer — 'one boo from a miner and that was all.'

At the time of the formation of the National Government, MacDonald had not of course contemplated the formation of any new party organization. His expulsion from the Labour Party, and the decision to have a General Election, compelled the formation of some organization to assist the Labour supporters of the Government. The National Labour Committee, as it was called, came into existence a few days after the dissolution. It was announced on October 9 that Markham was in charge of the organization. On October 11, *The Times* reported that Lord De La Warr was acting as Chairman, that Sir Robert Donald had taken over general supervision of the publicity arrangements, and that Mr Benjamin Musgrave had been appointed chief organizer.

The *Daily Herald's* allegations were promptly and vigorously denied. MacDonald said in an interview:

I have seen that report. It is alleged we have got promises to dip our hands into Tory funds and that we are practically a Tory adjunct — a sort of sub-species. It is absolutely untrue. We have no arrangements about funds. Some well-to-do members of the Labour movement who used to subscribe to Labour Party funds, and one or two friends of my own, have subscribed a fund which is not a large one, but which is quite adequate for our purposes.

MacDonald then went on to speak of Conservative opposition to National Labour candidates in certain localities. He also referred to the *Herald's* photograph:

> The photograph shows Mr Baldwin and myself sitting in adjoining chairs putting our heads together. We are evidently whispering. That photograph is used for the purpose of making certain suggestions to you. It was taken weeks before there was a change in the Government. It was taken on the platform of the Albert Hall when we were brought together to bear testimony to international peace.
>
> Somebody said it was going to be a savage election. Well, they are certainly showing their savagery. I am ashamed that any party should ever produce such a rag as this newspaper has become. It is a mean and contemptible expedient, more particularly when the issues are so great.

Statements followed from the National Labour Committee, from Sir Robert Donald, and from Lord Stonehaven on behalf of the Conservative organization. The National Labour statement read:

> We have not had a penny of Conservative money here, and so far as we know no Conservative money has been put up in the constituencies. Our trouble, like other parties at the moment, is to get enough money. We are absolutely independent financially, both as regards propaganda and organization. Our one object is to see that in the coming House of Commons the Prime Minister will have behind him an adequate representation of Labour men. We are truly an emergency organization, and in three weeks we shall disappear. At present we are definitely turning away offers from many who desire to speak or to run as candidates for us because they have not been associated previously with the Labour Party. Our only negotiations with the Conservative Party have been in regard to arranging for candidates and seeing that there is no clash against the National Government. There is nothing secret about that. It is being done all over the country.

Sir Robert Donald himself added:

> So far as I am concerned I would not be here if there were any connexion with the Tory Party machine. I have been fighting the Tory Party machine all my life, and I would not consent to be an annexe to it. It would be an extremely short-sighted policy for Mr MacDonald and his colleagues to allow themselves to be definitely allied to the Tory Party machine. Surely they have more political sense than to do that.

Conservative headquarters issued the following statement:

> Lord Stonehaven, Chairman of the Conservative Party, denies emphatically the statement that Conservative funds are being used to pay the expenses of National Labour candidates. Conservative funds are solely used in support of Conservative candidates.

It may be added that the *Manchester Guardian*, reporting on MacDonald's arrival at Seaham and his opening meetings, said that his campaign was going forward 'with great enthusiasm', and that cheers had drowned the hecklers.

Enough has been said to show that the more deplorable kinds of 'electioneering' were certainly not confined to the Government side. Mowat has written that there was a good deal of organized rowdyism at meetings on both sides. That may well be true; but there is no doubt at all that the most conspicuous instances of it occurred at Seaham and Derby, where MacDonald and Thomas were on some occasions prevented from speaking. Similar instances were reported at other places where they were supporting National Labour colleagues.

When the campaign began, the predominant feeling on the Labour Party side (and for that matter on the Government side also) was that MacDonald had little chance of being returned at Seaham. 'It seems impossible that *he* can win,' wrote Dalton in his diary after speaking at Seaham. The *Daily Herald* editorial on October 17 announced in heavy type:

> Seaham's answer is already certain. Mr MacDonald is already beaten. He knows it and is plainly showing that he knows it. . . . We trust that there will be no more attempts to silence Mr MacDonald. Let him be heard.

The Special Correspondent of *The Times* at Seaham (October 27) wrote:

> It can be said on the eve of the poll that if Mr MacDonald is re-elected his success must be considered one of the greatest victories in the political history of recent years.

Although, to the end, confidence was expressed in Labour Party circles that MacDonald would be beaten, no stone was left unturned to ensure his defeat. The T.U.C., in particular, mobilized its forces against him. Bevin and Citrine were among the many speakers who visited Seaham. Lady Passfield also took a hand, or, rather, her pen; and characteristically raised a personal note:

Why should the late Labour member for Seaham have superseded George Lansbury as First Commissioner of Works by the Marquis of Londonderry? I can only observe that, as the Bible says, 'Evil communications corrupt good manners.'

MacDonald expressed his regret at this 'unworthy reference to Lord Londonderry and myself', adding, 'Lady Passfield lays herself open very much to a similar retort. But what is the use of that?'

The Webbs, and more especially Beatrice (as is plain from her diary), had what almost amounted to an obsession about non-political social relationships. For years they had gossiped about and deplored the lack of social contacts between the leading figures in the Labour Party. In particular, Beatrice Webb was constantly harping on MacDonald's preferences for social contacts in other circles, although she dwelt most frequently on his associations with 'aristocratic society'. The Londonderrys were a special grievance. The Webb preoccupation with class and social distinctions, and the Webb form of snobbery, are alike plainly revealed in the diary. The long and deadly serious reflections on the 'curtseying' problem for the wife of a Minister and Peer are amusing enough. In regard to MacDonald, perhaps the most illuminating point is the Webbs' complete misunderstanding of his character in their assumption that he hankered after a title. They had the precise title all ready. Bernard Shaw, it is true, immediately after MacDonald's announcement of the decision to form the National Government, said that what would happen would be MacDonald's retirement to the House of Lords as Viscount MacDonald of Lossiemouth, but Shaw was never good at such things; and the Webbs knew that an earldom is the customary dignity conferred upon ex-Prime Ministers who are willing to accept peerages. Already, on December 14, 1930, Beatrice wrote in her diary: 'MacDonald would fancy himself as the Earl of Lossiemouth!' After the formation of the National Government (August 25) she was convinced that MacDonald would go to the Lords at the close of the episode, and, on the 27th, she 'wished him well among the Dukes and Duchesses', adding, 'If it cost me nothing I would endow him with an adequate income for his position as Earl of Lossiemouth on the condition that he made no kind of attempt to veer back to the Labour Movement.'

The real basis of the suggestion that the campaign was conducted on the National Government side with the weapons of abuse and fear is to be found, it seems, in the Snowden broadcast on October 17 and in Snowden's other election activities. The other specific points usually mentioned in this connexion are either election commonplaces paralleled on the other side or have been given a greatly exaggerated importance in retrospect.

Mowat has written that Snowden set the tone in his October 17 broadcast. If so, it was a very belated 'setting', for October 17 was the day after nominations, and half the campaigning time had sped. In fact, Snowden did not wait until the 17th; and the truth is that the Snowden pronouncements which incurred criticism were essentially replies to the statements of ex-Ministers and official Labour propaganda. And, whether or not the criticism was justified, it has to be remembered that Snowden occupied a position which, though of key importance, was curiously independent. He was not himself a candidate; and, though still Chancellor of the Exchequer, his relinquishment of that office after the Election was inevitable, whatever the result might be. Snowden was by no means closely associated with the National Labour Committee. Moreover, he was, as he described himself in his broadcast, a 'stern and unbending Free-Trader'. The line he pursued during the election was his own.

In his reminiscences, Amery has written: 'I was sickened by the sadistic malignity of Snowden's horribly effective broadcast attacks upon his old colleagues.'[1] That, it is true, was written only recently; and there was much criticism, though not as a rule in such strong terms, at the time, in quarters opposed to the Government. But it would not be easy to justify the expressions used by Amery. The text of the broadcast, so often condemned subsequently, but so seldom read, is set out in Appendix VII below; and readers may judge for themselves. It is interesting to note Beatrice Webb's verdict in her diary for October 18, 1931:

> Snowden's broadcast last night was a model of lucidity, delivered with conviction, without the unctuous insincerity of Simon or false rhetoric of J.R.M.; admirably planned and phrased.[2]

Mowat speaks of the 'bitterness with which he (Snowden) denounced life-long colleagues of a bare two months ago'; and there

---

[1] Op. cit., p. 70.
[2] Op. cit., p. 293.

is no doubt that Snowden felt bitter. At the same time, it is doubtful whether an impartial judge would say that he expressed himself bitterly in the broadcast itself. What is a little odd is that Mowat should have not a word to say about the bitterness with which Snowden and the other Labour Ministers had been denounced and were being denounced by 'lifelong colleagues of a bare two months ago.' As evidence of Snowden's bitterness Mowat produces two phrases; first, the description of the Labour Party's election programme as 'Bolshevism run mad'; and, secondly, the assertion that it would 'plunge the country into irretrievable ruin'. The broadcast has been labelled by that first phrase: indeed, it is the only statement in the broadcast which is usually recalled. And, although the omitted context to some degree moderates its impact, Snowden's use of the expression was and is justifiably objected to. The second phrase, taken in its context, clinched an argument which, though it may be dissented from, was perfectly legitimate. It was certainly paralleled by many of the expressions employed in Opposition broadcasts. In that respect, and for the rest, the Snowden broadcast may well be contrasted with that delivered by Lloyd George two days before. The invective, what there was of it, differed from much on the Opposition side only in its greater effectiveness.

Perhaps the Snowden broadcast was most effective in destroying Lloyd George's case, which had been based on the supreme importance of Free Trade. Snowden was a much more consistent and reliable Free-Trader than Lloyd George, and was generally recognized to be so. He insisted, however, that Free Trade was not the issue:

> That one issue on which you should vote is . . . whether we should have a strong and stable Government in this time of national crisis, or whether we shall hand over the destinies of the nation to men whose conduct in a grave emergency has shown them to be unfitted to be trusted with responsibility.

Snowden said he did not believe 'that the Conservative leaders would regard a majority obtained in the circumstances of this election as giving them a mandate to carry a general system of protection in the new Parliament'. Anyhow, he asserted, if Free-Traders followed Lloyd George's advice, they would not be able to do it by voting for the Labour Party, which was not a Free Trade party.

It is not at all surprising that the *Manchester Guardian* was extremely angry. Its editorial on October 20 began with a reference to 'the peculiar malignity of the apostate', and described Snowden as 'the complete apostate', who, 'far more thoroughly than Mr MacDonald, has turned his back on the aims and ideals of a lifetime.' 'Vitriolic and scornful', 'a great master of gibes, and flouts and jeers', 'not over scrupulous in his methods of attack', were some of its comments on Snowden. This was an outstanding instance of the pot calling the kettle black. The language employed by the *Manchester Guardian* during and after the election campaign was anything but temperate. Journalists, however, are habitually severe upon any politician who lapses into the kind of terminology they are themselves accustomed to use. Snowden's gravest offence, in the *Manchester Guardian*'s mind, was his attitude towards Free Trade. It considered his optimism to be terribly misplaced, and could only suggest that 'his political judgment has been warped by the unreasoning bitterness against the Labour Party that now consumes him'. The *Manchester Guardian* laid itself wide open to an obvious retort.

Although Snowden was unable to do any platform speaking, his election activities were far from confined to his broadcast. Indeed, according to his autobiography, he launched attacks upon his late Labour colleagues 'every day from the first day of the Election campaign to the eve of the poll'. On the day of his broadcast (October 17) his letter to National Labour candidates was published. On the 20th he had a widely reproduced article in the *Daily Mail*. He records that after each of the Labour broadcasts:

> I followed them up with replies in the Press exposing their inaccuracies and giving the facts about their commitment to economies which they were now repudiating.

The main details of this controversy have already been given. Snowden's general attitude may be exemplified by two passages. The first is the opening of his *Daily Mail* article:

> I can recall the features of every General Election during the last 50 years. I have never known one where a political party has sunk to such depths of deception as the leaders of the Labour Party have done on this occasion. The brazen way in which they are repudiating their own actions in the Labour Government is an instance of political depravity without parallel in party warfare.

Mr Clynes, in his broadcast talk last week, spoke of the scandalous disclosures of Cabinet proceedings. I agree with him. But the disclosures came first from the members of the late Government, perverted and discoloured to excuse their own disgraceful surrender to the dictation of the trade union caucus.

Incidentally, there was a curious note in the *Economist* on October 24 about these disclosures. Ponderously deploring the secrets of the Council Chamber being 'shouted from the housetops', this paper wrote about 'the precedent set by Mr Snowden and Mr Graham'. The note indicates no awareness of the fact that the 'disclosures' had begun long before the Election campaign: it is related exclusively to that campaign. Similarly, there is no recognition of the connected fact that the process of disclosure was certainly not started by Snowden.

The second passage is the concluding part of his Letter to Electors on Eve of Poll (October 25):

I did not exaggerate when I said that the issue on which you vote tomorrow is prosperity or ruin.

As one of the oldest members of the Labour Party, I deeply regret that its present leaders have failed in this national crisis. They have shown a lack of courage to face difficulties. They are not fit to be trusted.

They knew the situation was serious. They have admitted that. But they left others to do the necessary and disagreeable work.

They are the Party that ran away.

I have told you plainly what the issue of the Election is. I implore you, if you care for your country, if you do not want to see the country go to the dogs, vote for the candidates who support the National Government.

Although Snowden wrote in his autobiography that, in attacking his former colleagues, he acted in no vindictive spirit, there is no doubt that he had become exasperated and embittered by the course of events. He was convinced that a Labour victory would be disastrous: at the same time he had grave misgivings about the policy which the National Government would pursue. His bitterness was soon to be directed against the National Government itself, and more particularly against MacDonald, whose personal opponent he had always been.

Apart from Snowden's 'malignity', two other matters have been mentioned (by Mowat as by others) in support of the fear or panic theory of the Government's electioneering. The first is trivial. Quoting Mowat, 'MacDonald irrelevantly brandished a handful of German paper marks from the time of inflation before an audience.' This gesture, which the *Daily Herald* considered 'undignified', MacDonald made more than once to illustrate the perils of inflation: it was and has been interpreted as an attempt to mislead the electors into believing that the pound was then in danger of falling as precipitately and as far as the mark, despite MacDonald's clear statements to the contrary. The second was the 'Post Office Savings Bank scare', which demands fuller treatment.

The 'scare' was, quoting Mowat, 'that depositors would lose their hard-earned savings, which would be squandered by a Labour Government to pay for the dole — regardless of the fact that past Governments for many years had followed orthodox financial practice in using the funds in the Savings Bank for loans to the Treasury.' Although Snowden, as the villain of the piece, has often been accused of originating this so-called scare, it was Runciman who in fact raised the matter in a speech at South Shields on October 24. He did so because of a reference made by Henderson in his broadcast speech the day before. Dealing with the Labour Party's programme of public ownership, Henderson said:

> You are being told that your savings would not be secure if a Labour Government were returned to give effect to its policy. Have the depositors in the Post Office Savings Bank the slightest fear that their savings are imperilled because they are held by the Post Office which is a public service?

Henderson mentioned the Post Office Savings Bank because it was 'a public service', and he was making the point that the policy of public ownership and control involved no threat to savings. He was not refuting — or, at any rate, his point did not refute — the legitimate contention which had often been made that all savings would be imperilled by inflation and that the Labour Party's policy would, if applied, lead to inflation. That policy comprised a great deal more than public ownership and control.

Runciman's remarks were as follows:

> I happen to know that in the months of April and August last the Labour Government were anxious about the position of the Post Office Savings Bank deposits. This is what happened. A substantial part of the assets of the Post Office Savings Bank had already been

lent to the Insurance Fund. That brought home to the cabinet the
difficulties with which they would be faced if serious distrust of
British credit set in. If that was not enough to open their eyes to the
situation nothing would be, because there is nothing in which we trust
more than the inviolability of the Post Office Savings Bank.

It was an ambiguous and, therefore, a misleading statement. When
Snowden's attention was drawn to it, he chose to interpret it as a
general warning of the danger which had threatened all savings.
He said:

Mr Runciman's warning to depositors in the Post Office Savings
Bank and other thrift societies is well founded. The Labour leaders
when they ran away were well aware that I had warned them of the
peril which threatened the savings of the poor. That peril is passed,
due to the measures which the National Government has taken. There
is now no danger, but if the Labour Party, with its programme of huge
borrowing and increased taxation were returned, it would at once
become a real danger again.

Henderson, in reply, said that the Runciman and Snowden
statements 'regarding the people's savings' were 'simply an attempt
to alarm the electors at the eleventh hour':

The security of the Post Office Savings Bank deposits was never
threatened in the slightest degree by the Insurance Fund. Is it not
significant that Mr Snowden's statement, although it appears to confirm Mr Runciman's allegations, does not in fact do any such thing?
. . . The statement is merely a repetition of his malicious attacks upon
his old colleagues and his own party.

Henderson was right in suggesting that Runciman's remarks about
the loans to the Insurance Fund and the inviolability of the Post
Office Savings Bank might justifiably be given a different interpretation to that which Snowden apparently placed upon them.
Runciman's subsequent explanation (in Paddington on the 26th)
did little to clear up the ambiguity of his original statement. He
then said:

. . . very heavy loans were made to the Unemployment Insurance
Fund. Some of these payments to that fund by way of loan actually
came from the funds deposited in the Post Office Savings Bank. Out of
£284 million on deposit in the Post Office Savings Bank a very large
amount had, in the course of a year, been lent to the Unemployment
Insurance Fund. It was one of the objects of the National Govern-

ment to place the Unemployment Insurance Fund on a solvent basis and make sure that there were no more such lendings from the Post Office Savings Bank.

The Times reported on polling day (October 27) that MacDonald,

> in conversation with a Press representative, said it was perfectly true to say that Post Office and similar savings had been in jeopardy, and he could not understand how Mr Henderson could contradict it. That fact was one of the things which influenced the Labour Cabinet most during its meetings in August. The savings were quite safe now, but they were not safe until the National Government saved the situation and reduced expenditure on the unemployed.

In effect, MacDonald repeated Snowden's statement, which Henderson had not directly contradicted, although he had strongly objected to the form in which it had been made.

This was a storm in a tea-cup. It arose almost accidentally; and, although Runciman's remarks provoked legitimate objections, they certainly did not constitute a deliberate last-minute attempt to create panic. That the incident had any material influence upon the result of the election is most unlikely. General concern about savings probably made some contribution, but to what extent it is impossible to say. If, however, one were to attach any considerable importance to this feature of electioneering on the Government side, it would still be true that it was much more than balanced on the other side by the continuous propaganda, from start to finish, about the Bankers' ramp and the machinations of international finance.

The impact of the broadcast speeches cannot be assessed with any confidence. Snowden's, by general consent, was the most effective. It is similarly difficult to estimate the effect of the Chancellor's election activities in general. They were, after all, only one of several notably influential factors in the campaign. Snowden himself held the view that a large Government majority was never in doubt. 'From the beginning of the campaign,' he wrote, 'the Labour leaders were in a hopeless position.' But it is clear that the controversy between the Labour Ministers and their former colleagues was the crucial one, and equally clear that in that controversy the ex-Ministers fared badly. Snowden was not far wrong when he wrote:

Their attempts to wriggle out of their commitments, when members of the Government, to most of the economies the National Government had imposed, carried no conviction, but served to emphasize the public impression of their own insincerity.

But perhaps more important were the personality and prestige of the Prime Minister, which, as the *Economist* wrote after the election, had 'clearly weighed very heavily with the electors'. Nobody, however, expected the actual result. That, in Snowden's words, 'surpassed the wildest expectations'.

CHAPTER XVI

THE RESULT

'Tuesday, October 27, 1931, will go down to history as the date of the greatest electoral tide in the whole story of British democratic politics. . . . In the average size of the Government candidates' majorities and in the almost complete submergence of all the leading spokesmen of one of the great parties of the State, last Tuesday's election creates a record which has never been approached, and in all human probability will never be equalled again.' So wrote the *Economist* (October 31).

Government supporters won 556 of the 615 seats, as follows:

Conservatives	-	-	-	471
Liberal Nationals	-	-	-	35
Liberals	-	-	-	33
National Labour	-	-	-	13
Nationals	-	-	-	2
Independents	-	-	-	2
				556

Opposition candidates were returned in only 56 seats, as follows:

Labour	-	-	-	46
Independent Labour	-	-	6
Independent Liberals	-	-	4
				56

One successful Independent, Miss Rathbone, is not allocated to either side. Neither the New Party nor the Communist Party secured a single seat.

An electoral victory is often exaggerated in terms of seats, owing to the nature of the electoral system. In this respect, the General Election of 1931 was no exception to the general rule; and the

really impressive thing about it was the distribution of the popular
vote. The total poll was 72·28 per cent of the electorate, as compared with 79·21 per cent in 1929. The decrease in the total votes
cast was largely due to the fact that there were 67 unopposed returns as against 7 in 1929. Since 61 of these Unopposed members
were Government supporters, the voting figures considerably
underestimate the popular backing for the Government. The
figures were:

Conservative	- -	11,926,537
Liberal National	- -	809,102
Liberal	- - -	1,405,102
National Labour	- -	343,353
National	- - -	55,309
		14,539,403

The votes cast for Independent supporters of the Government are
not included.

The Opposition figures were:

Labour - - - -	6,362,561 } 6,648,023
Independent Labour -	285,462
Independent Liberal - - -	106,106
	6,754,129

The other figures were:

Independents	- -	254,671
Communist Party -	-	74,824
New Party -	- -	36,377

As compared with 1929, the Labour poll fell by approximately
1¾ million, but was still more than 1 million above that of 1924. The
total poll of the various sections of the Liberal Party declined by
just over 3 million, a decline largely accounted for by the great
reduction in the number of Liberal candidates. The Conservative
poll was up by over 3 million.

The Conservatives gained 208 seats, the Liberal Nationals 7, the
Liberals 3, Nationals 2, while the National Labour representation
was reduced by 2.

Had the Election been contested on ordinary party lines, the

Conservatives would probably have secured a majority in terms of seats. Amery was justified in believing that not merely possible but likely. In their straight fights against Liberals, the Conservatives had two gains and greatly increased majorities. In the three-cornered contests in which the three main parties were concerned, they won 44 out of 52, although only 22 of these seats had been Conservative-held in the previous Parliament, 21 of them on minority votes (all in 1931 converted into clear majority victories). It is most unlikely, however, that the Conservatives, fighting independently, could have secured a clear majority of the popular vote.

The magnitude of the Conservative successes, both in the number of seats won and in the size of the majorities secured, was due to the fact that the Conservatives were supporting the National Government. In constituencies where there was a straight fight between Conservatives and Labour (a little more than half the total), the vote for the former was very far from being a vote for the Conservative Party as such. Similarly, of course, votes for Liberal National, Liberal, and National Labour candidates engaged in straight fights against Labour were, in varying degrees but in large measure, votes for the National Government rather than for the particular party or group involved.

Where Liberals were engaged in three-cornered contests, the decline in the Liberal vote was in most instances considerable. That was undoubtedly a reflection of the division and confusion in the Liberal ranks. The Liberal Nationals lost two seats where they had to meet Conservative as well as Labour opposition: one of the defeated candidates being a Minister, A. E. Glassey, in East Dorset. The Liberals who followed Samuel lost nine seats in similar circumstances, including two Ministers, Milner Gray in Mid-Bedfordshire and E. D. Simon in Penryn. Samuel and Maclean, however, held their seats at Darwen and in North Cornwall respectively, the former with a majority of over 4,000, the latter more narrowly with a majority of over 1,000.

Superficially, National Labour emerged a little weakened, its membership in the House being reduced by two. Mowat has written of 'a pitiful remnant' — an odd expression, for 13 out of 15 is an unusually substantial 'remnant'. Moreover, four of the five National Labour 'losses' were due to withdrawals (including Colne Valley, Snowden's former seat); and the fifth to Conservative opposition. National Labour gains were more significant than the 'losses'. Two of them, at Ilkeston and the Forest of Dean, were Labour strongholds, and the third, South Tottenham, had been won by Labour in 1923 as well as in 1929. At least equally striking were the National Labour majorities in the 'safe' Labour seats of Seaham, Derby, and Finsbury, and in Malcolm MacDonald's constituency of Bassetlaw. The outstanding results of the Election, indeed, were those at Seaham (where MacDonald had a majority of 5,951); Derby (where Thomas headed the poll and secured a majority of 27,416 over his leading Labour opponent in that two-membered constituency); and Bassetlaw (where Malcolm Mac-Donald's majority was 13,554). The predominantly mining constituency of Seaham was, of course, one of the strongest Labour seats in the country, and MacDonald's success there was generally recognized to be the most spectacular result. The *Economist* wrote:

> Of the personal triumphs yielded by the election, that of the Prime Minister himself at Seaham must be considered the greatest, for he won the day against the full force of the official Labour machine.

He did so, moreover, with an improvised organization which could not hope to function on anything like equal terms with that of his Labour opponent.

Labour supporters of the Government had very few opportunities of voting for a National Labour candidate; but their influence was great and in many cases decisive. Only to a very superficial eye, or to a blind one, was it concealed because it had to be exercised, as a rule, in support of Conservative, Liberal National or Liberal candidates. The strength of the National Labour vote in the country was to some extent indicated by the two cases in which National Labour candidates opposed Conservative as well as Labour candidates. In Everton, where in 1929 Labour had polled 14,234 against the Conservative figure of 12,667, the result was:

Conservative - - -	12,186
Labour - - - -	7,786
National Labour - -	4,950

It will be noted that the Conservative vote here actually declined. In South-East Essex, where the National Labour candidate was not the former member but a new-comer with a very hastily improvised organization, the position was more complicated. In 1929 there had been a large Liberal vote: in 1931 there was no Liberal candidate. The electorate, moreover, was much larger in 1931 than in 1929. The results of the two elections are given below:

1929			1931		
Labour	-	18,756	Conservative	-	30,436
Conservative	-	18,130	Labour	- -	20,066
Liberal -	-	13,030	National Labour	-	6,539

But the clearest indications of Labour support for the Government came from the many Labour strongholds won by non-Labour National Government candidates. These included well over 30 constituencies in which Labour had had a majority of over 10,000 in 1929. They comprised seats like the mining constituency of Morpeth, where the President of the Miners' Federation, Edwards, lost his former majority of over 16,000; Gateshead, where Ernest Bevin was beaten by nearly 13,000 although Labour had had a majority of 16,749 in 1929; Nottingham West, where the retiring President of the T.U.C., Hayday, had his majority of over 10,000 turned into a minority of over 5,000; mining constituencies in Durham, Staffordshire and Lancashire; the Labour strongholds of the Potteries; Graham's seat in Edinburgh, Adamson's in West Fife, Greenwood's at Nelson and Colne, and Alexander's in Sheffield. Of similar significance was Labour's loss of such constituencies as Jarrow, St Helens, Barnsley, Whitechapel, and Bishop Auckland (where Dalton was narrowly beaten). Dalton wrote in his reminiscences:

> My blow was softened a little by the other results in County Durham. The loss of Blaydon, Durham, Houghton-le-Spring and Consett, all 'safer' seats even than Bishop Auckland, showed the force of the tide. And J.R.M. held Seaham! In County Durham we held only two seats — Chester-le-Street and Spennymoor — out of nineteen. The contagion of Seaham spread like a plague through Durham and Northumberland.[1]

No Conservative or Liberal, merely as such, could have won any of these seats: they were won because of the extensive Labour support for MacDonald and his associates; a fact which conditioned the political situation in the subsequent years.

The only Labour ex-Cabinet Minister to survive the disaster was Lansbury. He was accompanied by two other ex-Ministers: Attlee, who scraped back with a majority of 551 in Limehouse, and

[1] Op. cit., pp. 296-7.

Cripps, with a still smaller majority of 429 in Bristol; and by only five ex-Under-Secretaries: George Hall (unopposed in Aberdare), Morgan Jones in Caerphilly, J. J. Lawson in Chester-le-Street, Lunn (with a majority cut from over 18,000 to 2,000 in his Yorkshire mining seat), and Parkinson at Wigan. Only in Wales, the Yorkshire mining areas, and East London did the Labour Party largely hold its own: 31 of its 56 members came from those three regions.

No clearer demonstration could have been given of the vital distinction between the political parties and the electorate, between the party machine and its active supporters, on the one hand, and, on the other hand, the general body of party voters and sympathizers. Nor could there have been any clearer demonstration that the result of the election had not turned on the tariff issue, and still less on that of the cut in unemployment benefit and the other economy measures. Two comments merit quotation because they make the main point. Miss Violet Markham, writing to Dr Thomas Jones on November 1, said:

> . . . the more I think of the result the more sound and satisfactory I feel it is as an indication of the spirit of the nation. It's a magnificent demonstration that democracy faced with a big issue has the power to reject appeals to personal interest and vote for the nation first.[1]

Mrs Mary Agnes Hamilton, who lost her seat at Blackburn, wrote in her reminiscences:

> Summing up in 1918, Mrs Pethick Lawrence at the time remarked, very acutely, that what impelled voters was 'a passion for abstract justice'. This passion, selfless and wholly idealistic, was again and more markedly present in 1931; it bore Labour down. The appeal of the National Government carried everything before it because it was felt to be an essentially non-material appeal. Voters believed that the country was in danger. In that belief, they were ready to make sacrifices, even welcomed sacrifices. MacDonald interpreted their mood far more truly than did Labour party 'realists' who counted on a solid working-class vote against cuts in unemployment benefit. There is, in fact, no such thing as a 'solid working-class vote'; men and women vote as citizens. The citizen appeal goes further home, and over a far wider range, than any class appeal can do. In fact democracy is real.[2]

[1] Op. cit., pp. 20–1.
[2] Op. cit., pp. 248–9.

It is of some importance to note that while the spokesman of the defeated attributed the defeat to the electorate having been 'swept away by panic and fear', the victors interpreted their success as a test of democracy which the electors had passed with flying colours. The *Manchester Guardian* declared on October 28:

> By the side of the scare about the pound, the cry of 'Hang the Kaiser' and the Red Letter appear almost respectable. The campaign has been carried on in a mood of hysteria that makes one tremble for the sense of proportion of most of our political leaders.

The Times on the same day maintained that:

> The election has been in a very high degree a contest between the democrat and the demagogue. . . . British democracy has passed that test.

Such reactions, on both sides, are not at all unusual. In this particular instance, there was greater justification for the second than for the first. And, although it has been fashionable in more recent years for commentators to accept uncritically the angry verdict of the *Manchester Guardian*, the other interpretation was not only predominant at the time but was recognized by the more balanced minds among the defeated to have much validity.

To Mowat, 'the importance of the election was that it gave the Conservatives, under false colours, an overwhelming strength in parliament which they could hardly have won unaided.' Whether or not the colours were false, the Conservatives' overwhelming strength in Parliament, just because it had not been won unaided, did not give them the overwhelming power they might otherwise have been able to exercise. The importance of the election, from the party standpoint, was precisely that the victory was 'National' rather than Conservative. That was the note struck by the chief figures in the Government when the results were known. Mac-Donald himself declared:

> The very emphasis of the response is embarrassing, but I appeal for forbearance as well as confidence.
>
> To my political friends who have suffered such unusual reverses, and especially to those of them who with splendid faith and courage backed our appeal and helped to swell our victory, I give the assurance that our triumph will in no way mean that either the interests or the point of view of the working classes will be overlooked in the perform-

ance of the task which is before us. The figures show that a great proportion of them have been by no means deaf to our call, and therefore they share with the other classes of the community the triumph of yesterday's response.

Baldwin, in his message, said:

This is no party victory. It is an emphatic declaration by the people as a whole in favour of national co-operation in order to restore the fortunes of our country. . . . At home it will serve as a lesson to political parties that the common sense of the British people is proof against the propaganda of the demagogue. It will prove that the electors are not to be misled by specious promises or false appeals to selfish instincts . . . the electors have declared in no uncertain voice that the insidious doctrines of class warfare cannot make headway against the general desire for national co-operation at a time of national emergency. . . . The workers throughout the country have put their trust in the National Government: we must not fail them. The magnitude of the defeat makes it all the more imperative that we should be faithful to our trust.

Snowden's statement said:

This overwhelming majority for the National Government is not a party, but a national victory. Millions of men and women have voted for candidates with whose general political views they are not in agreement on the sole ground of showing to the world that Britain is determined to stand four-square and bring the nation through its difficulties. . . .

I do not rejoice at the disaster which has come to the Labour Party. I regret it because the Labour leaders have brought this catastrophe upon themselves and the party by their folly, lack of courage in leadership, and misunderstanding of the popular spirit. They hoped to exploit the unemployed for party advantage. The electors in the industrial areas, where unemployment is highest, have given the most emphatic condemnation of the Labour leaders. Millions of unemployed and former Labour voters have put national interests before party at this election without in the least changing their political and social ideals.

This is not the end of the Labour Party. It will rise again, but only with new leaders who have vision and courage. But it must be based on a citizen's and not a class outlook. This defeat of the Labour Party will be for its ultimate good if the lessons are learnt.

Before polling day, the *Economist*, by a process of elimination, had come to the conclusion that a majority for the Government would mean simply approval of the formation of the National Government, condemnation of Henderson and his associates, and desire for a strong administration. After the polling, it wrote:

the fact stands out clearly that the nation has demanded in the loudest possible tones a strong 'safety-first Government'. It has condemned the late Labour Government for its dalliance with an approaching financial crisis, and has visited upon the Ministers who refused to stand with Mr MacDonald the dire penalty of wholesale rejection.

The *Economist* was quite clear that 'the electorate has voted on national and not on party lines'. So, for that matter, was the *Manchester Guardian*, though it expressed the point in different terms:

But for Mr MacDonald and Mr Snowden, first through their appeal for faith in their integrity, and secondly through their envenomed campaign against their old colleagues as the architects of anarchy, there would probably have been no Tory victory.

CHAPTER XVII

CONCLUSION

'Any man in my position at the time, knowing all that I did, would have acted as I acted. However, I wish sometimes that someone else had been in my position at the time.' So MacDonald said to Nicolson when discussing the 1931 crisis with him many years afterwards.[1] So he implied in several statements made during the crisis itself, as, for example, in his opening election speech at Easington on October 12:

> I know a lot of you shook your heads over that National Government. If I might whisper in your ears — I may have shaken my own. Do you think that was the sort of thing we wanted? Not at all.

Unhappily, plaintively, many of his devoted friends and admirers in the Labour Party held, or tried to convince themselves, that he need not have acted as he did.

It must be granted that the situation confronting MacDonald in August 1931, was one of extraordinary complexity. He was at the head of a minority Government which had been restricted essentially, though not exclusively, to the task of 'keeping things going'. That task had been from the start highly uncongenial to considerable elements in his Party: it became more and more so. It was rendered far more difficult than it otherwise would have been by the immediate onset of the great world depression and afterwards by the effects of its rapid intensification. When the financial crisis came, the Labour Cabinet was in no position to deal with it on other than orthodox lines. It accepted the need to undertake the task, but failed to agree on the methods of accomplishing it.

Much criticism has been directed at the financial orthodoxy of the period, and at the banking policies which had been pursued. Whether justified or not, that criticism was of no assistance to the Government in coping with the immediate crisis: a point which MacDonald repeatedly made. No authority himself on such mat-

[1] Op. cit., p. 494 (footnote).

ters, as he told the nation in his broadcast address on the night of August 25, MacDonald took the advice of the recognized financial experts, after consulting, as he said, 'every shade of opinion.' That advice was overwhelmingly in accordance with traditional policies. Moreover, it was strongly endorsed by the Chancellor of the Exchequer, the Government's acknowledged financial authority. Mowat has rightly said that to blame those who gave the advice 'is to blame them for lacking a belief in economic theories which only became fashionable later'. Whether the advice given was sound or unsound is perhaps still an open question, for the newer theories, in so far as they have been tested, have not proved unqualifiedly successful. But to blame MacDonald and the Labour Cabinet for accepting that advice, as they did in principle, is not only to fall into the same error as that pointed out by Mowat but also to ignore the realities of the political situation. If it had been possible for the Cabinet to frame a policy on the somewhat fluctuating views of J. M. Keynes, it would have been quite impossible for it to have implemented such a policy. Only through the medium of a much stronger Government, which probably would have had to be something in the nature of the National Government, would such a development have been feasible.

It must be emphasized that financial experts and economists were agreed about the desirability of maintaining the Gold Standard. They were in more complete agreement than they had been in 1925 about the desirability of its restoration. On the position then, Professor Robbins has written:

At that time the idea of a managed currency never had a ghost of a chance of being adopted as a basis of policy. This for very good reasons. The state of the world at large was not such as to justify high hopes in the ability of Governments to manage inconvertible paper successfully. All the Great Powers, save America, had gone off the Gold Standard during the war. None of them had exhibited the capacity to keep the operation of the printing press within limits. At the time when the controversy in England was at its height, the standards of continental Europe were in a condition of the most violent fluctuation ever witnessed. Trade had shrunk to a fraction of its pre-war dimensions. The one hope of stabilizing business conditions seemed to be the elimination of these fluctuations. Gold stood for stability. The eyes of the world looked to Great Britain for leadership. Small wonder that responsible men charged with the conduct of policy, although ignorant for the most part of the profound theoretical strictures which could have been passed upon the plan for a managed currency, turned a deaf ear to all this talk and resolved upon a restoration of the Gold Standard.[1]

In the conditions of the summer of 1931, essentially the same kind of considerations prevailed. The continued adhesion of Britain to the Gold Standard, and the stability of sterling, were regarded as stabilizing factors of the utmost importance in the international financial chaos.

It must further be emphasized that, at the time of the crisis, no question was raised within the Cabinet about the possibility of going off the Gold Standard. As Lord Passfield said, such a step was apparently regarded as unthinkable. The Labour Cabinet were in full agreement about that. They were agreed also in turning down any devaluation of the pound. And, as Henderson said on September 8, they were in absolute agreement that the Budget must be balanced. The immediate task, one of rapidly increasing urgency, was to restore confidence and to check the drain of funds from London. The agreed policy was that of balancing the Budget and maintaining the stability of the pound in the interim by securing further large credits from New York and Paris.

The differences within the Labour Cabinet arose about the methods of achieving those two connected objects. MacDonald's task as Prime Minister was to secure Cabinet agreement on a policy which would enable the loans to be raised and which would be acceptable to the House of Commons. That involved discussions with the bankers' representatives in this country, and, through them, with the representatives of the foreign bankers. It also necessitated discussions with the leaders of the Opposition parties, not merely because the Government was dependent upon the support of at least one of them in the House of Commons, but also because the co-operation of both was obviously desirable. And on that point also, as has been seen, there was complete agreement within the Cabinet.

The tangle of dissension in the Cabinet concerning the detailed application of its agreed policy has been sufficiently analysed above. When the General Council of the T.U.C. declared its uncompromising opposition to the policy itself Cabinet agreement became well-nigh impossible. It may well be argued that in such circumstances the Labour Government ought to have resigned at once. That was the course Henderson seems to have favoured. In-

[1] Op. cit., pp. 77-8.

deed, it may be argued, and was in fact argued by some, that the
Government ought not even to have embarked upon the task; that
it should have resigned at the outset of the crisis and 'passed the
baby' to the Tories. That was naturally the view of those who had
either always been opposed to the minority government experiment
or had come increasingly to dislike it. Rightly or wrongly, Mac-
Donald persisted in his efforts to secure Cabinet unity, despite the
growing urgency of the situation. He did so until, by general consent, all expedients had failed and further effort had become not
only useless but dangerous. MacDonald, as he said, wanted the
Labour Government to stay in office; partly, no doubt, because of
international and Indian problems in which he was particularly
interested; but primarily because he desired the Government and
the Labour Party to deal successfully with the crisis. That was in
line with his general political attitude and a life-time's application
of it in building up and conducting the Labour Party. MacDonald
wanted his Government to face the unpleasant facts and to shoulder its responsibilities. In his son's words, his greatest wish was
that the Labour Government 'should have the honour and responsibility of taking us through the crisis'. To shirk the task would
have been, in his view, disastrous for the Party. That is why he
strove to the end to secure Cabinet agreement on the only lines
which were practicable; and he did so, in Passfield's words, 'with
great patience and ingenuity.'

When, on the night of Sunday, August 23, it became clear that
his final effort had failed, there was no alternative for him but to
tender his resignation. That he should do so was an agreed Cabinet
decision. There was no question of asking the King for a dissolution of Parliament. The nature of the crisis ruled that out any-
way, but there was no legitimate ground upon which such a
request could be based.

As to the nature of the new Government which would have to
be formed, there was at the time, and there has been subsequently,
much glib talk about a Conservative-Liberal coalition. Had Mac-
Donald not agreed to undertake the task of forming a National
Government, or had he proved unsuccessful in attempting the
task, Baldwin would undoubtedly have been commissioned to form
a new Administration. And we know that he would have accepted
the commission if assurances of Liberal support were forthcoming,
and on the understanding that he would be granted a dissolution as

soon as the immediate crisis was surmounted. It is most unlikely, however, that Baldwin would have been able to form a Conservative-Liberal coalition government. It is extremely doubtful if he would have been willing to try to do so, although the fact of Lloyd George's incapacity would have made him less unwilling than would otherwise have been the case. He might, it is true, have succeeded in bringing Simon and his associates into any Government he formed, had he wished to do so; but the danger of such a development, from the Liberal standpoint, was itself a factor of some importance in determining the Liberal Party's attitude to the crisis resulting from the Labour Government's collapse. Moreover, a divided Liberal Party would have been of no help to Baldwin in such circumstances, for any kind of Government he might form would have been dependent upon Liberal support.

It had been generally expected that if and when the Labour Government resigned, a Baldwin Government would take its place. When, however, it appeared highly unlikely that the Labour Cabinet would be able to reach agreement upon the measures required to deal with the financial crisis, the circumstances were such that the expedient of a National Government, always in the background as a possibility, emerged for the first time as a practical proposition. In view of the parliamentary situation, the urgency of the crisis, and the disastrous effects from that standpoint which would ensue were an immediate General Election to be held, an emergency all-party government was a natural and appropriate device for surmounting the difficulty which would arise if MacDonald proved unable to carry on with some kind of Labour administration. The facts of the situation were by themselves sufficient to explain and justify both Samuel's initiative, in the advice he tendered to the King at mid-day on August 23, and Baldwin's independent endorsement of that advice later the same afternoon.

Other considerations, undoubtedly, played their part in determining the actions of the two Opposition Leaders. Conservatives and Liberals alike preferred that the crisis should be dealt with by the Labour Government. The main body of Liberals, indeed, had special reasons for desiring that Government's retention of office. The leaders of both Opposition parties were alike willing to support the Government in taking whatever steps were likely to prove adequate. They were not at all eager, either separately or in combination, to assume the undivided responsibility for dealing with the crisis. And, in the event of the Government's resignation, both Baldwin and Samuel preferred a National Government under MacDonald to either a Conservative-Liberal coalition or a Conservative government dependent upon Liberal votes. The reasons for their preference are plain enough. A coalition (formal or informal) of the Conservative and Liberal parties would have had a relatively small majority in the existing House of Commons, and (as subsequent events underline) might well have been faced by a Labour Opposition largely intent on exploiting the unpopularity of the economy measures with a view to the impending Election. In such circumstances, a majority might well have proved unstable. A formal coalition between the two parties would have been repugnant to both, and extremely difficult to bring about. It was particularly distasteful to the main body of the Liberals, for such a coalition would necessarily have been headed by Baldwin, and would have been very heavily weighted against the Liberals, themselves anything but a happy family. A Conservative Government dependent on Liberal backing, while dangerous to the poor prospects of Liberal cohesion, would have rested on very insecure foundations. The tariff issue, bound to arise as soon as the immediate crisis was overcome, and possibly before, deeply divided the Conservatives from Samuel's supporters. Lloyd George, too, was an incalculable factor. Baldwin may well have been influenced by other considerations. Differences of view within the Conservative Party about the nature of any tariff proposals had been considerable and had by no means disappeared. The Party was also acutely divided on the subject of India, then urgently demanding attention; and on that subject Baldwin was in substantial agreement with MacDonald. But the main explanation of the advice given to the King by the two Leaders is to be found in their recognition of the urgency of the crisis combined with their fear of electoral repercussions. Mutual party mistrust and parliamentary difficulties were important subsidiary factors. In the circumstances, both statesmen considered that the retention of the Premiership by MacDonald offered the best prospect of securing a broad-based Administration. The soundness of this judgment was to be demonstrated late in the following September when, in a changed situation, the differences between the Conservatives and those Liberals who followed Samuel brought the National Government to the verge of collapse.

But, when MacDonald tendered his resignation on the night of August 23, the formation of a National Government in accordance with the advice of Samuel and Baldwin depended upon whether or not MacDonald could be induced to undertake the task. It is clear that MacDonald himself had formulated no plan in advance, and anticipated that he would be succeeded by Baldwin. The many attempts which have been made to prove the contrary are flimsily based and collapse under examination. They show only that Mac-Donald, like most people in the political world, had from time to time thought that a National Government might provide a way out of the difficulties produced by the complex party situation. It is also clearly established that even late on the night of August 23, after the suggestion of a National Government under his own leadership had been put to him, he was still undecided about his course of action. There is no doubt about his hesitation. His response to the appeals made to him was reluctant. The appearance of decisiveness to the general public was due to the conditions of urgency in which his decision had to be made. The decision itself was, in his own words, 'very painful.'

MacDonald's hesitation was natural enough. His position was one of peculiar difficulty. The circumstances in which the Labour Cabinet had authorized him to resign made impossible a National Government in the sense of a coalition of all three parties. He knew that most of his Labour colleagues and the great majority of the Parliamentary Labour Party would strongly disapprove of any Labour participation in a new Government. On the other hand, the Labour Party was the largest party in the House of Commons; the formation of a new Government presented obvious difficulties; a dissolution was out of the question; the crisis was becoming dangerously urgent; and it was impossible for MacDonald, as the retiring Prime Minister and leader of the largest party, to throw aside all responsibility for seeing to it that the King's Government was carried on and the crisis dealt with. These aspects of the situation could hardly have been absent from the minds of the other members of the Labour Cabinet. And that, undoubtedly, is why they agreed, or expressed no dissent, when MacDonald announced his intention to advise the King to confer with Baldwin, Samuel and himself; and similarly raised no objection when he told them that this advice had been given and accepted.

When confronted by the need to make his decision, MacDonald

had also to consider the consequences of a refusal on his part. If, in such circumstances, Baldwin accepted the commission to form a Government and succeeded in doing so, it could safely be assumed that his Government would submit to the House of Commons substantially the same proposals for balancing the Budget as the small majority of the Labour Cabinet had been prepared to accept. What then would have been the position and attitude of the Labour Party? Obviously enough, neither MacDonald nor Snowden could honourably oppose such measures. Nor, it would seem, could any of the ex-Ministers who in office had been willing to accept them. At the same time, those ex-Ministers who had threatened to resign if the proposals approved by the majority were adopted by the Cabinet would certainly maintain their opposition; and, Labour being out of office, they would almost certainly have the backing of the majority of the Parliamentary Labour Party. It may well have been thought that, even so, they could not honourably oppose a new Government's probable measures in their entirety, since they had been prepared to accept, provisionally at any rate, by far the greater part of them when in office. It is true that extra-Parliamentary influences, and most powerfully that of the General Council of the T.U.C., would have to be reckoned with. Relinquishment of office opened the path to repudiation of all responsibility for dealing with the crisis, or, at any rate, of all collaboration with other parties in relation thereto; and that there were elements in the Labour Party eager to pursue that path was well known.

The differences within the Labour Cabinet and the Labour Party were not, and could not be, resolved by the Cabinet's resignation. In the circumstances envisaged, they might even have been widened. If, as would certainly have been the case, MacDonald and his associates were to support a new Government's proposed measures, then, there seems little room for doubt, the Labour Party leadership would have passed into other hands. That of course is what MacDonald meant by saying to the Conservative and Liberal leaders, on the night of August 23, that 'it meant his death warrant'. None the less, MacDonald, with Snowden and Thomas, would have been a formidable combination, and would have had very considerable backing. They would probably have been able to rely upon the support of most, if not all, of the ex-Ministers who had been prepared to follow their lead. They would have had much support from the Parliamentary Party and still more from the

Party outside Parliament. For this, and other reasons already implied, the breach in the Labour Party would have been maximized. Nevertheless, it was this course of action which MacDonald, as we now know, was at first inclined to take. It was the course which his friends believed that night he would take. Undoubtedly, it was the course which Snowden would have preferred him to take.

Plainly enough, however, such a course of action offered no attractive prospect either from the personal or party standpoint. That MacDonald was not averse to remaining Prime Minister may readily be granted. In order to establish that point, there is no need to suggest that he was flattered into thinking that he was indispensable. But, apart from the personal factor, there was the Party which he had done so much to create and had led to Governmental status. Indeed, with MacDonald, the two things went together; and, as always, he looked ahead. There is an important clue to his attitude in the concluding passage of his letter to Shinwell on August 24:

> Having failed to meet the immediate situation we should have been swept away in ignominy before the end of this week by popular clamour, so that it can be proved later on, whatever offence we have caused at this moment, we have created the conditions under which the Party can continue as an Opposition and allow the public, saved from panic, to consider a return of our general policy when things have become more normal.[1]

This passage was written by one who, clearly, not only regarded himself as a leading and responsible figure in the Labour Party but was also prepared to defend his action from the Party standpoint. MacDonald viewed the situation as one in which popular judgment of the Party would be materially affected by the action taken by himself and his associates as leading members of it: and his suggestion was that, as a consequence of that action, the judgment would be much less adverse than it otherwise would have been. His assessment of the situation and prospects may be stated in some such terms as these: 'Had we all simply resigned (or been compelled to resign by popular clamour), the Party would have suffered very severely in the public estimation. We should have been condemned as people who had failed in our duty. Even if some of us had proceeded to support the measures proposed by a new

---

[1] Op. cit., p. 111. The whole letter is worth consulting as an expression of MacDonald's views on the day of his decision.

Government to deal with the crisis, the public impression of our failure and lack of political courage would have been disastrous. Those of us who have remained in office to apply the requisite measures will not only have helped to avert the panic which would have resulted from a financial crash, but will also have enabled the Party to function as a responsible Opposition and to recover its position in the public favour more speedily.'

The clear implication is that MacDonald did not contemplate severance from the Labour Party; but, on the contrary, expected to resume an active role in the conduct of the Party after the brief period then anticipated of the National Government's life. That, of course, was precisely what people like Beatrice Webb feared. There is little doubt that MacDonald had in mind the sort of situation which had arisen during the War as a consequence of Labour participation in the Coalition Government. Henderson, it is also clear, looked at the situation in the same way, merely as an 'interlude'. In this instance, moreover, as MacDonald emphasized in the Shinwell letter, and in public, the combination which he had decided to lead was one of individuals for a specific limited purpose and was to be of short duration.

It is necessary to look at the matter not with the hindsight derived from knowledge of the subsequent course of events but in the light of the situation as it was, or as it appeared to the leading participants at the time. When the National Government was formed, it must be repeated, it was not expected that the official Labour Party would adopt an attitude of unqualified and bitter opposition, and that all the resources of its machine would be utilized for the purpose.

In taking his momentous decision, MacDonald, whether or not he decided wisely, was moved primarily by his sense of duty. Diligent search for evidence of unworthy personal motives, and attempts to explain his conduct in terms of alleged weaknesses of character, have been unnecessary, indeed suspect, exercises. That conduct can be adequately explained on public grounds; and on those grounds also it can be legitimately criticized. When such a difficult choice as his had to be made, it is obvious that strong arguments could be presented against as well as for the choice he made, and that opinions would differ, and will continue to differ, about the wisdom of his choice. But, although MacDonald put first his responsibility to the nation, he was far from unmindful of the interests of the Labour Party, quite apart from his consistent conviction that the latter were inseparably bound up with the interests of the nation as a whole.

If the whole-hog opposition of the Party machine to the National Government largely nullified MacDonald's hopes and upset his calculations, that was not his fault. The record shows how the nature of that opposition contributed to the partial failure of the Government's efforts and transformed the political situation. The reader must be left to judge whether or not any act of omission or commission on MacDonald's part can provide a partial justification or excuse for his Party's behaviour. The author's own opinion is that, at most, only a plea of extenuating circumstances can be admitted.

It may be argued that MacDonald ought to have foreseen what his Party's reactions would be. His language at the time shows that he well knew that he would incur odium, that he would be subjected to bitter attacks from within his Party. But that would be no new experience for him. MacDonald knew his Party. He was fully aware that his decision would involve his deposition from the leadership. That, indeed, was generally and immediately recognized. It was 'a patriotic act of self-sacrifice' of which, we are told, he spoke to his Cabinet colleagues, and in which he gave them a general invitation to participate. Nor would loss of the leadership be a novel experience for MacDonald: he had lost it in 1914, only to regain it in 1922. But neither he nor any of his associates anticipated that their former colleagues would seek to repudiate all responsibility for the policy which the Labour Cabinet had failed to implement. It was that, as has been seen, which outraged Snowden. Nor did they envisage the depths to which so many of their inevitable critics would sink in personal abuse.

The special grounds of complaint advanced against MacDonald in regard to his decision to form the National Government are that he did not previously consult any of his Labour colleagues and that he made no attempt to secure the approval of the Parliamentary Labour Party or of the Labour Party as such. The answer to the first point is that, in the circumstances, the provisional decision was necessarily made without such consultation, and that consultation necessarily followed before the final decision was made. The answer to the second point is that any such attempt would plainly have been futile, particularly in view of the rapidly and publicly announced decision of the directing Labour executives to go into 'vigorous opposition', and, therefore, undesirable.

That raises a point of much importance. It was because there was no prospect of bringing the Labour Party as such into a coalition that the National Government was formed as a combination of individuals. It was for the same reason that MacDonald limited his invitations to Labour colleagues to join him, and also his appeals for wider Party backing. Some of his invitations, it is true, were rejected; but expectation or fear of refusal does not account for the limitation. MacDonald was naturally reluctant to urge others to involve themselves unnecessarily in his action and its consequences. Some Labour associates were essential; others were or would have been welcome; but, apart from all questions of personal consequences, considerations of far-reaching importance were involved and made restriction desirable.

That such wider political considerations appealed strongly to MacDonald is a circumstance which will occasion no surprise to those acquainted with his political outlook and career. In the Labour and Socialist movement in this country (and for that matter abroad as well), MacDonald had been the leading theoretical exponent and the outstanding practitioner of the methods of parliamentary democracy. He had aimed at making the Labour Party one of the two main parties in the State, and, as such, a party prepared fully to accept the responsibilities of government. The Party's failure (as he regarded it) to face up to those responsibilities in the crisis of 1931 was, no doubt, a grievous disappointment to him. But he did not consider it a final defeat nor a failure fatal to the Party. It was rather an experience (avoidable but not wholly surprising in view of the severity of the test) incidental to the Party's growth, one the lessons of which could, though they might not be, learned. MacDonald had no wish to create any wide or lasting breach in the Labour Party. He had been the chief architect of its rise to governmental status, and he was, moreover, both a firm believer in party and a staunch adherent of the so-called two-party system, though not (partly for those very reasons) dominated by the partisan spirit. The greater the number of moderates associated with him in the National Government, the more influential would the Left Wing become in the main body of the Labour Party and the greater would be the danger that the Party might be drawn into anti-parliamentary courses and his whole life-work ruined. For this reason, MacDonald sought to make the breach as narrow as possible.

This is not mere supposition. It is the only pattern into which the known facts can be fitted. It provides the reason why Mac-Donald refrained from engaging in a direct personal effort to obtain the maximum measure of support from the Parliamentary Labour Party. It provides the basic explanation of the advice he gave to the junior Labour Ministers in the early afternoon of August 24. It explains why he made no attempt, when, contrary to his original expectations, the breach with his Party became complete, to establish a new party. And it may well be contended that his foresight in August of 1931 met with its reward. It is true that, for a few years after the crushing Labour defeat that October, the Labour Party appeared to be greatly under the influence of anti-parliamentary tendencies, but the moderate forces within the Party gradually re-established their ascendancy, until it has become possible for Left Wing critics to speak, with substantial justification, of the predominant 'MacDonaldism' of the Party.

From every standpoint save that of the narrowest partisans, who were not by any means confined to the Labour Party, an extremely strong case can be presented for MacDonald's decision to form the National Government, and for the actions of Samuel and Baldwin in advising its formation and securing the support of their respective parties for it. More open to criticism from the Party standpoint was MacDonald's decision in the following October to go to the country as head of the National Government. It was that decision and its outcome which alienated much of the support and sympathy which had still existed for him within the ranks of the Labour Party. The resentment engendered during the campaign was rendered bitter, extravagant and enduring as a consequence of electoral disaster, with all that that involved in terms of personal disappointments and even hardships. Yet, in the changed circumstances, the holding of a General Election could not long have been postponed, whether or not the National Government had continued in being. Those who so severely denounced the resort to the electorate because, in their view, it would gravely imperil the stability of the pound were proved completely wrong. For Mac-Donald himself, the only alternative would have been retirement from office, and the termination of the National Government with its purpose unachieved, or only partially achieved.

MacDonald's dilemma was presented by the *Economist* on October 3, 1931, in the following terms:

> The Prime Minister was thus faced with a very delicate situation, in which three courses were open to him. Should he resign? If so he would plunge the country into a party election, stultify his own sacrifices for the nation, and incur the risk of a Labour victory and the annulment of much of the good work done by his National Government. Secondly, should he surrender to the Protectionist clamour, replace Mr Snowden and the present Liberal Ministers by *soi disant* Liberals, and lead an appeal to the country on behalf of a practically Conservative administration possessing a thin veneer of national unity? On all grounds such a course was repugnant to Mr MacDonald personally and presented obvious disadvantages and risks from the national point of view. A third alternative remained, and that was to make one last supreme effort to create a real unity, to induce Liberals and Conservatives to reach a compromise on the tariff issue, and thereby to be enabled either to carry on with the present administration, or, at worst, to make a three-party appeal to the electorate.

The preceding breach with the Labour Party was not due to MacDonald but to the Party. For the failure of the National Government to prevent the abandonment of the gold standard, and its consequential prolongation, the Labour Party was to some extent responsible. And it was wholly responsible for the need to secure popular endorsement of the formation of the National Government and popular sanction for its continuance. In view of the nature of the attacks made upon him by the Labour Opposition, MacDonald would naturally have welcomed the opportunity to demonstrate that his actions were approved not only by the bulk of the electorate but in particular by a great body of Labour opinion. On the other hand, he viewed with a repugnance not shared by Snowden an Election in which he would lead not only his own Labour supporters but the Conservative and Liberal parties also against the Labour Party. Once again, it was a painful decision to have to make. As the *Economist* said, 'for the second time in a few weeks' MacDonald was 'faced with a situation calculated to make the most exacting demands upon his patriotism and statesmanship'. Once more he vacillated. Once again, too, the determining factor was his conception of the national interest. And seldom, if ever, has the electorate given so overwhelmingly decisive a verdict as that given to his National Government, and very largely to him personally as its head, on October 27, 1931.

With the consequences of this electoral triumph the present book is not directly concerned. Several volumes would be required to do full justice to the versions of British politics in the 'thirties which are now current.[1] None the less, a few brief comments seem desirable.

After the Election, the National Government was reconstructed (see Appendix VII). The most important changes were (1) the inclusion of Sir John Simon and other Liberal Nationals (Simon became Foreign Secretary in place of Lord Reading, and Walter Runciman was appointed President of the Board of Trade instead of Sir Philip Cunliffe-Lister), and (2) the inevitable retirement of Philip Snowden from the Chancellorship of the Exchequer and his replacement by Neville Chamberlain. Snowden went to the House of Lords with the office of Lord Privy Seal.

It has become a commonplace of political controversy in these days to suggest that the National Governments from 1931 to 1939, though ostensibly Ministries of All the Talents, were governments of mediocrities from which the real political talent of the country was missing. Apart from the Labour Opposition and Lloyd George (and, at a later stage, the official Liberal Opposition), this absent talent appears to have been embodied only in Churchill, Amery, and Sir Austen Chamberlain. The basis of the suggestion, of course, is the fact that Churchill was out of office during those years. Nowadays, one reads *ad nauseam* of the 'exclusion' of Churchill, Amery and Austen Chamberlain. The fantastic lengths to which this process has gone may be illustrated by Sir Robert Boothby's recent assertion that the National Government of 1931 was formed in order to keep Churchill out of office. It is perhaps not altogether surprising that the name of Lloyd George is omitted from the list of the 'excluded', for he had openly and strongly opposed the National Government during the Election campaign. But it is also true that both Churchill and Amery were only lukewarm and limited supporters of the governmental alliance. Austen Chamberlain's case was different; it was one of voluntary retirement from office in order to ease the Prime Minister's task of

---

[1] The author has dealt exhaustively with one group of legends in his *Democracy and Foreign Policy* (1952), a study of the Sino-Japanese Dispute, 1931–33. In his article and subsequent correspondence, *Telling the Truth to the People: The Myth of the Baldwin 'Confession'* (The Cambridge Journal, Vol. II, Nos. 2 and 4, November 1948 and January 1949), he has also exposed one extremely influential set of distortions concerning the General Election of 1935.

Cabinet-making. He remained a highly influential, though not always uncritical, supporter of the administration. Churchill and Amery, on the other hand, were in marked and outspoken disagreement with important features of Government policy. In Churchill's case, the disagreement was acute on both the problem of India and that of armaments policy.

The most remarkable point to note is that the parties and groups (and most individuals) who have in more recent years condemned Churchill's 'exclusion' from office were, at the time, and more particularly during the Second National Government from 1931 to 1935, scathing in their condemnation of Churchill himself, partly on account of his attitude towards India, but still more vehemently because of his attitude towards disarmament.

The National Governments have been made scapegoats for the failure to prevent the Second World War. Mowat has rightly written that in retrospect the National Government 'has been blamed for all the misfortunes of the time, partly because its opponents rose to power by reiterating their version of its history and its period'. But, in regard to foreign affairs, and especially in regard to armaments, the policies which critics have since argued ought to have been pursued were at the time bitterly and persistently opposed by the overwhelming majority of them. Those who, for example, denounced Simon's handling of the Manchurian issue objected even more strongly to the line taken on that matter by Churchill and Amery, whose views, indeed, were used by them as a stick with which to beat the Foreign Secretary. The devotees of the League of Nations Union were outraged by the scorn with which Amery and Churchill treated the 'unrealities' of the Disarmament Conference and, later, 'collective security.' To those who nowadays savagely condemn the National Government of 1931–35 for 'not rearming' (or, with much less frequency but greater accuracy, for the belatedness and inadequacy of rearmament), it must be pointed out that the only practicable alternative Government (a Labour Government, or, conceivably a Labour-Lloyd George Coalition) would have been resolutely opposed to any measure of rearmament. Mowat has referred to the White Paper, *Statement Relating to Defence*, published on March 4, 1935, over MacDonald's initials, as 'a document of epochal significance'. He comments that 'the apostle of peace signed as one of his last state papers the announcement that Britain must rearm'. It is regrettable that he did not

2A

mention the bitterly hostile reception given to that White Paper by the Labour and Liberal Oppositions and by the League of Nations Union. In the General Election of 1935, the reader may be reminded, one of the most popular Opposition points was that if the National Government were successful Churchill ('National Swashbuckler No. 1') would be brought back to office. But then, in those days, even Neville Chamberlain could be described in an official Labour broadcast as a 'militarist'.

The difficulties which had confronted MacDonald prior to the General Election in preserving the co-operation of the official Liberal Party, and that of Snowden, with the National Government have been set out above. They turned primarily on the tariff issue, and, not having been resolved, were bound to recur. Certain emergency measures were taken by the new Government in this field without much trouble; but the recommendation of a Cabinet committee in favour of a general 10 per cent duty on all goods other than those exempted on a free list led to a Cabinet crisis. On January 21, 1932, Snowden, Samuel, Maclean and Sinclair threatened resignation; and MacDonald notified the King that he might have to tender the resignation of the Government as a whole. On the following day, however, a suggestion first put forward by Neville Chamberlain was adopted: this allowed the dissentient Ministers to speak and vote against the proposals of the majority. Criticism was naturally directed against this 'agreement to differ' as a breach of the practice of collective Cabinet responsibility. Limited, however, to the particular issue, and defended as an expedient justifiable only in the exceptional circumstances, it aroused little public interest; and it served to maintain the Government intact for nearly the whole of the remainder of its first and vital year of office. But the Agreements reached at the Ottawa Imperial Economic Conference, involving the extension of preferences, proved too much for the Free Trade Ministers. Despite MacDonald's efforts, they could not be persuaded to remain. On September 28, 1932, Snowden, Samuel and Sinclair resigned (Maclean had died in the preceding June), together with seven Liberal junior Ministers.

The withdrawal of the official Liberals at this stage did not constitute a serious blow to the National Government. Baldwin had suggested to MacDonald beforehand that the boat might 'well sail henceforward on a more even keel', and his forecast proved accurate.[1] The Liberal press, it is true, became more outspokenly critical, but it had never been favourably disposed. It is true also that Snowden embarked upon a course of bitter denunciation, with, however, relatively little and diminishing effect. Samuel, it may be noted, did not lead his Party into general opposition to the Government until November 1933, and then because of the latter's alleged lack of zeal in the cause of disarmament.

It is customary, and extremely plausible, to contend that from this point onwards the National Government became, to all intents and purposes, a purely Conservative administration. MacDonald himself had feared that might happen, and that his own position as Prime Minister would become more and more anomalous and degrading.[2] Certainly, the defection of the Samuelite Liberals weakened both the 'national' basis of the Government and MacDonald's personal authority. With what G. M. Young has described as his 'logical, analytic, Scotch mind', the Premier had set out the problem to Baldwin before the resignations took place.[3] Baldwin, however, was much less apprehensive, and decisively rejected any suggestion that MacDonald should retire from the Premiership. The co-operation between the two leaders remained the central core of the administration. Although opponents and critics might regard, or profess to regard, Sir John Simon and the Liberal Nationals as indistinguishable from Conservatives, and MacDonald and his Labour colleagues as helpless prisoners of the Tories, the Government continued to be a broadly-based coalition. The party labels of its members had, in reality, little significance. In the formulation and conduct of policy, this National Government appears to have functioned with a high, indeed unusual, measure of harmony. Its approach to the problems of the time was empirical, moderate, progressive. In terms of party development, it represented a most important further stage in the broadening and modernization of British Conservatism. And, during these years, it expressed the views of the great body of central opinion in the country. The character and policy of the Government may be exemplified by its handling of the Indian question. MacDonald was able to continue and develop his Indian policy with the steadfast backing of Baldwin and the skilled assistance of Hoare; and, in view of the inherent

[1] G. M. Young, *Stanley Baldwin*, p. 172.
[2] Letter to the King, September 11, 1932, quoted by Nicolson, op. cit., p. 498.
[3] Op. cit., pp. 170–1.

difficulties, and of the prolonged and resourceful obstruction of Churchill and his Conservative Right-Wing supporters, the Government of India Act of 1935 was one of this administration's greatest achievements.

It has long been fashionable to think and write of the 'thirties as a period of almost unrelieved economic depression and social misery, the 'hungry 'thirties', as they have so frequently been called. The impression thus conveyed is highly deceptive. The element of truth in it is derived from the obstinate problem of the distressed areas, the unemployment so heavily concentrated there, and the consequential social evils. But in this country the impact of the world economic depression was relatively mild; and Britain was the first of the more important industrial communities to emerge from it. Steady, though uneven, recovery marked the years of the Second National Government, particularly from 1933 onwards. By 1935, the number of insured persons unemployed was progressively declining, employment and production had passed beyond the 1929 level, and output per head had increased by nearly 20 per cent. Britain's share of the reduced world trade rose slightly; the terms of trade were favourable; and in 1935 there was a favourable balance of payments. With the fall in the cost of living, the real income of the working classes was rising; and for all save the unemployed and those on short time conditions showed a marked improvement. There was a notable and continuous growth in the consumer and service industries, and a remarkable housing boom. In regard to the unemployed, the cuts in the rates of benefit were abolished in 1934; and, by the Unemployment Act of that year, the Government created the Unemployment Assistance Board for the administration of relief payments, although political disturbances occurred in relation to the initial scales proposed. In 1935, all the salary and pay cuts imposed in 1931 were removed.

How far this limited but considerable recovery was due to Government action is a question to which conflicting answers may be given; but the Government's contribution was certainly not negligible. Far from being rigidly orthodox in financial policy, the National Government experimented with and developed the techniques required for a managed currency. Deflationary measures were soon modified, and a cheap money policy inaugurated and maintained. The Bank Rate was lowered to 5 per cent on February 18, 1932, and by rapid stages to 2 per cent in the following June, at which figure it remained. Fears of high protection proved ground-less. Tariff policy, and other expressions of the prevalent economic nationalism, can fairly be described as moderate. Forecasts that the 'National' regime would be 'reactionary' turned out to be even more erroneous. Indeed, to the Conservative Right Wing and to the more doctrinaire Liberals the Government's policy seemed scandalously semi-socialistic. In industry and agriculture alike, there was active interventionism. Several important measures of nationalization were carried through; and the development of what later came to be called the 'Welfare State' was resumed and accelerated.

Part of the credit for the improved economic and social conditions must undoubtedly go to the National Government; and, therefore, to the statesman whose courageous decisions in 1931 made its formation and maintenance possible. Indeed, the verdict pronounced by one eminent and detached judge on MacDonald's general policy in the years 1929–31 may well be endorsed. It was, Professor J. A. Schumpeter wrote, probably 'one of the best per-formances in the history of democratic politics, and one of the best examples of action responsibly decided on from a correct percep-tion of an economic and social situation', though 'to the radical critic who failed to link up that policy with the comparative mild-ness of the depression in England and with the steadiness of the subsequent recovery, there was nothing in it except weakness, in-competence, hidebound traditionalism, if not traitorous abandon-ment of the socialist cause'. Schumpeter expressed the hope that historians would learn to do justice to the statesmanship of Mac-Donald as they have done to that of Sir Robert Peel.[1]

[1] *Capitalism, Socialism and Democracy*, 2nd Edition, pp. 367–70.

APPENDIX I

THE MONARCH AND THE CRISIS

A. Mr Leonard Wolff

The formation of the first National Government gave rise to certain criticisms of both the King and the Prime Minister on constitutional grounds. Criticisms of George V on such grounds have now almost petered out, although Herbert Morrison has recently presented, on wider political grounds, some half-heartedly critical comments on the King's actions, and, still more recently, Graeme Moodie has endeavoured to reopen the whole subject. For many years, however, such criticisms enjoyed considerable popularity. Writing in 1951, Lansbury's biographer referred to 'the widespread belief that it was the King, who, stepping away from the traditional neutrality of the Crown, was responsible for MacDonald's astonishing final action'. There was, he said, 'nothing to establish or contradict' this belief.[1]

The initiative in criticism of the monarch appears to have been taken by Leonard Wolff in some brief notes written soon after the new Government was formed, and before the General Election.[2] Wolff described what had happened as an ominous and dangerous 'constitutional revolution'. King and Prime Minister were both censured. Action such as they had taken, though it may have been 'technically constitutional', made impossible 'a fair and honest working of a democratic system on the model of the British Constitution'. Wolff's argument was based upon a contention that 'the whole of our political system, in so far as it is democratic, rests upon the party system'. The Prime Minister, so the argument ran, is Prime Minister, not as an individual, 'but because he can count on the support of a party.' That was ambiguously phrased. It would certainly be difficult to point to any Prime Minister who has lacked 'the support of a party'. MacDonald was never in that posi-

[1] Op. cit., p. 261.
[2] *Political Quarterly*, II, No. 4. Oct.-Dec. 1931.

tion. In his next sentence Wolff made a quick transition, customary also with those who have repeated or developed his argument, from '*a* party' to '*his* party':

> When Mr MacDonald found that he wished to pursue a policy which was solidly opposed by practically the whole of his party, he should on democratic principles have told the King that he could not carry on the Government and have resigned. It was quite open to him to tell the King that he was prepared to support as an individual any Government formed to carry out that policy or take office in it as an individual. But that is not what happened. Mr MacDonald was induced . . . to form a National Government, which meant a Government of all parties. If Mr Baldwin entered the Government as Leader of the Conservative Party and Sir H. Samuel as Acting Leader of the Liberal Party, what was Mr MacDonald's position? It was that of Leader of the Labour Party. Even to state the bare facts is almost equivalent to stating baldly that the thing was a fraud.

As stated by Wolff, the facts are rather threadbare; and the argument presented is a confused one. When, it may be asked, did Mac-Donald find himself in the position alleged? His policy was supported by a majority of the Labour Cabinet; but, since it was not supported by the Cabinet as a whole, he *had* resigned. Wolff can hardly have meant that MacDonald should have resigned again *after* he had formed the National Government, for he is criticizing that Government's formation. And even then it was not true that MacDonald's policy was solidly opposed by practically the whole of his party. The meaning attached by Wolff to the term 'a National Government' is familiar in its ambiguity. The Government formed by MacDonald under that designation was not 'a Government of all parties', but was specifically and repeatedly declared to be a Government of individuals drawn from all three parties. Baldwin and Samuel entered it as individuals: so did MacDonald: Baldwin, of course, was Leader of the Conservative Party, and Samuel was Acting Leader of the Liberal Party; and both remained so, since they were able to secure the support of their respective parties. MacDonald was still the Leader of the Labour Party, but, as everybody knew, would not be able to retain that position after forming (or participating in) the new Government, because the great majority of his party would be against him doing so, whatever their views might be on the nature of his policy.

Wolff had no objection to MacDonald supporting 'as an individual' any Government formed to carry out his policy. He had no objection to MacDonald taking office in such a Government 'as an individual'. Why then should he have objected so strongly to Mac-Donald, as an individual, forming such a Government? Why should he have regarded MacDonald's action in doing so as un-democratic and, therefore, contrary to the spirit if not to the letter of the Constitution? Presumably because, on his interpretation, MacDonald acted, or purported to act, not 'as an individual' but as 'Leader of the Labour Party', though he was, or at any rate would be, no longer effectively leader. Though, on agreeing to form the National Government, MacDonald could no doubt formally have resigned his leadership, it is difficult to conceive how, 'as an indi-vidual,' he could have divested himself of his capacity or quality of having been Leader of the Labour Party. Yet Wolff, while objecting to MacDonald forming a National Government, did not object to him participating in such a Government or supporting it from outside. Why the first of these courses should be considered 'undemocratic', and the others 'democratic', is incomprehensible.

Wolff, however, proceeded to a criticism, in form conditional, of the King's part in the formation of the new Government:

> It is said that the King personally induced Mr MacDonald to do this. If so, he was doing something which may prove highly dangerous to the Crown. For, in effect, he was making an individual Prime Min-ister though he had no support for his Government in the House of Commons, except by a process of camouflage and jugglery.

Wolff ended by suggesting that the precedent might be developed to introduce 'a system not materially different from that of a dicta-torship'. This, again, is difficult to follow: indeed, it seems to be hysterical nonsense. MacDonald plainly had support for his new Government in the House of Commons; much greater support than he had had for his old Government. And it would have been impossible for Wolff to explain how any other person, whether or not the leader of a party, could have formed a Government enjoy-ing a greater measure of support in the existing House of Com-mons. Indeed, it was precisely because no one else could command greater support there that MacDonald was induced to form the National Government. Wolff, of course, had to concede that Mac-Donald had 'support for his Government', but only, he suggested, as a result of 'a process of camouflage and jugglery'. What he meant by that he did not explain, but his previous remarks imply that what he had in mind was that support for MacDonald was forthcoming only because he had been fraudulently presented as being still the Leader of the Labour Party in fact as well as form. That, however, was plainly not the case. The facts spoke for themselves. MacDonald had been Leader of the Labour Party for the preceding nine years, and Prime Minister of a Cabinet the majority of whom had approved his policy; he still had the backing of important colleagues and many supporters in the Labour Party; and he enjoyed the support of the other two parties.

Wolff, it will be noted, did not go so far as to assert that the King's action in inducing MacDonald to form the National Government and MacDonald's action in allowing himself to be induced were contrary to constitutional practice. He was really arguing that any such actions ought to be considered unconstitutional because they were 'undemocratic', an opinion apparently based on the view that no one should ever be appointed Prime Minister unless he has the support of the party to which he has belonged and still belongs at the time of his appointment. Wolff's vaguely-formulated conception of the place of party in democratic politics was to be endorsed, though not significantly developed, by a more influential writer.

B. PROFESSOR H. J. LASKI

At the time of the National Government's formation, some commentators in the popular press had stressed the part played by George V. The *Daily Express*, for example, wrote on August 25:

> What then made Mr MacDonald choose the path of party ostracism instead of throwing in his hand and leaving the task to Mr Baldwin? THE ANSWER is the insistence of His Majesty that there should be no dissolution or General Election and that all the Party leaders should combine to meet the emergency. The truth is that during the last few days the King has been in fact as well as in form the ruler of his people.

Harold Laski appears to have adopted this view of what had happened; and, in his booklet, *The Crisis and the Constitution*, which receives fuller consideration in Appendix IV below, he roundly denounced the King's behaviour.

Writing soon after the General Election, Laski declared that the National Government was 'born of a Palace Revolution'. Rarely, he wrote, had Crown influence exerted so profound an influence in modern times. MacDonald was described as 'the King's nominee for the place of Prime Minister', and was likened to 'Lord Bute in 1760 or the younger Pitt in 1783'. In Laski's view, MacDonald was given a significance more than purely personal only by that 'which the King chose to attach to him at a period of crisis'.

Laski admitted that he did not know any of the details. It was apparently sufficient for him that MacDonald had had 'repeated conversations' with 'the Palace'. He made no pretence of knowing what advice (if any) had been tendered to the King. None the less, he declared that the new Cabinet 'was made at the instance of the Crown without any sort of consultation with the Ministers who were ousted from power'.

This last phrase indicates Laski's one specific objection to the King's conduct, viz.: that the King had not consulted Henderson or any of his associates. In the form given it by Laski the argument is not at all impressive. Despite his absence from the country at the time of the crisis, he must have known that the Labour Cabinet, too hopelessly divided to carry on, had agreed, late on August 23, that MacDonald should resign, and had thereby ousted themselves from power. It is scarcely conceivable that Laski should have thought Henderson either willing or able to form an administration; and it is clear that Henderson would not have served under MacDonald in a National Government. The purpose of any consultation of Henderson or any other ex-Minister would have been, therefore, to obtain advice about the character of the new Government which had to be formed. Although Laski did not express himself very clearly on the point, his view presumably was that Henderson, if he had been asked for his advice, would have advised against the formation of a National Government under MacDonald's leadership; and would have done so on the ground that the Labour Party as such would not support MacDonald. Some subsequent commentators have attached much importance to these considerations. Their assumption has been that George V did not realize that the bulk of the Labour Party would oppose MacDonald and would resent his appointment. It is probable that something of this kind was in Laski's mind.

The King was of course free to send for Henderson or any other ex-Minister and seek advice. He was under no constitutional obligation to do so. Nor was it necessary for him to do so for the purpose or purposes apparently envisaged by Laski. Moreover, any such consultation presented difficulties, apart from the time factor. Henderson was not the Leader of the Labour Party. On the other hand, he was the most prominent member of the dissentient minority in the Labour Cabinet, whose threatened resignations had brought about its downfall. In the circumstances, consultation of any ex-Minister involved the risk of being construed as interference in the internal affairs of the Labour Party.

Laski could not go so far as to assert that the King had acted unconstitutionally in not consulting Henderson or any of his associates; he knew that was quite untenable ground; but he appears to have sought to convey that impression indirectly by contending that MacDonald 'had ceased in fact, and ceased, almost immediately in theory, to be the Labour Leader, once he separated himself from his Labour colleagues'. That was putting the cart a little before the horse. At the time of his decision to head a National Government, MacDonald had not 'separated himself from his Labour colleagues'; nor, by taking that decision, did he in fact separate himself from all his colleagues or necessarily from any of them. According to Laski, MacDonald, when commissioned to form the National Government, was not 'a party leader' but only 'a very eminent private Member' of the House of Commons. Even if one interprets the phrase 'a party leader' to mean 'the Leader of a Party', that was not strictly the case; but had it been so, and in so far as it was bound to become so, Laski's objection would still have been invalid from the constitutional standpoint.

There is nothing unconstitutional in a Government headed by 'a very eminent private Member'; and one famous subsequent instance was to have Laski's ardent approval. His 1932 criticism of George V was both imaginative and vague. It goes without saying that the King played an important part in the formation of the National Government. Faced with the inability of the existing Labour Government to carry on, it was his constitutional duty to take the requisite steps towards the formation of a new administration. Plainly enough, however, Laski had no reliable knowledge early in 1932 of the part actually played by George V.

When, in 1938, he published his *Parliamentary Government in England*, his attitude on this subject was substantially unchanged. It is true that he referred to 'wide divergencies of opinion about the King's action', and said that it was 'difficult to pronounce any opinion upon it with certitude'. He admitted that it was not known whether MacDonald's leadership of the National Government was the result of advice tendered by him to the King or of a suggestion made by the King to him. He appears to have had a glimmering that the advice might have come from some other quarter. Discussing the Liberals, he expressed the view that there was no reason to suppose that they indicated a preference for MacDonald as leader. It was afterwards disclosed, however, that that was precisely what the Liberals did do, through their Acting Leader, Samuel.[1] None the less, Laski made the following assertion:

> It appears, in any case, to be universally admitted that the King played a pivotal part in securing the assent of Mr Baldwin and Sir Herbert Samuel to his (MacDonald's) assumption of the Premiership.

In Baldwin's case, Laski might have attempted to justify this assertion by reference to the Conservative Leader's public explanations of his decision at the time; but no such justification could be given in Samuel's case. Laski actually relied once more on the dubiously relevant contention that

> no attempt was made by the King to elicit the views of the great bulk of the Labour Party who transferred their allegiance from Mr MacDonald to Mr Arthur Henderson.

That transference, of course, came afterwards.

Despite his admitted lack of the relevant knowledge, Laski then declared:

> It appears certain that the impetus to the peculiar form of the new administration came wholly from the King. Mr MacDonald was as much the personal choice of George V as Lord Bute was the personal choice of George III.

A 'Palace Revolution' he still thought a not unreasonable description of what took place. The curious and wholly inadequate ground for that view was that

> a Baldwin Premiership was confidently expected at least as late as the night before the break-up of the Labour Government.

[1] Curiously, in the letter to Frankfurter already mentioned, and written on October 6, 1931, Laski said: 'The King sent for Baldwin and Samuel, who urged on him Mac as Premier, the others to serve under him.' From whatever source he had derived this information, Laski appears to have forgotten it very quickly.

The implication seems to be that the King intervened almost at the last moment to prevent a Baldwin Government. Incidentally, all this did not deter Laski from suggesting that for many months a National Government had been contemplated by 'Palace circles', by MacDonald, and even by Baldwin.

Shortly before his death in 1950, Laski delivered the lectures subsequently published under the title *Reflections on the Constitution*. Only a faint echo of his former contentions was then heard. He 'believed' that 'the effective source of the change (of Government) was the influence of King George V'. As yet, however, we had 'no official knowledge of what transactions took place at the Palace'. That perhaps was formally true; but Laski completely ignored Samuel's *Memoirs*, published in 1945. On the other hand, he thought it only fair

> to note that, in a published account, Mr Sidney Webb does not share my view that the King directly interfered to bring out the remarkable arrangement, and that a careful authority, Sir Ivor Jennings, supports Mr Webb.

It would have been only fair to have pointed that out long before 1950. Webb's account had actually been published early in 1932, and Sir Ivor Jennings had expressed his own view soon afterwards in the same year. Neither, of course, had any special information about what had happened. It is highly probable that Laski's criticism of the monarch was merely incidental to his criticism of MacDonald, who was certainly his main target.

C. LORD PASSFIELD

In an unpublished commentary on the crisis, written in September of 1931, Sidney Webb (Lord Passfield) said:

> What happened on Monday morning at Buckingham Palace is easily seen. When the Prime Minister formally tendered his resignation the King, with whom MacDonald has always been in high favour, pressed him not to abandon the Monarch, and suggested a 'National Government', for which Kings always have a hankering and on which MacDonald had already talked with him. The King doubtless made a like appeal on patriotic grounds to the four leaders of the two oppositions to which they had (little or) no hesitation in responding. Everything went, so far, according to the plan which MacDonald had, in my opinion, gradually been concocting for months previously.[1]

[1] The reference to the *four* leaders is an obvious slip. Baldwin and Samuel alone were involved.

Webb was more cautious in his published account (*What Happened in 1931: A Record*). On the subject at issue, he did not commit himself definitely, nor perhaps at all, for there was a prefatory remark, as follows:

> What happened at Buckingham Palace on Monday morning, 24th August, can be known only to the actual participators.

The passage then proceeded:

> What is said is that the King, with whom the Prime Minister had been in constant communication but who never went outside his constitutional position, made a strong appeal to him to stand by the nation in this financial crisis, and to seek the support of leading members of the Conservative and Liberal Parties in forming, in conjunction with such members of his own Party as would come in, a united National Government. The King is believed to have made a correspondingly strong appeal to the Liberal and Conservative Leaders.

No authority is given for this: nor does the passage make it quite clear that Webb himself held that the King had kept within the limits of his constitutional position. Like other distinguished persons who burst into print about the same time, Webb knew nothing of what had taken place at the King's interviews with Samuel and Baldwin on the previous day (August 23).

Webb's 'What is said' passage (but not the prefatory remark) figured prominently in subsequent discussions. In particular, it was to be quoted, without comment, by Sir Ivor Jennings in the first (1936) edition of his important book, *Cabinet Government* (pp. 38–9). Curiously, Sir Ivor has retained the passage in his revised (1951) edition, although it is not actually set out there in the form of a quotation; and has done so, apparently, on the unconvincing ground that it had 'received no contemporary denial'.

D. SIR IVOR JENNINGS

Early in 1932, Sir Ivor Jennings had himself written that there was 'no evidence that the King acted otherwise than with due constitutional propriety'.[1] He pointed out that, when a Cabinet decides to resign, the King is free 'to consult what party leaders he pleases to determine what Government Parliamentary exigencies demand'; indeed, that 'he is entitled to consult whom he pleases'. In Jennings's

[1] 'The Constitution under Strain', *Political Quarterly*, April-June 1932.

view, it was not George V but MacDonald who had 'strained the Constitution'.

In the first edition of *Cabinet Government*, Sir Ivor reiterated these points and cited the precedents. The available information, he wrote, 'suggests that the formation of the National Government was, at least in respect of the King's action, quite constitutional.' The qualification should be noted. 'It is irrelevant', Sir Ivor declared, '(except as evidence of Mr MacDonald's good faith or otherwise) to ask at whose suggestion the National Government was formed.' Again the qualification is important.[1]

In his revised edition, with Lord Samuel's information both available and quoted, Sir Ivor wrote (p. 41):

> It is clear that the King acted constitutionally, but it would be possible to give a different opinion on Mr MacDonald's action.

He also retained (p. 44) the passage quoted above containing the reference to Mr MacDonald's 'good faith or otherwise'. And to this he appended a footnote stating that 'criticisms of the formation of the 1931 Coalition rest upon Mr MacDonald's action in relation to his colleagues', and giving references to Snowden's autobiography, the Laski booklet, and his own 1932 article.

Sir Ivor Jennings thus acquits George V of the charge of having acted unconstitutionally, but suggests that such a charge might be brought against MacDonald. No charge is actually formulated. Nor is MacDonald's good faith directly challenged. It is a strange procedure, made all the more unsatisfactory by the nature and influence of the treatise in which it is followed. And, if criticisms of the formation of the National Government rest (as Sir Ivor suggests, whether or not he endorses them) upon 'MacDonald's action in relation to his colleagues', a question arises as to their relevance to any charge of 'unconstitutional' action on the part of the then Prime Minister.

E. Mr Herbert Morrison

In his book *Government and Parliament*, Mr Herbert Morrison deals at some length with the part played in the 1931 crisis by George V. His conclusion is:

> On a balance of considerations, therefore, my own view is that in this instance King George V received bad advice and that he himself made

[1] Op. cit., pp. 39–40.

a mistake in accepting it, though I would not go so far as to assert that his action was unconstitutional. He may have taken the view (from which I would respectfully differ) that the crisis required a National Government, and that it would be helpful if Mr MacDonald (for whom he had a warm regard) continued as Prime Minister. I have set out my own view though I recognize that many authorities may not agree with it.

Morrison's argument is on a rather different footing from those previously considered. His criticism of the King is somewhat tentative. None the less, he suggests that George V ought to have rejected the advice tendered to him by Samuel and Baldwin, and, in a formal sense, by MacDonald. And he also raises the point about consultation of ex-Ministers. He writes:

> It may well be that the King had the impression that Mr MacDonald would carry a majority, or at any rate a substantial proportion, of the Parliamentary Labour Party with him, and had that been true it would have strengthened the case for his action. But this did not prove to be so. He would have been wise to have ascertained what was likely to happen by inquiry of one or more Labour Privy Councillors likely to know. He might have asked the Prime Minister to ascertain the view of the Labour Cabinet; but no action was taken to ascertain the general Labour view. King George V was, I feel sure, actuated by sincere motives. And certainly the financial and economic situation of the country was serious. Nevertheless, I think his judgment was at fault. He was himself, I apprehend, over-favourable to a very speculative course of action. The very formation of what was styled the National Government was a highly controversial step; it led to bitter parliamentary debates, for Mr MacDonald did not carry the Labour Party with him.

There is no evidence to support the view that the King was unaware that the great majority of the Parliamentary Labour Party would be opposed to the formation of the National Government; nor for the view that he failed to realize that the great majority of the Labour Cabinet would similarly be opposed to it. Such evidence as there is, and all the probabilities, point the other way. That such opposition existed was well known to all the political leaders, and, indeed, to the politically-experienced in the country generally. It was in spite of that fact, and because MacDonald might nevertheless command much support from Labour in the country, that Chamberlain appealed to him on the night of August

23. That 'no action was taken to ascertain the general Labour view' is one of those assertions which can be neither proved nor disproved, but what matters is whether or not the essential facts of the situation were known and appreciated by George V. It is highly improbable that the King's Secretary was unaware of them. It is equally unlikely that MacDonald himself failed to make the position clear; and the same is true of Baldwin and Samuel. The nature of the provisional agreement to form a National Government (at the Palace on the morning of August 24) strongly suggests that the King was fully apprised of the state of affairs as it affected the Labour Cabinet and the Parliamentary Labour Party.

But Morrison's main contention raises an obvious point. He is really suggesting that George V ought to have played a more decisive part; that he was entitled to exercise his own personal judgment even to the extent of rejecting the advice of the Leaders of the two Parties which together had a majority in the House of Commons, and also the formal advice of his Prime Minister. Presumably, had he done so, Morrison would not have regarded his action as unconstitutional, and doubtless Morrison would have been right, but, if so, it is difficult to understand why Morrison should entertain even the slightest doubt that the King acted constitutionally in accepting the advice tendered to him. Supposing, however, that the King had done what Morrison thinks he ought to have done; supposing that he had rejected the advice to ask Mac-Donald to form a National Government, and had asked Baldwin to form a Conservative-Liberal coalition; what then? Baldwin might conceivably have accepted the task, and Samuel might conceivably have agreed; but the first is unlikely, and the second more unlikely still. Suppose, then, a Baldwin refusal or failure to form such a Government. In such circumstances the King would have been forced back to accept the advice he had rejected; unless, indeed, he succeeded in persuading MacDonald to decline the task. Morrison's argument comes very near suggesting that George V ought to have done his utmost to dissuade MacDonald from undertaking the leadership of a National Government. Laski no doubt would have considered such action on the King's part perfectly constitutional.

The Morrison argument is simply an argument that, to use his own words, 'the natural and appropriate parliamentary solution' of the crisis resulting from the resignation of the Labour

2B

Cabinet 'was that the Conservatives should take office, probably with Liberal support'. Naturally enough, that is the solution which Morrison himself would have greatly preferred. He attempts, however, to state a case for it on public grounds. It is that 'the national necessity really did not, as I see it, require the formation of what was called the National Government', since 'a Conservative-Liberal Coalition could have done all that the so-called National Government did'. And this opinion is supported by the contention that MacDonald 'had ceased to possess representative parliamentary value', and that 'Mr MacDonald and his few supporters brought no real strength to the new Government, though their action much increased the bitterness in Parliament and the country'. However, it is extremely doubtful if a Conservative-Liberal coalition could even have been formed without MacDonald's assistance and under someone else's leadership. And Morrison badly contradicts himself when he writes later on:

> While the defections from the Labour Party were so small that they could not be described as a split, the consequence of Mr MacDonald, Mr Snowden, and Mr J. H. Thomas associating themselves with the Conservatives at the subsequent election led to a dramatic Labour Party defeat so far as seats were concerned.

If MacDonald had ceased to possess representative parliamentary value when he formed the National Government, he very soon reacquired it, and did so in unprecedented degree. And with his 'few supporters', he brought a strength to the new Government without which, as events prior to the election demonstrated, it would have failed to survive. Morrison's half-hearted criticism of King George V is really only a peg upon which he has hung a rather belated expression of his views on the crisis.

F. MR GRAEME MOODIE

In his re-examination of the crisis of 1931, already alluded to, Graeme Moodie shows himself reluctant to endorse what he grants is now the generally accepted view that George V acted with complete constitutional propriety. He is not prepared to place the exclusive responsibility upon MacDonald 'for any undesirable features about the manner of his own selection', and that selection itself he plainly considers to have been constitutionally undesirable.

MacDonald, it is said, 'was the personal choice of the King to the extent that he was preferred to Baldwin.' This remark is perhaps open to misinterpretation. Moodie apparently means that George V had an effective choice between a National Government under MacDonald and a Baldwin Government, and preferred the former:

> There is nothing to indicate that Samuel, despite his preference for a National Government, would not have supported Baldwin if MacDonald had refused to become National Prime Minister, or had not been asked to do so. And Baldwin explicitly stated his willingness to become Prime Minister, even although the King had opened their conversation by asking if he were prepared to serve under Mac-Donald. It is therefore virtually certain that had King George not favoured a National Government under MacDonald, he could as well have selected Baldwin, and that Baldwin would have succeeded in forming a new Government.

In fact, of course, Baldwin expressed a willingness to form a Government only if MacDonald refused to do so. Incidentally, there is no conclusive evidence that the King 'opened' his conversation with Baldwin in the manner described.

Moodie is well aware of the advice tendered to the King by Samuel and Baldwin. He holds, however, that George V was constitutionally free to reject that advice, and implies that he ought to have rejected it. He insists that the King was perfectly entitled to act upon his preference, but implies that his preference was ill-founded. His points are put for the most part in a conditional form:

> if the King had in fact known that MacDonald would not be followed and had still selected him, then he could hardly have remained immune from criticism.

'Followed' by whom? The answer is, apparently, 'by the Labour Party.' Did the King know that MacDonald would not be so followed? Moodie is unsure about that. The King, in his view, should certainly have known that MacDonald might not have 'the full, or even substantial, backing of his own party in the formation of an "all-party" Government'. Anyhow, it would have been appropriate for him to find out whether that was so or not. Moodie therefore suggests that the King was at fault in not undertaking consultations for the purpose of discovering

> the extent to which a given individual would, if appointed Prime Minister, possess the approval and support of his own party.

He argued that in the circumstances it was more than usually desirable for the monarch to 'question the credentials of a potential Prime Minister', because

> the Prime Minister's *own party* may have no power to remove him should it turn out that he no longer possesses the qualifications for leadership.

And, in Moodie's view, he lacks the essential qualification if he 'no longer possesses the confidence of his own party'.

The argument is substantially the same as Wolff's. It rests on a contention that no individual should be appointed Prime Minister unless he has the backing of the party to which he belongs when appointed. Like Wolff, Moodie recognizes that this is not a constitutional rule; but he argues that it ought to be. He pleads for a 'new rule', which he formulates, in its 'simplest form', as follows:

> that a Prime Minister should at all times, as a matter of principle, be selected only with the approval and support of his own party.

A footnote adds:

> Or, possibly, with the approval and support of a majority of his own party. Some vagueness in the rule is probably inevitable, and is not untypical of the British Constitution. Like most rules, too, this one needs to be subject to the qualification 'whenever possible'.

Such a rule, even in its qualified form, would constitute a deplorable, indeed intolerable (and therefore impracticable) limitation of the rights and powers of the citizens and their representatives. The proposal springs from a much exaggerated emphasis upon the role of political parties in a democracy. It ignores both the minority status of any political party and the oligarchic tendencies at work in any party machine. It would make the statesman the prisoner of his party organization. It would impose a disqualification wholly inconsistent with the political rights of the individual and the effective performance of his duties. It is designed to restrict the monarch's present constitutional freedom to select as Prime Minister the individual who, in his judgment and in the light of such advice as he may obtain, is best fitted to form a Government and to secure majority support for it in the House of Commons. And the motive behind the proposal is protection of party interests.

Moodie attempts to justify his suggested new rule by reference to MacDonald's selection. He evidently endorses the view that George V's 'offence'

> consisted of the separation of MacDonald from the vast majority of his followers, of the treatment of MacDonald as an individual, with individual claims to the office of Prime Minister, rather than as an actual or potential party leader in which capacity alone he should have been selected (or rejected). This violation of the party bond . . . is liable to be interpreted as a partisan action and, in any case, is dangerous to democratic government and not fully compatible with the proper working of the constitution.[1]

Whether or not it is true that MacDonald was or became separated from 'the vast majority of his followers' depends in large measure upon one's interpretation of the term 'followers'. That MacDonald had been and still was formally the leader of a party, and was certainly the potential leader of a party, are facts which are obvious enough. His acceptance of the Premiership of the National Government did not violate any party bond, if by that expression is meant either a breach of his party's rules or his resignation from the party. His selection, therefore, involved no violation by the King of 'the party bond'. The violation came from the Labour Party organization — a month later. If, however, it be contended that the King's appointment of MacDonald 'violated the party bond' in the sense of producing a split in the Labour Party, the answer is that the split was already there and, indeed, was the cause of the political crisis with which the King had to deal. And, if it be held that the King's action made the split wider than it otherwise would have been, the answer is that the facts strongly suggest the opposite conclusion.

But the main point is that this argument implies that the King should have so acted as to avert or minimize a split in the Labour Party. He should have refrained from asking MacDonald to form a National Government in order to maintain or promote the unity of the Labour Party. What we have, in effect, is a plea that the monarch should have put the interests of the Labour Party before those of the nation. Had the King done so, he would certainly have incurred, and would have merited, censure for partiality. The cleav-

---

[1] That Moodie accepts this is plain from a subsequent passage in which he envisages the possibility of a Labour leader 'once again' being 'thus separated from his party' and of a Conservative Party refusing to acquiesce 'in a similar violation of their party bond'.

age in the Labour Cabinet, and the wider internal differences in the Labour Party, actual and potential, were factors which the King had to take into account; but it would have been contrary to his constitutional duty had he treated them as of paramount or decisive importance.

George V's failure to act partially has, it is true, been criticized as an act of partisanship. Moodie quotes, without actually endorsing, Morrison's statement that the King became involved in what many of his subjects

> regarded as an unnecessary and unpleasant political manoeuvre by Mr MacDonald and his new allies, calculated to inflict grave injury on the Labour Party and to benefit the Conservatives — as it did.

Morrison only specifically commits himself to the view that the formation of the National Government in fact injured the Labour Party and helped the Conservatives; not that it was 'calculated' to do so. It need not have injured the Labour Party at all; although that Party would undoubtedly have suffered in any event from the failure of the Labour Cabinet to cope with the crisis. That it did so was due to the nature of the Party's opposition to the National Government and to the General Election which that provoked.

In support of his proposed new constitutional rule, Moodie himself has a curious passage:

> it is worth noting that one effect of MacDonald's selection as leader of a new government, with a different composition and a different policy from his old one, was to enable him successfully to evade personal responsibility for the former policies which he himself, along with Snowden in particular, had largely framed and actively pursued. In effect he was allowed to make his party the scapegoat for his own mistakes. With more justice, the normal and generally accepted British practice is almost the exact opposite.

The National Government, however, was formed to deal with an emergency situation. That was its sole purpose, and speedy accomplishment of it was anticipated. Its policy for dealing with the crisis was not different from but almost identical with that accepted in principle by the whole Labour Cabinet. It was a policy, moreover, most of the details of which had been 'provisionally' accepted by the whole Labour Cabinet, and practically all of which had been approved by a majority of that Cabinet. Any attempt to evade responsibility for previous policies was plainly made by the Labour ex-Ministers, but with a striking lack of success. In the longer run, however, they were much more successful in making MacDonald the scapegoat for their previous policies, both prior to and during the crisis, whether or not such policies may be regarded as mistakes. Moodie, presumably, has in mind, not policy in regard to the crisis, but policies prior thereto. It is difficult to see how the formation of the National Government enabled MacDonald to evade responsibility for the prior policies of the Labour Government. But the Labour Party's opposition to the National Government's crisis policy, involving as it did repudiation of the Labour Government's crisis policy, naturally led to criticism of the latter Government's former policies being directed against the Labour ex-Ministers to a much higher degree than would otherwise have been the case.

Finally, Moodie is very anxious that the monarch should be shielded 'from criticism or the suggestion of partiality'. He grants that such criticism may be

> entirely unfounded, directed at a failure to act partially, confined to a totally unimportant minority, or quite contrary to all the accepted principles and practices of the constitution.

He considers it none the less important that a monarch should not act in such a way as to arouse the opposition of 'any powerful group in the community', because that might lead to the undermining of the whole position and strength of the monarchy. And, although Moodie grants that criticism of the King's action in 1931 has not had any such effect, he thinks it possible that any repetition of it might do so. He is therefore prepared to concede that 'one disaffected group' (presumably whether justified or not in its disaffection) is entitled to insist upon a change in the constitution to meet its views, provided, apparently, that there is the possibility of the change securing wider acceptance later.

LORD SAMUEL'S MEMOIRS

Attempts to condense into a few pages the story of complex events always present difficulties and dangers. If the attempt be made by one who has authoritative information to impart, there is the special danger that any consequential inaccuracies may be repeated by others and that any ambiguities may result in misleading interpretations. The account of the 1931 crisis given by Lord Samuel in his *Memoirs* comes within this category; and, unfortunately, is free neither from incidental inaccuracies nor from the ambiguities arising from the process of condensation. The matter is of considerable importance because Samuel's account has been unquestioningly accepted by subsequent commentators, notably (subject to one expression of doubt) by Sir Ivor Jennings.

Samuel deals (p. 202) with the initial conversation he had with MacDonald and Snowden on August 13 (see above, pp. 66–7). He proceeds:

> In the next week the currency position was no better, while the political situation was worsened by a grave division in the Cabinet. The Prime Minister and the Chancellor of the Exchequer had presented a bold and comprehensive plan, which would cover the deficits completely, but only a minority of their colleagues supported them. The rest, led by Arthur Henderson, then Foreign Secretary, objected to some of the cuts in expenditure, amounting to about one-third of the effective savings that were proposed. The most important of these was a reduction in the scale of unemployment allowances, which were then absorbing £2½ million a week. Prices generally had fallen, and with them the cost of living, and the reduction was defended on that ground. On August 19th the Cabinet sat for nine hours, but could not reach agreement. The representatives of the other parties were summoned to a joint conference at Downing Street on the following morning.

And then, after a passage emphasizing the general agreement, both

inside and outside the Cabinet, on the question of maintaining the
value of the £, Samuel goes on:

> At our conference at Downing Street on August 20th, we went
> through the Chancellor of the Exchequer's proposals point by point.
> The Conservative and Liberal Leaders agreed to recommend our
> parties to support them. The disagreement in the Cabinet continued.
> We met again on August 21st, and twice on the 22nd. At the final
> meeting, at nine o'clock that night, the Prime Minister told us that
> the Cabinet deadlock could not be overcome and that he had decided
> to resign.

In the earlier part of the first passage quoted above, Samuel was
attempting to cover the whole week from Monday, August 17, until
Saturday, August 22; and he was also endeavouring to summarize
the divisions in the Cabinet which arose during that period. He was
not purporting to give any detailed account of the Cabinet discussions. Only at the end of the passage did he refer to any specific
meeting of the Cabinet, that on August 19, before going on to deal
with the conferences of the party leaders; and no subsequent Cabinet meeting is specifically mentioned. Furthermore, his references
to the meeting on August 19 and to subsequent Cabinet proceedings were merely incidental: he said only that agreement could not
be reached and that the disagreement continued.

The first meeting of the Cabinet during the crisis was the meeting on August 19. Samuel's remarks about the divisions in the
Cabinet during the week have been wrongly interpreted in some
quarters (doubtless because they came first in Samuel's order) to
relate to that meeting on August 19. In fact they relate to the Cabinet meeting on August 21. The proposals submitted to the Cabinet
on the 19th did not include any cut in the standard rates of unemployment allowances. Nor did Henderson on the 19th lead the
opposition to the proposals. It was on the 21st that the proposals
were 'reduced' by 'about one-third', as Samuel told the Liberal
Party meeting on August 28 (see p. 106 above). It is particularly
unfortunate that Samuel, in his *Memoirs*, passes over completely
the crucial events of August 20. In regard to the Cabinet meeting
on the 21st, when the 'one-third reduction' was agreed to, there is
no evidence to support the statement that only a minority of the
Cabinet supported the original proposals. On this point Samuel
was misleading. There *is* evidence (see p. 102 above) that, at the
meeting on the 21st, the inclusion in the proposals of a cut in the

rates of unemployment benefit was *opposed* by 'a substantial minority', and that that question was accordingly dropped.

The second passage from the *Memoirs* quoted above contains some unfortunate errors. Samuel's comments on the three-party conference on August 20 certainly convey the impression that the Conservative and Liberal leaders agreed, *at that conference*, to recommend their parties to support the Chancellor's proposals. They did not in fact do so. As Samuel himself said on September 14, the conference was adjourned so that the Opposition leaders could consult their colleagues and give the proposals further consideration. After these consultations, it is true, they were prepared to recommend support of the proposals, although determined at the same time to raise the question of cuts in the rates of unemployment benefit. But, of course, when the three-party conference was resumed on the evening of August 21, it was confronted by the 'one-third' reduction (so-called) in the Cabinet's proposals. This again emphasizes the misleading effect of the order followed by Samuel in presenting his account.

Samuel writes that the three-party conference 'met again on August 21st, and twice on the 22nd'. In fact, the conference met twice on the 21st, but only once on the 22nd; and the point is of much importance because of what Samuel says took place at the supposed second meeting on the 22nd. The three-party conference, which had adjourned on August 20, reassembled on the 21st at 5 p.m. Confronted by an unexpected situation, the conference was adjourned (see pp. 105–7 above) at 6.30 p.m. It met again at 9.30 p.m., when the Opposition leaders declared the Cabinet's proposals to be inadequate and announced their intention to oppose them. The meeting of the conference on August 22 was the meeting summoned to enable the Prime Minister and Snowden to make their enquiry about the attitude of the Opposition leaders to the revised (and final) tentative proposals. It took place during the luncheon period, roughly from 12.40 to 1.40 p.m. (see p. 122 above). No further meeting of the three-party conference was held that day; nor, indeed, at all.

It is clear that Samuel has muddled up the events of the two days. Quite apart from the fact that no meeting of the three-party conference was held late on the evening of August 22, it is most unlikely that the Prime Minister should have spoken to anyone then of a Cabinet deadlock and of a decision to resign. The Cabinet had adjourned to await the reply from New York; a reply which was not expected, and did not come, until late in the evening of the next day, August 23. What the Cabinet might then do, should the reply be favourable, was uncertain, but there was clearly a possibility that they might endorse the tentative proposals which had been put forward. The official statement issued after the Cabinet had adjourned on the afternoon of the 22nd was by no means unhopeful (see above, p. 125). Late on the night of the 21st, however, when the three-party conference did meet, the position had been much less promising. There had certainly then been a deadlock as between the Cabinet and the Opposition parties, although there is no clear evidence that MacDonald had told the Conservative and Liberal leaders of a deadlock within the Cabinet or that he had decided to resign. He may well have told them that such a deadlock was possible and even likely; and he certainly mentioned the possibility of resignation on that occasion. According to Chamberlain's diary, however, he did not think that resignation would help (see above, p. 108).

The confusion arising from Samuel's mistake about the dates is increased by his subsequent comments. He wrote (p. 204):

> The King, who had just gone to Balmoral, returned to London that night, and next morning, Sunday, August 23rd, received the Prime Minister. Mr MacDonald offered his resignation, and that of the Government; he advised His Majesty to consult the representatives of the other two parties as to the course to be taken. Accordingly Mr Baldwin and I were summoned to the Palace. Mr Baldwin being then on his way back to London, my interview took place at 12.30 that day and his in the afternoon.

In view of the situation on the night of August 22, MacDonald is most unlikely to have offered his resignation first thing the next morning, August 23. He did not in fact do so. Formally, Samuel is correct in saying that MacDonald advised the King to consult the two Opposition leaders, although he apparently did so in response to George V's own suggestion. But when Samuel and Baldwin had their successive interviews with the King (at noon and 3 p.m. respectively), the situation they had to consider was not one in which MacDonald had offered his resignation but one in which it was possible, and perhaps likely, that he would have to do so. MacDonald did not offer his resignation until very late that evening (10.20 p.m.).

Samuel's account in the *Memoirs* proceeds as follows:

I felt no doubt that the members of the Liberal Party in the House of Commons would support an all-party Government, formed with the single purpose of overcoming the financial crisis. A purely Conservative Administration, or a combination of Conservatives and Liberals only, would not be as effective; and a general election would offer no solution at all of the immediate urgent problem. The best prospect of securing a broad-based Government would be if there were no change of Premier. I advised His Majesty to that effect. Mr Baldwin was of the same opinion. Mr MacDonald himself had expressed to us on the previous evening much doubt as to the course he should pursue; but he now fell in with the proposal, and the King acted on the advice unanimously tendered to him.

It has already been pointed out (p. 129 above) that Samuel's account of the advice he tendered to the King at his interview on August 23 is in one extremely important respect incomplete. He omitted having expressed the view that the best solution would be for MacDonald, either with his existing or a reconstituted Labour Cabinet, to propose the economies required (a view which provides confirmation, were any needed, that MacDonald had not then offered his resignation).

Samuel's final sentence in the passage last quoted adds to the muddle about dates. 'The previous evening' would be that of August 22, but MacDonald did not meet the Opposition leaders that evening. He did meet them very late on the evening of August 23, after he had been to the Palace to tender his resignation and after the Cabinet had subsequently adjourned; and it is known that he was then in doubt as to the course he should pursue (see above pp. 151–4). Obviously, Samuel has again got the date wrong; and the resulting confusion is increased by the remark that MacDonald 'now fell in with the proposal' to head a National Government, 'and the King acted on the advice unanimously tendered to him.' 'Now' suggests that these things happened on the 23rd. They actually occurred on the 24th. It was not until the conference at the Palace on the morning of the 24th that the Opposition leaders knew that MacDonald was prepared to fall in with the proposal for a National Government: very late on 'the previous evening' he had still been in doubt. And it was later on the morning of the 24th that, in a formal sense, the unanimous advice of the three leaders was tendered to the King.

'CABINET GOVERNMENT'

Sir Ivor Jennings, it has been seen, dismissed criticisms on constitutional grounds of the King's actions in the 1931 crisis, but suggested that criticisms might be formulated on such grounds against MacDonald. Sir Ivor's references to the crisis in his *Cabinet Government* demand attention. This work of his is widely and deservedly regarded as the best available book on our political system. Most unfortunately, Sir Ivor's revised edition (1951) was produced before the publication of Sir Harold Nicolson's *King George V*; but lack of the information thus made available hardly provides a sufficient explanation of Sir Ivor's treatment of the crisis.

Since Sir Ivor refers his readers to his own 1932 article, it may be well to look first at that. Sir Ivor there suggested that the formation of the National Government had led to 'an exaltation of the powers of the Prime Minister to an extent alien to the ideas of the nineteenth century'; indeed, that we were 'nearing a dictatorship'. He granted that exactly what happened on August 24, 1931, was known only to two persons; and, after considering the probabilities, concluded:

> The most that could be said against Mr MacDonald is that he went to Buckingham Palace prepared to form a National Government if he were given the opportunity.

Jennings objected, however, to the statement (officially issued on the previous day, August 23) that Sir Herbert Samuel and Mr Baldwin were summoned to the Palace on the advice of the Prime Minister. It was, he wrote, constitutionally unnecessary that MacDonald should have been asked; and he added:

> The fact that such a notice was issued from Downing Street is only one example of the emphasis which the present Prime Minister has invariably given to his own office.

The point is not impressive. It may well be true that the King was under no obligation to ask for MacDonald's approval before consulting Baldwin and Samuel on August 23. He may none the less have done so; and, if so, MacDonald can hardly be blamed for the terms of the announcement. As already pointed out, we do not know exactly what happened in this respect. Nicolson conveys the impression that the initiative in regard to the consultation of Baldwin and Samuel came from the King. Dawson's diary confirms that impression. When he wrote, Jennings had before him not only the official announcement but also (as we know from his article) the report of the Parliamentary Correspondent of *The Times* (August 25) which contained the statement that the King returned to London determined to see the leaders of all parties, 'though he properly sought and received the advice of his Prime Minister before doing so.' While that, if it be correct, exemplifies the King's care to act with due constitutional propriety, it provides not the slightest warrant for censure of MacDonald.

Sir Ivor Jennings's other grievance in his 1932 article was that

> the account given in the newspapers, obviously inspired from Downing Street, stated that the Prime Minister then (i.e. after the conference between the King and the three party leaders on the morning of August 24) returned to a Cabinet meeting and 'called for the resignations of all ministers'.

This was the phrase used by *The Times* Correspondent in the report already mentioned on August 25. To Sir Ivor in 1932 MacDonald's action, if correctly reported, was 'another gross and undesirable breach of conventions'. On this point he dissented from the view expressed by Professor Laski (in *The Crisis and the Constitution*) that the Prime Minister had an independent right to hand to the King the resignation of his Ministry.

In the revised edition of *Cabinet Government*, however, Jennings completely abandons that position. He explains that ministerial offices are in fact always considered to be held at the Prime Minister's disposal, and that a Prime Minister can, by a personal resignation, force a dissolution of the Government.[1] The objection

---

[1] 'The Cabinet depends on the Prime Minister because it is, technically, a meeting of "His Majesty's confidential advisers" summoned by the Prime Minister to consider what advice shall be given to the King; but legally the ministers as such do not depend on the Prime Minister for their offices. They are appointed by the King and they hold office during His Majesty's pleasure.

he raised in 1932 was flimsily based, anyhow, on a phrase used by a journalist in a report which was not checked with known facts. The report was not correct. And it is odd that Jennings ignored the statement which had then already been made by Sidney Webb that 'late on Sunday evening, 23rd August', the Labour Cabinet 'in order not to render urgent public business impossible, empowered the Prime Minister to tender to the King his own resignation, which automatically includes the termination of office of the whole Ministry.' When he came to write *Cabinet Government*, Jennings said (p. 66, First Edition) that in 1931 the Cabinet had 'instructed the Prime Minister to tender their resignations'. His reference in this connection was to Snowden's autobiography (pp. 950–2). And this passage, with its reference, is retained in the revised edition, in which, moreover, Jennings states (p. 40) that 'on Sunday, 23rd August' the Labour Government 'authorized the Prime Minister to resign'.

In 1932, in a long development of his second grievance, Jennings argued that

> it is not for the Prime Minister, with or without the King, to dismiss his Cabinet because he no longer agrees with them.

This contention, sound or unsound, was strangely irrelevant. That the Labour Cabinet, on the evening of August 23, had reached a

Until they are allowed to resign or are dismissed, therefore, they remain in office. In fact, however, their offices are always considered to be held at the Prime Minister's disposal. If he desires to replace a minister by another, he simply informs the two persons concerned. The minister then surrenders his seal, if he has one, and the King gives it to the other person; or, if there is no seal, the new minister kisses hands. Whether the retiring minister is said to have resigned or to have been dismissed is therefore a matter of no importance. Frequently he writes to the Prime Minister saying that he is glad to place his office at the Prime Minister's disposal in order to facilitate the reconstitution of his Government; but it makes not the slightest difference if he does not, for it is no longer His Majesty's pleasure that he be employed in that office. This applies *a fortiori* where the Prime Minister formally resigns (whether on his own behalf, or on that of his Government) and is commissioned to form a new Government. This usually happens only when it has been decided to reconstitute the Government on a different political basis. . . . Mr MacDonald resigned in 1931 (though whether on behalf of himself or on behalf of his Government is not clear) in order to form the "National" Government' (pp. 71–2).

'It follows that, though it is usual for the Cabinet to resign, the Prime Minister can, by a personal resignation, force a dissolution of the Government' (p. 74).

'In 1931 . . . the Cabinet instructed the Prime Minister to tender their resignations. . . . Usually, the retiring Prime Minister takes with him the resignations of his colleagues, but they are not immediately accepted. . . . What really happens is that the retiring ministers receive notice, through the resignation of the Prime Minister, that they may be dismissed: whether they politely offer to resign or not makes no difference' (p. 75).

final deadlock and could not continue was a matter of public knowledge when Sir Ivor was writing. To portray the situation as one in
which the Prime Minister found himself in opposition to the rest of
the Cabinet and therefore decided to get rid of them is nonsense. It
would have been almost equally nonsensical to have suggested that
the Prime Minister's object was 'to get rid' of the dissentient
minority in the Cabinet. It appears, however, that Jennings was
annoyed by an incidental comment in the report of *The Times*
Correspondent. Discussing premature reports of the Cabinet's resignation which were current on the morning of August 24, this
Correspondent said that

> it was even arguable at that stage that there need be no resignation of
> the Government at all, since the existing Prime Minister had made up
> his mind that he could carry on the administration, replacing his dis-
> sentient colleagues by Ministers drawn from other parties.

The Correspondent was correct in suggesting that the possibility of
such a procedure was arguable. To Jennings, incredible though it
may now seem, this newspaper assertion was evidence that 'we are
nearing a dictatorship'.[1] Sir Ivor, however, was dealing not with
the facts but with a journalist's comment. So far as his 1932 article
is concerned, no valid criticism of MacDonald emerges.

In the first (1936) edition of *Cabinet Government* Sir Ivor Jennings gave as his authorities Snowden's autobiography and Sidney
Webb's 1932 'record'. In the revised (1951) edition he added Lord
Samuel's memoirs. His treatment of the subject in the first edition
is very brief and inadequate but less open to objections than is his
revised version. Both begin with the same words:

> The Labour Government was in difficulties on account of the finan-
> cial situation. The majority would not accept a proposal to reduce
> unemployment insurance benefit; and on Sunday, August 23rd, it
> authorized the Prime Minister to resign.

---

[1] 'Can a Conservative Prime Minister inform the King that he has turned
socialist and proposes to substitute socialist members for his conservative colleagues? Who is the Prime Minister that he may "make up his mind" to change
the nature of his government? He is there because the policy of his party has
received the most substantial measure of agreement in the country and in Parliament. If they can no longer secure such agreement, then they must resign,
leaving the King to consult such persons as he pleases in order to find out what
combination will meet with Parliamentary approval and, ultimately, the approval
of the electorate.' That, however, is precisely what had happened; and it would
have been more appropriate for Jennings to have dealt with what had actually
occurred than with what a journalist said might have occurred.

It was a bad start. Readers would be entitled to conclude that the authorization to resign arose out of the refusal of a majority of the Cabinet to accept some proposal or other to reduce unemployment insurance benefit. In fact, the majority of the Labour Cabinet voted, on Sunday, August 23, in favour of proposals which included a cut in the standard rates of benefit. It was a minority who voted against and, by threatening resignation, prevented an agreed decision and made it impossible for the Cabinet to continue. This was public knowledge at the time of the crisis. It is true that the majority was a small one, as Snowden, one of Sir Ivor's authorities, said in his autobiography. In this matter, apparently, Sir Ivor followed the account given by Webb without noting its ambiguity and without checking it against Snowden or against the information given at the time of the crisis. According to Webb's 1932 'record', the Labour Cabinet 'refused to accept' the cut in the rate of unemployment benefit. That was true of the Cabinet as a whole, but it was not true of the majority of the Cabinet. Webb went on in the same sentence (and Jennings followed suit) to his already quoted remark about the Cabinet authorizing the Prime Minister to tender his resignation.

After this beginning, Jennings introduced a new passage in his revised edition before resuming his account of what happened on August 23. The first sentence reads as follows:

> The Prime Minister and the Chancellor of the Exchequer (Mr Snowden) had previously been in consultation with the Opposition leaders, apparently with the approval of the Cabinet committee dealing with the matter.

Why, one wonders, should Jennings have been in any sort of doubt on this point? His reference is to Lord Samuel's memoirs (p. 202), but plenty of confirmation was available to him from other sources. Apart from the obvious consideration that the continuous effort to secure the co-operation of the other parties could not have been made without the approval of the Cabinet Committee, and later of the Cabinet itself, Sir Ivor had available, together with much other evidence, Henderson's unequivocal statement in the House of Commons on September 8, 1931: 'I must say that we were all agreed that that course should be followed.'

The new passage went on:

> At a meeting held on 19 August, however, the committee's proposals

2C

were disapproved of in important respects by a majority of the Cabinet led by Mr Arthur Henderson. On the 20th, 21st and 22nd there were further meetings between the Prime Minister and the Chancellor of the Exchequer on the one hand and the Opposition leaders on the other, at which the Opposition leaders agreed with the minority of the Cabinet. Though Viscount Samuel says that the two ministers 'represented the Government', the evidence seems to suggest that they did not and that they were using the Opposition leaders to force their own policy on the Cabinet.

To attempt a summary in three sentences of the complex events of those four days was rash in the extreme. The omissions are particularly striking. The errors are serious. Worse still is the highly tendentious last sentence of comment, based upon 'evidence' the nature of which is not indicated save for the incidental allusion to Lord Samuel.

There is no evidence that a majority of the Cabinet disapproved any of the committee's proposals on August 19. What is known is that some of the proposals failed to secure the agreed support of the Cabinet. No evidence was available in 1949 (when Sir Ivor was revising his book), nor has any been forthcoming since, that Henderson led the opposition to important committee proposals on that day. There is none in his official biography, nor in Snowden's autobiography. Webb makes no mention of the August 19 meeting in his 'record'. As already noted, Lansbury's biographer states that Henderson's opposition appeared only at a later stage, and confirmation of that is available from other sources. Henderson, after all, was one of the five members of the Cabinet Economy Committee whose proposals were submitted to the Cabinet for consideration on August 19. What were the important proposals of which the majority of the Cabinet are said to have disapproved? On what proposals did the Opposition leaders in the following days agree with the 'minority of the Cabinet'? In view of Sir Ivor's initial remarks, his readers are certainly likely to conclude (1) that the disagreements in the Cabinet related throughout to a proposal to reduce the rates of unemployment benefit, and (2) that the majority of the Cabinet were opposed throughout to that proposal. Both conclusions would be incorrect, as has been demonstrated above. One cannot be sure that they represent Sir Ivor's own view of what happened: his method is so telescopic and his language too vague. Probably, however, Sir Ivor has relied upon Lord Samuel's memoirs. It will be seen that he has done so in other respects, and with unfortunate results. In this particular instance, Sir Ivor has misinterpreted Samuel's remarks about the divisions in the Cabinet (see pp. 376–8 above), applying them to the meeting on August 19, and has repeated Samuel's misleading reference to a minority of the Cabinet.

Jennings also introduced a doubt whether MacDonald and Snowden 'represented the Government' in the discussions with the Opposition leaders. It is difficult to understand how a Government can be more effectively represented than by the Prime Minister and (in circumstances of financial crisis) by the Chancellor of the Exchequer. A Cabinet objecting to the Prime Minister and Chancellor acting as their representatives at conferences of party leaders would promptly cease to exist. There is no evidence of any objection having been raised in this instance. In so far as the Cabinet had reached no agreed decisions on the issues involved, its representatives, whoever they might have been, were bound to be in an extremely difficult position. In the concluding stages, MacDonald and Snowden were actually to be authorized by the Cabinet to make proposals to the Opposition leaders without any assurance that if the latter agreed to the proposals the Cabinet itself would endorse them. One does not know who Sir Ivor considers would have been able effectively to 'represent the Government' at each successive meeting as its internal differences persisted and widened. In this connection, surely, the numerical strengths (whatever they may have been) of the various and fluctuating opinions in the Cabinet are irrelevant. Jennings makes the insinuation that MacDonald and Snowden 'were using the Opposition leaders to force their own policy on the Cabinet'. It would have been at least as plausible for him to suggest that the Opposition leaders were using MacDonald and Snowden for that purpose. But the fact is that the Prime Minister was confronted by the dual task of securing agreement within the Cabinet and agreement between the Cabinet and the Opposition parties.[1] Incidentally, it would be erroneous to

[1] Critics of the Prime Minister and Chancellor sometimes denounce them as Machiavellian schemers and at other times sneer at them as pathetic errand-boys. An example of the latter is provided by G. D. H. Cole (op. cit., p. 253): 'Soon the leading figures in the Government — MacDonald, Snowden and Thomas — had reached the ignominious position of going to and fro between the Tories and Liberals and the bankers on the one hand, asking with how small cuts in expenditure they would put up, and their Cabinet colleagues on the other, asking how large cuts they would endorse under the influence of these pressures.'

assume that MacDonald and Snowden were in anything like complete agreement about the policy to be pursued. One of Mac-
Donald's chief problems was that of resolving the differences
between Snowden and his opponents in the Cabinet.

Like Samuel, Jennings makes no reference to the extremely
important developments on August 20. He thus ignores completely,
for example, the part played by the General Council of the Trades
Union Congress. Nor does he deal with the crucial Cabinet meeting, and its consequences, on August 21. He passes on (in the same
new passage in his revised edition) to August 22, as follows:

> Late on the 22nd the Prime Minister informed the Opposition leaders
> that the Cabinet deadlock could not be overcome and that he had
> decided to resign.

This is plainly taken from Samuel's memoirs. The same words are
used. The same mistake in the date is made. The Prime Minister
did not see the Opposition leaders late on the 22nd; and, late on the
21st, when he had seen them, he did not tell them he had decided
to resign. In this passage, Jennings has followed Samuel blindly.

We come to Sunday, August 23. In his first edition Sir Ivor
Jennings wrote:

> The King had returned from Balmoral the previous day and on the
> Prime Minister's advice had summoned the leaders of the Opposition
> parties. Mr Baldwin and Sir Herbert Samuel had visited the King
> before the Cabinet meeting. The Government had been in communi-
> cation with the leaders of the Opposition, and there is nothing to show
> that this meeting had anything to do with a prospective resignation of
> the Government. The official announcement explained that the King
> 'wishes to hear from them themselves what the position of their
> respective parties is'.
>
> When Mr MacDonald presented to the King the resignation of the
> Cabinet, he advised the King to see Mr Baldwin and Sir Herbert
> Samuel, with Mr MacDonald, the next morning, and the Prime
> Minister so informed the Cabinet.

This was a careful passage to which no serious objection can be
raised. Unfortunately, it is scrapped in Sir Ivor's revised edition,
where a much longer passage is substituted. The first part of this
new version reads as follows:

> On the 23rd he (i.e. the Prime Minister) had an audience with the
> King and, according to Lord Samuel, 'offered his resignation and that

of the Government; he advised His Majesty to consult the representatives of the other two parties as to the course to be taken.' Whether
this is what really did happen is not at all clear. The official announcement merely said on the 23rd that the King had summoned the leaders
of the Opposition parties because he wished 'to hear from them themselves what the position of their respective parties is'. It seems probable that Mr MacDonald had informed the King that he had decided
to resign and advised His Majesty to consult Mr Baldwin and Sir
Herbert Samuel. They advised that a broad-based Government with
Mr MacDonald as Prime Minister should be formed. Mr MacDonald,
who had expressed doubts about this course the previous evening,
acquiesced.

In this passage, Jennings again follows Samuel's memoirs, but this
time with incomplete confidence. His doubts are not at all surprising. What is surprising is that they failed to lead him to look
more closely at Samuel's account and to check it with the available
facts. As emphasized above, MacDonald did not offer his resignation when he saw the King on the morning of August 23; nor did
he inform the King that he had decided to resign. And it was not on
the evening of the 22nd but on that of the 23rd when MacDonald
expressed his doubts to the Opposition leaders about his future
course of action.

Concerning the Buckingham Palace Conference on Monday
morning, August 24, Jennings wrote in his first edition as follows:

What happened at this meeting is not exactly known.

(At this point follows the already quoted 'What is said' passage
from Webb's 1932 'record')

What is certain is that at a Cabinet meeting immediately afterwards
Mr MacDonald reported that he had kissed hands as Prime Minister
of a Cabinet of individuals, and that Mr Baldwin and Sir Herbert
Samuel had agreed to serve.

Jennings showed a proper caution in not seeking to go beyond the
then known facts; although in one not altogether unimportant detail he did so, for MacDonald had not then kissed hands as Prime
Minister of the new Government. The Labour Cabinet was still
formally in being. MacDonald's resignation had not been accepted
by the King on the previous night; nor was it accepted by him that
morning. Jennings doubtless relied upon Webb's statement that
MacDonald, at the final meeting of the Labour Cabinet, had in-

formed his colleagues that 'he had actually "kissed hands" as Prime Minister of a National Government'.

In his revised edition, however, Jennings has obviously tried to adapt his former treatment of the matter to the comments made by Samuel in his memoirs. It was not a successful effort. His revised version reads:

> According to the official announcement, he (i.e. MacDonald) resigned on the 24th and had been commissioned to form a new Government. The exact arrangement had been discussed at a conference of the three leaders at Buckingham Palace, the King presiding for a few minutes and then leaving the leaders to settle the matter. The Cabinet was informed after the Prime Minister had kissed hands. It is clear that the King acted constitutionally, but it would be possible to give a different opinion on Mr MacDonald's action. Lord Samuel comments as follows:
>
> 'It was alleged in some quarters . . . that the King had used his influence to bring about the end of the Labour Administration and the formation of the National Government. With full knowledge of the facts I can testify that that was not so. Mr MacDonald's resignation (*sic*) was the necessary consequence of an irreconcilable division in his Cabinet. The King then acted in strict accordance with precedent in following the advice of the outgoing Premier: that was to bring into consultation the spokesmen of the two parties which together could furnish a majority in the House of Commons, able to sustain a new Administration. The invitation to the Prime Minister to return to office, and to form an Administration on an all-party basis, was the course advised by them. So far as I was myself concerned, neither directly nor indirectly did any expression reach me of any personal opinion or wish of His Majesty. In every particular the principles and practices of our democratic constitution were scrupulously followed.'
>
> No difficulty whatever would have arisen if Mr MacDonald had presented the resignation of his Government and had given no advice. The King would then have sent for Mr Baldwin, as Leader of the Opposition, who could have advised a coalition under Mr MacDonald had he been so disposed. As things were, Mr MacDonald's advice, behind his Cabinet's back, led to a different interpretation, which received no contemporary denial.

(Sir Ivor then repeats the 'What is said' passage from Webb which he had quoted in his first edition, but this time does not set it out as a quotation.)

Samuel's comments quoted in this passage are in certain important respects inaccurate. The advice given to the King by himself

and Baldwin in favour of an all-party administration under Mac-
Donald was tendered by them in the early afternoon of August 23.
It was tendered *before* the division in the Labour Cabinet had become irreconcilable, *before* MacDonald first offered his resignation.
They did not advise that MacDonald should be invited to return to
office. MacDonald had not then left office nor announced any
decision to do so. He had advised the King to consult the Opposition leaders (probably, as we have seen, on the King's own initiative) because of the possibility that the Labour Cabinet might have
to resign. That advice was not tendered by 'the outgoing Premier':
it was tendered by a Prime Minister who was not then at all sure
whether or not he would be going out.

Apparently (though very strangely) unaware of all this, Sir Ivor
Jennings's comments are hopelessly confused. No difficulty, he
says, would have arisen if MacDonald had given no advice when
he presented the resignation of his Government. His meaning
seems to be that there would then have been no difficulty at the
time in understanding what had happened; but why he should
think that is a mystery. The Webb 'interpretation' which, he says,
'received no contemporary denial', did not rest in the slightest
degree upon any advice given or withheld by MacDonald: it related entirely to the action attributed to the King — that of having
made a strong appeal to MacDonald, and to the leaders of the other
parties, to form a National Government.

But what advice of MacDonald's is Sir Ivor talking about? If, as
appears to be the case, it is the advice to the King to consult the
Opposition leaders, that advice was not given when MacDonald
tendered the Government's resignation. Sir Ivor's 1932 criticism
of MacDonald will be recalled. He then objected to the statement
(issued on the morning of August 23) announcing that the King,
on MacDonald's advice, had asked the Opposition leaders to see
him. His argument was that the King had no need to ask for Mac-
Donald's approval before consulting the Opposition leaders. If,
therefore, MacDonald had refrained from giving his advice (or if
the King had not asked for MacDonald's approval) it would have
made no difference. At that time Sir Ivor made no suggestion that
the incident occurred after MacDonald had tendered the Government's resignation, nor did he speak about the advice having been
given by MacDonald 'behind his Cabinet's back'. On the assumption that the King asked MacDonald for his approval, Jennings

would hardly maintain that the Premier's correct response would have been that he must first consult his Cabinet.

If, on the other hand, Sir Ivor is talking about the advice given to the King by MacDonald when the latter first tendered his resignation (late on the evening of August 23) — the advice to confer next morning with the Opposition leaders and himself — why does Sir Ivor introduce the phrase 'behind his Cabinet's back'? Not only did MacDonald inform the Cabinet of the advice he had given (as Sir Ivor himself mentioned in his first edition), but he also informed them beforehand that he was going to give it (as Sir Ivor must have read in Snowden, one of his authorities). Moreover, had MacDonald refrained from giving that advice, there was nothing to prevent the King from himself proposing a conference of the three party leaders next morning: indeed, on Sir Ivor's earlier argument, he could have summoned such a conference without obtaining MacDonald's approval.

Sir Ivor argues that if MacDonald had given no advice, then the King would have sent for Baldwin and asked for his advice. Probably, though not necessarily, so. But what difference, one wonders, would it have made to the outcome? Anyhow, Sir Ivor, confused by Lord Samuel, does not seem to realize that the King had already obtained Baldwin's advice, and Samuel's also, about the best course to be pursued in the event of the Labour Government's resignation.

One is left with some final queries. Does Sir Ivor Jennings consider that it was unconstitutional for MacDonald to have given the King advice? Or that it would have been unconstitutional had he tendered any advice 'behind his Cabinet's back'? If the answers are in the negative, what has he in mind when he says that it is possible to hold the opinion that MacDonald's action was unconstitutional?

'THE CRISIS AND THE CONSTITUTION'

Attention must be given to the views on the 1931 crisis expressed by the late Professor Laski, not only because of the considerable and lasting influence those views have had both in this country and in the United States of America, but also because Laski, in his booklet, *The Crisis and the Constitution*, presented the only seriously-argued criticism on constitutional grounds of MacDonald's action. His criticism of King George V has already been examined.

The first point which arises is that Laski, like some other commentators, was ambiguous and misleading about the circumstances in which the Labour Cabinet came to an end. Like Jennings, he conveys the impression that MacDonald had a majority against him at the decisive Cabinet meeting on Sunday, August 23. His language was so characteristically elusive that it must be quoted:

> There came into the field, whether from international or other pressure we do not fully know, a recommendation for a reduction in unemployment pay against which there was a majority in the Cabinet (p. 13).

In view of the report of the May Committee, not to mention other known developments and also the disclosures about Cabinet discussions, this is oddly put; but the reference to a majority of the Cabinet being opposed to a reduction in unemployment pay raises several questions. What was the particular proposal against which this supposed majority existed? It is, of course, clearly established, and was clearly established when Laski wrote, that the whole Cabinet agreed, provisionally at any rate, to certain reductions in unemployment pay. At what stage in the proceedings did this alleged majority exist? Was Laski writing of the proposal to reduce the standard rates of unemployment benefit? And was he referring to the Cabinet meeting on Sunday, August 23? Having regard to the facts known at the time, it may well be thought that the answers to these two last questions could not possibly be in the affirmative; but it seems that they must be, because Laski went on in his next sentences to say:

> Mr MacDonald found himself faced by the threat of vital resignations if he acceded to the proposed reduction. He himself favoured it, as did some of his colleagues; but it was known that a majority of the party in the House of Commons would vote against the reduction. As time was of the essence of the position . . . Mr MacDonald offered his resignation to the King.

It will be noted that in these sentences there is no definite assertion that a majority of the Cabinet were opposed to the suggested reduction. There was, we are told, a 'threat of vital resignations', which is true enough; but we are not told how many threatened to resign. 'Some' of MacDonald's colleagues, it is said, 'favoured' the reduction; but again we are not told how many. But, in view of the previous sentence with its reference to 'a majority' being opposed to the reduction, the natural conclusion for any reader to draw was that a majority of the Cabinet were opposed to 'the reduction' at the Cabinet meeting preceding MacDonald's offer of resignation, that is, at the meeting on the evening of Sunday, August 23. Yet Laski knew quite well that the majority of the Cabinet were prepared to accept the reduction at that meeting. A little later (p. 15) Laski wrote:

> Defeated in his own Cabinet, he (i.e. MacDonald) did not simply resign and ask that Mr Henderson be commissioned to take his place.

Here again the reader would have to be forgiven for concluding that a majority of the Cabinet voted against MacDonald at the decisive meeting on August 23. In fact, MacDonald was 'defeated in his own Cabinet' only in the sense that he was unsuccessful in obtaining an agreed decision.

The main part of the last quoted sentence introduces Laski's criticism of MacDonald. He proceeds:

> That, on the precedents, would have been one normal course for him to follow.

How far it may be considered 'a normal course' for a Prime Minister, on resigning in accordance with an agreed decision of his Cabinet, to propose as his successor the leader of the minority in that Cabinet whose dissent had brought about the agreed decision to resign, is a matter of opinion. Laski would have been very hard put to it to find any precedent, particularly in the case of a minority government. It is impossible to take seriously Laski's suggestion that MacDonald should have advised the King to ask Henderson to form a Government. But Laski certainly appears to have been labouring under the delusion that Henderson was the leader of a majority in the Cabinet; and, as will be seen, he persistently ignored the fact that the whole Cabinet agreed to MacDonald's resignation. He went on:

> Alternatively, had he consulted the Labour Cabinet, their knowledge of the position would probably have resulted in the advice of total resignation with the suggestion that if asked for advice, he give to the King his counsel to summon Mr Baldwin to form an administration in which Labour would have had no share.

It will readily be granted that in 1932 Laski had not the same knowledge about what actually happened as is available to-day. But he must have known of Webb's statement (in his 'record') that the Labour Cabinet had empowered the Prime Minister to tender his resignation to the King. And, in view of his close contacts with ex-Ministers, it is extremely difficult to believe that he could have been unaware of the fact, subsequently to be disclosed, that the Cabinet agreed to the advice which MacDonald proposed to tender, and actually did tender, to the King, viz.: the advice to summon a conference with Baldwin, Samuel and himself the next morning. When consulted, the Labour Cabinet did not in fact give MacDonald the advice which Laski suggests they would probably have given him if they had been consulted.[1]

The truth is that for Laski there were only two legitimate courses open to MacDonald. He wrote later in his booklet (pp. 32–3):

> Mr MacDonald informed the King of the disagreements in the Labour Cabinet, and appears to have indicated the necessity of resignation.

[1] Moodie (op. cit., p. 16) is still unaware, apparently, even that the Labour Cabinet agreed to MacDonald's resignation, for he considers 'relevant' Jennings's 1932 argument that 'a Prime Minister has no right to tender the Cabinet's resignation . . . without first consulting the Cabinet'.

At that stage it may be argued, there were two courses open to him. He could, with the assent of his colleagues, have tendered his resignation to the King and, if his opinion was invited, advise the latter to send for Mr Baldwin, as the head of the next largest party in Parliament. So to have acted ought to have implied that Mr MacDonald had obtained the assent of his colleagues to that course. For the essence of his position was that he was Prime Minister as Leader of the Labour Party, and to ignore the opinions of his colleagues would have been to constitute himself the dictator of the party's fortunes. Or, alternatively, he might have felt that in view of the difference between himself and his Cabinet, and the meagre support within it upon which he could count, he should himself resign as Prime Minister, advise the King to send for Mr Henderson, and leave the latter to carry on as best he could with a reconstituted Cabinet. Either of these courses would have been strictly constitutional since it would have taken account of the fact that Mr MacDonald was not the Prime Minister as Mr MacDonald, but as Leader of a Party within whose discretion it was to unmake him as leader if it so desired. Mr MacDonald took neither course.

This passage repeats and elaborates Laski's previous contentions. In regard to the alternative course, it will again be noted that Laski writes as though MacDonald had had only minority backing in his Cabinet, indeed only 'meagre' backing, and almost as if it had been a case of MacDonald versus the rest. In suggesting this alternative course, Laski was making a merely formal point. He knew perfectly well that Henderson could not have carried on with a reconstituted Labour Cabinet, and would never have entertained the notion. In regard to the first course, MacDonald (as Laski certainly should have known) *had* tendered his resignation to the King 'with the assent of his colleagues', and (as Laski conceivably may not have known) had also obtained the assent of his colleagues to giving the King, if asked, advice of a different kind to that suggested by Laski. But the emphasis in this passage upon party leadership as the basis of the Premiership brings us to what seems to be the heart of Laski's case.

Laski continued the first passage quoted above from his booklet in these terms:

It did not occur to his Labour colleagues that Mr MacDonald would, without consulting them, place their opponents in power under his leadership.

For, clearly, the whole theory of collective Cabinet responsibility is gravely attenuated if, in any serious position, the Prime Minister is the master of its life and fortune. The conception which underlies Mr MacDonald's action is that since his colleagues did not agree with him, their utility as colleagues was necessarily ended. He acted in relation to them as an American President might act to recalcitrant colleagues without the constitutional sanctions which the former possesses. It is true, of course, that Mr MacDonald, by so doing, risked his future position in the Labour Party. But he also risked, not only the right of his Cabinet to live; he also assumed that he was entitled to transform the largest party in the House of Commons into the opposition without the assent of his colleagues, or of the party itself. He acted, not in co-operation with those who had made him their leader, but against them. He built his strategy not on the forces of his friends, but the strength of his enemies. The underlying thesis of his action was, no doubt, that he was himself indispensable in a position of national emergency, but it is a dangerous thing in a democratic State when any man, however eminent, builds his strategy upon the basis of his own indispensability (pp. 15–16).

Then, a little later (p. 19):

The real indictment against Mr MacDonald during the emergency is that he never seems to have acted upon the assumptions which colleagueship upon the basis of collective responsibility necessarily implies.

The references to 'opponents' and 'enemies' reveal an uncompromisingly partisan approach, and also a failure to recognize the facts of the party situation in August of 1931, but the main point to note is that Laski merged the break-up of the Labour Cabinet with the formation of the National Government as though it were all a single transaction, and one, moreover, resulting from MacDonald's 'strategy'. As for this supposed strategy having been based upon MacDonald's thesis of his own indispensability, all that needs to be said is that if MacDonald ever became convinced that he was indispensable he took a lot of convincing. One would almost gather from this passage once again that MacDonald had found himself opposed by all his colleagues in the Labour Cabinet and had therefore decided to get rid of them. Indeed, Laski wrote a few pages further on (p. 21) that MacDonald 'unhesitatingly threw his Labour Cabinet to the wolves'. It is odd to speak about 'the right of his Cabinet to live' when very nearly half of the Cabinet, by threatening resignation, had brought about its death. It is equally absurd to speak of MacDonald transforming the Labour Party into the opposition. That the resignation of the Labour Cabinet was inevitable in the circumstances was generally agreed: it did not follow at all from the formation of the National Government that the Labour Party was compelled even formally to constitute itself 'the Opposition', still less that it had to go into active, vigorous opposition. The decision rested with the Labour Party itself; and it was made by the Labour Party itself in spite of MacDonald's hopes and pleas. Furthermore, it was made with great rapidity, with a haste which might well be described as politically indecent.

Granted the position late on the night of August 23, with MacDonald authorized to resign, Laski's charge against him boils down to one of neglect to consult his Labour colleagues about the formation of the National Government. It relates to the events of August 24.

> No emergency (wrote Laski, p. 19), however desperate, can excuse his failure to consult them about a change of front so vital as that upon which he embarked.

Waiving what Laski called the 'thesis of emergency', and also his dubiously valid notion of a vital 'change of front', it is still difficult to see what useful purpose would have been served by consultation of the divided Labour Cabinet. It is obvious that there would have been no agreed decision in favour of the formation of an all-party administration; nor in favour of MacDonald's participation in such a Government in any capacity. It was quite clear, indeed, that a majority of the Labour Cabinet would have been opposed to either course. That had been made plain during the Cabinet discussions. The theory of collective Cabinet responsibility did not imply an obligation on MacDonald's part to acquiesce in any decision of that sort, any more than it implied an obligation on the part of Henderson and his associates to give way to the majority about the economy proposals. The latter had indicated their intention to exercise their undoubted right to resign, and had thus made it impossible for the Cabinet to continue. The Cabinet had made itself collectively responsible for the decision to resign, Ministers having placed their resignations in MacDonald's hands. It can even be argued that the Cabinet had made itself collectively responsible for the advice tendered by MacDonald for a conference between the King and the three Party Leaders. But, while the Cabinet was still formally in existence on the morning of August 24, it had ceased, save for formal purposes, to function as a collectivity. It is difficult to understand how the collective responsibility of the Labour Cabinet could have been involved in the formation of a new Cabinet. And, from the constitutional standpoint, MacDonald was fully entitled to take whatever action he thought fit in regard to participation in a new administration. By failing as a body to follow his lead, the Labour Cabinet had created a situation in which, unless he was prepared to acquiesce in what to him was an irresponsible course of action, he had to choose between alternatives neither of which, he well knew, would be approved by majority opinion in his Party. Those alternatives were, either to participate in a new administration or to support such an administration from outside. Either course involved the risk, and even the certainty, of losing the Labour Party leadership.

The point about consultation has been dealt with at greater length elsewhere (see pp. 156–62 and 348–50). The emergency aspect of the situation cannot be dismissed so lightly as Laski dismissed it. All three Party Leaders entered into their provisional agreement to form a National Government on the morning of August 24 without prior consultation of their party colleagues. That is why it was provisional. The official announcement did not say that a National Government had been formed: it said that the formation of such a Government was under consideration. All three statesmen had to seek support. Baldwin and Samuel could make a confident appeal to all their colleagues, although of course they could not be sure of a favourable response in all cases, and Samuel may well have been in some doubt about the attitude of his incapacitated leader, Lloyd George. But all three were well aware that MacDonald would appeal in vain to the majority of his colleagues. That Mac-Donald proceeded to form the new Government without any previous consultation of Labour colleagues is simply not true. It would have been quite futile for him to have consulted the Labour Cabinet as a whole. What he did was to consult his leading supporters in that divided Cabinet; and without their agreement it is difficult to see how he could have gone forward.

Laski gave little consideration to the situation which would have resulted if MacDonald had refused to participate in a National Government and a Baldwin Cabinet had been formed (see p. 345 *et seq* above). In an interesting passage, he wrote as follows:

Nor does the thesis of emergency rule out alternative conduct on Mr MacDonald's part. If he so desired, he could have advised the formation of a Baldwin Cabinet. He might have served in it; he might, as a private member, have given it independent support.

One is entitled therefore to assume that Laski would have had no great objection to MacDonald taking either of those courses; and that may well have been so, for Laski's real grievance was Mac-Donald's continued tenure of the Premiership, and he would certainly have welcomed any action on MacDonald's part which involved his deposition as Leader of the Labour Party and his relegation to the position of a private Member. None the less, the passage is a curious one when considered in relation to Laski's general argument. The next sentence stated the criticism of Mac-Donald in these terms:

> What he did was bound to have the impact upon his party that was least desirable — the impression that he was lending to its opponents a force which was its creation and that at a period when it would need all its strength to safeguard its principles from attack.

This objection needs further examination, but, whatever its precise meaning may be, it certainly seems to apply with almost equal force to participation by MacDonald in a Baldwin Cabinet, though perhaps not to his support of such a Cabinet 'as a private Member'.

A basic inconsistency underlies the whole of Laski's criticism of MacDonald's action. While attacking MacDonald in his capacity as Party Leader, he insists that he had become merely a private Member. He objects to MacDonald's appointment as Prime Minister of the National Government on the ground that he was no longer the leader of a party. On that ground he questions the constitutionality of the appointment. At the same time he criticizes MacDonald precisely because he was something more than a private Member, because he had at his disposal 'a force which was his party's creation', presumably the influence derived from having been Party Leader; and criticizes him also for not having, as Leader, consulted his Party.

Despite the apparent equanimity with which Laski wrote of MacDonald serving under Baldwin or giving a Baldwin Cabinet independent support, he knew quite well that either course would have met with the disapproval of the majority of the Labour Party. And Laski, like other critics, often appears to contend that Mac-

Donald ought to have refrained from any action clearly unacceptable to majority Labour opinion. This is probably the real basis of the suggestion that he acted 'unconstitutionally'. It implies that the primary, if not the exclusive, responsibility of the party member is to his party. That Laski himself would have been prepared to accept that implication is highly dubious. It may be that he only considered it applicable to party leaders, or, at any rate, to party leaders of whose actions he disapproved. But, if action contrary to the views of the party majority be justifiable in other cases, it is all the more so in the case of a leader, who bears a heavier responsibility, and who, risking and probably incurring the loss of his position as leader, is most unlikely so to act unless the matter is gravely important and urgent.

MacDonald, of course, was fully aware that his decision would involve his deposition as Leader of the Labour Party. That was, indeed, generally and immediately recognized. For reasons which will appear, Laski repeatedly stressed the point that MacDonald entered the new Government not as a Party Leader but only as a very eminent private Member of the House of Commons. From a different standpoint, MacDonald had himself emphasized this fact at the time. The new Government was specifically declared to be not a coalition of parties but a Government of individuals. Baldwin and Samuel, as well as MacDonald, agreed to enter it on that basis (Samuel, of course, was only the acting leader of his party). Neither MacDonald nor any of his Labour associates considered that their participation in the Government would involve permanent separation from the Labour Party. They did not conclude that it involved separation at all, in the sense of resignation or expulsion from Party membership. That indeed was also Henderson's view. It has to be remembered also that, at the time of the National Government's formation, there was no certainty about the attitude which the Labour Party would adopt towards it. It was assumed that the Party would formally constitute the Opposition, under new leadership;[1] but that it would embark upon active whole-hog opposition to the Government's proposals did not necessarily follow. There was the possibility that its hostility would be concentrated upon the particular matters about which the Labour Cabinet had failed to

---

[1] It is of some interest to recall that during Churchill's war-time coalition the Labour Party conducted formal Opposition activities, although it was officially supporting the Government and its chief leaders were in office.

2D

agree. These raised no real difference of principle, as the *New Statesman* and some other opponents of the new Government conceded at the time. MacDonald said at Easington on October 12, 1931, that he had expected ex-Ministers to 'stand up to what they had done before they went' and not to offer any 'factious opposition'. Any other line of action was bound to place all ex-Ministers in a highly embarrassing situation. It did so. Laski, however, as his quoted remarks make plain, was one of those who favoured all-out opposition to the new Government, and by implication condemned the policy pursued by the Labour Cabinet as a whole. He appears to have held the view that vital principles were at stake. He certainly took the line that since the new Government comprised 'enemies', that is to say, Conservatives and Liberals, it had to be vigorously opposed.

Laski was of course fully entitled to question the political wisdom of MacDonald's decision. His argument that MacDonald's action was unconstitutional is another matter. That argument (also alluded to, though not specifically endorsed, by Sir Ivor Jennings) was, in fact, simply an argument that, constitutionally, the Prime Minister must be the recognized leader of a party. At the outset of his discussion of the matter in his booklet (p. 11), Laski declared:

> The thesis of our constitution is the straightforward one that the King must choose as his Prime Minister the man whom the party which is in a position to carry on the Government designates as its leader.

What happens then, it must be asked, when no party is in a position by itself to carry on the Government? That, after all, was the situation in August of 1931. A few pages later (p. 16) Laski wrote:

> In modern times, no man has become Prime Minister merely as a person; it is to his position as a party leader that he owes his Premiership.

'*A* party leader' is not the same thing as *the* Party Leader. Laski no doubt had remembered Lloyd George. There are cases, of course, in which the Premier has become the Leader of his Party immediately after, and perhaps because of, his appointment; but such may be excluded from consideration. There has since been the case of Churchill in 1940, of whose appointment Laski warmly approved, and of whose acceptance of the Conservative Party leadership after Neville Chamberlain's death he warmly disapproved.

Certainly, MacDonald was as much a Party Leader in 1931 as Lloyd George in 1916. He was, indeed, still in form *the* Leader of the Labour Party, whereas Lloyd George did not attain the position of Leader of the Liberal Party until many years after he had become Premier, although he had formed a party of his own in the interim. Laski referred (p. 15) to the formation of the Lloyd George Cabinet in 1916, but distinguished it from the formation of the National Government on the ground that the former was 'largely a reshaping of the previous administration'. 'Largely' is rather good. Anyhow, the National Government itself was not an entirely new team: it involved no change in the Premiership, and the policy it was formed to apply was virtually identical with that approved by the majority of the previous Cabinet. Presumably, however, the Lloyd George Cabinet was considered constitutional because the previous Government had been a coalition. In the case of the National Government, the previous Government had been a 'minority' Government dependent upon the support of another party, with which it had eventually entered into formal collaboration. The difference, from a constitutional standpoint, between largely reshaping a coalition government and reshaping largely a minority government (itself necessarily an informal coalition) was not explained: it is not explicable.

Laski repeatedly insisted, plausibly enough, that MacDonald's political significance 'once he dissented from the policy of his party' became 'purely personal'.[1] He suggested indeed that Mac-Donald's influence was derived merely from his party ('a force which was its creation'). That would be an odd view to take of the usual relationship between a party and its leader: in the case of MacDonald and the Labour Party it is so odd as to be plainly jaundiced.

In a passage which again reveals the real nature of his grievance, Laski wrote (p. 34):

One could have understood Mr MacDonald supporting a Baldwin Government as a private individual; one could even have understood him entering a Baldwin Government as a Minister, the more strongly to emphasize his separation from his former colleagues. But it is diffi-

[1] But, when MacDonald was appointed Prime Minister of the National Government, he had not 'dissented from the policy of his party'. His party, very quickly afterwards, dissented from *his* policy, and from the policy pursued by the Labour Cabinet.

cult to understand his re-emergence as Prime Minister without a party behind him. For party lies at the very base of our political system.

MacDonald was not of course separated from all of his former colleagues. He had in fact no desire to emphasize his separation from the rest of them, expecting it to be of short duration. Evidently Laski appreciated that MacDonald's acceptance of the Premiership of the new Government, a Government of individuals drawn from all three parties, weakened any such 'emphasis'. He went on to suggest as the only explanation of MacDonald's 're-emergence' as Premier that the King chose to attach a more than personal significance to him, and to describe MacDonald as 'merely' a person who had become 'the King's favourite'. It is true that, as noted already, Laski had previously written, more than once, of MacDonald's assumption that he was indispensable to the solution of the crisis. Presumably, too, there were others who either shared that view of MacDonald or were persuaded to accept it.

Before Laski wrote his booklet, the preliminaries to the General Election had plainly demonstrated that MacDonald's personal influence, however derived, was very considerable indeed, if not decisive. And the General Election itself had provided an even more striking demonstration of its power, particularly among the Labour voters in the industrial areas. Laski, however, would only concede that MacDonald 'doubtless assumed that it was as a National Government that he obtained his majority'. So, it may be said, did everybody else; and neither he nor they needed to make any assumption when the fact was so dramatically and clearly revealed. Laski did not challenge the 'assumption'; but, adhering to his 'party' theory of our political system in defiance of the realities so emphatically disclosed by the election results, he maintained that without a party MacDonald had no power save that derived from the willingness of Conservatives and Liberals to support him. If that support were withdrawn, he argued, MacDonald would cease to be the 'King's favourite', and that would mean his downfall. To escape from dependence on the King, the argument proceeded, MacDonald would have to build a new party of his own; and, at the time of writing, Laski thought it possible that MacDonald might attempt to do so at some future stage. It should be noted that, although, in the changed circumstances which led to the continuance of the National Government and the General Election, MacDonald and his Labour associates had to form an *ad hoc* electoral organization, and although an organization was maintained during the years of the resulting National Government's existence, it was not officially described as a party, nor usually referred to as such. MacDonald made no attempt to form a permanent party or group: he had no desire to do so.

It will be seen that the criticism of MacDonald on constitutional grounds is pitifully thin. It is a classic example of the use of the term 'unconstitutional' to describe what one does not like. The exaggerated place in the constitution assigned by Laski to party is one of many indications that party interests, as he conceived them, were to him of primary concern. It is also an illustration of the tendency of party militants to forget that, in relation to the electorate as a whole, the political parties are small minorities. If freely-operating parties are essential to democracy (as indeed they are), they also constitute potential dangers to democracy, because of the excesses of partisanship to which they are prone; because, in short, they may not, and often do not, behave democratically. Party is not the basis of our political system: that basis is to be found rather in the subordination and limitation of partisanship.

One remaining passage in Laski's 1932 booklet calls for attention. He wrote (pp. 19–20):

> How little, indeed, Mr MacDonald and Lord Snowden thought of colleagueship was shown by their conduct after the formation of the Coalition, and particularly during the General Election. For neither of them had the slightest scruple in revealing the details of Cabinet discussions to the secrecy of which they were bound by the most elementary principles of English public life. Lord Snowden, with vehement affirmation from Mr MacDonald, discussed in public not only the proceedings of the Cabinet, but the motions proposed, the votes taken, and the personalities involved in each of these. That was a revelation of the attitude of mind in which they approached the making of an agreed policy. So little did they care for the implications of past colleagueship that they were prepared, in effect, to violate the oath of secrecy which they had taken as Privy Councillors in order to gain support for the new administration.

No passage perhaps provides so striking a revelation of Laski's own mood, mind, and methods of controversy as does this severely-phrased indictment. The facts in regard to the disclosures of the

Labour Cabinet's proceedings, and alleged violations of the oath of secrecy, have been set out above. Anyone who takes the trouble to check the record will find that Laski's version of what happened is grossly inaccurate.

It is difficult, as Sir Ivor Jennings has pointed out, to prevent revelations of Cabinet discussions when they are matters of political controversy, and Sir Ivor's illustrative reference reads:

> After the resignation of the Labour Government and the formation of the National Government in 1931, both ministers and ex-ministers disclosed the proposals upon which they had tentatively agreed and those upon which they had not been able to agree.[1]

It has been shown that the main points about these proposals had previously been reported in the press, and that, although more detailed information was forthcoming during the debates, nearly all the matters so disclosed were already known to persons outside the Labour Cabinet and were not revelations of Cabinet secrets. But it has also been shown that, in so far as further disclosures were made, the process was begun and persisted in by ex-Ministers. Ministers were involved, often under protest, only in reply to statements made. Henderson's disclosures (the real start of the whole business) were notably extensive and detailed; and Laski's omission of any reference to them exemplifies his lack of even an elementary sense of fair-play in this matter. The charges made by him (and others) against MacDonald and Snowden about the disclosure of Cabinet secrets break down completely under examination. In Mac-Donald's case it would be difficult to discover any plausible basis for the accusation: his attitude was consistently correct; and he behaved, moreover, with exemplary dignity under great and growing provocation. It may be noted that Laski had to bring Snowden into the picture in this connexion — the Chancellor is otherwise only mentioned perfunctorily two or three times in *The Crisis and the Constitution*. But Snowden certainly took no initiative in revealing anything that had taken place in the Labour Cabinet: and he made no fresh disclosures and avoided all recrimination until he made his crushing reply to a bitter personal attack on October 2.

During the General Election campaign, inevitably, the subject of the Labour Cabinet's proceedings was prominent; but in this phase also the statements of Labour Ministers were made in

[1] *Cabinet Government*, Revised Edition, p. 250.

answer to ex-Ministers. Snowden, not himself a candidate and unable to do any platform speaking, was particularly active in this connexion. His successive corrective statements were, it is true, most vigorously expressed, but, once again, he confined himself almost entirely to restating facts already known. Only in regard to the votes on tariff proposals did he give further details, and, even so, the main points he referred to had already been disclosed in the press.

It would seem, according to Laski, that MacDonald and Snowden should have been striving, not only in the period immediately following the formation of the National Government, but also during the subsequent General Election campaign, to arrive at an agreed policy with their late colleagues. Not a word is said, however, about the fact that the latter, as early as August 26, had committed themselves to a policy which was a complete repudiation of the one they had been pursuing when in office. That made any subsequent agreement well-nigh impossible. MacDonald and Snowden, wrote Laski, had little thought of colleagueship. Yet Laski himself had written a few pages earlier (p. 13) that these colleagues of theirs had formally expelled them from the Labour Party.

THE PLOT THEORY

It would be to invite legitimate criticism to omit from a book on the 1931 crisis an adequate treatment of one important feature, perhaps the most conspicuous feature, of subsequent controversy. That feature is the charge, presented in a variety of forms, that MacDonald had planned the National Government long in advance. The 'Bankers' ramp', the conspiracy of the international financiers, was soon relegated well into the background.

Mowat (p. 395) says that 'the theory of a deep-laid plot' on Mac-Donald's part began with Sidney Webb's *Political Quarterly* article early in 1932. So far as written statements are concerned, that seems to be true. But the charge was current before then. It was frequently met with during the General Election campaign in the previous October. Henderson himself, as we have seen, came very near endorsing it in his Burnley speech on October 13, and provoked a reply from MacDonald.[1]

In his 'record', Sidney Webb wrote of

> the whole unfolding within sixty-three days of a single drama, in all its development foreseen in advance, it is safe to say, only by the statesman who was at once its author, its producer, and its principal actor.

He proceeded to suggest that MacDonald had decided to do his best to smash the Labour Party, after thirty years upbuilding of it; and that the idea of a National Government seemed 'to have been germinating in the Prime Minister's mind for months before the blow was struck'. Later he referred again to 'the drama' that Mac-Donald himself had 'staged'.

Perhaps the first thing that strikes one about this is that, if it is true, MacDonald must have been a master-schemer; a plotter of almost unparalleled genius. And, indeed, that is precisely the con-

---

[1] See pp. 314–6 above.

clusion at which the Webbs arrived as a consequence of the theory which they gradually formulated in the weeks following the crisis. Sidney said in his 'record' that his 'drama' found 'no parallel in anything in the Parliamentary annals of this or any other country'. Beatrice's diary for October 28 (the day after polling day) contains the following passage (clearly the foundation of that which was to appear in her husband's 'record'):

> MacDonald, at once author, producer and chief actor, of this amazing political drama, had shown consummate art: he had been aided and abetted with acid malignity by Philip Snowden; a malignity which could only be accounted for by the return of his recent illness.[1]

Before the election (October 10), she wrote that MacDonald 'had carried out the intrigue with supreme cunning — with a self-deception about his own patriotism which is almost disarming'. By the following March (7th) she could write of MacDonald's 'long continued and masked treachery'. And, on the 19th, in a relatively benign mood:

> I have ever a sneaking admiration for MacDonald, as perhaps the greatest and most artistic of careerists — a veritable genius — he has completely fulfilled his abiding vision of himself as a great political personage.[2]

One might well be tempted contemptuously to put aside this melodramatic interpretation of the crisis of 1931, but it still has its protagonists, as a recent publication shows.[3] In the case of the Webbs, it is possible to trace the gradual formulation of the deep-laid plot theory; and the story, as will be seen, exemplifies a much wider process.

In Beatrice Webb's diary for August 27, 1931, three days after the formation of the National Government, this entry appears:

> Arnold reports that Lansbury told him that J.R.M. spoke to him casually at the end of July after the issue of the May report, as to the desirability of a National Government if the financial position became serious. Lansbury rejected the notion as impossible and J.R.M. dropped the question. By the light of this incident the P.M.'s letter to S.W. July 14, which puzzled us, seems to indicate some such solution, put forward tentatively. 'You may think I have been doing nothing,' he

---

[1] Op. cit., p. 294.
[2] These passages from the diaries are not included in the published selection.
[3] R. T. McKenzie, *British Political Parties* (see Appendix VI below).

wrote, 'but as a matter of fact I have been working at it for week-end after week-end and am at a complete dead end. We have not the material in our party that we ought to have. The solution will have to come, I am afraid, by moves which will surprise you all. I am still working at it however.'[1]

MacDonald's letter of July 14 to Sidney Webb has already been quoted.[2] In this diary entry on August 27, Beatrice omitted the preceding sentence of the paragraph:

As you know, I am in a most awful difficulty about the House of Lords.

That, however, was the key sentence. It was the problem of the House of Lords upon which MacDonald said he had been working and was still working. It was 'the most awful difficulty' of the Upper House for which MacDonald feared a surprising solution might have to be provided. In this July 14 letter he made no direct allusion to the reconstruction of his Government; and the paragraph from it incompletely quoted by Beatrice Webb on August 27 related specifically to the House of Lords. At the time the Webbs recognized that. Their interpretation of MacDonald's concluding remarks was that MacDonald was thinking of resigning the Premiership to Henderson and going to the House of Lords as Foreign Secretary.[3] In one of their many intimate talks with Henderson this possibility had been mentioned; and they had then (in the previous November) been told by Henderson that Mac-Donald had said that either he or Henderson would have to go to the House of Lords.[4] Henderson, it is known, desired in May of 1931 to go to the House of Lords; and in the diary for September 20, 1931, it is recorded that Henderson then told the Webbs

that before the crisis he had hoped to go on, as Foreign Secretary, in the House of Lords, and devote himself to the Party machine and had never wished to be Leader, but only the manager of the Party.[5]

[1] Op. cit., p. 285.
[2] See p. 51 above. The letter was set out in full in the diary for July 20, op. cit., p. 276.
[3] Op. cit., p. 276.
[4] Diary, November 23, 1930; and referred to, op. cit., p. 276.
[5] Op. cit., p. 287. Some further light on this matter is provided by other entries in Beatrice Webb's diaries. On April 18 (op. cit., p. 270), it is said that Henderson wanted some of the younger Trade Unionists in the House of Lords. On September 23, Beatrice recorded (not selected for publication) that Citrine had told her that MacDonald had formally offered him and Bevin peerages, which they had both refused. Since such an offer can hardly have been made *after* the crisis, it confirms that MacDonald had been 'working at it', and, as he said without success.

This curious post-crisis reinterpretation of MacDonald's July 14 letter became one of the few pieces of 'evidence' produced in support of the 'plot' theory. It was to be publicized (usually to the accompaniment of inaccurate references to the occasion of the letter and with incorrect dates) by others to whom in some form the Webbs must have communicated it. It crops up again in Mowat's history as 'the testimony of Sidney Webb'. In Mowat's reference, MacDonald's letter in reply to Webb's plea for retirement of May 31 appears to have been mixed up with the July 14 letter (which appears to have been primarily one of birthday greetings to Webb). It also comprises what purports to be a quotation from the July letter, taken from Mrs M. A. Hamilton's biography of Henderson. Mowat's passage reads:

> He (Webb) wrote to MacDonald in June, stating that he wished to retire; MacDonald asked him to stay on a little longer, since he was planning to reconstruct the government, 'and I may soon take a decision that will surprise you.'

Mowat has relied on Mrs Hamilton, who wrote (p. 394):

> Thus, in June 1931, Lord Passfield wanted to retire. MacDonald wrote to him, begging him to stay on a little longer. For reconstruction of the Government 'we have not got the men and I may soon take a decision that will surprise you'.

This inaccurate version of the July 14 letter was Mrs Hamilton's own chief piece of 'evidence'. It was also Dalton's; and Dalton plainly implies that he was given it by Webb himself. His passage reads:

> Webb had been trying for months to resign on grounds of age, and in June, 1931, wrote to J.R.M. insisting that he must be free by the autumn. And J.R.M. replied, in June, begging him to stay on a little longer, 'The truth is that we have not got the men, and I may soon take a decision that will surprise you.'[1]

Since Dalton proceeds to refer to a dinner with Molly Hamilton at which the subject was discussed, it may well be that the latter got her 'evidence' from Dalton. The same merging of MacDonald's two letters will be noted.

It will also be noted that the Webbs' reinterpretation of the July 14 letter was avowedly inspired by a report from Lord Arnold of

[1] Op. cit., p. 286.

something told him by Lansbury about an alleged comment by MacDonald at the end of July. In the diary for September 7, 1931, a little over a week after the Arnold entry, Beatrice wrote:

> Lansbury told me that Stafford Cripps had told him that he had definite knowledge that J.R.M. contemplated a National Government two months ago.

that is, not far from the end of July. It is all very round about. Indeed, in view of the relationship between Cripps and the Webbs, the possibility cannot be excluded that on September 7 the full circle was completed — that what Cripps had gathered from the Webbs, as a consequence of what Lansbury had told Arnold, had come back to the Webbs via Lansbury.

In her diary entry on August 27, after the Arnold report, and the reinterpretation of the July 14 letter, Beatrice Webb added:

> I don't believe that Mac. deliberately led the Cabinet into a trap: *tried* to get them into agreeing to economies in the process of bargaining with the U.S.A. financiers, all the time intending to throw his colleagues over and form a National Government — but *he drifted into doing it* — largely because he is secretive — he never *can* be frank — yet he will let the cat out of the bag in a moment of queer indiscretion to someone who is a comparative stranger like Sidney or even an enemy like Lansbury.

Those were early days. The 'veritable genius' was then capable of being indiscreet even to an enemy like Lansbury. In July, moreover, as all concerned well knew, there had been much talk about the possibility of a National Government.

In an unpublished document, written early in September 1931, Webb wrote that it was now plain to him that MacDonald had had the idea of placing himself at the head of a National Government for at least a couple of months before it happened, and probably from the beginning of the session of 1931. Later in the same document he said it was now clear to him that MacDonald had

> from the outset, not only the idea of a National Government in his mind but also the confident expectation, amounting practically to conviction, that his Cabinet would enable him to make such a Government inevitable, according to his own steering, by refusing to agree to the economies insisted on, both by the Liberal and Conservative leaders, with whom he was in almost hourly communication, and by the American bankers.

This sounds much more like a master-schemer at work. But what was the nature of the evidence which had made plain to Webb what had not been plain before? The only indication is provided by an insertion, in pencil, after the words 'It is now plain to me', as follows:

> from various cryptic utterances to various persons, which the subsequent events have both elucidated and recalled to memory.

One would have liked some evidence even in support of the 'almost hourly communication'. In his 'record', Webb varied this by writing that Neville Chamberlain had been 'almost hourly in consultation with the Prime Minister'. Evidence of that, too, would have been welcome.

Webb's published 'record' at the beginning of 1932 provided no scrap of supporting evidence for his suggestion that MacDonald had planned the National Government in advance. What he wrote in that 'record' was immediately challenged by Malcolm Mac-Donald in a letter dated January 6, 1932. Malcolm MacDonald told Webb that he had immediately recorded his conversations with his father during the last days of the Labour Government; and that the records made it quite clear that:

> the Prime Minister was fighting as hard as he could to keep the Labour Government in office. He had no desire for any change of Government, and indeed took risks to keep the Labour Government going, so anxious was he that he and his colleagues should stick together to carry the country through the crisis. When in the last two or three days he feared that he would not be able to carry a sufficient majority of his colleagues with him, my record of his talks shows that what he contemplated in that case was the resignation of the whole Government. He believed that Mr Baldwin would immediately become Prime Minister and that he himself would probably be back in Lossiemouth two or three weeks afterwards, more or less in retirement. There was no suggestion of any other alternative until within the last few hours.

Malcolm MacDonald added that it was clear to him

> that the Prime Minister's greatest wish throughout the crisis was that the Labour Government should have the honour and responsibility of taking us through the crisis, and that he had not any preconceived plan for an alternative.

As previously noted, he referred to Neville Chamberlain's Dumfries speech in confirmation.

Lord Passfield's reply (dated January 9) was, in its brief relevant passage, as follows:

> What you report as to your father's communications to you about the final Cabinet meetings is most interesting, and, needless to say, I entirely accept your statement. And, of course, there were various projects for a National Government during the first six months of 1931, by Garvin, Churchill, Beaverbrook, &c., having different objectives, with which nobody can suppose that your father had any connection, if indeed he ever heard of some of them.

That might appear to be conclusive; but Webb made no public withdrawal or even modification of his charge. There exists the draft of a reply to Malcolm MacDonald which was not sent, and which throws considerable light on Webb's attitude. In this draft Webb began his discussion of the matter in these terms:

> Let me say that the Prime Minister's behaviour at the final Cabinet meetings seems to me — as I recollect it — to have corresponded exactly with what you report of his contemporary communications to you. He gave me the impression at the time (so fully that I thought of no other) that he was trying his utmost with great patience and ingenuity to get general agreement among his colleagues on anything that would, in his judgment, sufficiently meet the needs of the situation. That is why he succeeded to a great extent — as it appeared at the moment — in inducing his colleagues to agree provisionally, and with many reserves, to a large part of what seemed to be requisite. . . . I certainly thought that the Prime Minister was doing his best to bring about some agreement. Thus, I quite accept your account of your father's communications to you whilst the Cabinets were being held.

After saying that he could give only 'an avowedly hypothetical account' of what happened during the Sunday night and at the Palace on the Monday morning, Webb said that he could not easily believe 'that the apparent initiative of the King that morning arose without previous consultation then or weeks before with the Prime Minister'. It was, he went on, 'the duty of the King to discuss such a matter with the Prime Minister before plunging it upon him and the Opposition leaders.' This, of course, was all supposition and opinion. Webb did not know what had happened: in particular he was unaware of the advice tendered to the King by the Opposition leaders early on the Sunday afternoon. And it is difficult to understand why he should have thought that the King had a *duty* to discuss the formation of a National Government or any new Government with the party leaders *before* the resignation of the Labour Cabinet, or before that resignation seemed imminent, much less *weeks* before.

The draft of the unsent letter proceeds:

> But when did the idea first arise? Gradually various previous utterances by the Prime Minister were recalled by sundry persons (as well as by myself) which gave me the impression that the idea of a National Government had been in the Prime Minister's mind for at least two months.[1]
>
> Notice, by the way, that there had been several different National Governments projected during the year, by Garvin, by Winston Churchill, by Beaverbrook and so on, having different objectives. I am not connecting the Prime Minister with any of these. My interpretation of what I know is merely that the idea of a National Government as a way out of the actual difficulties was 'played with' in the mind of the Prime Minister as one of several possible alternatives.

It will be noted that the only evidence brought forward by Webb is provided by various unspecified previous utterances by MacDonald 'gradually recalled' by 'sundry persons', including Webb himself. It will also be noted that Webb only attempts to justify an 'impression' or 'interpretation' that the idea of a National Government had been for some time in MacDonald's mind 'as one of several possible alternatives'. But there was no need to attempt any such justification. As pointed out above, it would have been very strange indeed if the idea of a National Government as a possible way out of the actual difficulties had not occurred to MacDonald and to all other politicians in all parties. It had certainly occurred to Webb himself, as his wife's diary shows. Moreover, according to that same source, confirmed as we have seen from other sources, the idea had been mentioned more than once within the Labour Cabinet itself.

The conclusion of the draft of the unsent letter is particularly interesting. Webb wrote:

> I do not know whether you see any difficulty in reconciling such a state of mind with the action (as to which we agree) taken during the

---

[1] The phrase 'a long time' had been deleted.

last week of the Cabinet. To me the two seem quite compatible. Psychologically it is a case of a complicated mind, habitually running together all possible alternative courses, within the range, of course, of what is for the country's welfare, tentatively following out one, and then another; and not coming to any decision between them, as to what to do when the actual crisis comes — meanwhile taking wholeheartedly the action necessary from day to day — so as to have ready at the final moment, with rival courses still open, fairly well informed and mature decision, according to the hypothesis ultimately chosen.

I can quite understand the necessity of considering possible alternative courses of action, long before the moment arrives when a choice becomes imperative. It is important gradually to accumulate information as to all conceivable courses, in order to be ready with a decision at short notice. It is awkward that secrecy should be involved, but the conditions make it imperative. And I do not mean to imply that entirely wrong courses should be admitted as possible alternatives. But whatever seems to be for the welfare of the nation must be the decision.

Such an argument is no adequate defence of the language used by Webb in his 'record'. Still less is it a justification of the developed 'plot' theory. And even the suggestion that MacDonald was 'ready with a decision at short notice' was an assumption unwarranted by the facts then known, one which Chamberlain had already shown to be unwarranted, and one which authoritative information subsequently made available has shown to be unsound.

In the unpublished September document already mentioned, Webb wrote that he did not wish to suggest that in accepting the headship of a National Government MacDonald had done wrong on his own assumptions of what the country required; but that he did not find it easy to excuse his 'duplicity'. Surely, he wrote, MacDonald

ought to have placed the plan of a National Government before the Cabinet, and consulted them as to its pros and cons, almost as soon as he formed the plan in his own mind. Even if he foresaw that they would mostly disapprove (and this had been made manifest in the last days when Lees Smith had insisted on warning the Cabinet against any idea of a coalition of parties)[1] it seems to me that they were entitled to be made aware of what the Prime Minister had in mind.

This, of course, is merely the old point about 'consultation', coupled with the assumption that the Premier had 'formed a plan'

[1] A further indication that the subject had been raised in Cabinet.

for a National Government before the Palace conference on the morning of August 24. The now well-established fact is that Mac-Donald lost no time at all in informing his Cabinet and consulting immediately afterwards those members of it who were likely to join him in the proposed new Administration.

Mowat has rightly pointed out that the 'plot' theory was greatly strengthened by the appearance in 1934 of Snowden's autobiography. Snowden's remarks (most of which have already been quoted)[1] certainly gave it countenance. He suggested that Mac-Donald had anticipated the final disagreement in the Cabinet and had made his plans to deal with it; that he neither showed nor expressed any regret at it; and set about the formation of the National Government with enthusiasm. For these reasons, and because MacDonald had not informed any of his Labour colleagues of his intention, and further because MacDonald did not attend the meeting of the Parliamentary Labour Party on August 28 (which Snowden himself did not attend), Snowden wrote:

> Taking all these things together, I think they give ground for the suspicion expressed by Mr Henderson and other Labour Ministers that Mr MacDonald had deliberately planned the scheme of a National Government.

It should be noted that Snowden only said that, in his opinion, these things 'gave ground for the suspicion'. Mowat is inaccurate in writing that Snowden gave it as his opinion that MacDonald had 'deliberately planned the scheme'. Snowden added that Mac-Donald's mind

> for a long time before this crisis arose had been turning to the idea of a new party orientation and government by what he called a Council of State.

This, presumably, was a reference to MacDonald's opening speech to the new Parliament in 1929, the relevant passage in which has been quoted above (p. 40). Snowden himself, however, had used the expression 'a Council of State', and he related in his book how his own appeal on July 30, 1931, to the Opposition parties to co-operate was misinterpreted as an appeal for the formation of a National Government. MacDonald's plea in 1929 was simply one that the more serious problems of the day should not be discussed in a partisan spirit.

[1] See p. 142 and p. 190 above.

2E

But perhaps the most influential of all the comments on the 1931 crisis has been the story told by Snowden in his autobiography in support of his impression that MacDonald felt no regret at the break with his Labour colleagues. The tale was this:

> The day after the National Government was formed he (MacDonald) came into my room at Downing Street in very high spirits. I remarked to him that he would now find himself very popular in strange quarters. He replied, gleefully rubbing his hands: 'Yes, to-morrow every Duchess in London will be wanting to kiss me!'

Naturally enough, this story was gleefully seized upon by Mac-Donald's critics, and has been reproduced on countless occasions. Obviously, however, the words attributed to MacDonald could well have been spoken in a manner which would give them a very different meaning to that Snowden wished to convey. The remark to which they are alleged to have been a response should be noted. It is, of course, well known that Snowden was no friend of Mac-Donald's, and it is generally agreed that his autobiography was written when he had become an extremely embittered man. Snow-den's 'venom', when directed against the Labour ex-Ministers, has been much condemned: his 'venom' against MacDonald has been warmly welcomed in the same quarters and extensively exploited. Certainly, in telling the 'Duchess' story, Snowden's sense of humour, which was notably keen and frequently displayed in private, was for the time being in abeyance. It seems to have been so throughout his treatment of the crisis and its aftermath. An interesting parallel to the 'Duchess' story is provided by Snowden's treatment of an incident in which Henderson was involved. He describes in his autobiography (p. 983) how deeply he resented the weak surrender of the Labour ex-Ministers 'to the dictation of the Trade Union Congress'. He then quoted what Henderson had said on the subject in a newspaper interview, and proceeded:

> A week later, when addressing the Trade Union Congress at Bristol, he (Henderson) was reported as saying: 'I am going to see whether the minds of the General Council and my own have been travelling on similar lines. But, of course, that was only to be expected in view of the fact that these gentlemen here (pointing to the platform) are our bosses.'

Perhaps the report read by Snowden did not indicate (as did the official report) that this remark was greeted with laughter, nor that this laughter was renewed when Henderson added:

> Although the papers have circulated that yarn, they have failed to appreciate the fact that there is often a considerable difference between the outlook of the boss and the outlook of the servant.

But, if so, it would be an insufficient excuse for Snowden's attempt to treat Henderson's remark as an admission that he regarded the members of the General Council as his bosses. The well-known sense of humour was dormant. It is perhaps important to realise that Henderson had actually been speaking of the tariff issue. To Snowden that issue was not an appropriate one for the employment of humour.

An important clue to the development of the 'plot' theory has been provided by Mrs Hamilton, Henderson's biographer. Dealing with the final meeting of the Labour Cabinet on August 24, when MacDonald announced the proposed formation of the National Government, she wrote (p. 384):

> This was heard with stupefaction. . . . For all who sat at the table, indeed, a light, entirely new and more than ambiguous, was suddenly cast backwards over the long days of crisis. How far beyond them it might reach none could guess; but suspicion threw its sinister colouring on every incident of the recent past, and called up many a trifling indication, hardly noted at the time.

Then (pp. 385–6):

> This was dirty, poisonous. When MacDonald calmly told men with whom he had worked in many cases for more than a quarter of a century . . . that he now proposed to head a Government composed of their bitter and lifelong political opponents,[1] there was, inevitably, a stunned sense of having somehow been tricked. This, they felt, was what he had been planning; this was what he had, throughout, been leading up to. Unjust this view may have been. But at the time, to minds naturally simple and straightforward, it leapt as the one possible explanation of conduct they could not otherwise explain.

Later, it is true (p. 394), Mrs Hamilton wrote:

> That new combinations had long been in his mind was no secret to

---

[1] This phrase is worth noting. The Government it was proposed to form, and which was formed, was not so composed. The phrase implies uncompromising hostility to any form of Coalition Government. Yet Henderson himself had already been a leading member of such a Government; and some of his then colleagues were to be leading members of another.

his closer associates; in 1931, even his acquaintances were aware of this.

The 'stupefaction' is therefore somewhat surprising. As evidence, Mrs Hamilton produced the Webb reinterpretation of Mac-Donald's July 14 letter. And the truth is that the 'evidence' against MacDonald in this connexion has nearly all been 'called up' by minds 'cast backwards', whether or not such minds were 'naturally simple and straightforward'; and none of it will bear the construction put upon it in subsequent controversy. The 'plot' theory is indeed the outcome of 'suspicion' throwing 'its sinister colouring' on every 'trifling indication' which could be recalled.

Dalton has written (p. 286) of 'a great cloud of witnesses'. He proposed to confine himself to those who had given him evidence directly. The first (as already pointed out) was Webb with the reinterpretation of the July 14 letter. The second is Mrs Hamilton, who, at dinner on November 5, 1931, said, according to Dalton's record:

> One night last March she went into J.R.M.'s room at the House, and he said, 'Baldwin was sitting in that chair an hour ago. He came to ask me whether I wouldn't form a National Government.' This was obviously a fly, but she only laughed and said, 'what a ridiculous idea!' and he dropped the subject.[1]

Dalton's next piece of evidence is that he was told by Joe Compton on August 25, 1931, that the latter's room (he was Chairman of the House of Commons Kitchen Committee) had been used 'for several nights a week' by MacDonald for small private dinners with Tory and Liberal leaders, and that special precautions had been taken by MacDonald's staff to keep the door closed 'whenever any member of the Government went by'. Here we are certainly in the sphere of melodrama. It was not apparently known who among the Opposition leaders attended these dinners — with one exception. At this point Dalton ceases to rely on evidence directly conveyed to him.

---

[1] Mowat has written (pp. 396–7) that there were meetings between MacDonald and Baldwin as early as November 1930, when the leaders were in growing difficulties with their own followers: 'after one of these MacDonald told Mrs Hamilton that Baldwin had suggested that they should get together to solve their common difficulties, and asked her to sound out people in the party.' Mowat gives no reference. In her Henderson biography (p. 394), Mrs Hamilton wrote: 'He (MacDonald) had also thrown out feelers to lesser folk, who, mistakenly, did not take them seriously.' This seems to be an allusion to the incident related to Dalton over the dinner-table.

Lloyd George, he writes, told Henderson, after the Election, that he had attended one of these dinners, and had said it was no use discussing National Government and suchlike subjects without Henderson, 'whereat J.R.M. shut up like an oyster.' Dalton then quotes a comment alleged to have been made by J. H. Thomas to Ernest Hunter of the *Daily Herald* 'in the small hours of July 16th' — 'in the Bar'! Finally, Dalton comes to Snowden's comments in his autobiography; and, of course, to the 'Duchess' story.

It is all very flimsy. And the 'casting backwards' was carried, in these circumstances, 'far beyond' the 'long days of crisis'. MacDonald, it was suggested, had always hankered after some 'new combination'. People delved into the distant past in search of evidence, going back even to the years before the First War.

The conclusions reached by Mowat on this subject are sound enough. In his opinion the 'evidence' produced

> proves only that a National Government of some sort had been discussed in high political circles for some time, and that MacDonald expected some crisis. With the chronic weakness of the Labour Government's majority, speculation about its future was not unnatural.

In regard to MacDonald's decision at the height of the crisis, he writes:

> That he had decided upon it earlier, as opposed to being vaguely predisposed towards it, cannot be proved. And for two reasons. First, supposing one can start a crisis (and MacDonald had not started this one), one cannot be sure how it will develop. . . . Second, and more important, there seems to have been no anticipation of the solution actually followed, on the part of the Conservatives, until Sunday, August 23.

Mowat concludes:

> There is no proof that MacDonald, or any of the others, had planned it so beforehand. But they were perhaps not very surprised at the outcome.

Doubtless, however, Mowat underestimates the 'cunning', the 'masked treachery', the 'consummate art', with which the 'veritable genius' had conceived and carried through his 'long concocted plan'.

'BRITISH POLITICAL PARTIES'

T he deep-laid plot theory was accompanied by, indeed necessitated, charges against MacDonald of 'insincerity', 'perfidy', 'treachery'. His character and political record immediately began to be savagely assailed, even by former colleagues. It may well seem an unprofitable exercise to pay much attention to this aspect of the controversy about 1931, but it was a notable feature of the Election campaign itself in that year, and its prominence in the subsequent literature of the subject makes complete neglect of it impossible.

Perhaps the best, and certainly the most convenient, way of dealing with it is to examine what has been written about it by R. T. MacKenzie in his 1955 book on *British Political Parties*. This treatise has considerable importance as the most recent, and a most interesting, study of the two main British parties of the present time. McKenzie is primarily concerned with leadership. In his discussion of the leadership of the Labour Party, the central figure is inevitably MacDonald; and the long sections on the emergence and exodus of Labour Leaders are mainly devoted to Mac-Donald. Yet no adequate accounts are given of the two outstanding crises in MacDonald's career as Leader, those of 1914 and 1931.

We are told (p. 305) that MacDonald resigned the chairmanship in 1914 'in disagreement over the party's war policy', and there is a brief footnote giving an uninformative sentence or two from the Parliamentary Party's report on the event. Another reference (p. 345) is followed by the sentence:

> It is unnecessary to review in detail either the reasons for Mac-Donald's resignation in August 1914 or his activities during the course of the war.

Neither MacDonald's reasons nor his activities are in fact reviewed at all; but the plea that no such review was necessary must be questioned. After all, McKenzie dwells much on MacDonald's character; repeatedly questions his sincerity; and makes insinuations about his ambitions for office. MacDonald's resignation in August 1914 and his subsequent attitude towards the war are, surely, highly relevant. But one may grant that it is particularly difficult to fit this phase of MacDonald's career into McKenzie's picture, deeply influenced as it is by post-1931 Labour fashions. McKenzie rightly emphasizes the degree of harmony in which the opposing Labour factions worked together during the 1914–18 war: to him it was 'surprising' — doubtless a natural reaction for him in the light of what happened in 1931.

More striking, however, than McKenzie's reserve about 1914 is his treatment of MacDonald's action in 1931. Allusions to the latter, invariably of an uncomplimentary nature, abound; and certain features of the 1931 crisis receive considerable attention. But no attempt is made to present the facts of the crisis; and, in consequence, the relations between MacDonald and his Party are inadequately explained. At one point (p. 373), McKenzie announces:

> It is unnecessary to attempt to assess the sincerity of MacDonald and the action he took in 1931.

This illustrates McKenzie's curious preoccupation with the question of MacDonald's 'sincerity', but, in view of that preoccupation, one can hardly agree that examination of the 1931 crisis from that angle is unimportant. The truth seems to be that McKenzie, while neglecting to discuss the question, assumes throughout that the answer to it is adverse to MacDonald. His treatment of the crisis itself almost makes one doubt if he has taken the trouble to ascertain what actually happened; and one suspects that he has been loth to question even in his own mind the versions which have been popularized by MacDonald's critics. And, while trying carefully to present the views of the critics rather than his own, he slips up often enough to reveal his endorsement or acceptance of their views.

Thus, one reads (p. 317) of

> MacDonald's 'betrayal' of the Labour movement in 1931

and (p. 323) of

> ... a quite understandable revulsion against what the party considered to be ... his intolerable betrayal of the party.

In a footnote on the next page, one reads of

... the shock of what Attlee has called ... 'the greatest betrayal in the political history of this country'.

There is another reference (p. 364) to the great 'betrayal', McKenzie again using the inverted commas. So far so good, so to speak, but in the course of another passage (p. 370) he writes of

a forewarning of MacDonald's ultimate willingness to jettison the Labour Party and the ideals for which it stood.

Later (p. 378) he expresses the view that MacDonald might conceivably have carried a considerable part of the Parliamentary Labour Party with him in 1931

had he not *preferred* to desert them (McKenzie's italics).

Further on (p. 443) he writes of

the final crisis when MacDonald, Snowden and Thomas were preparing to 'go over to the enemy'.

Subsequently, however (p. 445), he reverts to the more cautious method when he writes

its (the Labour Cabinet's) leaders 'betrayed the party to the enemy'.

But McKenzie reveals himself at an early stage. In his introductory remarks on the Labour Party leadership (pp. 299–300), he says:

MacDonald ... had no difficulty in retaining office as Leader (despite the deep gulf which opened between him and his followers) until he chose in his own time to leave his party in 1931.

Now McKenzie must know perfectly well that MacDonald did not leave his Party in 1931. MacDonald was expelled from his Party. McKenzie will have read about that in several of his much-quoted authorities, e.g. Snowden and Dalton. He will have read in the latter's book about Henderson's opposition to the expulsion: he even quotes incidentally (p. 353) the statement attributed by Dalton to Henderson, 'we must not drive (MacDonald) and the others out.' He can hardly have missed Dalton's reference to MacDonald's anger at the news of the expulsion. There is not, in fact, the slightest evidence of any intention or desire on MacDonald's part to leave his Party. Yet McKenzie can commit himself to the assertion that MacDonald left his Party, and, moreover, 'chose his own time' to do so. In such circumstances, it is not perhaps surprising that there is not a single reference in his long book to the Labour Party's expulsion of MacDonald and his associates — unless one counts a repetition of Dalton's phrase 'expelled himself'. But one would have expected McKenzie to have given some attention to a Party's expulsion of a former Leader — an unparalleled event — made all the more striking by reason of the facts that the individual concerned had been the particular Party's first effective leader, had functioned as leader for the previous nine years, and at the time of the expulsion had only very recently been deposed. One would also have wished to know more about the 'deep gulf', and, whatever that may have been, to have some evidence for the view that it had 'opened'.

It is not a good start, and the resulting impression is all too fully confirmed by what follows. An extremely peculiar reference appears on p. 317, as follows:

> Had MacDonald's second Government proved a success, or alternatively had he resigned the office of Prime Minister in August 1931 and gone to the country as Leader of the Labour Party, he would in all probability have won and retained an authority as secure and untrammelled as that ever accorded any Liberal or Conservative leader.

McKenzie's alternative is puzzling. As students constantly have to be reminded, a Prime Minister cannot 'resign' and then 'go to the country'. He can, as a rule, take either the one course or the other. If McKenzie means that, in August 1931, MacDonald could have asked for a dissolution, he apparently forgets what the circumstances were. With the financial crisis at an acute state, a dissolution of Parliament would have been disastrous, and it had to be avoided if at all possible. That was one of the major political facts in the situation. But how could MacDonald have gone to the King and asked for a dissolution? What ground for the request could he have advanced, other than the fact that his Cabinet was hopelessly divided? Had MacDonald been so foolish as to ask for a dissolution, the King would certainly have refused the request. McKenzie may conceivably mean that MacDonald, having resigned, might have remained Leader of the Labour Party and as such contested the next General Election whenever it occurred. That doubtless was a possibility. But McKenzie, whatever his meaning, plainly fails to consider the immediate national interest, the complexity of the political situation resulting from the resignation of the Labour Cabinet, and the responsibility resting upon all the political leaders, particularly upon the outgoing leaders of the largest party in the House of Commons, to provide a government and to deal promptly with the crisis. Relinquishment of office did not, and could not, resolve the differences within the Labour Party. If the course envisaged had been followed, moreover, the breach in the Party would in all probability have been greatly widened, for MacDonald and his leading associates would neither have been able nor willing to do what the Labour Opposition to the National Government actually did, that is, oppose the measures which a majority of the Labour Cabinet had approved and even measures which the whole Cabinet had either endorsed or provisionally accepted.

McKenzie deals (pp. 353-5) with the election of Henderson as Leader of the Labour Party on August 28, 1931. His failure to present a straightforward account of the crisis is revealed again in this connexion. He tells us that at the meeting of the Parliamentary Party that day, the Chairman of its Consultative Committee reported on the Committee's work 'during the days immediately preceding the downfall of the Labour Government', and then moved a resolution 'approving their action and recommending that the party go into opposition to MacDonald's new Government'. No indication is given of the nature of the Committee's 'work' before the break-up of the Labour Cabinet, nor of its 'action' (whether before or after the Cabinet's downfall is not specified). McKenzie omits all reference to the joint meeting of the General Council of the T.U.C., the National Executive of the Labour Party, and the Consultative Committee of the Parliamentary Party, which had been held on August 26, and at which the decision had been taken vigorously to oppose the new Government. Similarly, he has nothing to say about the manifesto approved next day (August 27) by the three bodies and issued to the press, a manifesto which in effect endorsed the attitude of the General Council, repudiated the policy of the Labour Cabinet, and implied a criticism of all the ex-Ministers. These events were not only of the utmost importance in the development of the situation, and to the relations between MacDonald and his Party; they are also directly relevant to one of McKenzie's major topics, the autonomy of the Parliamentary Labour Party.

McKenzie is strangely reticent about the part played in the 1931 crisis by the General Council of the T.U.C. Indeed, he has almost nothing to say on the general subject of the influence of that body. There is a footnote reference, it is true (pp. 325–6), to an article containing a warning against the 'tendency' of the Labour Party in the years before the Second War to become a very humble servant of the T.U.C. In regard to 1931, McKenzie must be well aware that the alleged 'dictation' of the General Council was a prominent issue at the time. And there is no doubt at all that the attitude of the General Council on August 20 greatly influenced the Labour Cabinet's discussions on the following day, despite the Cabinet's repudiation of any interference on the part of outside bodies. That McKenzie should quote words used by Citrine on October 14, 1931, when he said:

The Labour movement could reasonably complain of dictation. It resented the attempted dictatorship of Mr MacDonald. . . .

is a little amusing, since Citrine was replying to the charge of T.U.C. dictation, his previous sentence on that occasion being:

Nor was it true that Mr MacDonald's separation from the Labour Party had been brought about by anything in the nature of T.U.C. dictatorship.

When dealing with the meeting of the Parliamentary Labour Party on August 28, it is true, McKenzie mentions that the members of the General Council of the T.U.C. had been invited to attend, and quotes Dalton's reference to this as 'an innovation', suggested by Henderson, 'to mark unity.' But he makes no comment, although one would have thought that this unprecedented event would have had a special interest for him. Similarly, in a later section of his book (pp. 443–4), he alludes in passing to the General Council's part in the 1931 crisis. He is then discussing the National Executive Committee of the Labour Party, which he describes as having been 'little more than a baffled and horrified spectator', adding:

Certainly it played a much less significant role than did the General Council of the T.U.C.

But the only information we are given about the General Council's role (taken, mainly in the form of direct quotation, from Dalton's memoirs) is that, after the joint meeting with the N.E.C. on August 20, addressed by MacDonald and Snowden, the General Council sent a deputation, in a highly critical mood, to Mac-Donald. That information is merely incidental: McKenzie is concerned with the N.E.C.; and he concludes his paragraph with the sentence:

> Then, as throughout the lifetime of the Government, there was not the slightest question of extra-parliamentary control of the Government or of the PLP by the mass organization outside.

That may be so; but there most certainly was a question of extra-parliamentary control of the Government and of the Parliamentary Labour Party by the General Council of the T.U.C.

One of MacDonald's most interesting actions during the crisis of 1931 was his address to the non-Cabinet and junior Ministers in the early afternoon of August 24. McKenzie mentions this meeting (pp. 363–4) because Attlee, according to Dalton's records, asked a question on that occasion, and he is discussing Attlee. No indication is given, however, of MacDonald's speech on that occasion. McKenzie does not even quote Dalton in that connexion. Yet MacDonald's action in advising these Ministers to dissociate themselves from the National Government was surely worth consideration by one so much concerned about Mac-Donald's 'character' and 'sincerity', and with his attitude towards his Party. It may well be, however, that this episode is not easily reconciled with the 'betrayal' judgment which McKenzie endorses.

In his concluding passages on MacDonald's 'exodus', McKenzie quotes at length David Kirkwood's view that if MacDonald had attended and addressed the P.L.P. meeting on August 28, 1931, he would have carried the party with him. Most other survivors of the meeting, he adds, deny that there was the slightest chance of MacDonald carrying any considerable part of the P.L.P. with him. McKenzie then proceeds:

> Perhaps *at that late date* he could not have done so. But what if Mac-Donald had been less aloof from his followers during the preceding months? He might have set about attempting to carry them with him rather than so obviously seeking to rid himself of them. It is worth remembering that a considerable part of the Cabinet stood with Mac-Donald in the final critical vote on the proposal to cut the unemploy-

ment benefit. He might have set about much earlier convincing them and the members of the PLP that only a coalition government could deal with what was widely considered to be the nation's desperate economic dilemma. It is at least an open question whether he might not have succeeded in such a campaign. . . . It is at least conceivable that he might have carried a considerable part of the PLP with him had he not *preferred* to desert them. (McKenzie's italics.)

The whole tenor of this remarkable passage implies that Mac-Donald's decision to form the National Government was the outcome of a long-contemplated desire to head a coalition government (although it certainly does not suggest that he displayed the skill which might have been expected from an arch-schemer). The charge is also specifically made that MacDonald was anxious to separate himself from his Party. These accusations are familiar enough, and have received adequate attention above. The important point is that McKenzie, in an academic work of no little importance, appears to have accepted them unquestioningly. Such supporting evidence as may be discovered in his volume is ludicrously inadequate. The overwhelming evidence on the other side is completely ignored, although McKenzie cannot be entirely ignorant of it, for he has at least read Nicolson's book and the Neville Chamberlain biography. One would have expected him to give some slight consideration to MacDonald's own statements on the subject, but these are not mentioned at all.

McKenzie's main task in relation to MacDonald is to explain his long and almost unchallenged leadership of the Labour Party down to 1931. The problem, as he sees it himself, is presented (p. 366) in these terms:

It seems particularly strange that no serious effort was made to unseat MacDonald between 1924–29, and that no one should ever have stood against him at the annual elections for the chairmanship of the PLP. In retrospect even MacDonald's colleagues were baffled to account for their failure to challenge his authority over so long a period.

Though he strives hard, McKenzie clearly fails to provide what he would consider a satisfactory solution. To the problem as he states it, there can be, indeed, no acceptable solution. His approach blinds him to the simple explanation, which is that in the bitterness arising from the formation of the National Government (and still more from Labour's crushing defeat in the subsequent Election)

MacDonald's critics, including many of his colleagues, have presented and popularized a much distorted picture of him. McKenzie may not wholly accept that picture, but he assumes its substantial faithfulness. That is why he finds it so strange that no serious effort was made to evict MacDonald from the leadership. There is no other reason why it should be considered strange at all. It also explains why he finds rather unconvincing the apologies of MacDonald's former colleagues, who have certainly been baffled to account for their conduct. MacDonald made a justifiable allusion to this matter during the Election campaign of 1931, when he said:

> men and women who were prepared to lick my boots three months ago are coming to tell you about things they discovered five or ten years ago but were discreet enough to keep buried in their hearts until two or three weeks ago.[1]

If what former colleagues said and wrote about MacDonald after 1931 were true, they had much to answer for — and no creditable answer to give. But was it true? McKenzie ought to have devoted much more attention to that question than he appears to have done, if, indeed, it ever arose in his mind. After all, as has been noted, MacDonald's critics involved themselves in all kinds of inconsistencies. McKenzie might have noted the clue provided by Mary Agnes Hamilton. But he himself provides some striking instances of searching into the distant past for possible evidence against MacDonald. Moreover, he relies excessively upon MacDonald's chief detractors. His leading authority throughout is Mrs Webb, whom he describes himself as 'one of MacDonald's bitterest critics', and, it may be added, a critic of long standing. Mrs Webb is supplemented by Snowden, whom McKenzie calls 'bitter' and 'misanthropic'; by Dalton, although no reference is made to 'the sheer joy' with which that frankly ambitious politician says he hailed, in 1931, the prospect of getting rid of MacDonald, Snowden and Thomas; by MacNeil Weir, charitably described by McKenzie as a 'prejudiced witness'; by Ernest Bevin, who sought Snowden's help to unseat MacDonald, although, as we are reminded, he disliked the former almost as much as he disliked the latter; and by Mary Agnes Hamilton, who, incidentally, wrote two books on MacDonald which McKenzie does not mention.

Now, McKenzie recognizes that the chief reasons why Mac-

[1] Speech at Wheatley Hill, reported October 21, 1931.

Donald acquired, recovered, and retained his leadership of the Labour Party were his Parliamentary skill, his intellectual powers, and his untiring energy. The odd thing is that these qualities, and others which do not go unnoticed by McKenzie, are not enough for him; but what he writes or quotes in regard to them will probably come as a considerable shock to nearly all his younger readers. Such a fantastically absurd view of MacDonald has become current that they will be greatly surprised at the repeated references to his 'intellectual ascendancy'. From this standpoint, McKenzie may be congratulated. He endorses Balfour's remark, 'a born Parliamentarian.' He has obviously been much impressed by Mrs Webb's often reiterated verdict — before 1931 — that MacDonald was 'head and shoulders above the rest' of his Labour colleagues, a verdict all the more impressive because of its reluctance. MacDonald, McKenzie grants, was 'obviously superior in parliamentary skills to any possible rival.' Mrs Webb, despite her almost continuous endeavours, could find no one else even 'remotely acceptable'. McKenzie repeats his verdict: MacDonald 'was obviously superior in personal accomplishments to all possible rivals'. That is why he is forced back to criticism of MacDonald's character. It is why, from the outset, he questions MacDonald's 'sincerity', or, to be more accurate, assumes his 'insincerity'. Almost every reference to MacDonald's abilities or achievements is accompanied by some reminder or warning of his alleged untrustworthiness. It would be intolerably tedious to go through the instances.

When McKenzie comes to his central problem about MacDonald (p. 366) and points out how baffled his colleagues were, in retrospect, to account for having failed to challenge MacDonald's authority over so many years, he supports his point by quoting from a letter written by Lansbury to Cripps in December 1932. MacDonald was therein described as 'a terrible mixture of vanity, cowardice, and utter lack of principle', and Lansbury said he was 'terribly distressed that a man with his mentality should have led us all for so many years'. McKenzie may have been impressed by that. No one closely associated with the Labour Party during those years is likely to be. Lansbury was always a bitter, most unsaintlike, opponent of MacDonald, though he knew how hopeless it was formally to challenge his authority.

McKenzie then 'casts backwards' to 1912 and the inevitable Mrs

Webb, who, as early as that year, 'had had no doubt about Mac-Donald's insincerity.' McKenzie solemnly writes:

> She wrote in her diary in October of that year: 'J. R. MacDonald has ceased to be a Socialist.'

It would be difficult to name a British Socialist whose right so to describe himself or herself has not been denied or questioned by other British Socialists. The title was often denied to the Webbs. As this book is being written, the intellectuals of the Labour Party are still engaged upon what has already become a long process of 're-thinking' what Socialism means. It is amusing to find Shinwell informing us in his autobiography that MacDonald did not consider Snowden to be a Socialist but a Liberal, and that Snowden always thought exactly the same about MacDonald. McKenzie's quotation is made still more diverting by Mrs Webb's quoted addendum:

> The Trade Union M.P.s never were Socialists: Snowden is embittered and Lansbury is wild. . . .

One might be tempted to conclude that by 'sincerity' McKenzie means acceptance of Mrs Webb's conception of Socialism. But, in the next sentence, he tells us that Mrs Webb and others continued to have 'the deepest reservations about MacDonald's suitability as Leader and the sincerity of his support for the Labour Party', which is not at all the same thing. And here the first supporting evidence is Mrs Webb's report that MacDonald, during the Labour Party Conference in June 1920, told her with 'angry contempt' that 'he thought it might be better to make a new combination and "smash" the present Labour Party'. The context of this utterance is not explained by McKenzie. Mrs Webb, however, explained it at considerable length. MacDonald had been subjected to what she described as 'this ugly, published snub'.[1] McKenzie's omission of any account of the circumstances of this reported remark of MacDonald's is hardly defensible. The Parliamentary Labour Party in June of 1920 (which was responsible for the snub) was not exactly an inspiring spectacle; and MacDonald's reference to the *present* Labour Party should be noted. The importance seemingly attached to this unusual expression of anger and im-

[1] *Beatrice Webb's Diaries, 1912–1924*, pp. 181–2.

patience on MacDonald's part is in itself significant of McKenzie's straw-clutching.

Having advanced from 1912 to 1920, McKenzie promptly 'casts backward' again — even further backwards. MacDonald, he writes, 'appears to have toyed with the idea (of a new combination) as early as 1910–11.' Once again we have Mrs Webb, this time with the report of a conversation in October *1921* with Henderson, in which:

> Henderson told us that MacDonald (about 1910–11) proposed to enter a coalition Cabinet with Lloyd George and Balfour (to oust Asquith) and offered him (Henderson) an Under-Secretaryship! Henderson refused decisively and declared that any such action would destroy the Labour Party and that he would not consent to it. J.R.M. tried to get George Roberts, who also refused. No more was heard of it.

Beatrice Webb 'cast backwards' to this herself in her diary for October 28, 1931, on hearing the General Election results, though only in developing her view that had it not been for the smashing of the Liberal Party by Lloyd George in 1918 the Labour Party would have continued to be merely a left wing of the Liberal Party, 'and not very left at that!' Henderson, it seems, had recalled the same incident in January, 1930, according to Dalton (p. 289). The occasion was a conversation at the Embassy in Paris between Tyrrell (the Ambassador), Henderson and Dalton. The latter recalled it after quoting the 'Duchess' story. His record reads:

> Uncle then related how in 1910 there was much talk behind the scenes of a new Government, which should be created to settle the Irish question. It would include, besides Liberals, Balfour and some of the younger Tories, and J.R.M. would be Chief Secretary for Ireland. Right in the centre of the picture, chief hero or chief scapegoat. J.R.M. was very anxious to go in. He asked Uncle to come and have a talk about it. He said that he, J.R.M., would be in the Cabinet. No other member of the Labour Party would, but Uncle could have any job he liked outside the Cabinet, if he would put the party machine at the disposal of the new Government. Uncle refused, and strongly advised J.R.M. to drop the whole idea. Anyhow, the idea dropped him!

Dalton's footnote ascribes the authorship of this project to Lloyd George.

McKenzie himself has a footnote in which he points out that

2F

Lord Elton (dealing with another and longer version of the same story given by Henderson's biographer[1]) stoutly denies that Mac-Donald ever entered into such discussions with the Liberals, but adds

> it is difficult to believe that Henderson, who so faithfully refused to join in any move to unseat MacDonald, should have invented so damaging a story against MacDonald and passed it on to Mrs Webb in 1921.

The story clearly has reference to Lloyd George's well-known coalition project during the Constitutional Conference of 1910. We are given a statement alleged to have been made by Henderson 11 years later, and reported by another party, Mrs Webb. We have another report, in rather different terms, from Dalton 9 years further on; and a third, from Mrs Hamilton, 8 years after that. It is perhaps a pity that McKenzie has provided no further information about Lord Elton's denial. Elton pointed out[2] (*inter alia*) that he had obtained emphatic denials from both Lloyd George and Churchill (the two active promoters of the project), from Lord Crewe (so closely in touch with Asquith at the time), from Thomas, and from George Barnes (then Chairman of the Labour Party) that any proposal was made to include MacDonald. McKenzie is disposed to prefer reliance upon Henderson's memory. He relies particularly upon Henderson's refusal to join in any move to unseat MacDonald when the latter became Leader; but Henderson's attitude in that respect did not prevent him from indulging in private gossip about and criticism of MacDonald, as the Webb and Dalton diaries make abundantly clear. It is obvious, however, that some conversation about the coalition project in 1910 took place between MacDonald and Henderson. It would have been rather surprising if they had not discussed the matter at all. Lord Elton's plausible suggestion is that MacDonald, as a precautionary measure, may have asked Henderson for his opinion of such a proposal as that referred to. It may even be that Lloyd George and the others forgot that any suggestion had ever been made at the time to include a Labour representative, if in fact any such suggestion was made. Clearly, to those who conceived the project, Labour participation was a minor issue.

[1] Op. cit., pp. 73-4.
[2] *The Life of James Ramsay MacDonald*, pp. 183-5.

What, however, does it all signify? Perhaps the most interesting point arising is the view (evidently shared by McKenzie) that for a Labour leader even to contemplate entry into a coalition government is to give evidence of 'insincerity'. The amusing thing is that it was not MacDonald but Henderson who first actually entered a coalition government. It would not be convincing to argue that a coalition for purposes of conducting a war is on a totally different plane from a coalition designed to settle a grave internal crisis and to prevent a war. Indeed, McKenzie reminds us later (footnote, p. 402) that Beatrice Webb regarded the Labour Party's entry into the Lloyd George coalition in December 1916 as a betrayal of the interests of the British working class! In passing, it may be noted that McKenzie's interest in MacDonald's 'sincerity' has not led him to make any allusion to MacDonald's refusal of the place offered him in Asquith's Government in August 1914. Presumably he considers that, like MacDonald's whole attitude at the time, to be irrelevant.

McKenzie then turns to the situation after MacDonald's first term as Prime Minister (in 1924), asserting that there was widespread dissatisfaction with MacDonald's leadership at the highest party levels. It is unnecessary to follow his argument in detail. That there was criticism of MacDonald and his leadership goes without saying. There always had been. There was bound to be. How widespread it was is another matter. McKenzie, as usual, relies overmuch on those who were always MacDonald's opponents, Snowden, Ernest Bevin, H. N. Brailsford — even J. B. Figgins of the N.U.R. He could have done much better than he does, even from his own standpoint. And, within a year of the fall of the first Labour Government, so McKenzie gathers from Mrs Webb, 'MacDonald had completely re-established his ascendancy.' But, McKenzie adds, 'there were lingering doubts in the minds of many of MacDonald's supporters.' Why? Because of 'Biscuits!' For the greater part of two pages, McKenzie pursues the subject of the baronetcy conferred upon MacDonald's old friend, Sir Alexander Grant, and the latter's allotment of shares in his biscuit company to endow a Daimler motor-car for MacDonald's use during his lifetime. The passage (pp. 369–70) is the most extraordinary one in McKenzie's book. Its whole drift is to suggest that MacDonald had done something dishonourable or at least something quite inconsistent with his association with the Labour Party and bound to provide justifiable suspicion of his integrity and sincerity. McKenzie finds it strange that most of MacDonald's colleagues seemed unconcerned, 'even in retrospect,' which, however, should surely have given him furiously to think. His final sentence reads:

> But to others there can be no doubt that the Daimler incident must have come as a forewarning of MacDonald's ultimate willingness to jettison the Labour Party and the ideals for which it stood.

That is a glaring *non sequitur*; but it is much more: it involves an accusation against MacDonald which McKenzie makes no attempt to examine fairly, indeed, no real attempt to substantiate. He does not appear to be aware of the facts of the Daimler incident. He is either ignorant of, or ignores, the detailed account given by the man who was, in his own words, 'entirely responsible' for Grant's gift.[1] If he had been content to criticize MacDonald for his carelessly innocent handling of this incident, he could readily have been forgiven. That, however, would hardly have served his purpose. His actual treatment of the matter also shows a lack of any sense of proportion. MacDonald's followers were much more perturbed by the incident of the five cruisers (unmentioned by McKenzie) than by the Daimler motor-car. If McKenzie felt it necessary to devote nearly two pages to the car, he might usefully have examined the real reasons for the gift, which are certainly relevant to the topic with which he is so much concerned. And he could surely have found space briefly to record that MacDonald returned the Daimler quietly, without any publicity, at the end of his period of office in 1924.

In 'casting backwards', McKenzie then beats his own record by going back, *via* Snowden, to 1908, this time in an attempt to justify his assertion that during the years between the two Labour Governments MacDonald was increasingly exasperated with others in addition to the admittedly tiresome I.L.P. He quotes MacDonald's reported reference in 1908 to 'the whirlpool of class-conscious trade unionists around him'. It seems that what in his judgment was permissible in Beatrice Webb's case was to be condemned in MacDonald's, for he quotes (p. 305) Mrs Webb's reference to 'all those underbred and under-trained workmen who sur-

---

[1] Sir Ronald Waterhouse. The account is to be found in Nourah Waterhouse, *Private and Official*, pp. 296–300.

round him (MacDonald)' — and (p. 402) her references to 'pecuniary interest and class illusion' and the 'maddening muddle-headedness which makes them (the Labour men) quite incapable of asking for terms for their own class before they consent to take office'. The difference for McKenzie, conceivably, is that MacDonald disliked class-consciousness in all its forms, whereas Mrs Webb approved certain of its political manifestations. He is presumably aware that MacDonald was a consistent opponent of the 'class-conscious' approach to politics.

McKenzie concludes this patchwork argument with the assertion to which it was doubtless designed to lead up:

And when MacDonald found that he could not wean his followers from 'the teachings of a quarter of a century', he did not hesitate to break with them and to establish the National Government.

Leaving aside the 'did not hesitate' and the 'to break with them', McKenzie would be hard put to it to explain what teachings of MacDonald's over a quarter of a century he discovered he could not wean his followers from. It could easily be demonstrated that MacDonald's attitude towards the issues raised by the political and economic crisis of 1931 was fully consistent with his declared views over the previous quarter-century; and McKenzie's favourite authority, Beatrice Webb, would warmly have endorsed such a demonstration.

McKenzie grants that 'disillusionment' with MacDonald, before the 1931 crisis, was largely confined to 'the inner circle of the Party'. He admits that MacDonald's hold on the party outside Parliament was overwhelmingly strong. Wisely, he doubts whether MacDonald could have been unseated by means of a Palace Revolution even if Henderson had been willing to take the lead in such a move. The implications of these remarks are far-reaching, and, one would think, of major importance in a study of leadership. Unfortunately, McKenzie does not pursue them further. He is altogether too much concerned with 'the inner circle' or with those who considered that they belonged there. This is exemplified by his repeated references to MacDonald's 'aloofness', which he plainly believes to have been a major factor in the development of the breach in 1931.

The charge of 'aloofness' is of course frequently made against Party leaders. It is more common even than the charge of 'vanity'.

MacDonald is certainly not unique in this respect. As Mary Agnes Hamilton pointed out before he became Prime Minister, 'Leadership mechanically creates an isolation round the leader.' Were there not complaints, and extremely bitter ones too, about Attlee's 'aloofness'? The leader's colleagues (most of them) desire to be 'in the know', to be on terms of intimacy with him, or at least to be 'considered'. McKenzie, discussing the dissatisfaction of backbench militants at what they feel to be 'their intolerable exclusion from the councils of the party', (p. 449) rightly acknowledges that 'the existence of this perpetual unhappiness and sense of grievance among the back-bench militants is the normal condition of every parliamentary party'. But he does not appear to acknowledge that it is also 'the normal condition' of those who are not 'back-bench militants' and who think they have a special claim to consideration and to the Leader's confidence. In the case of MacDonald and the Labour Party, such people were unusually numerous; and the feelings of disappointed ambition and wounded vanity were all the more widely distributed. Someone once said, moreover, that there are 'no friendships at the top' in politics. If one may judge from Dalton's second volume of memoirs[1] the relations between Attlee, Morrison, Bevin, Dalton himself, and Cripps were even less satisfactory than those of the 'Big Five' of the Labour Government in 1929–31. Was Attlee, one wonders, on terms of intimate friendship with any of his leading colleagues? McKenzie quotes Mrs Webb about the general lack even of ordinary social contacts between the leading figures in the Labour Party. There was nothing novel about this during the first two Labour Governments.

It may well be, however, that MacDonald was in some special sense 'aloof'; and one would have wished that McKenzie had made some allusion to Mary Agnes Hamilton's extremely interesting comments on the subject in the book on MacDonald which she published in 1923.[2] She suggested that perhaps 'the most solid and serious criticism' levelled at MacDonald was that he did not know how to break down the isolation which is always created round the leader. Her explanation was his 'shyness', 'purely instinctive', with 'nothing conscious', 'nothing intentional', about it; but, none the less, 'an Achilles heel in a leader and in the given case the source of

---

[1] *The Fateful Years, 1931–1945* (published 1957).
[2] This book, like her subsequent (1925) book, written under the pen-name 'Iconoclast', is not listed in his bibliography, which also omits all but one of MacDonald's own works.

most of the misunderstandings both within his own party and without.' But the important point, in regard to what McKenzie has to say on the matter, is that Mrs Hamilton made her analysis of this trait in MacDonald *before* he became Prime Minister. Mac-Donald's 'aloofness' was already — and had been for a long time — the subject of critical comment. It did not develop during his Premiership; and, in so far as it may have appeared to become more pronounced, that can easily be accounted for in terms of the almost intolerable pressure upon his time. That did not prevent disgruntled persons, as Nourah Waterhouse says, from suggesting that he 'favoured the fleshpots of Mayfair when he was grossly overworking'.

APPENDIX VII

A. — The Labour Government, August 1931

Prime Minister: J. Ramsay MacDonald
Lord President of the Council: Lord Parmoor
Lord Chancellor: Lord Sankey
Lord Privy Seal: Thomas Johnston
Chancellor of the Exchequer: Philip Snowden
Home Secretary: J. R. Clynes
Foreign Secretary: Arthur Henderson
Dominions Secretary: Lord Passfield
Colonial Secretary: J. H. Thomas
Secretary for War: Thomas Shaw
Secretary for India: W. Wedgwood Benn
Secretary for Air: Lord Amulree
Secretary for Scotland: William Adamson
President of Board of Trade: William Graham
President of Board of Education: H. B. Lees-Smith
First Lord of Admiralty: A. V. Alexander
Minister of Health: Arthur Greenwood
Minister of Agriculture: Christopher Addison
Minister of Labour: Margaret Bondfield
First Commissioner of Works: George Lansbury
Minister of Transport: Herbert Morrison

B. — The First National Government, August–November, 1931

The Cabinet
Prime Minister: J. Ramsay MacDonald
Lord President of the Council: Stanley Baldwin
Lord Chancellor: Lord Sankey
Chancellor of the Exchequer: Philip Snowden
Home Secretary: Sir Herbert Samuel
Foreign Secretary: Lord Reading
Dominions and Colonies Secretary: J. H. Thomas

Secretary for India: Sir Samuel Hoare
President of Board of Trade: Sir P. Cunliffe-Lister
Minister of Health: Neville Chamberlain

Ministers not in Cabinet
Lord Privy Seal: Lord Peel (Con.)
Secretary for War: Lord Crewe (Lib.)
Secretary for Air: Lord Amulree (Lab.)
First Lord of Admiralty: Sir Austen Chamberlain (Con.)
Secretary for Scotland: Sir Archibald Sinclair (Lib.)
President of Board of Education: Sir Donald Maclean (Lib.)
Minister of Transport: P. J. Pybus (Lib.)
Minister of Agriculture: Sir John Gilmour (Con.)
Minister of Labour: Sir Henry Betterton (Con.)
Minister of Pensions: G. C. Tryon (Con.)
Chancellor of the Duchy of Lancaster: Lord Lothian (Lib.)
First Commissioner of Works: Lord Londonderry (Con.)
Attorney-General: Sir William Jowitt (Lab.)
Solicitor-General: Sir Thomas Inskip (Con.)
Postmaster-General: W. Ormsby-Gore (Con.)
Paymaster-General: Sir J. Tudor Walters (Lib.)
Lord Advocate for Scotland: Craigie M. Aitchison (Lab.)
Solicitor-General for Scotland: J. C. Watson (non-party)

Junior Ministers
Parliamentary Under-Secretaries of State:
  Home Affairs: Oliver Stanley (Con.)
  Foreign Affairs: Anthony Eden (Con.)
  Dominion Affairs: Malcolm MacDonald (Lab.)
  Colonies: Sir Robert Hamilton (Lib.)
  Air: Sir Philip Sassoon (Con.)
  Scotland: A. N. Skelton (Con.)
Financial Secretary, War Office: A. Duff Cooper (Con.)
Parliamentary and Financial Secretary, Admiralty: Lord Stanhope
  (Con.)
Parliamentary Secretaries:
  Board of Trade: G. Lloyd George (Lib.)
  Mines Department: Isaac Foot (Lib.)
  Overseas Trade Department: Sir E. Hilton Young (Con.)
  Health: E. D. Simon (Lib.)

Transport: Sir G. Gillett (Lab.)
Education: Sir Kingsley Wood (Con.)
Labour: Milner Gray (Lib.)
Assistant Postmaster-General: H. Graham White (Lib.)
Treasury:
 Parliamentary Secretary: Sir B. Eyres-Monsell (Con.)
 Financial Secretary: Major Walter Elliot (Con.)
 Lords Commissioners:
  Capt. David Margesson (Con.)
  Sir George Penny (Con.)
  A. E. Glassey (Lib.)
  Lord Titchfield (Con.)
  Capt. D. Euan Wallace (Con.)
 Assistant Whips:
  Sir George Bowyer (Con.)
  Sir Victor Warrender (Con.)
  Capt. A. U. M. Hudson (Con.)
  Lord Elmley (Lib.)
  Sir M. McKenzie Wood (Lib.)
H.M. Household:
 Treasurer: Major Sir Geo. Hennessy (Con.)
 Comptroller: Major Goronwy Owen (Lib.)
 Vice-Chamberlain: Sir Frederick Thomson (Con.)
 Lord Chamberlain: Earl of Cromer (non-political)
 Lord Steward: Earl of Shaftesbury (non-political)
 Master of the Horse: Earl of Granard (non-political)
 Captain of the Gentlemen-at-Arms: Earl of Cavan (non-political)
 Captain of the Yeomen of the Guard: Lord Loch (non-political)

C. — SECOND NATIONAL GOVERNMENT, NOVEMBER 1931

Prime Minister: J. Ramsay MacDonald (Nat. Lab.)
Lord President of the Council: Stanley Baldwin (Con.)
Lord Chancellor: Lord Sankey (Nat. Lab.)
Lord Privy Seal: Lord Snowden (Nat. Lab.)
Chancellor of the Exchequer: Neville Chamberlain (Con.)
Home Secretary: Sir Herbert Samuel (Lib.)
Foreign Secretary: Sir John Simon (Lib. Nat.)
Dominions Secretary: J. H. Thomas (Nat. Lab.)

Colonial Secretary: Sir P. Cunliffe-Lister (Con.)
Secretary for War: Lord Hailsham (Con.)
Secretary for India: Sir Samuel Hoare (Con.)
Secretary for Air: Lord Londonderry (Con.)
Secretary for Scotland: Sir Archibald Sinclair (Lib.)
President of Board of Trade: Walter Runciman (Lib. Nat.)
President of Board of Education: Sir Donald Maclean (Lib.)
First Lord of Admiralty: Sir B. Eyres-Monsell (Con.)
Minister of Health: Sir E. Hilton Young (Con.)
Minister of Agriculture: Sir John Gilmour (Con.)
Minister of Labour: Sir Henry Betterton (Con.)
First Commissioner of Works: W. Ormsby-Gore (Con.)

SNOWDEN'S BROADCAST
OCTOBER 17, 1931

In front of me, as part of the wireless arrangement, is a red light, and a red light is a warning of danger to be avoided. I am going to give you this warning to-night. I am going to talk to you for a few minutes about this General Election. I don't think I can say much that is new to you. The issue is very simple, and it has been stated through the wireless this week with admirable clearness by Mr Baldwin and Sir John Simon. This is an unusual Election, and I can well understand that you feel rather puzzled about it. An ordinary General Election is quite a simple matter. We have the three Parties running independently. Each has its distinct programme of ordinary political questions. Most of us are Party men and women, and we vote the Party ticket. But at this Election the old Party divisions have been largely obliterated. New and strange issues have to be decided.

I have been a strong Party man, and I never expected to find myself in the political company I am keeping to-day. But I never had a shadow of doubt about the wisdom and rightness of my action. I joined the National Government to carry out the financial policy I pressed on my late colleagues in the Labour Government. They knew this policy was necessary. But when it came to the point of having to face up to it they hadn't the courage to face the unpopularity and opposition which necessary measures of economy would naturally meet with in certain quarters. To call a halt in expenditure on the social services and to make cuts in the dole and reductions in pay here and there seemed, in the absence of knowledge of how necessary they were, to be inconsistent with Labour policy.

So it would have been in ordinary times. But these are not ordinary times. However anxious we may be to advance the social services we cannot do it when the resources from which the cost must come are drying up. A nation, like an individual, cannot go on increasing expenditure when income is falling, unless it wants to be landed into bankruptcy. It became clear to me in the early part of this year that we were on the edge of national bankruptcy, and drastic measures would have to be taken if that catastrophe were to be averted.

The vast increase in unemployment with its enormous cost to the Exchequer, the rapid fall in revenue through the decline in the profits of industry, had upset all Budget calculations. In a speech in the House of Commons in February, I called attention to the position and urged Parliament to give serious consideration to it. I pointed out that we had committed ourselves to expenditure which might be tolerable in a time of prosperity and abounding revenue, but which we could not stand in a period of intense depression. Economy in expenditure was absolutely necessary. It was the only way in which we could conserve our resources and prevent a complete collapse of our social services.

I may mention the fact now because no harm is likely to be done since we have balanced the Budget, but the situation was so serious that by the middle of November, if we had allowed things to drift, there would have been no money to pay the unemployment benefits. What we have done has saved the unemployed from that plight.

You have been told by a spokesman of the Labour Party this week that the resources of the country are enormous and that we have money enough to go on spending to our hearts' content. This is appalling ignorance or wilful deception. It is true the resources of the country are great; but the fact is that they cannot continue to be mortgaged for current expenditure. Let me give you a few striking facts. When I first entered Parliament in 1906, twenty-five years ago, the total national expenditure for the year, excluding the Post Office, was £123,000,000. This year it is £804,000,000 — nearly seven times more. The Income-Tax then was 1s. in the £1; to-day it is 5s., with an additional Surtax running up to 5s. 6d. in the £1. In 1906 the whole cost of the social services was only £18,000,000. This year it is £237,000,000 — over thirteen times more. In 1906 there was no unemployment benefit. This year the country is paying £132,000,000 for this item — more than the whole national expenditure twenty-five years ago. In 1906 national and local taxation took one-thirteenth of the national income — that is, the incomes of everybody in the country aggregated together. This year nearly one-third of the national income is taken in rates and taxes. Only two-thirds is left to maintain the population and to provide capital and wages for industry. We are far away the most heavily taxed nation in the world. All this taxation has to come out of industry. There is nowhere else it can come from.

In July our own financial difficulties were aggravated by the serious financial panic on the Continent. I need not go into that story. It has been told to you often in the last few weeks. In August the situation became so pressing that measures had to be taken at once. The majority of the Labour Government, after agreeing to most of the economies, shirked the responsibility of placing the proposals before Parliament, so the Prime Minister dissolved the Government.

It became necessary to form a new Government at once. So the National Government was formed to deal with the situation. By drastic economies, and by heavy taxation spread fairly over the whole population, the Budget has been balanced. I know that the economies we have had to make are disagreeable. It has been no pleasure to impose them. They were necessary to prevent a far more serious reduction in working-class conditions. They are far less drastic than reductions which the Labour Government of Australia has been compelled to make, and far less than the economies made in Germany. After the cuts have been made the unemployed in this country are far more generously provided for than in any other country. In America they are left to private charity or to beg or starve. After the reductions in unemployment pay the benefits now are 17 per cent more in value than the Labour Government in 1924 considered adequate, and at a time when there was a Budget surplus of £30,000,000 — not a deficit of £170,000,000.

It is being said that the National Government has failed to save the pound. It is true we have been driven off the Gold Standard, and the external value of the pound has fallen. But its internal value has not depreciated. The purchasing power of the pound at home is still worth 20s. The action of the National Government in balancing the Budget has prevented a tremendous increase in the cost of living.

The question is being asked: Why have a General Election now? The answer is that the National Government was formed without any direct mandate from the nation. The crisis was urgent and acute. There was no time to appeal to the country. Now that we have secured a certain measure of stability we desire to give the electors the opportunity to express their opinion on the National Government and to give it their definite authority to continue and complete its work. The Government has not put before the electors a programme for the establishment of a new earth in the new Parliament. It leaves that to others who have no responsibility and who know they are not likely to be called upon to redeem their promises.

I would warn the electors against being influenced by other considerations than the one issue. That one issue on which you should vote is, as I have stated elsewhere, whether we should have a strong and stable Government in this time of national crisis, or whether we shall hand over the destinies of the nation to men whose conduct in a grave emergency has shown them to be unfitted to be trusted with responsibility. I regret that other issues are being raised in this Election. The position is too serious to have the national unity threatened by divisions on a subject which is no essential part of the work in front of the National Government.

There is no more stern and unbending Free-Trader than I am. If Free Trade or Protection were the issue at this Election I should be on the side of Free Trade. We all joined the National Government on the understanding that controversial Party questions were to be set aside until we had completed the task of restoring national solvency. I do not believe that the Conservative leaders would regard a majority obtained in the circumstances of this Election as giving them a mandate to carry a general system of Protection in the new Parliament. Such a radical departure from our established fiscal system could not be made without an emphatic and unequivocal decision of the electorate. But I would warn Free-Traders that if they do attach importance to this question at this Election, if they follow the advice of Mr Lloyd George and vote for the Free-Trade candidate, they will not be doing that by voting for the Labour Party.

The Labour Party is not a Free-Trade Party. Its candidates are saying that from a thousand platforms. They have issued an Election programme which involves the most extreme form of Protection. Immense subsidies are to be given from the taxes to keep up the prices of agricultural produce; the staple manufacturing industries and the transport services are to be taken over and sub-sidized from the same source. A month ago the Trade Union Council was preparing a tariff policy. When the General Election became imminent they dropped that in order to pose as an anti-tariff Party.

Mr Henderson is quoted in the *Daily Herald* this morning as having said that if he were faced with a large cut in unemployment pay or a 20 per cent revenue tariff as an emergency expedient he was going to try the value of that expedient. Now he is denouncing tariffs as an expedient to raise prices and lower wages. He was pre-pared a month ago to raise the cost of living to the unemployed and to all employed workers by 20 per cent rather than adopt the straightforward course of reducing the benefits by 10 per cent. This is the Party which Mr Lloyd George recommends the Elec-tors to support as a sound Free-Trade Party.

I hope you have read the Election programme of the Labour Party. It is the most fantastic and impracticable programme ever put before the electors. All the derelict industries are to be taken over by the State, and the tax-payer is to shoulder the losses. The banks and financial houses are to be placed under national owner-ship and control, which means, I suppose, that they are to be run by a joint committee of the Labour Party and the Trade Union Council. Your investments are to be ordered by some board, and your foreign investments are to be mobilized to finance this mad-cap policy. This is not Socialism. It is Bolshevism run mad.

I have been an advocate of a sane and evolutionary Socialism for forty years, but I have always attacked such a revolutionary policy as is set out in this manifesto. Well might Mr Lloyd George say the other evening that there is no likelihood of the country giving this programme a majority. Nothing could better show the utter lack of understanding of the national and international financial situation than such a programme as this. At a time when national retrench-ment is vital, when above all else confidence in our sanity is needed, this programme is issued, a programme which, were it taken seriously, would destroy every vestige of confidence and plunge the country into irretrievable ruin.

May I say a word in conclusion to my old friends in the ranks of the Labour Movement? My recent action may seem to them incon-sistent with my past. I assure them it is not. I am supporting this National Government as a temporary expedient to do the work which I would fain have seen a united Labour Government undertake. I am doing this because I do not want to see the work of a life-time brought to rack and ruin. To none more than to the working-classes is it more vital that a strong National Government should be returned. I ask them to believe that I give them this advice under a profound conviction that in doing so I am still serving the best interests of the working-classes and safeguarding their future progress. Good Night.

INDEX

PRINTED IN GREAT BRITAIN BY ROBERT MACLEHOSE AND CO. LTD
THE UNIVERSITY PRESS, GLASGOW